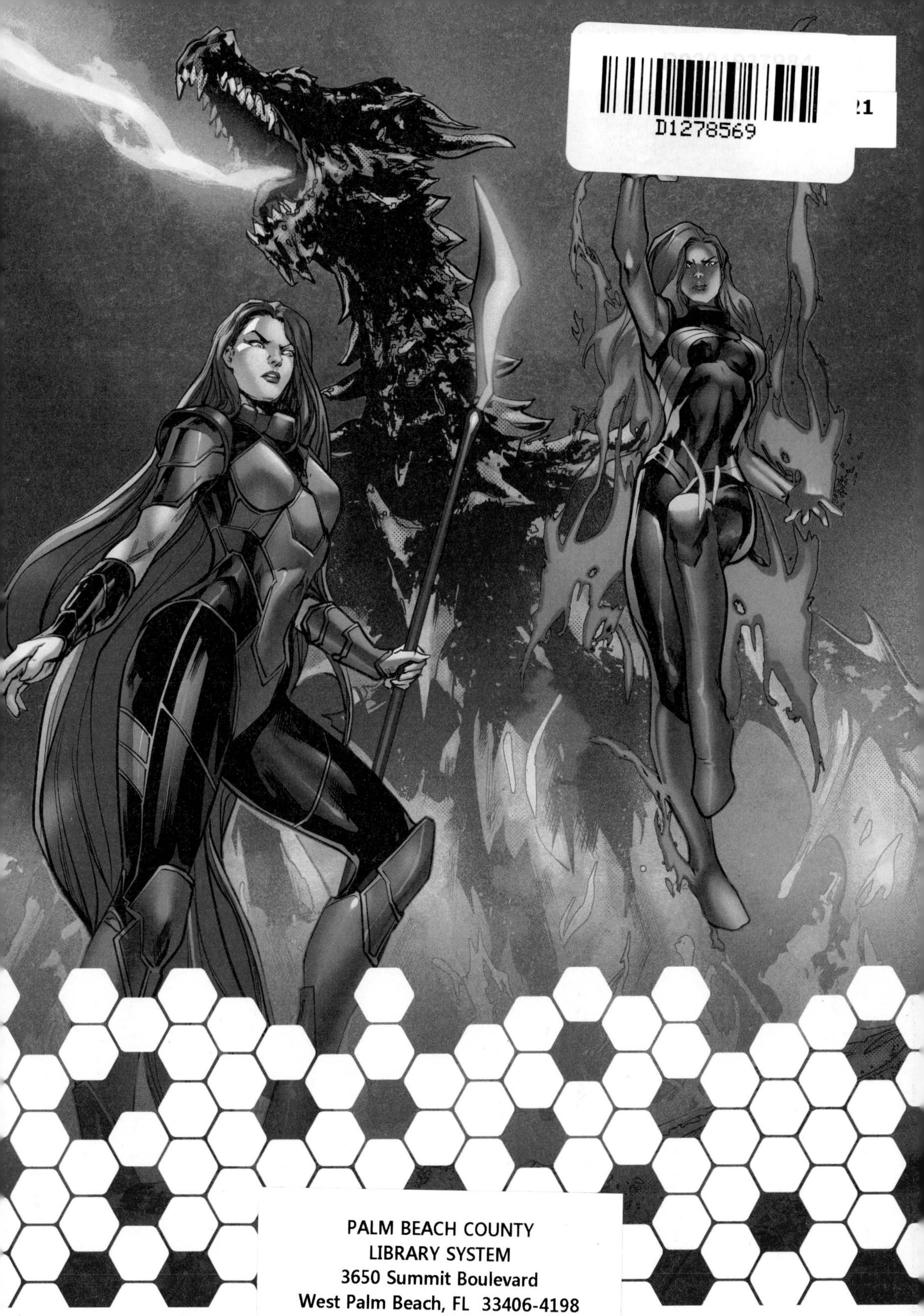

gen:LOCK

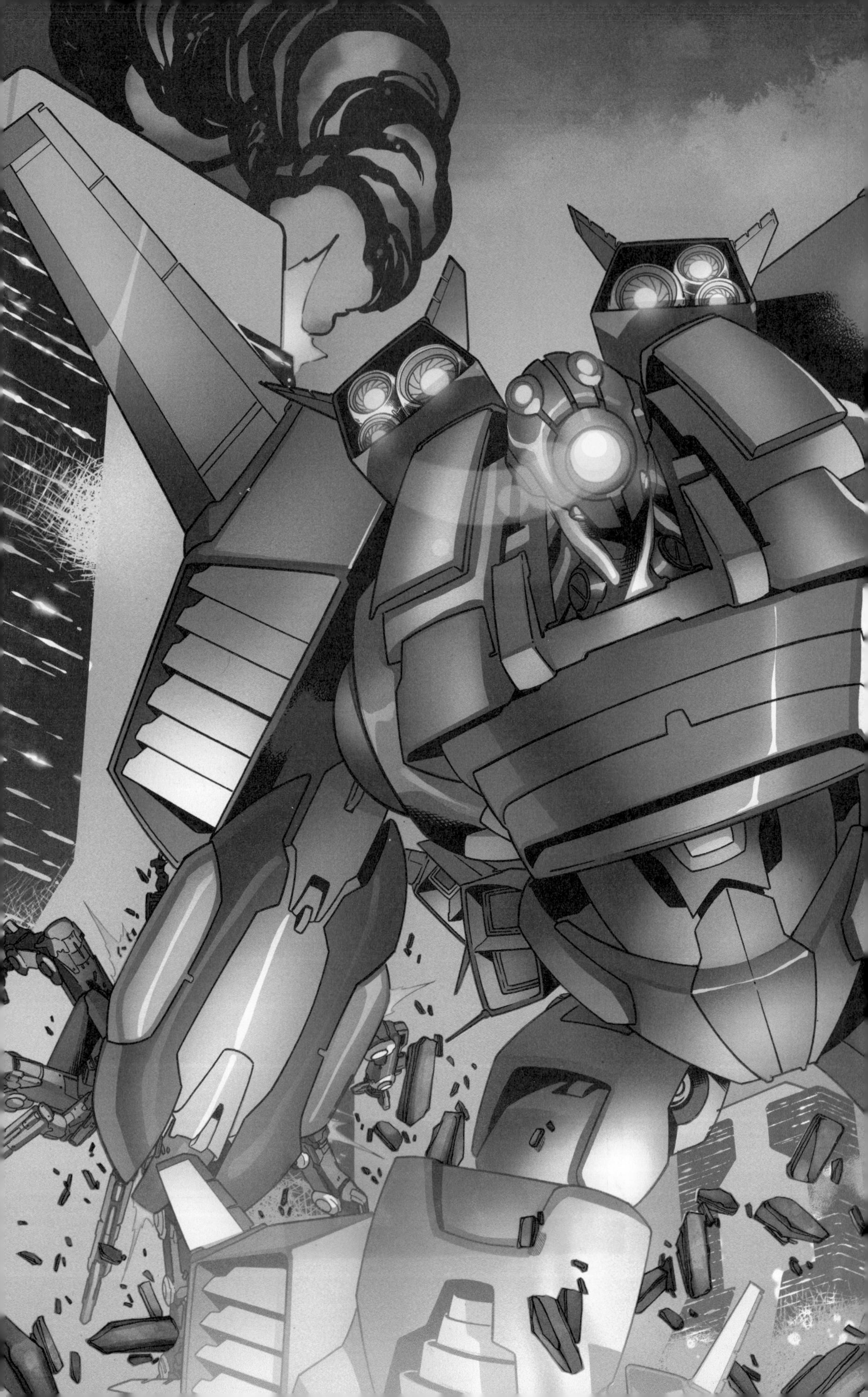

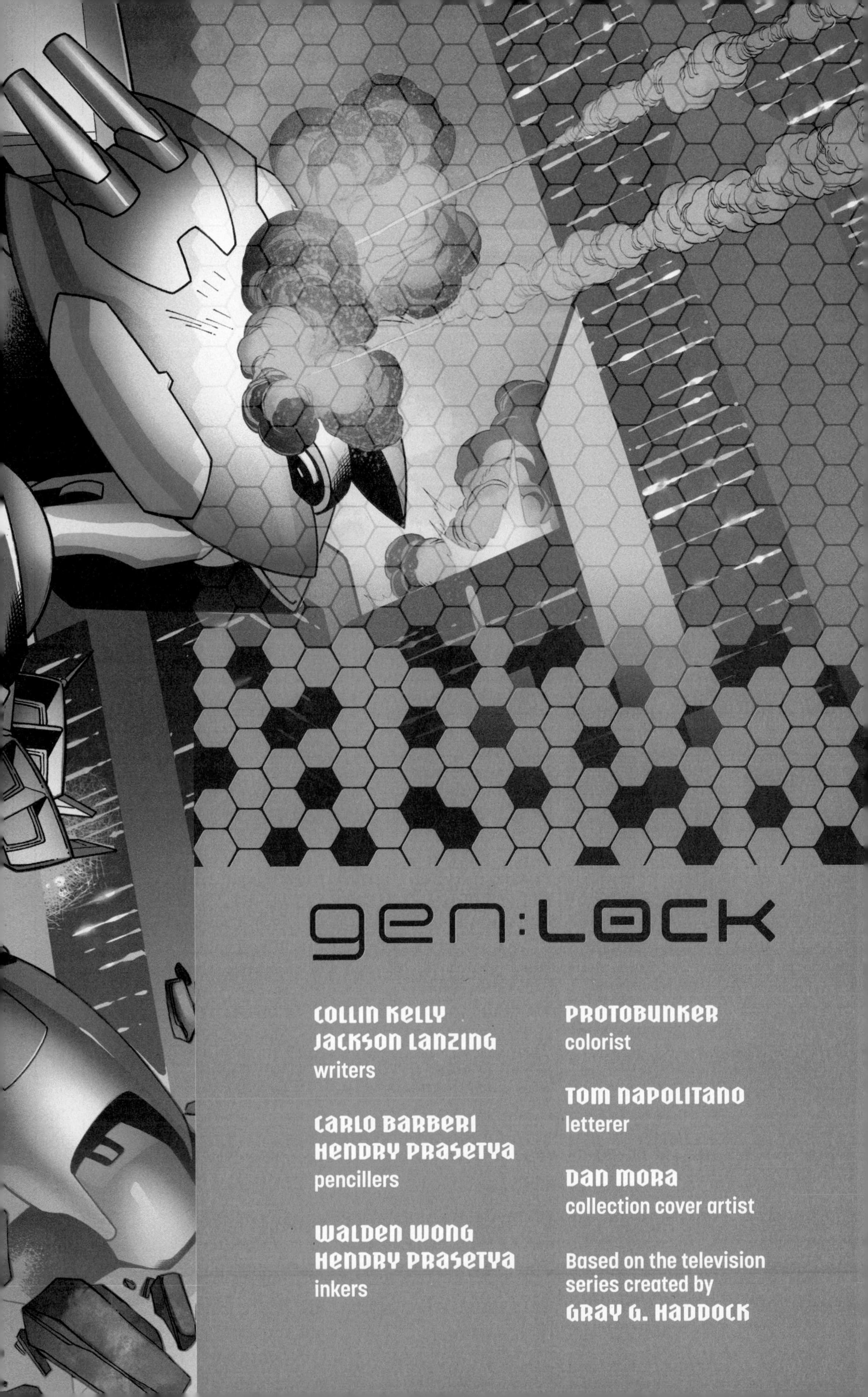

gen:LOCK

COLLIN KELLY
JACKSON LANZING
writers

CARLO BARBERI
HENDRY PRASETYA
pencillers

WALDEN WONG
HENDRY PRASETYA
inkers

PROTOBUNKER
colorist

TOM NAPOLITANO
letterer

DAN MORA
collection cover artist

Based on the television series created by
GRAY G. HADDOCK

ANDREW MARINO	Editor – Original Series
JEB WOODARD	Group Editor – Collected Editions
FRANCESCA DiMARZIO	Editor – Collected Edition
STEVE COOK	Design Director – Books and Publication Design
SUZANNAH ROWNTREE	Publication Production
BOB HARRAS	Senior VP – Editor-in-Chief, DC Comics
JIM LEE	Publisher & Chief Creative Officer
BOBBIE CHASE	VP – Global Publishing Initiatives & Digital Strategy
DON FALLETTI	VP – Manufacturing Operations & Workflow Management
LAWRENCE GANEM	VP – Talent Services
ALISON GILL	Senior VP – Manufacturing & Operations
HANK KANALZ	Senior VP – Publishing Strategy & Support Services
DAN MIRON	VP – Publishing Operations
NICK J. NAPOLITANO	VP – Manufacturing Administration & Design
NANCY SPEARS	VP – Sales
JONAH WEILAND	VP – Marketing & Creative Services
MICHELE R. WELLS	VP & Executive Editor, Young Reader

gen:LOCK

DC Comics, 2900 West Alameda Ave., Burbank, CA 91505
Printed by LSC Communications, Owensville, MO, USA. 7/17/20. First Printing.
ISBN: 978-1-77950-308-4

Library of Congress Cataloging-in-Publication Data is available.

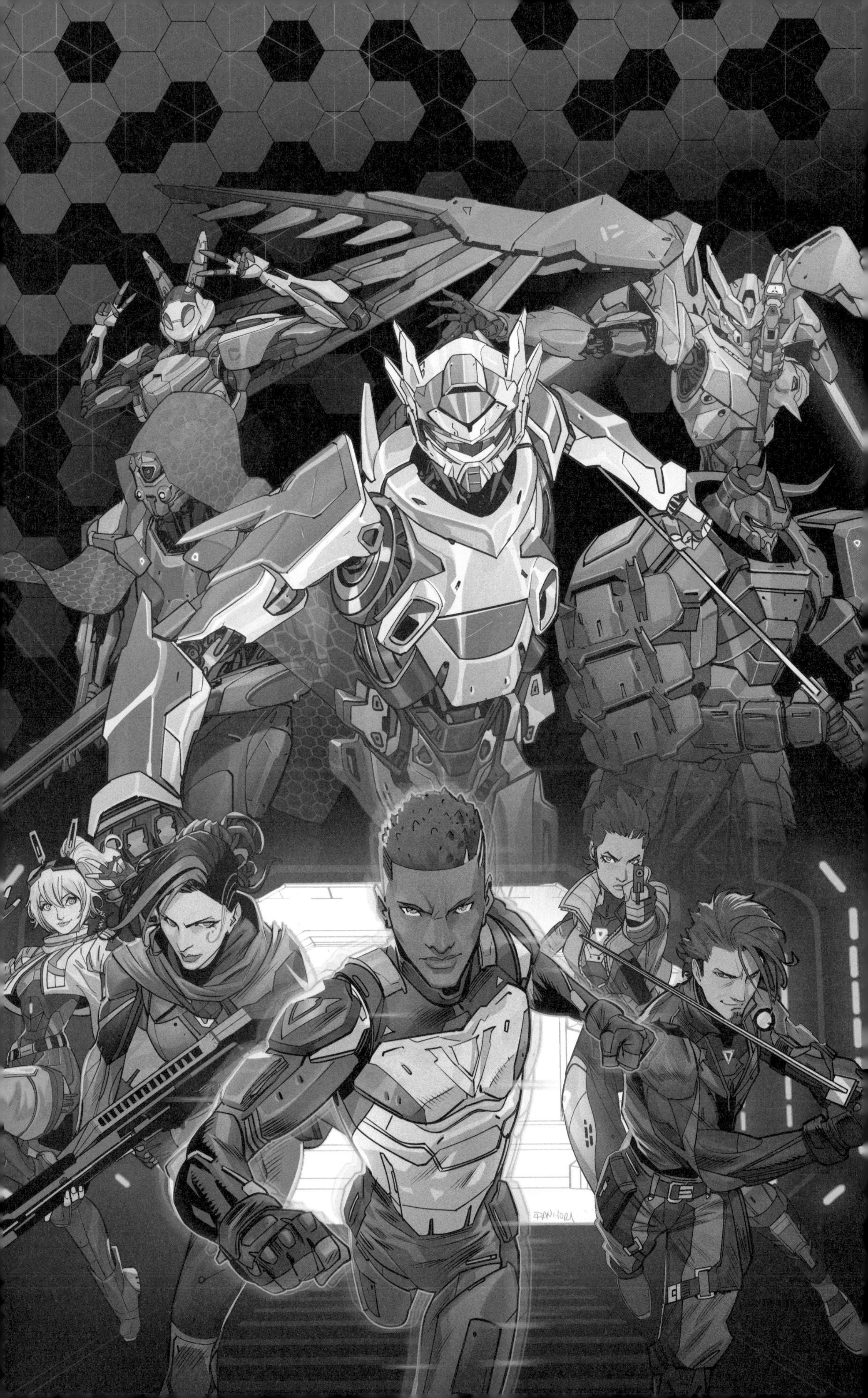

V

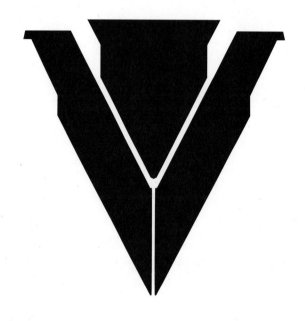

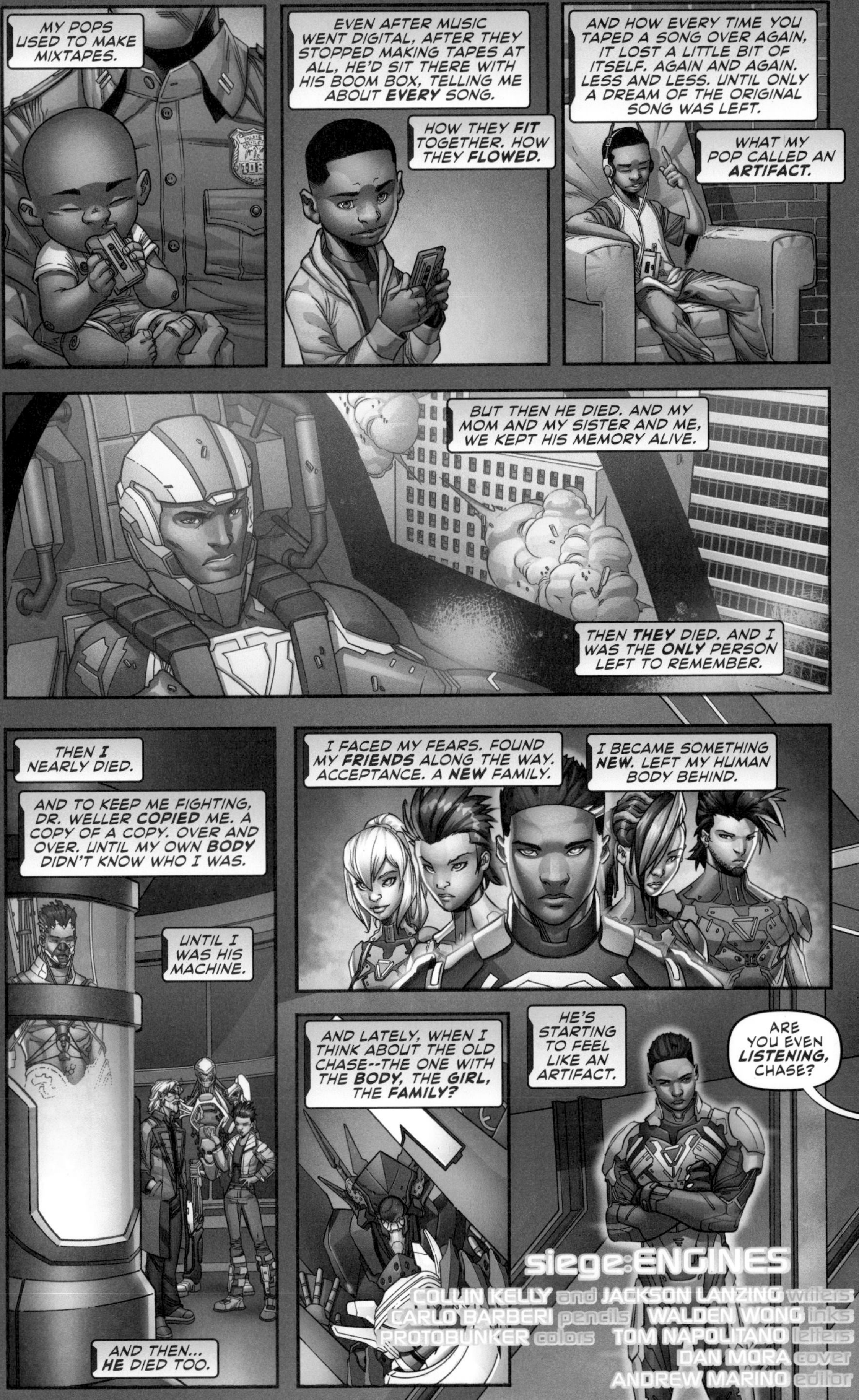
MY POPS USED TO MAKE MIXTAPES.
EVEN AFTER MUSIC WENT DIGITAL, AFTER THEY STOPPED MAKING TAPES AT ALL, HE'D SIT THERE WITH HIS BOOM BOX, TELLING ME ABOUT EVERY SONG.
HOW THEY FIT TOGETHER. HOW THEY FLOWED.
AND HOW EVERY TIME YOU TAPED A SONG OVER AGAIN, IT LOST A LITTLE BIT OF ITSELF. AGAIN AND AGAIN. LESS AND LESS. UNTIL ONLY A DREAM OF THE ORIGINAL SONG WAS LEFT.
WHAT MY POP CALLED AN ARTIFACT.
BUT THEN HE DIED. AND MY MOM AND MY SISTER AND ME, WE KEPT HIS MEMORY ALIVE.
THEN THEY DIED. AND I WAS THE ONLY PERSON LEFT TO REMEMBER.
THEN I NEARLY DIED.
AND TO KEEP ME FIGHTING, DR. WELLER COPIED ME. A COPY OF A COPY. OVER AND OVER. UNTIL MY OWN BODY DIDN'T KNOW WHO I WAS.
UNTIL I WAS HIS MACHINE.
AND THEN... HE DIED TOO.
I FACED MY FEARS. FOUND MY FRIENDS ALONG THE WAY. ACCEPTANCE. A NEW FAMILY.
I BECAME SOMETHING NEW. LEFT MY HUMAN BODY BEHIND.
AND LATELY, WHEN I THINK ABOUT THE OLD CHASE--THE ONE WITH THE BODY, THE GIRL, THE FAMILY?
HE'S STARTING TO FEEL LIKE AN ARTIFACT.
ARE YOU EVEN LISTENING, CHASE?
siege:ENGINES
COLLIN KELLY and JACKSON LANZING writers
CARLO BARBERI pencils WALDEN WONG inks
PROTOBUNKER colors TOM NAPOLITANO letters
DAN MORA cover
ANDREW MARINO editor

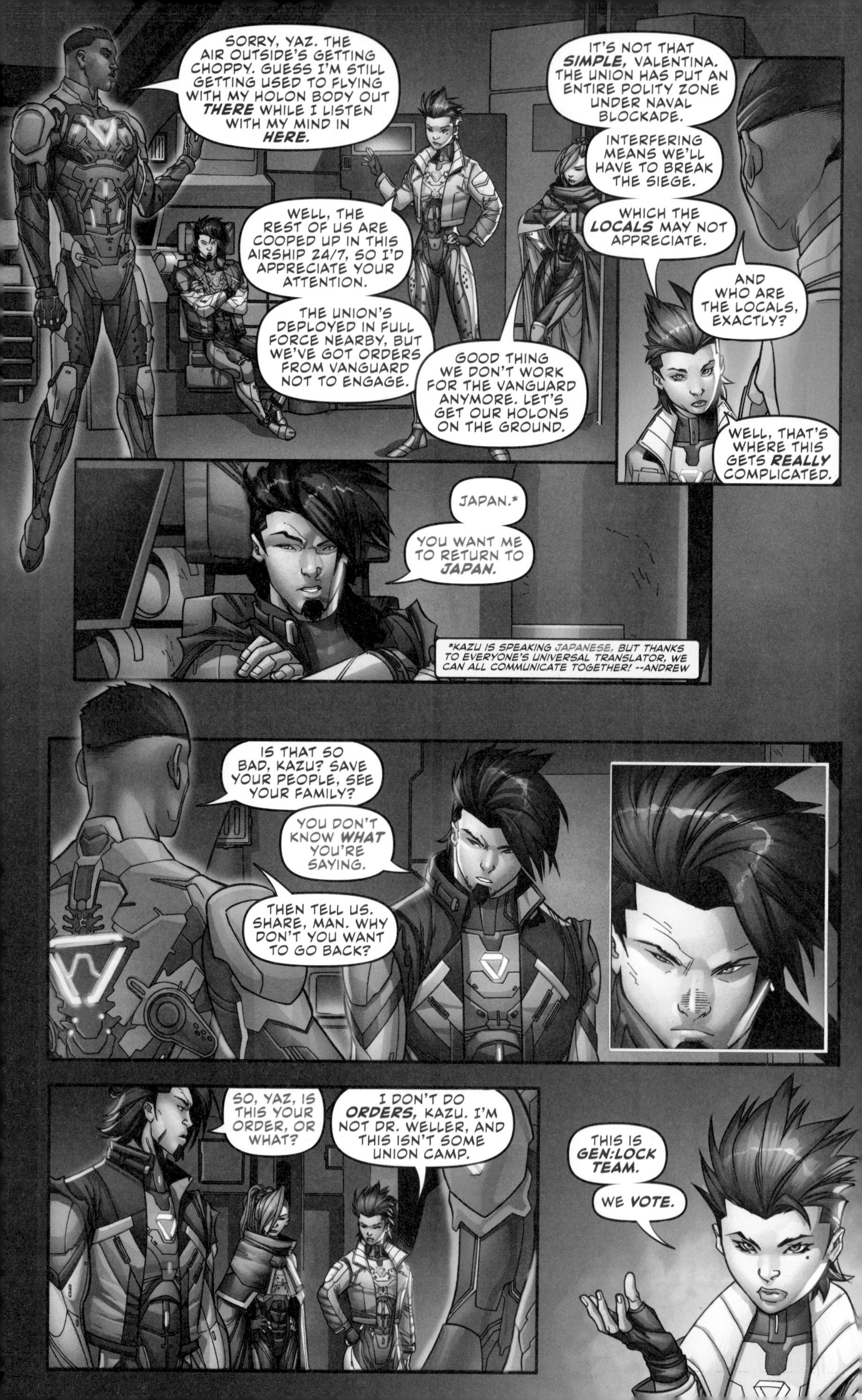
SORRY, YAZ. THE AIR OUTSIDE'S GETTING CHOPPY. GUESS I'M STILL GETTING USED TO FLYING WITH MY HOLON BODY OUT THERE WHILE I LISTEN WITH MY MIND IN HERE.
WELL, THE REST OF US ARE COOPED UP IN THIS AIRSHIP 24/7, SO I'D APPRECIATE YOUR ATTENTION.
THE UNION'S DEPLOYED IN FULL FORCE NEARBY, BUT WE'VE GOT ORDERS FROM VANGUARD NOT TO ENGAGE.
GOOD THING WE DON'T WORK FOR THE VANGUARD ANYMORE. LET'S GET OUR HOLONS ON THE GROUND.
IT'S NOT THAT SIMPLE, VALENTINA. THE UNION HAS PUT AN ENTIRE POLITY ZONE UNDER NAVAL BLOCKADE.
INTERFERING MEANS WE'LL HAVE TO BREAK THE SIEGE.
WHICH THE LOCALS MAY NOT APPRECIATE.
AND WHO ARE THE LOCALS, EXACTLY?
WELL, THAT'S WHERE THIS GETS REALLY COMPLICATED.
JAPAN.*
YOU WANT ME TO RETURN TO JAPAN.
*KAZU IS SPEAKING JAPANESE, BUT THANKS TO EVERYONE'S UNIVERSAL TRANSLATOR, WE CAN ALL COMMUNICATE TOGETHER! --ANDREW
IS THAT SO BAD, KAZU? SAVE YOUR PEOPLE, SEE YOUR FAMILY?
YOU DON'T KNOW WHAT YOU'RE SAYING.
THEN TELL US. SHARE, MAN. WHY DON'T YOU WANT TO GO BACK?
SO, YAZ, IS THIS YOUR ORDER, OR WHAT?
I DON'T DO ORDERS, KAZU. I'M NOT DR. WELLER, AND THIS ISN'T SOME UNION CAMP.
THIS IS GEN:LOCK TEAM.
WE VOTE.

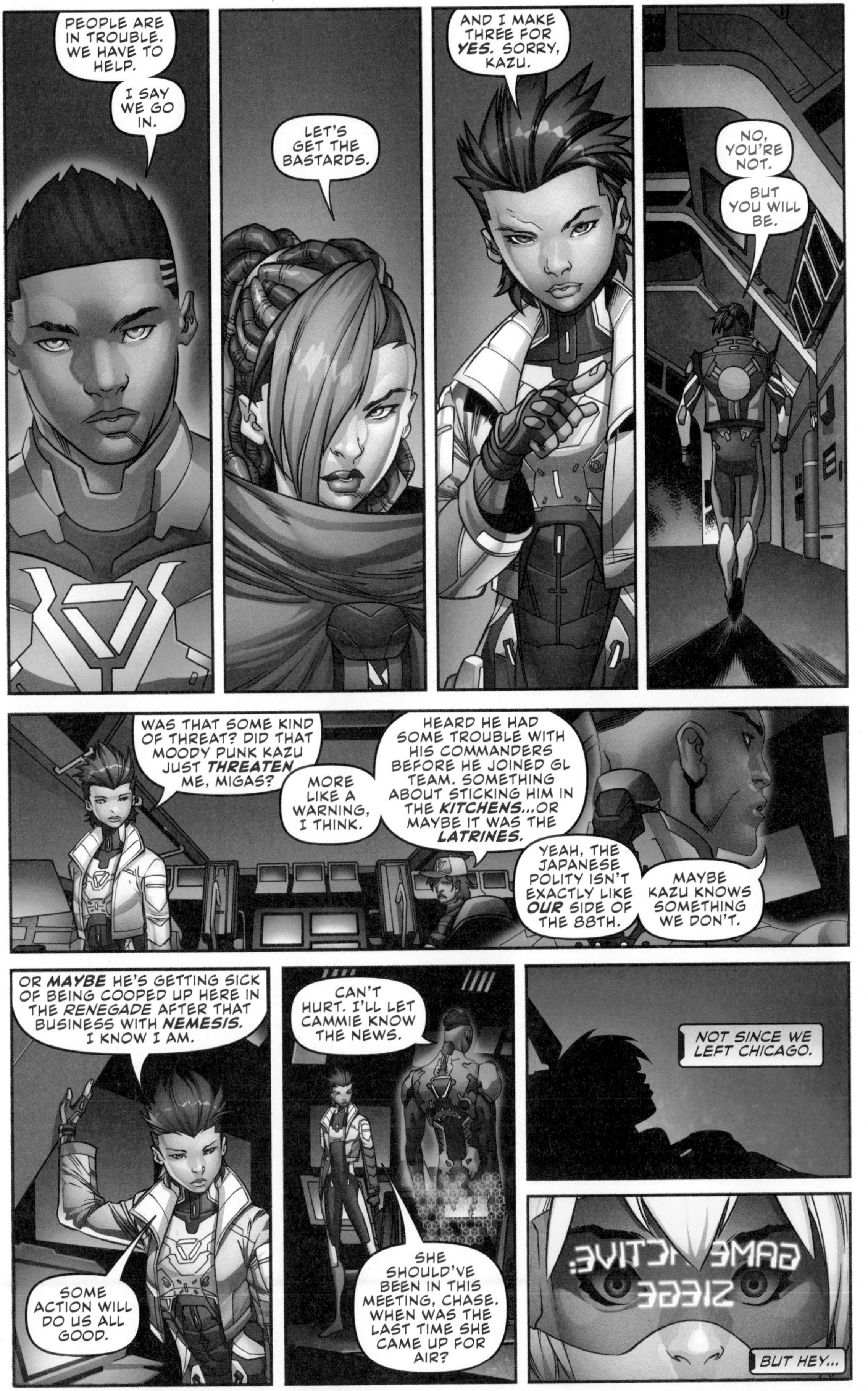

PEOPLE ARE IN TROUBLE. WE HAVE TO HELP.
I SAY WE GO IN.
LET'S GET THE BASTARDS.
AND I MAKE THREE FOR YES. SORRY, KAZU.
NO, YOU'RE NOT.
BUT YOU WILL BE.
WAS THAT SOME KIND OF THREAT? DID THAT MOODY PUNK KAZU JUST THREATEN ME, MIGAS?
MORE LIKE A WARNING, I THINK.
HEARD HE HAD SOME TROUBLE WITH HIS COMMANDERS BEFORE HE JOINED GL TEAM. SOMETHING ABOUT STICKING HIM IN THE KITCHENS...OR MAYBE IT WAS THE LATRINES.
YEAH, THE JAPANESE POLITY ISN'T EXACTLY LIKE OUR SIDE OF THE 88TH.
MAYBE KAZU KNOWS SOMETHING WE DON'T.
OR MAYBE HE'S GETTING SICK OF BEING COOPED UP HERE IN THE RENEGADE AFTER THAT BUSINESS WITH NEMESIS. I KNOW I AM.
SOME ACTION WILL DO US ALL GOOD.
CAN'T HURT. I'LL LET CAMMIE KNOW THE NEWS.
SHE SHOULD'VE BEEN IN THIS MEETING, CHASE. WHEN WAS THE LAST TIME SHE CAME UP FOR AIR?
NOT SINCE WE LEFT CHICAGO.
BUT HEY...

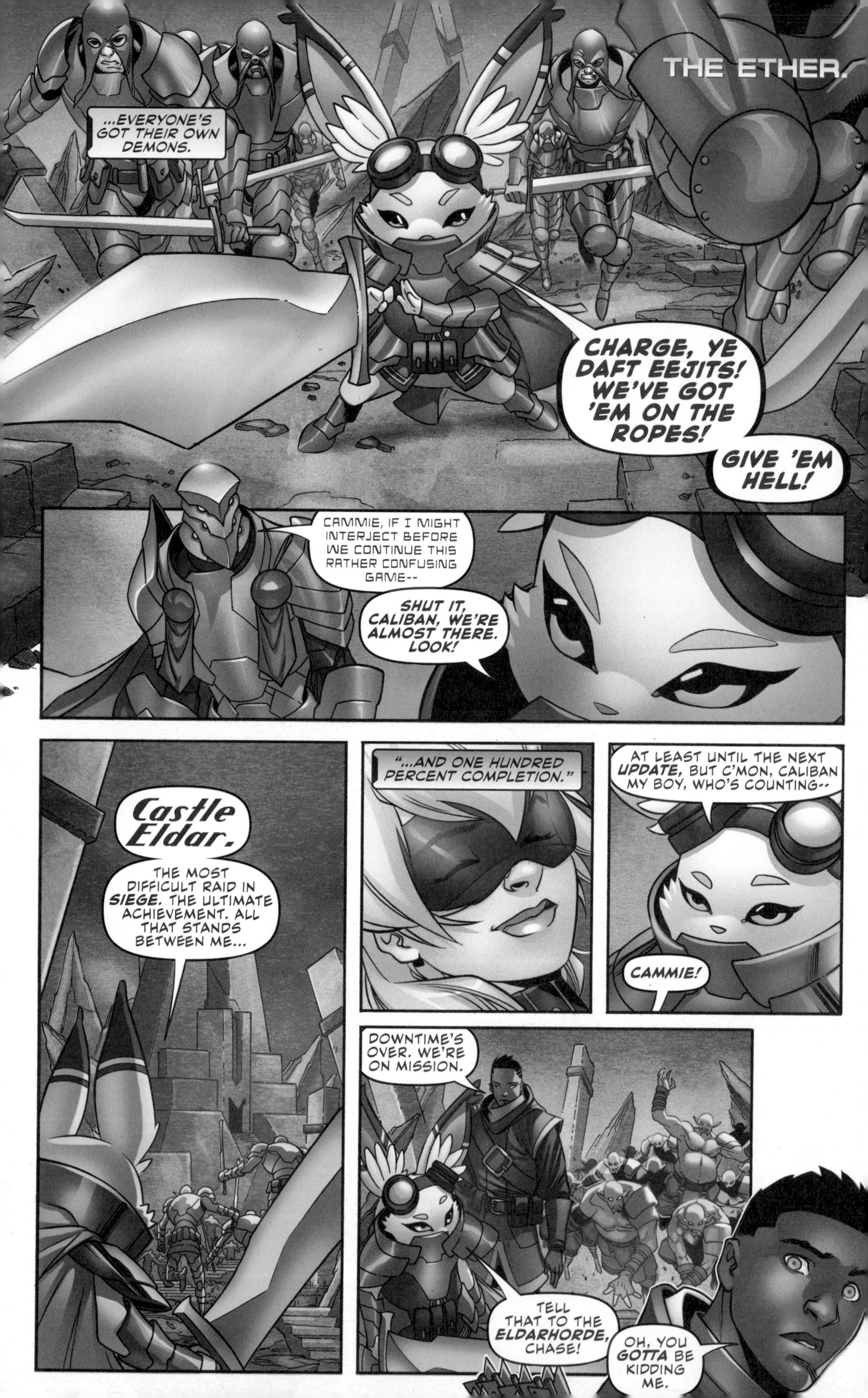
THE ETHER.
...EVERYONE'S GOT THEIR OWN DEMONS.
CHARGE, YE DAFT EEJITS! WE'VE GOT 'EM ON THE ROPES!
GIVE 'EM HELL!
CAMMIE, IF I MIGHT INTERJECT BEFORE WE CONTINUE THIS RATHER CONFUSING GAME--
SHUT IT, CALIBAN, WE'RE ALMOST THERE. LOOK!
Castle Eldar.
THE MOST DIFFICULT RAID IN SIEGE. THE ULTIMATE ACHIEVEMENT. ALL THAT STANDS BETWEEN ME...
"...AND ONE HUNDRED PERCENT COMPLETION."
AT LEAST UNTIL THE NEXT UPDATE, BUT C'MON, CALIBAN MY BOY, WHO'S COUNTING--
CAMMIE!
DOWNTIME'S OVER. WE'RE ON MISSION.
TELL THAT TO THE ELDARHORDE, CHASE!
OH, YOU GOTTA BE KIDDING ME.

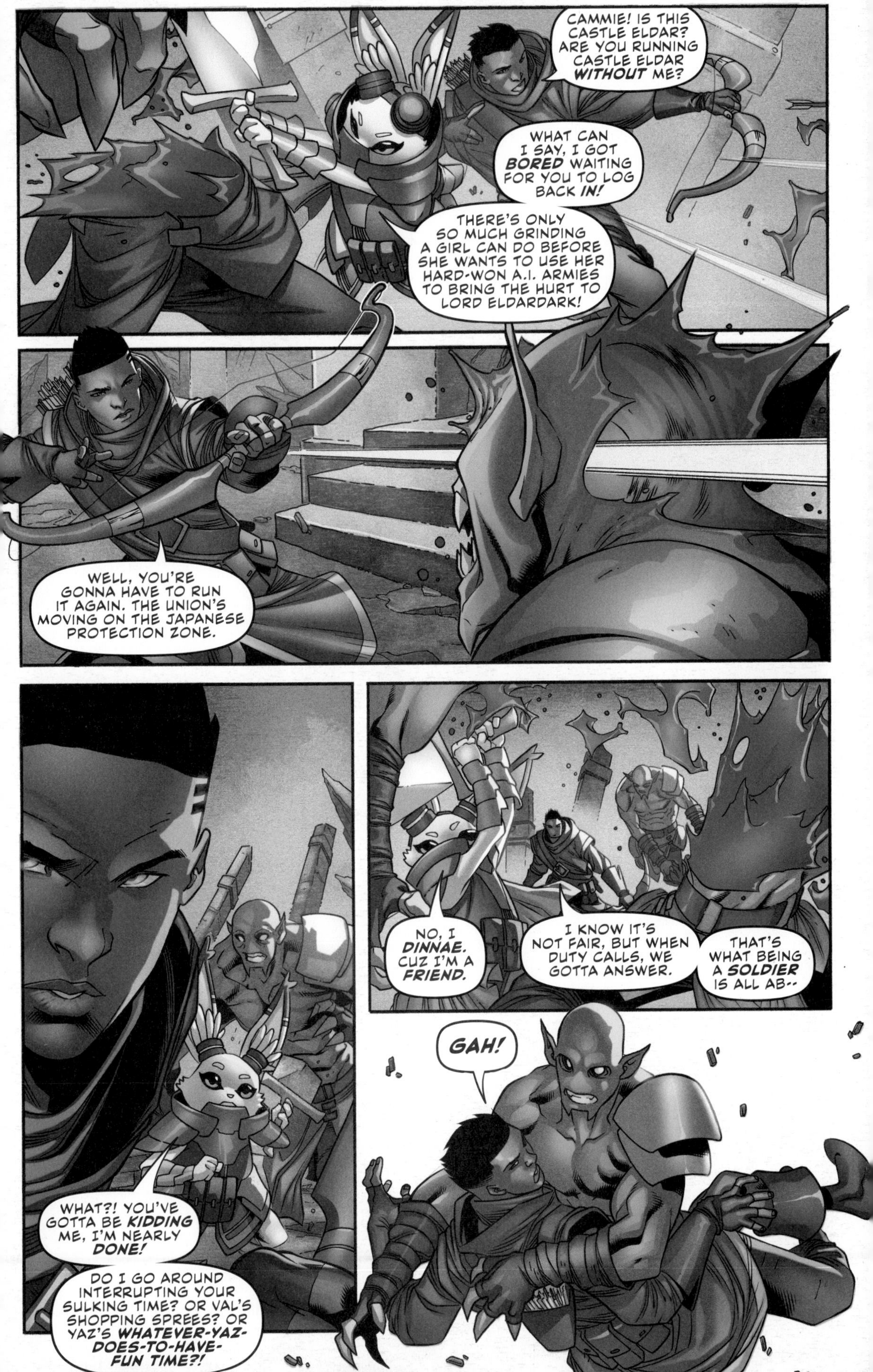

CAMMIE! IS THIS CASTLE ELDAR? ARE YOU RUNNING CASTLE ELDAR **WITHOUT** ME?
WHAT CAN I SAY, I GOT **BORED** WAITING FOR YOU TO LOG BACK **IN!**
THERE'S ONLY SO MUCH GRINDING A GIRL CAN DO BEFORE SHE WANTS TO USE HER HARD-WON A.I. ARMIES TO BRING THE HURT TO LORD ELDARDARK!
WELL, YOU'RE GONNA HAVE TO RUN IT AGAIN. THE UNION'S MOVING ON THE JAPANESE PROTECTION ZONE.
WHAT?! YOU'VE GOTTA BE **KIDDING** ME, I'M NEARLY **DONE!**
DO I GO AROUND INTERRUPTING YOUR SULKING TIME? OR VAL'S SHOPPING SPREES? OR YAZ'S **WHATEVER-YAZ-DOES-TO-HAVE-FUN TIME?!**
NO, I **DINNAE.** CUZ I'M A **FRIEND.**
I KNOW IT'S NOT FAIR, BUT WHEN DUTY CALLS, WE GOTTA ANSWER.
THAT'S WHAT BEING A **SOLDIER** IS ALL AB--
GAH!

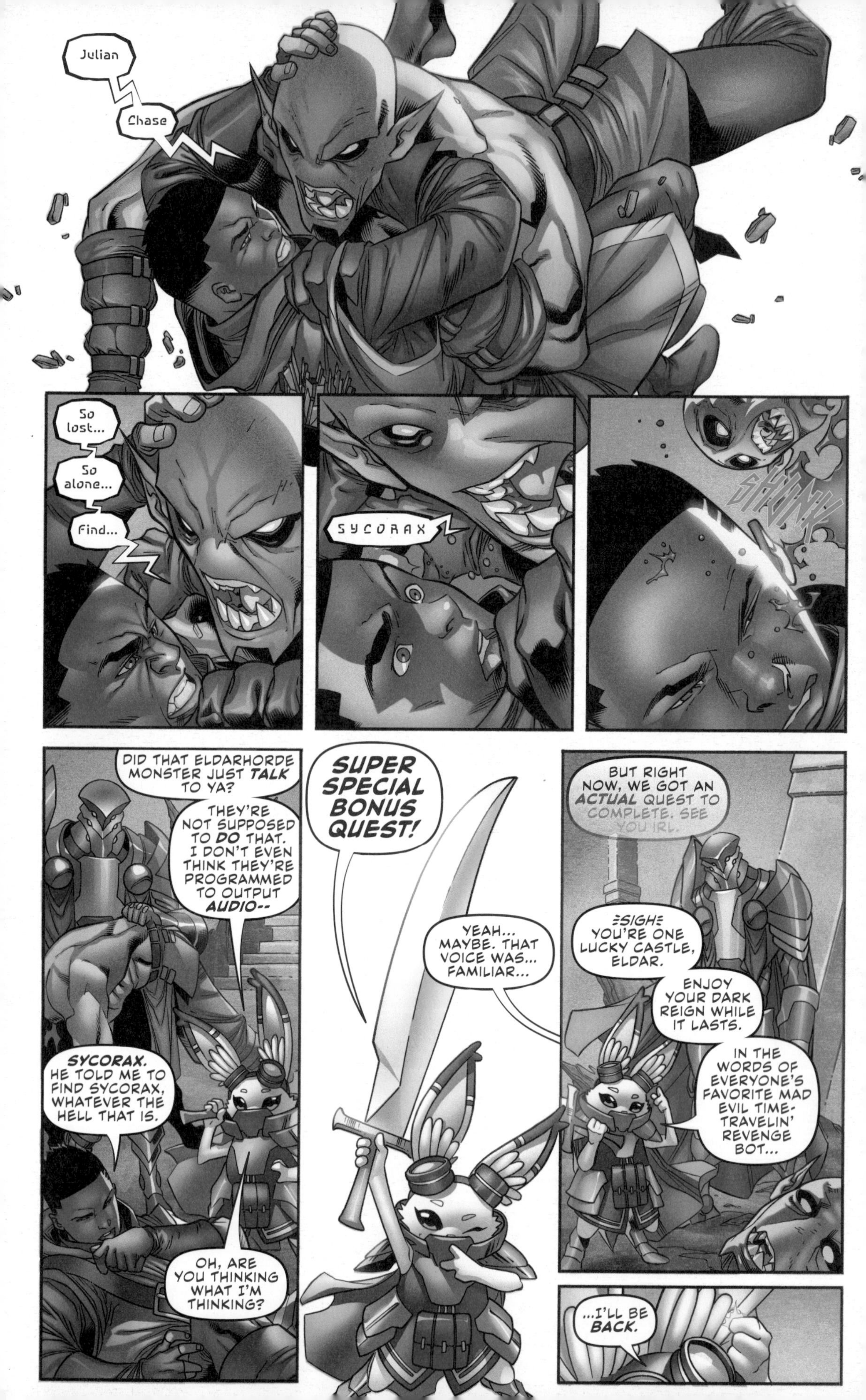
Julian
Chase
So lost...
So alone...
Find...
SYCORAX
SHUNK
DID THAT ELDARHORDE MONSTER JUST TALK TO YA?
THEY'RE NOT SUPPOSED TO DO THAT. I DON'T EVEN THINK THEY'RE PROGRAMMED TO OUTPUT AUDIO--
SYCORAX. HE TOLD ME TO FIND SYCORAX, WHATEVER THE HELL THAT IS.
OH, ARE YOU THINKING WHAT I'M THINKING?
SUPER SPECIAL BONUS QUEST!
YEAH... MAYBE. THAT VOICE WAS... FAMILIAR...
BUT RIGHT NOW, WE GOT AN ACTUAL QUEST TO COMPLETE. SEE YOU IRL.
SIGH YOU'RE ONE LUCKY CASTLE, ELDAR.
ENJOY YOUR DARK REIGN WHILE IT LASTS.
IN THE WORDS OF EVERYONE'S FAVORITE MAD EVIL TIME-TRAVELIN' REVENGE BOT...
...I'LL BE BACK.

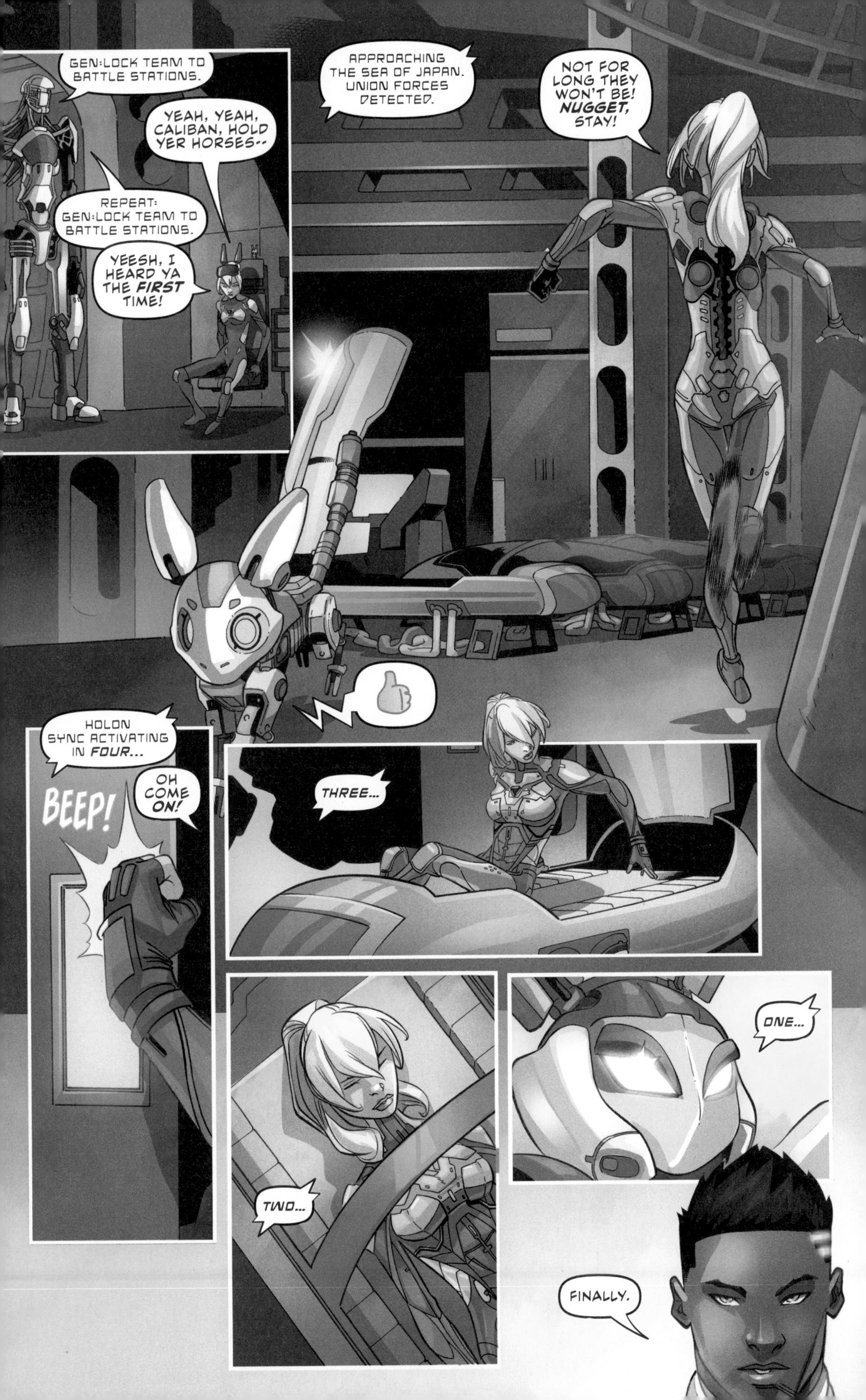
GEN:LOCK TEAM TO BATTLE STATIONS.
YEAH, YEAH, CALIBAN, HOLD YER HORSES--
REPEAT: GEN:LOCK TEAM TO BATTLE STATIONS.
YEESH, I HEARD YA THE FIRST TIME!
APPROACHING THE SEA OF JAPAN. UNION FORCES DETECTED.
NOT FOR LONG THEY WON'T BE! NUGGET, STAY!
HOLON SYNC ACTIVATING IN FOUR...
BEEP!
OH COME ON!
THREE...
TWO...
ONE...
FINALLY.

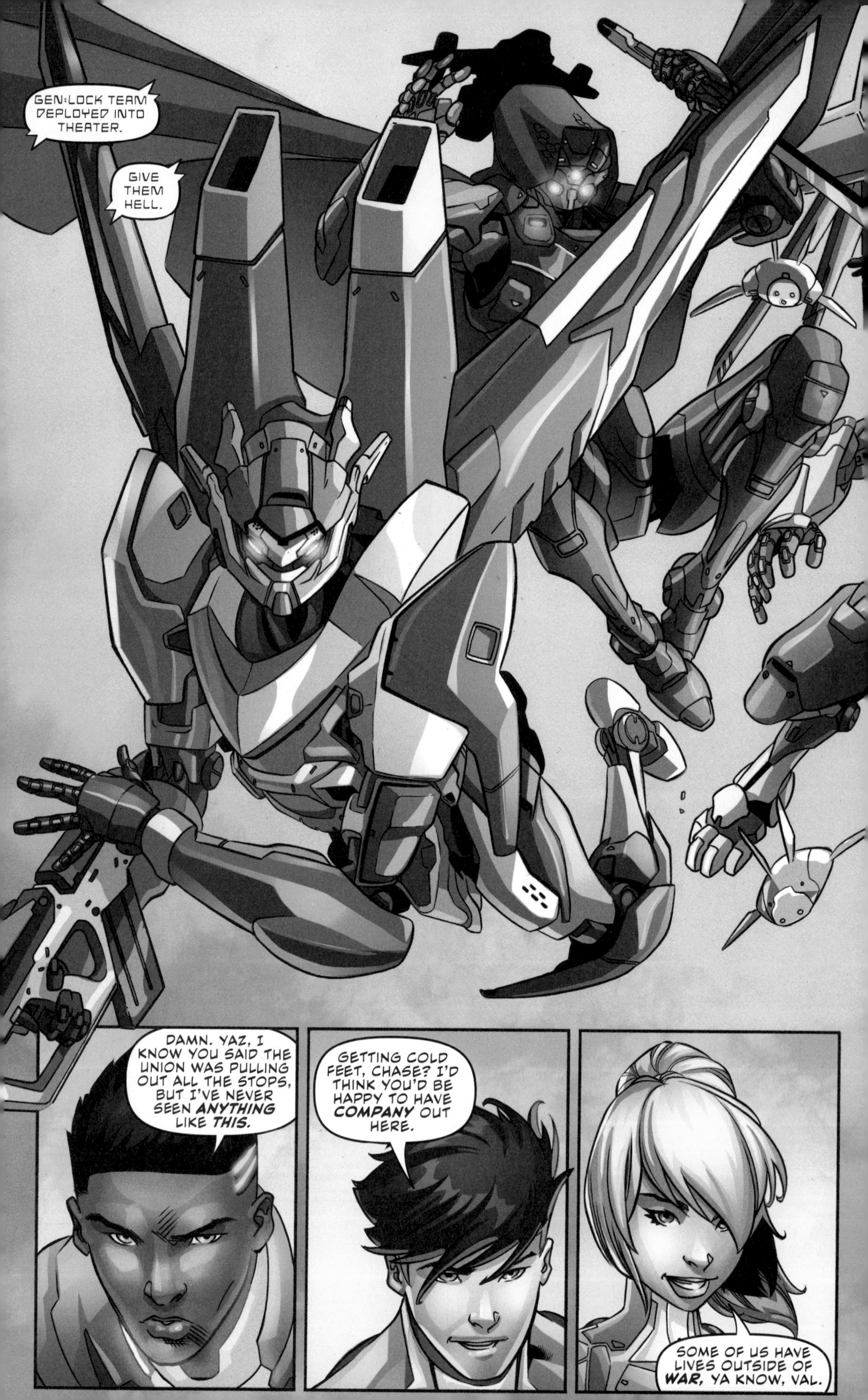
GEN:LOCK TEAM DEPLOYED INTO THEATER.
GIVE THEM HELL.
DAMN. YAZ, I KNOW YOU SAID THE UNION WAS PULLING OUT ALL THE STOPS, BUT I'VE NEVER SEEN ANYTHING LIKE THIS.
GETTING COLD FEET, CHASE? I'D THINK YOU'D BE HAPPY TO HAVE COMPANY OUT HERE.
SOME OF US HAVE LIVES OUTSIDE OF WAR, YA KNOW, VAL.

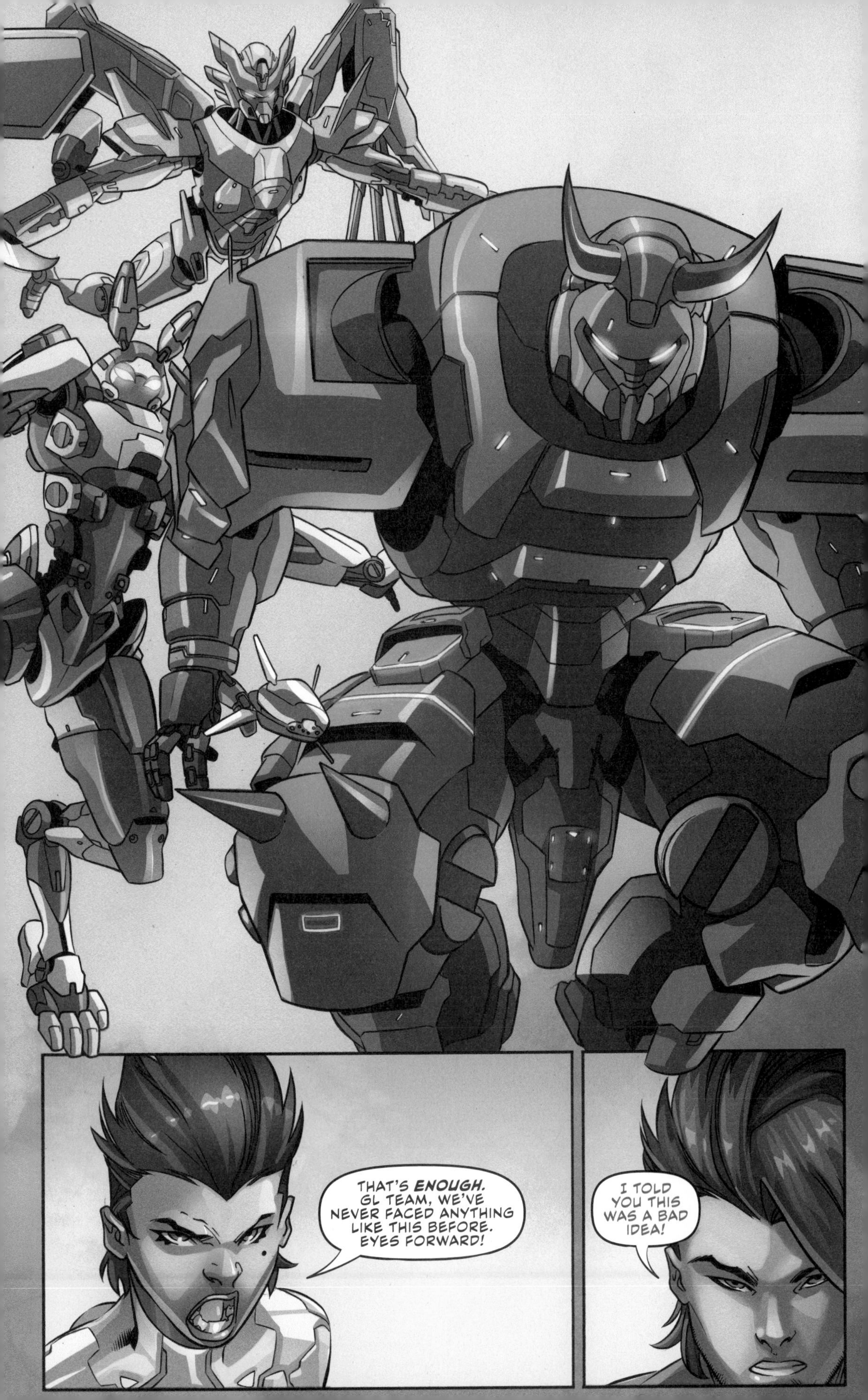
THAT'S ENOUGH. GL TEAM, WE'VE NEVER FACED ANYTHING LIKE THIS BEFORE. EYES FORWARD!
I TOLD YOU THIS WAS A BAD IDEA!

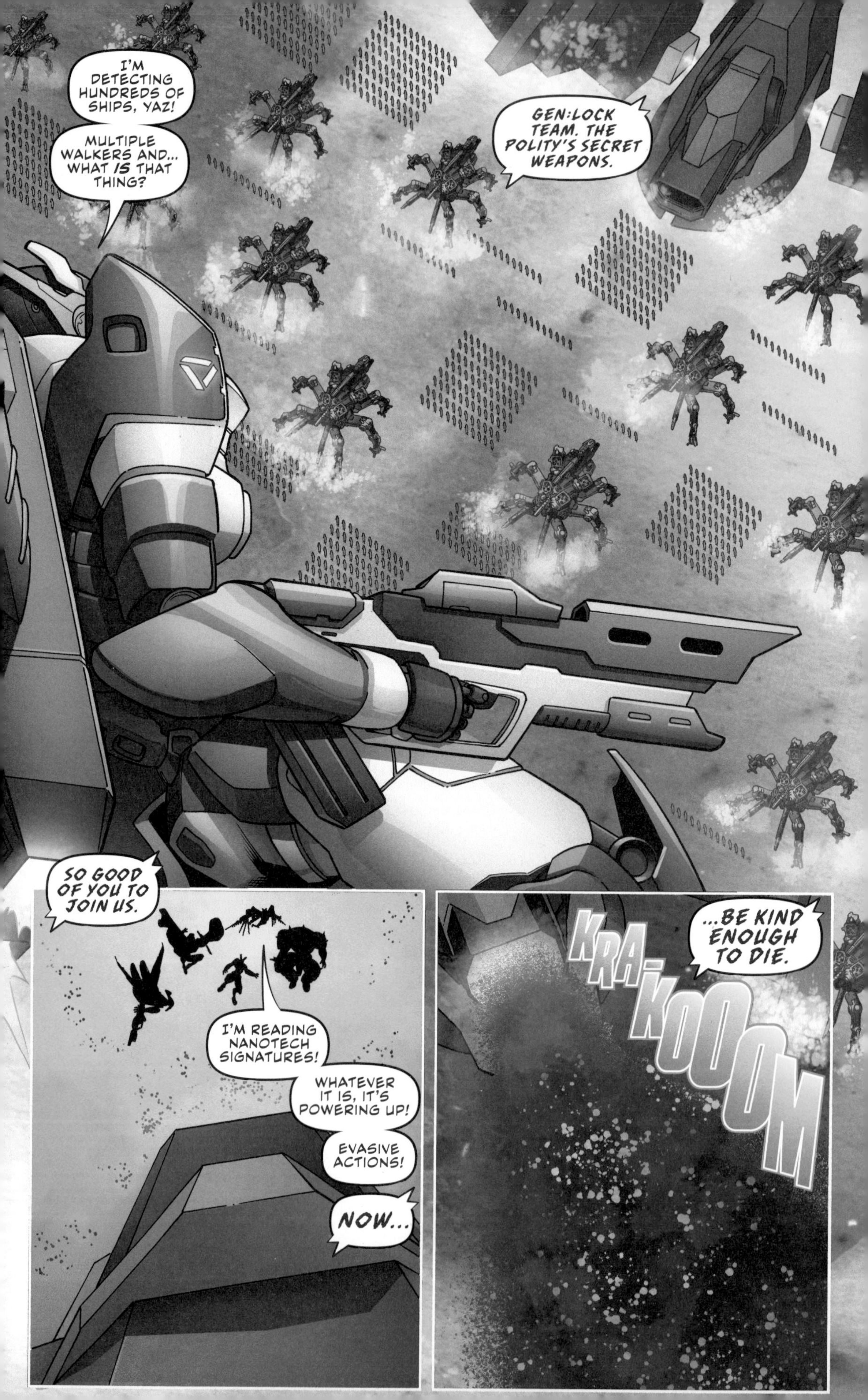
I'M DETECTING HUNDREDS OF SHIPS, YAZ!
MULTIPLE WALKERS AND... WHAT *IS* THAT THING?
GEN:LOCK TEAM. THE POLITY'S SECRET WEAPONS.
SO GOOD OF YOU TO JOIN US.
I'M READING NANOTECH SIGNATURES!
WHATEVER IT IS, IT'S POWERING UP!
EVASIVE ACTIONS!
NOW...
...BE KIND ENOUGH TO DIE.
KRA-KOOOOM

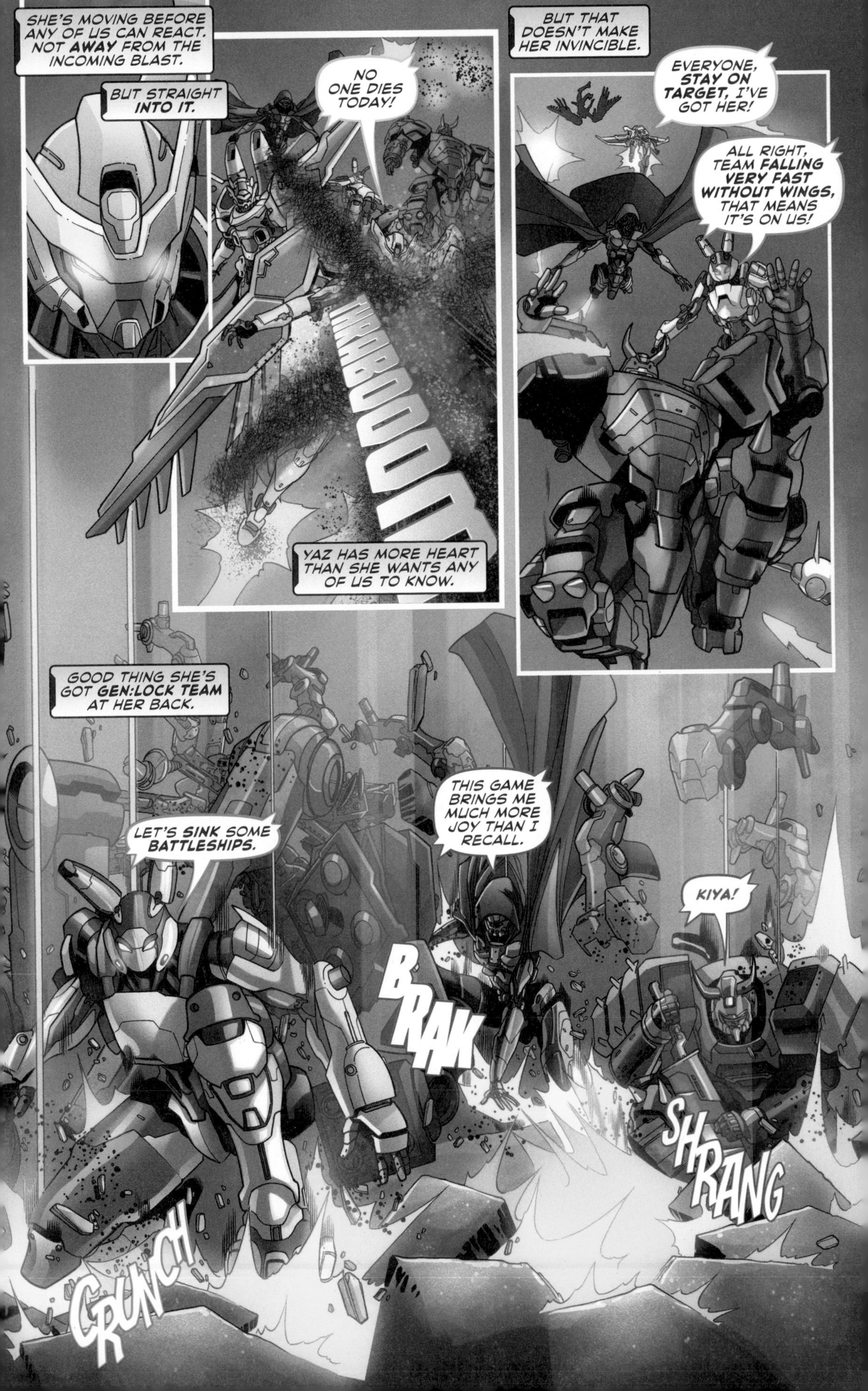
SHE'S MOVING BEFORE ANY OF US CAN REACT. NOT AWAY FROM THE INCOMING BLAST.
BUT STRAIGHT INTO IT.
NO ONE DIES TODAY!
THRABOOOM
YAZ HAS MORE HEART THAN SHE WANTS ANY OF US TO KNOW.
BUT THAT DOESN'T MAKE HER INVINCIBLE.
EVERYONE, STAY ON TARGET, I'VE GOT HER!
ALL RIGHT, TEAM FALLING VERY FAST WITHOUT WINGS, THAT MEANS IT'S ON US!
GOOD THING SHE'S GOT GEN:LOCK TEAM AT HER BACK.
LET'S SINK SOME BATTLESHIPS.
THIS GAME BRINGS ME MUCH MORE JOY THAN I RECALL.
KIYA!
BRAK
SHRANG
CRUNCH

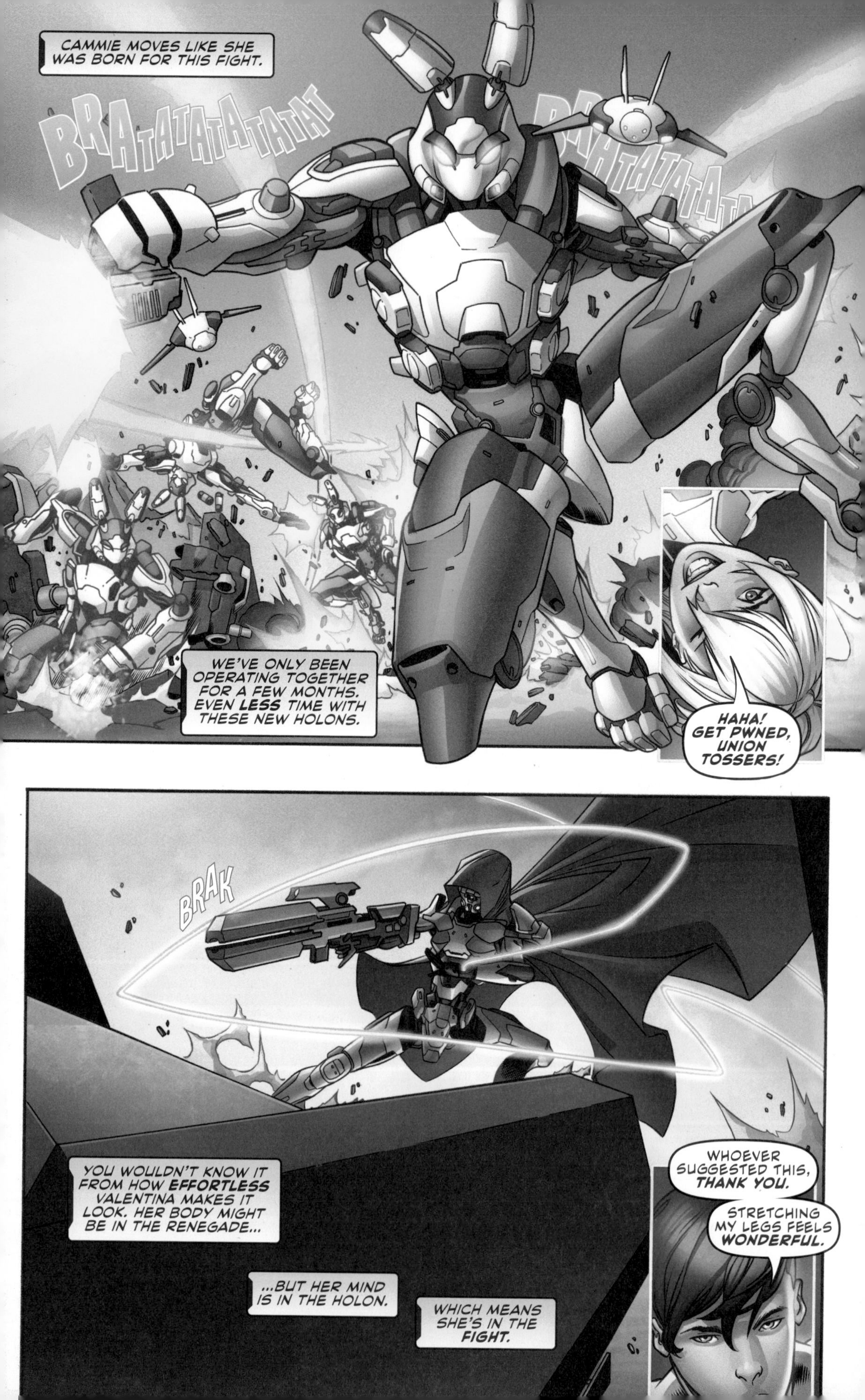

CAMMIE MOVES LIKE SHE WAS BORN FOR THIS FIGHT.
BRATATATATATATAT
BRATATATATA
WE'VE ONLY BEEN OPERATING TOGETHER FOR A FEW MONTHS. EVEN LESS TIME WITH THESE NEW HOLONS.
HAHA! GET PWNED, UNION TOSSERS!
BRAK
YOU WOULDN'T KNOW IT FROM HOW EFFORTLESS VALENTINA MAKES IT LOOK. HER BODY MIGHT BE IN THE RENEGADE...
...BUT HER MIND IS IN THE HOLON.
WHICH MEANS SHE'S IN THE FIGHT.
WHOEVER SUGGESTED THIS, THANK YOU.
STRETCHING MY LEGS FEELS WONDERFUL.

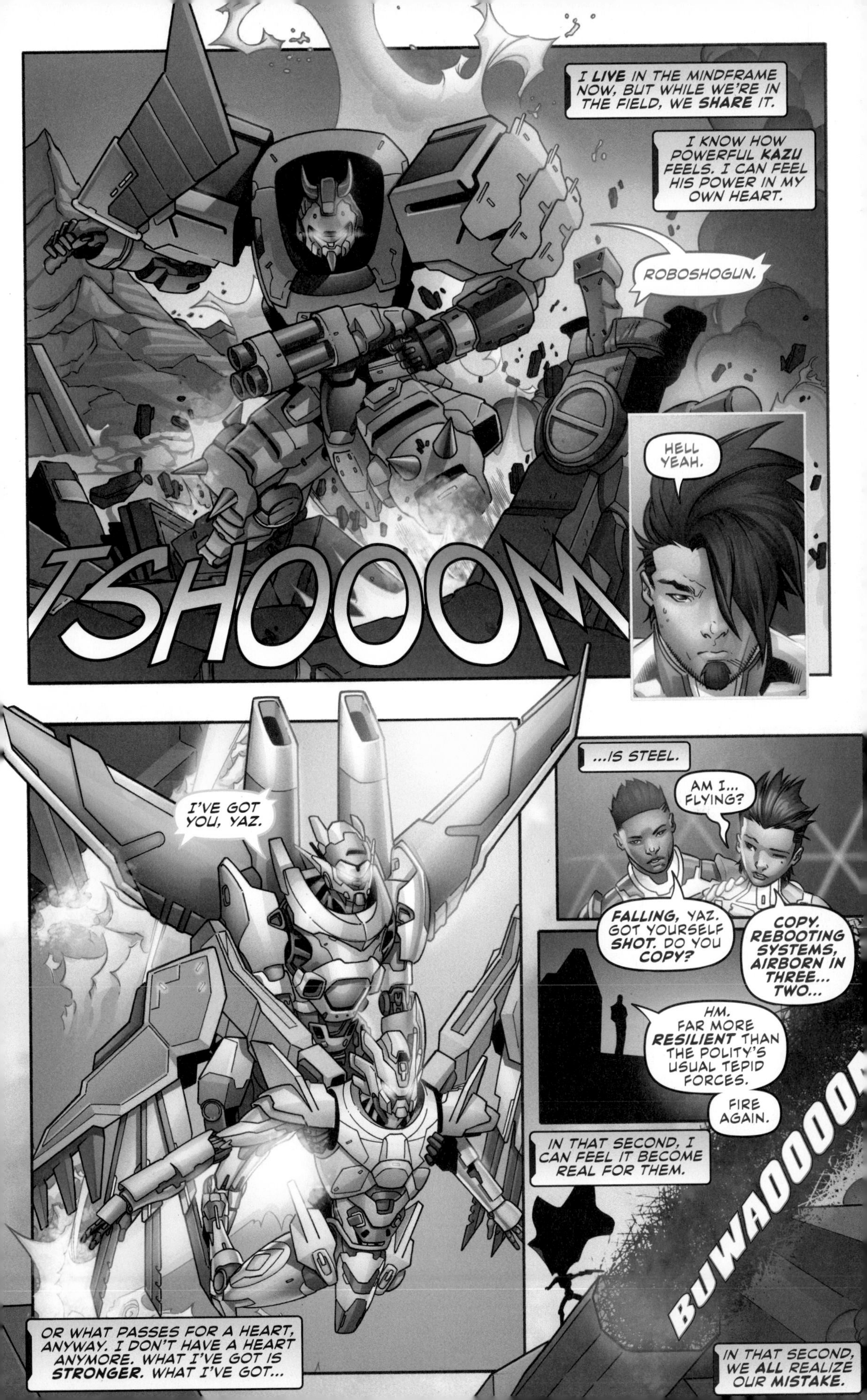
I LIVE IN THE MINDFRAME NOW, BUT WHILE WE'RE IN THE FIELD, WE SHARE IT.
I KNOW HOW POWERFUL KAZU FEELS. I CAN FEEL HIS POWER IN MY OWN HEART.
ROBOSHOGUN.
TSHOOOM
HELL YEAH.
OR WHAT PASSES FOR A HEART, ANYWAY. I DON'T HAVE A HEART ANYMORE. WHAT I'VE GOT IS STRONGER. WHAT I'VE GOT...
I'VE GOT YOU, YAZ.
...IS STEEL.
AM I... FLYING?
FALLING, YAZ. GOT YOURSELF SHOT. DO YOU COPY?
COPY. REBOOTING SYSTEMS, AIRBORN IN THREE... TWO...
HM. FAR MORE RESILIENT THAN THE POLITY'S USUAL TEPID FORCES.
FIRE AGAIN.
IN THAT SECOND, I CAN FEEL IT BECOME REAL FOR THEM.
BUWAOOOOO
IN THAT SECOND, WE ALL REALIZE OUR MISTAKE.

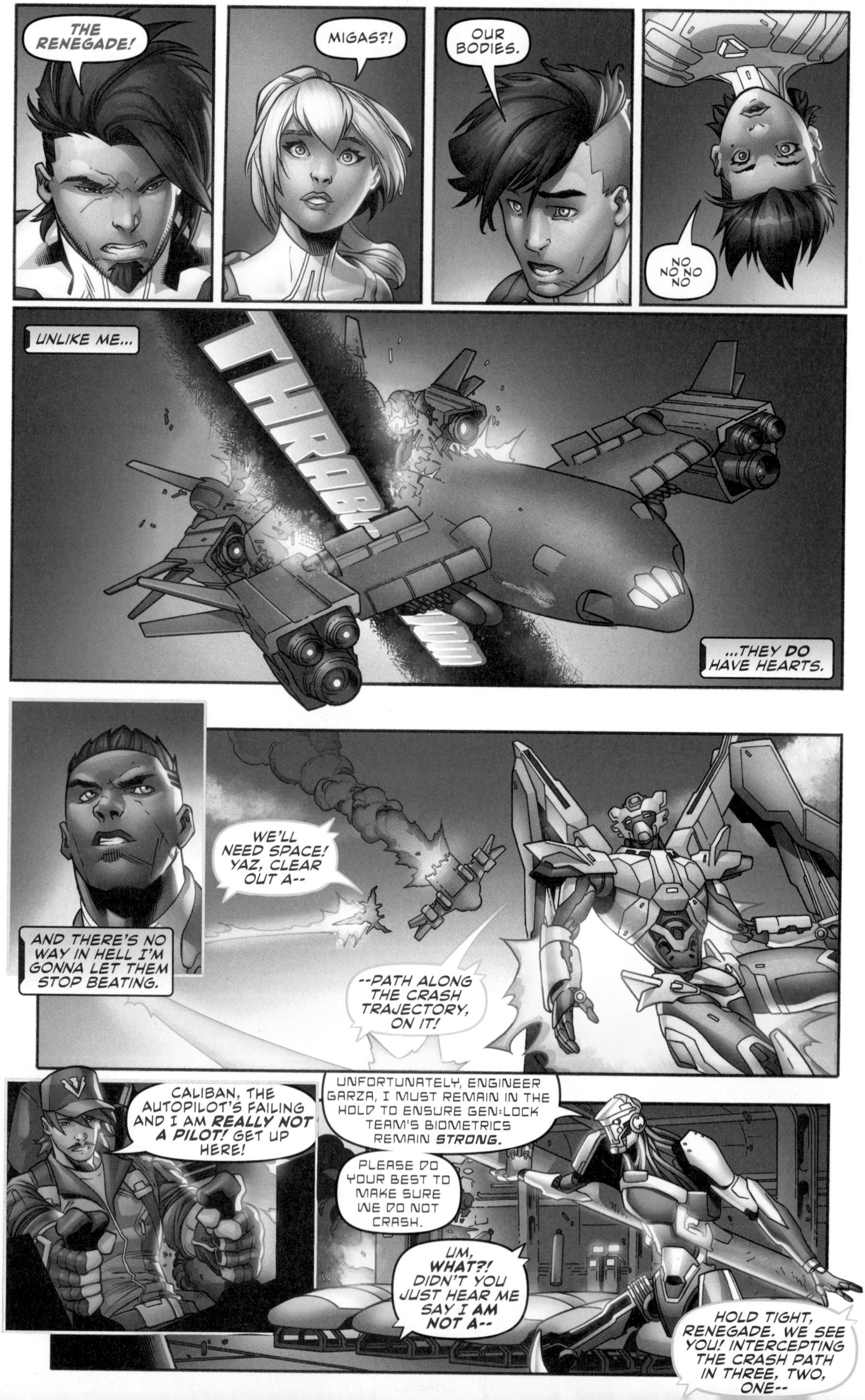
THE RENEGADE!
MIGAS?!
OUR BODIES.
NO NO, NO NO
UNLIKE ME...
THROBB
...THEY DO HAVE HEARTS.
WE'LL NEED SPACE! YAZ, CLEAR OUT A--
AND THERE'S NO WAY IN HELL I'M GONNA LET THEM STOP BEATING.
--PATH ALONG THE CRASH TRAJECTORY, ON IT!
CALIBAN, THE AUTOPILOT'S FAILING AND I AM REALLY NOT A PILOT! GET UP HERE!
UNFORTUNATELY, ENGINEER GARZA, I MUST REMAIN IN THE HOLD TO ENSURE GEN:LOCK TEAM'S BIOMETRICS REMAIN STRONG.
PLEASE DO YOUR BEST TO MAKE SURE WE DO NOT CRASH.
UM, WHAT?! DIDN'T YOU JUST HEAR ME SAY I AM NOT A--
HOLD TIGHT, RENEGADE. WE SEE YOU! INTERCEPTING THE CRASH PATH IN THREE, TWO, ONE--

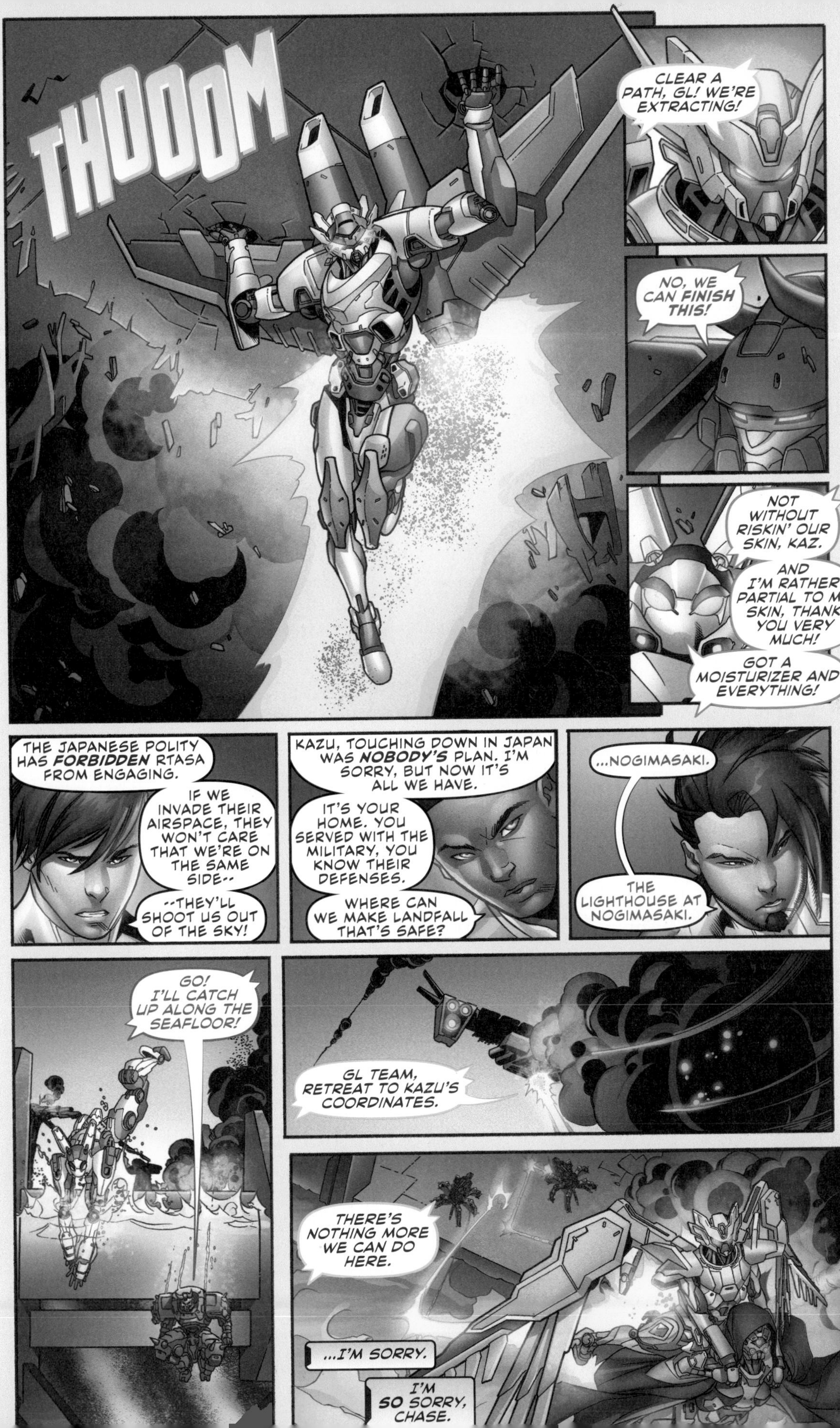
THOOOM
CLEAR A PATH, GL! WE'RE EXTRACTING!
NO, WE CAN FINISH THIS!
NOT WITHOUT RISKIN' OUR SKIN, KAZ.
AND I'M RATHER PARTIAL TO MY SKIN, THANK YOU VERY MUCH!
GOT A MOISTURIZER AND EVERYTHING!
THE JAPANESE POLITY HAS FORBIDDEN RTASA FROM ENGAGING.
IF WE INVADE THEIR AIRSPACE, THEY WON'T CARE THAT WE'RE ON THE SAME SIDE--
--THEY'LL SHOOT US OUT OF THE SKY!
KAZU, TOUCHING DOWN IN JAPAN WAS NOBODY'S PLAN. I'M SORRY, BUT NOW IT'S ALL WE HAVE.
IT'S YOUR HOME. YOU SERVED WITH THE MILITARY, YOU KNOW THEIR DEFENSES.
WHERE CAN WE MAKE LANDFALL THAT'S SAFE?
...NOGIMASAKI.
THE LIGHTHOUSE AT NOGIMASAKI.
GO! I'LL CATCH UP ALONG THE SEAFLOOR!
GL TEAM, RETREAT TO KAZU'S COORDINATES.
THERE'S NOTHING MORE WE CAN DO HERE.
...I'M SORRY.
I'M SO SORRY, CHASE.

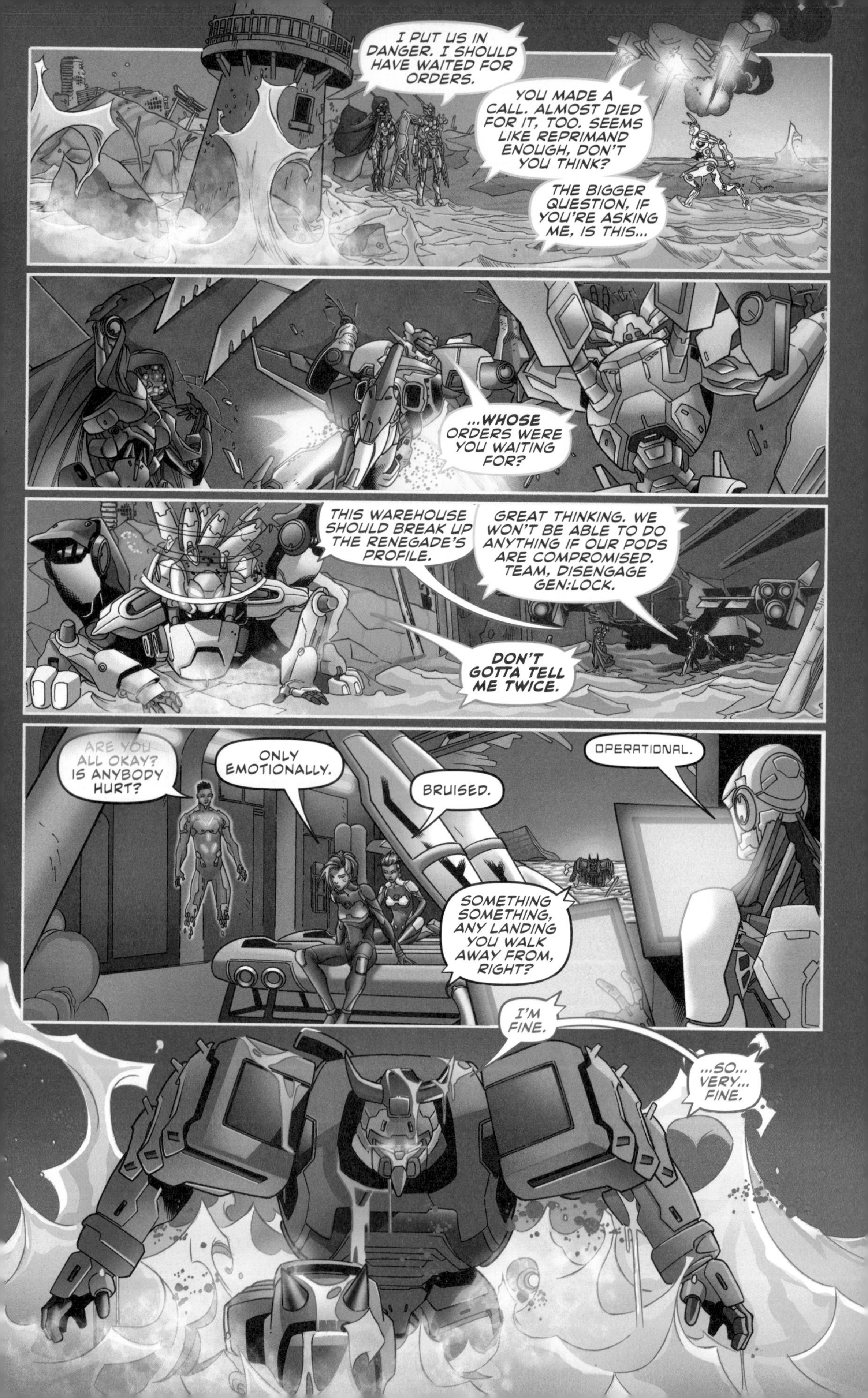
I PUT US IN DANGER. I SHOULD HAVE WAITED FOR ORDERS.
YOU MADE A CALL. ALMOST DIED FOR IT, TOO. SEEMS LIKE REPRIMAND ENOUGH, DON'T YOU THINK?
THE BIGGER QUESTION, IF YOU'RE ASKING ME, IS THIS...
...WHOSE ORDERS WERE YOU WAITING FOR?
THIS WAREHOUSE SHOULD BREAK UP THE RENEGADE'S PROFILE.
GREAT THINKING. WE WON'T BE ABLE TO DO ANYTHING IF OUR PODS ARE COMPROMISED. TEAM, DISENGAGE GEN:LOCK.
DON'T GOTTA TELL ME TWICE.
ARE YOU ALL OKAY? IS ANYBODY HURT?
ONLY EMOTIONALLY.
BRUISED.
OPERATIONAL.
SOMETHING SOMETHING, ANY LANDING YOU WALK AWAY FROM, RIGHT?
I'M FINE.
...SO... VERY... FINE.

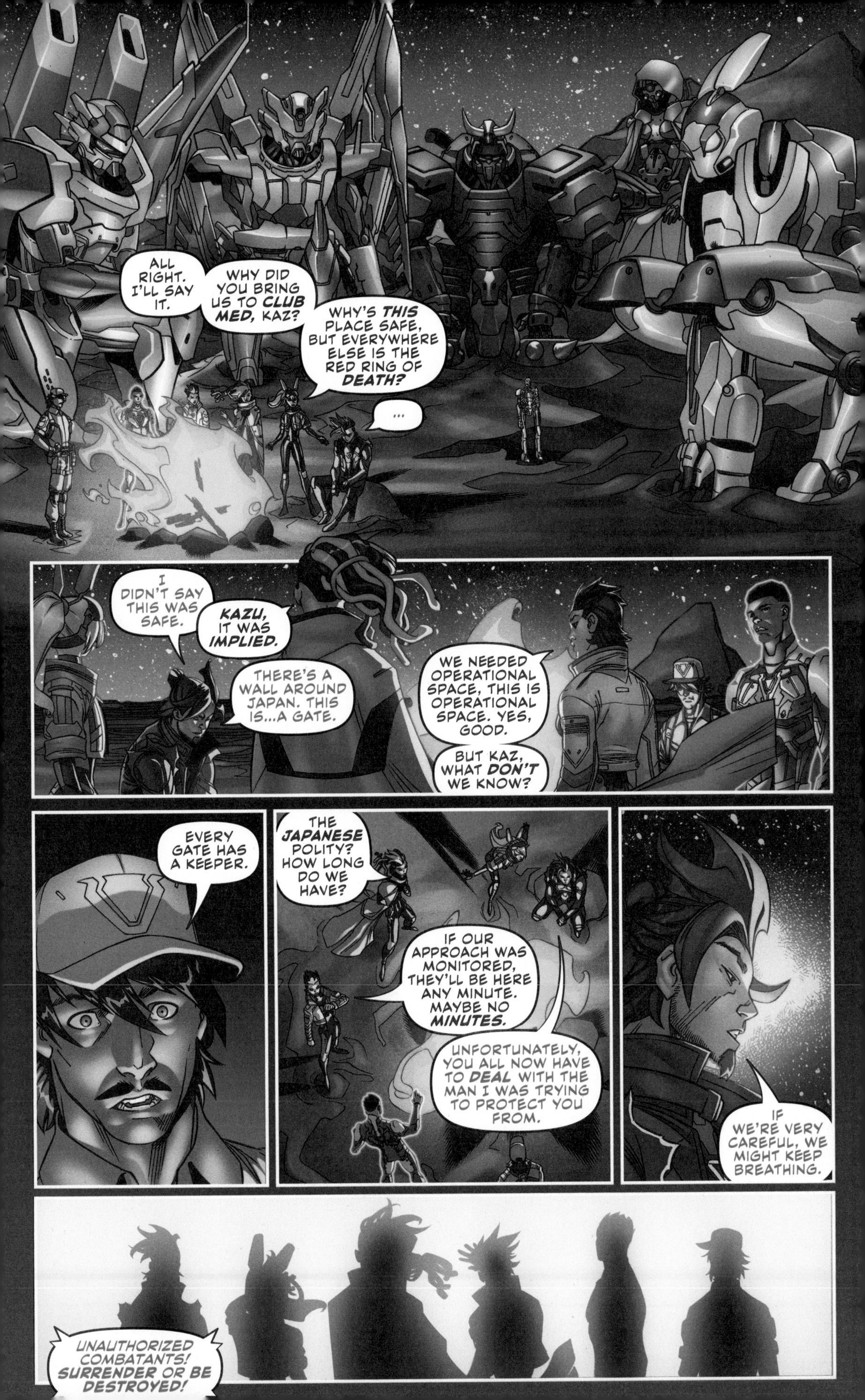
ALL RIGHT. I'LL SAY IT.
WHY DID YOU BRING US TO CLUB MED, KAZ?
WHY'S THIS PLACE SAFE, BUT EVERYWHERE ELSE IS THE RED RING OF DEATH?
...
I DIDN'T SAY THIS WAS SAFE.
KAZU, IT WAS IMPLIED.
THERE'S A WALL AROUND JAPAN. THIS IS...A GATE.
WE NEEDED OPERATIONAL SPACE, THIS IS OPERATIONAL SPACE. YES, GOOD.
BUT KAZ, WHAT DON'T WE KNOW?
EVERY GATE HAS A KEEPER.
THE JAPANESE POLITY? HOW LONG DO WE HAVE?
IF OUR APPROACH WAS MONITORED, THEY'LL BE HERE ANY MINUTE. MAYBE NO MINUTES.
UNFORTUNATELY, YOU ALL NOW HAVE TO DEAL WITH THE MAN I WAS TRYING TO PROTECT YOU FROM.
IF WE'RE VERY CAREFUL, WE MIGHT KEEP BREATHING.
UNAUTHORIZED COMBATANTS! SURRENDER OR BE DESTROYED!

I REPEAT: ACKNOWLEDGE SURRENDER OR BE DESTROYED!

WE SURRENDER!

ARE WE... USING KAZU AS A UNIVERSAL TRANSLATOR?

WE ARE.

...THAT IS SO COOL.

GOOD. AN UNCHARACTERISTICALLY WISE MOVE.

LISTEN, YOU'VE GOT THIS ALL WRONG. WE'RE GEN:LOCK TEAM, OPERATING IN TANDEM WITH RTASA.

WE DIDN'T MEAN TO BREACH YOUR AIRSPACE--

--OR TALK TO YOU AT ALL, REALLY--

BUT NOW WE'RE HERE, ON THE WRONG SIDE OF THE BLOCKADE.

SERGEANT IIDA.

GENERAL ANNO.

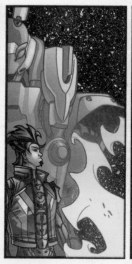

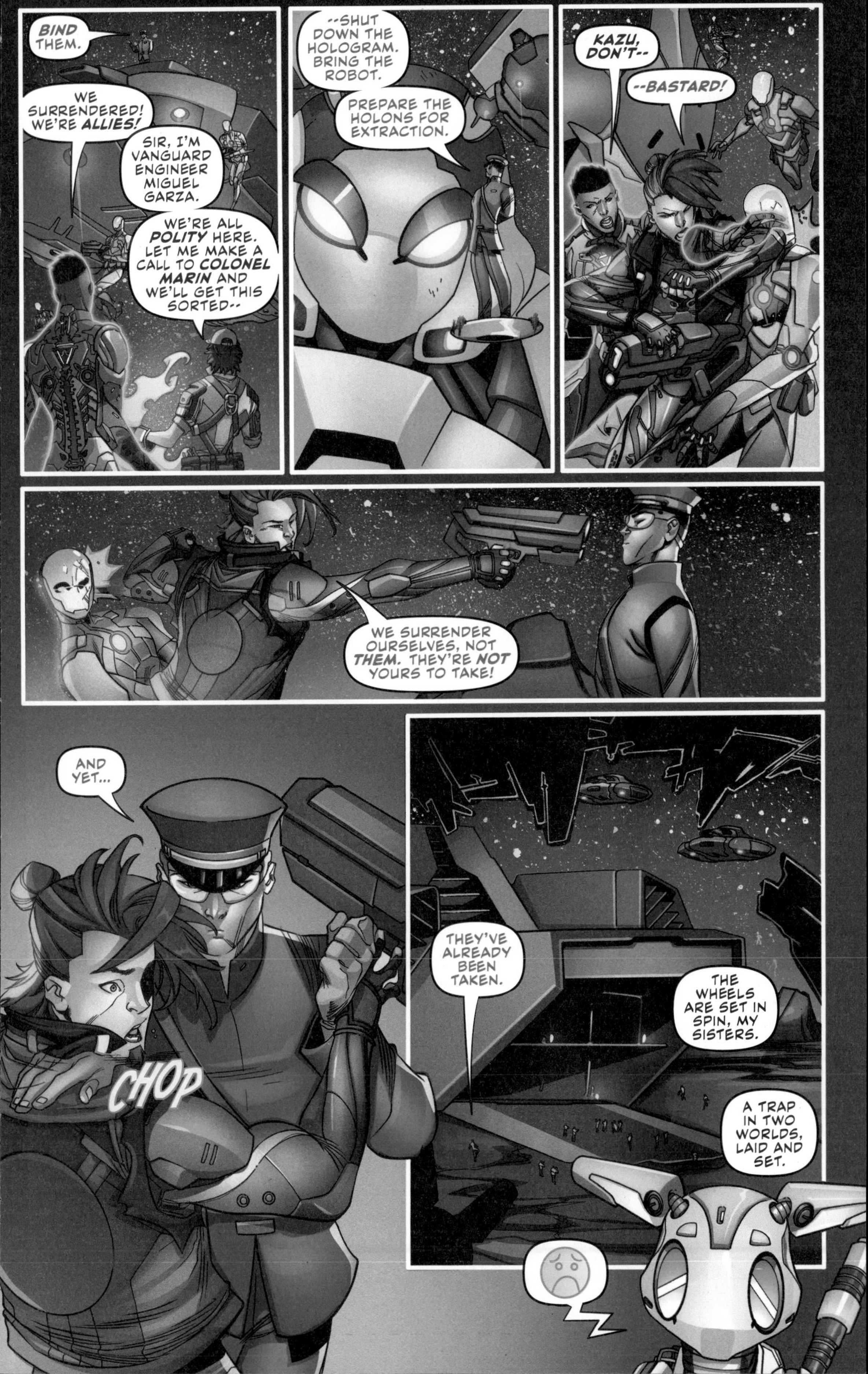
BIND THEM.
WE SURRENDERED! WE'RE ALLIES!
SIR, I'M VANGUARD ENGINEER MIGUEL GARZA.
WE'RE ALL POLITY HERE. LET ME MAKE A CALL TO COLONEL MARIN AND WE'LL GET THIS SORTED--
--SHUT DOWN THE HOLOGRAM. BRING THE ROBOT.
PREPARE THE HOLONS FOR EXTRACTION.
KAZU, DON'T--
--BASTARD!
WE SURRENDER OURSELVES, NOT THEM. THEY'RE NOT YOURS TO TAKE!
AND YET...
CHOP
THEY'VE ALREADY BEEN TAKEN.
THE WHEELS ARE SET IN SPIN, MY SISTERS.
A TRAP IN TWO WORLDS, LAID AND SET.

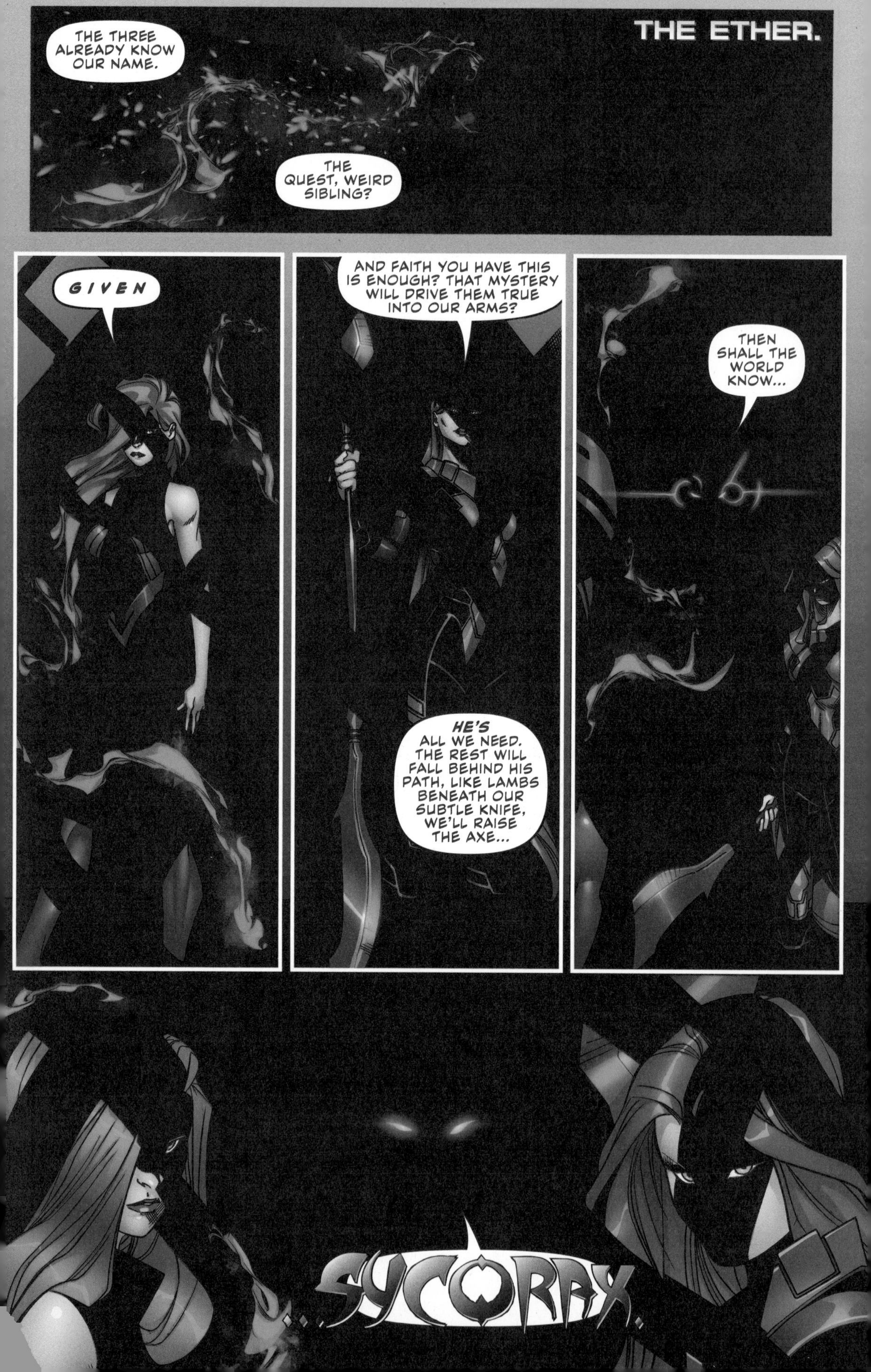
THE ETHER.
THE THREE ALREADY KNOW OUR NAME.
THE QUEST, WEIRD SIBLING?
GIVEN
AND FAITH YOU HAVE THIS IS ENOUGH? THAT MYSTERY WILL DRIVE THEM TRUE INTO OUR ARMS?
HE'S ALL WE NEED. THE REST WILL FALL BEHIND HIS PATH, LIKE LAMBS BENEATH OUR SUBTLE KNIFE, WE'LL RAISE THE AXE...
THEN SHALL THE WORLD KNOW...
SYCORAX.

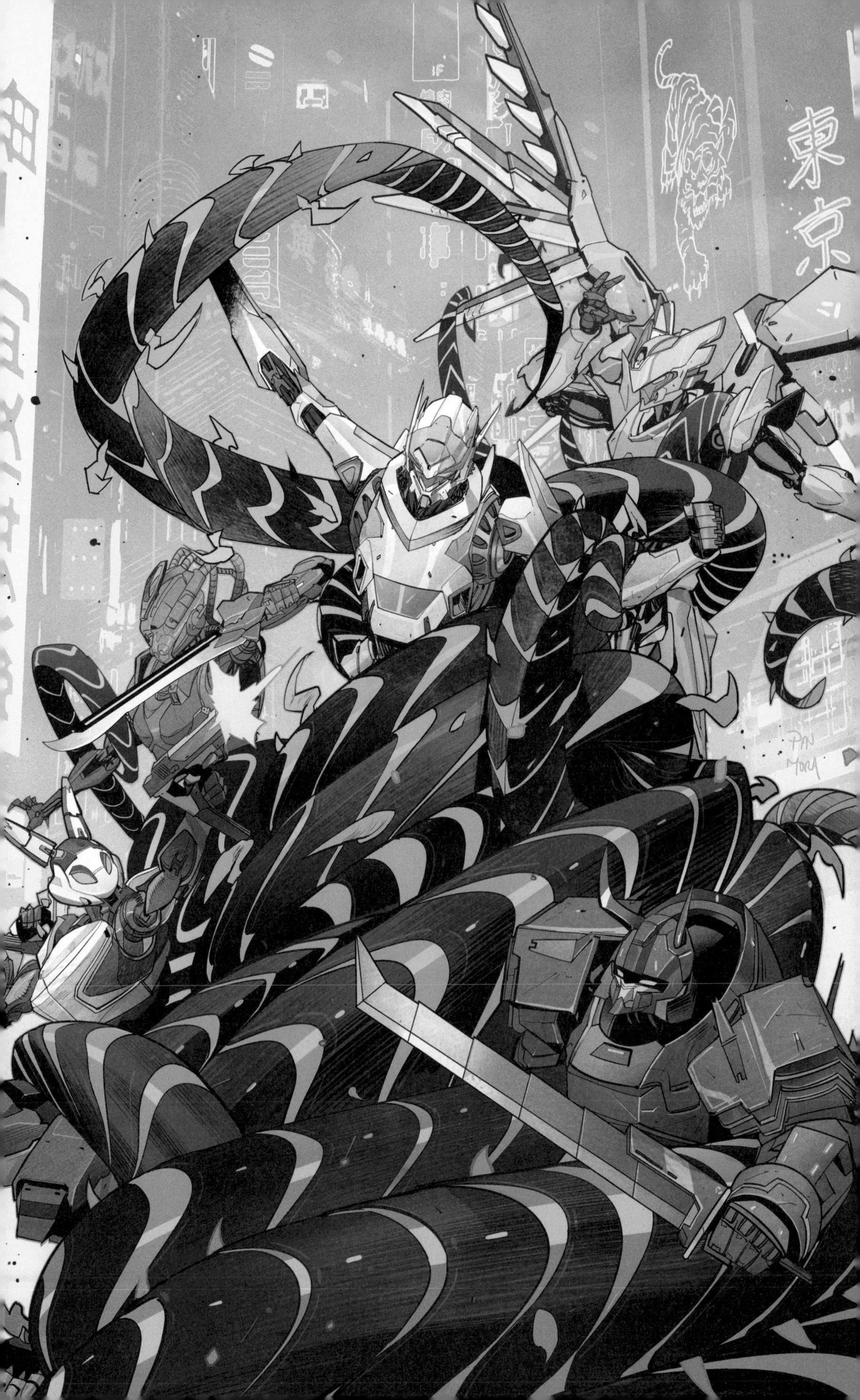

東京

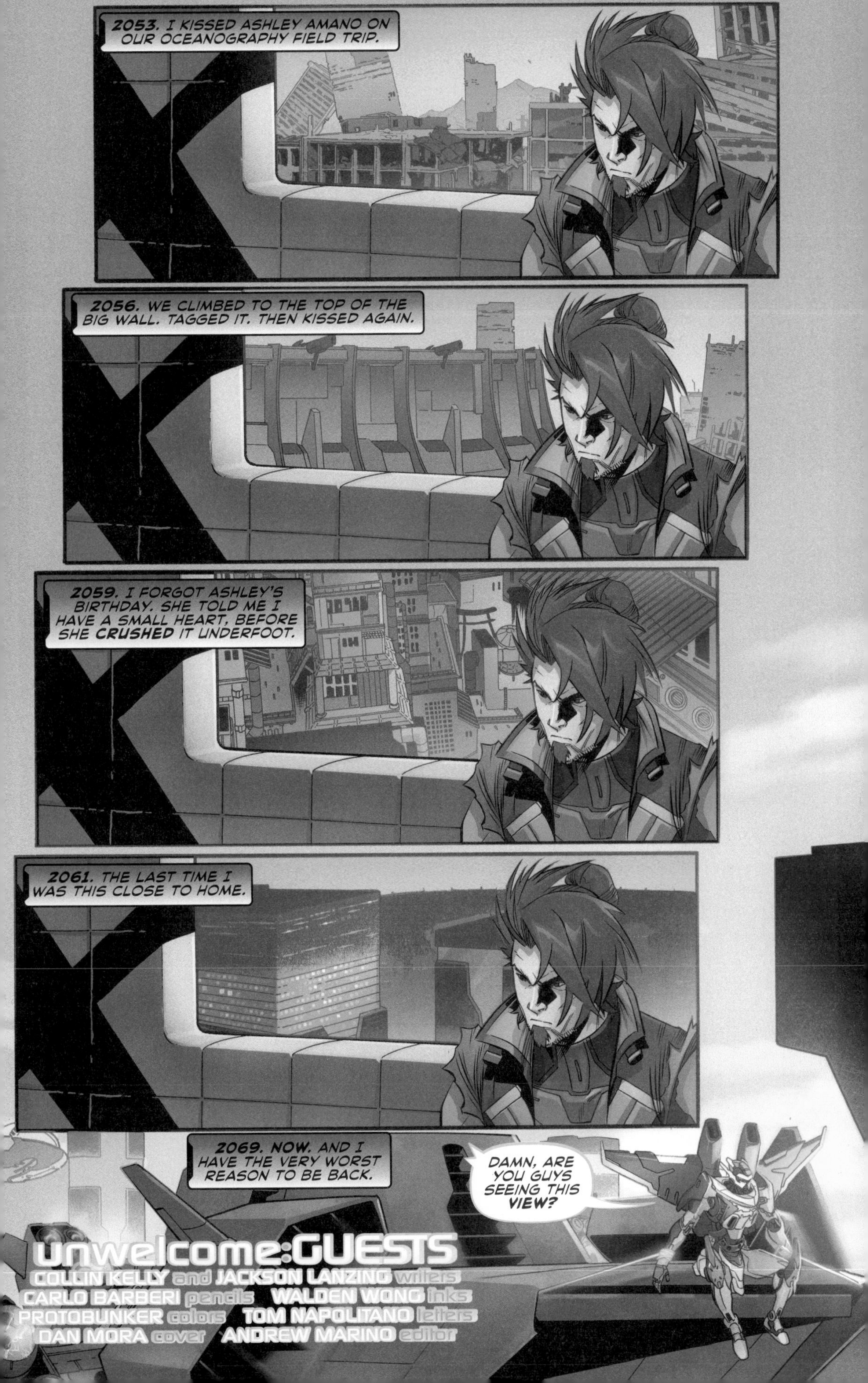
2053. I KISSED ASHLEY AMANO ON OUR OCEANOGRAPHY FIELD TRIP.
2056. WE CLIMBED TO THE TOP OF THE BIG WALL. TAGGED IT. THEN KISSED AGAIN.
2059. I FORGOT ASHLEY'S BIRTHDAY. SHE TOLD ME I HAVE A SMALL HEART, BEFORE SHE **CRUSHED** IT UNDERFOOT.
2061. THE LAST TIME I WAS THIS CLOSE TO HOME.
2069. NOW. AND I HAVE THE VERY WORST REASON TO BE BACK.
DAMN, ARE YOU GUYS SEEING THIS **VIEW?**
unwelcome:GUESTS
COLLIN KELLY and JACKSON LANZING writers
CARLO BARBERI pencils WALDEN WONG inks
PROTOBUNKER colors TOM NAPOLITANO letters
DAN MORA cover ANDREW MARINO editor

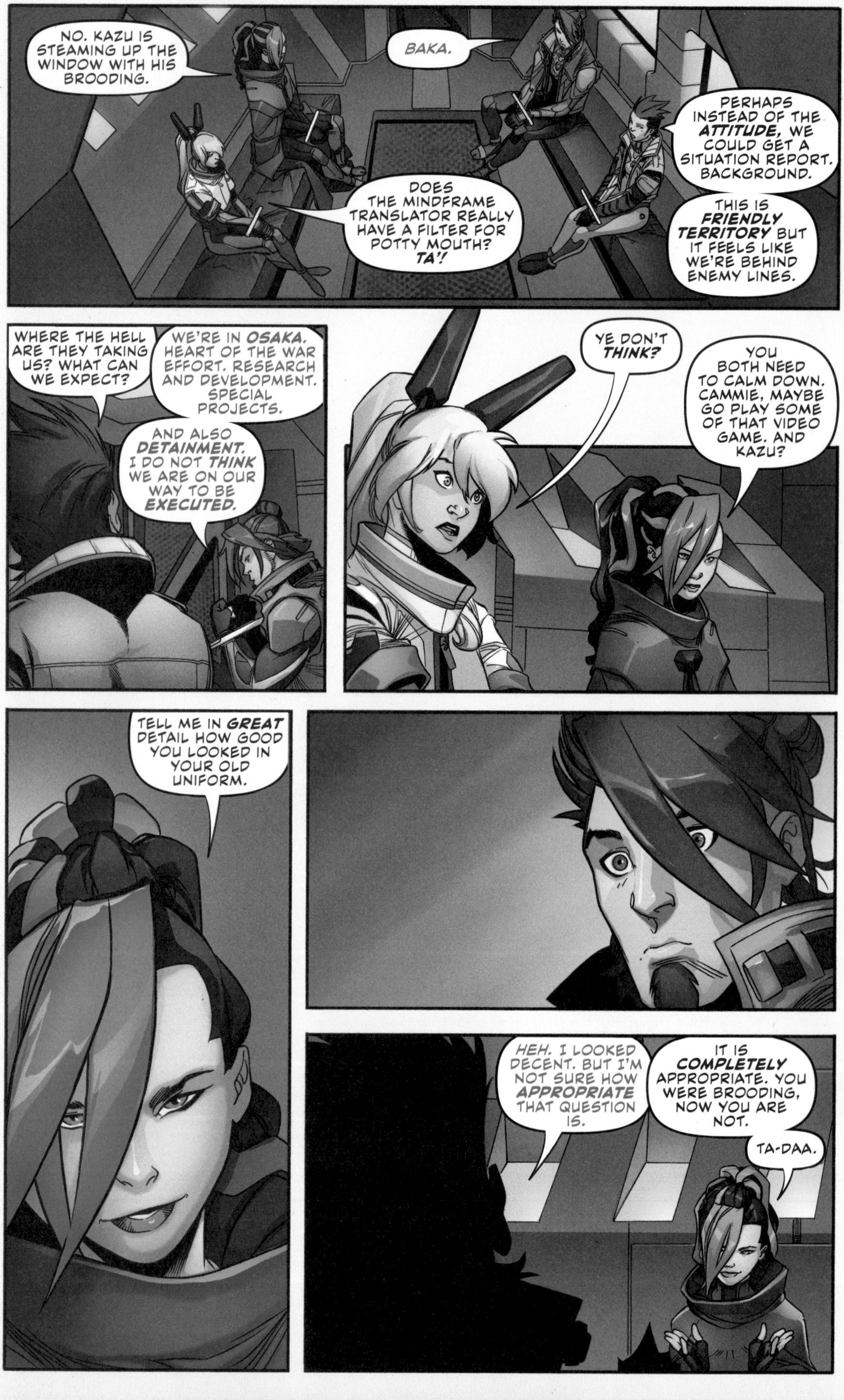
NO. KAZU IS STEAMING UP THE WINDOW WITH HIS BROODING.
BAKA.
PERHAPS INSTEAD OF THE ATTITUDE, WE COULD GET A SITUATION REPORT. BACKGROUND.
DOES THE MINDFRAME TRANSLATOR REALLY HAVE A FILTER FOR POTTY MOUTH? TA'!
THIS IS FRIENDLY TERRITORY BUT IT FEELS LIKE WE'RE BEHIND ENEMY LINES.
WHERE THE HELL ARE THEY TAKING US? WHAT CAN WE EXPECT?
WE'RE IN OSAKA. HEART OF THE WAR EFFORT. RESEARCH AND DEVELOPMENT. SPECIAL PROJECTS.
AND ALSO DETAINMENT. I DO NOT THINK WE ARE ON OUR WAY TO BE EXECUTED.
YE DON'T THINK?
YOU BOTH NEED TO CALM DOWN. CAMMIE, MAYBE GO PLAY SOME OF THAT VIDEO GAME. AND KAZU?
TELL ME IN GREAT DETAIL HOW GOOD YOU LOOKED IN YOUR OLD UNIFORM.
HEH. I LOOKED DECENT. BUT I'M NOT SURE HOW APPROPRIATE THAT QUESTION IS.
IT IS COMPLETELY APPROPRIATE. YOU WERE BROODING, NOW YOU ARE NOT.
TA-DAA.

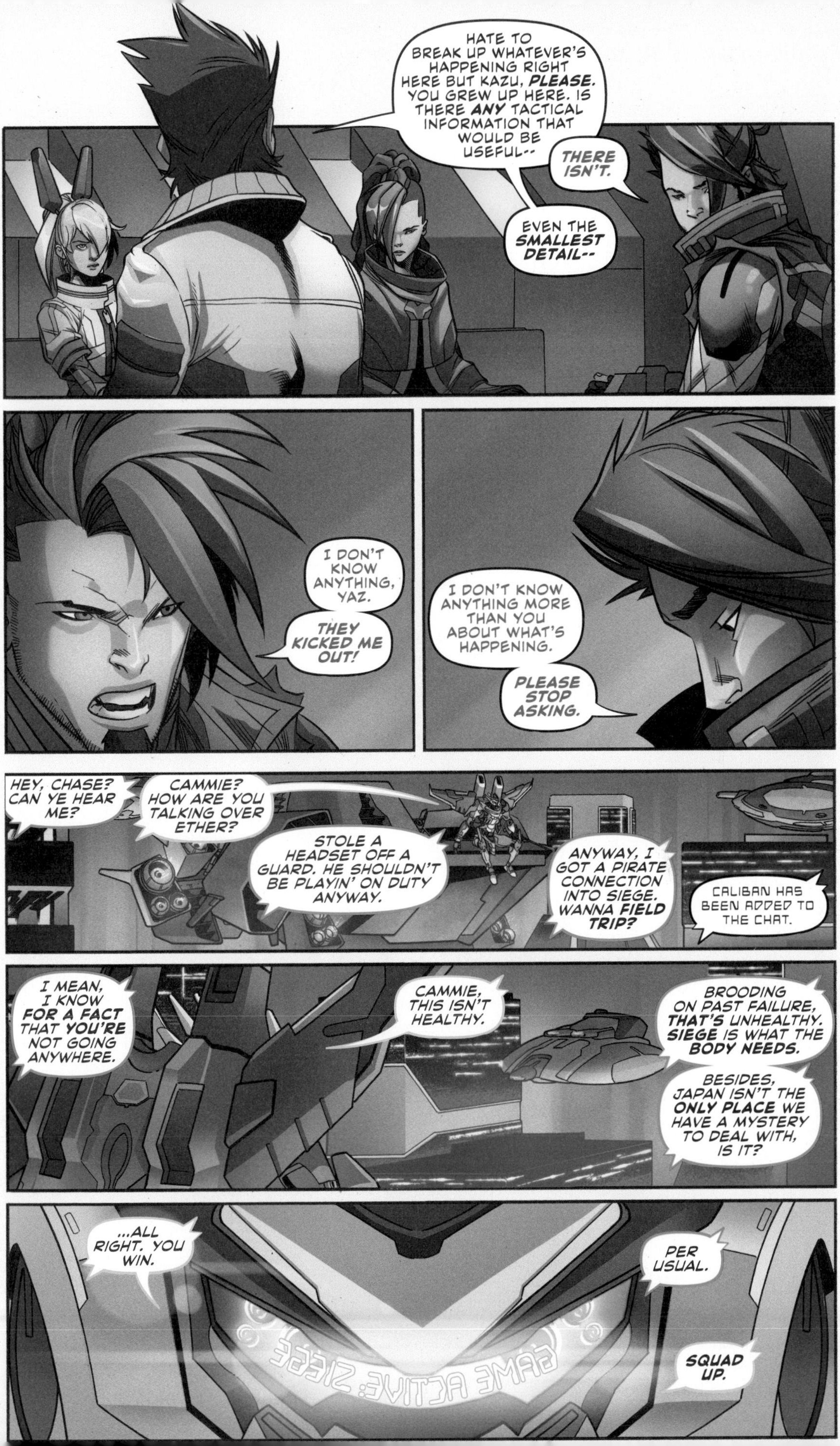
HATE TO BREAK UP WHATEVER'S HAPPENING RIGHT HERE BUT KAZU, PLEASE. YOU GREW UP HERE. IS THERE ANY TACTICAL INFORMATION THAT WOULD BE USEFUL--
THERE ISN'T.
EVEN THE SMALLEST DETAIL--
I DON'T KNOW ANYTHING, YAZ.
THEY KICKED ME OUT!
I DON'T KNOW ANYTHING MORE THAN YOU ABOUT WHAT'S HAPPENING.
PLEASE STOP ASKING.
HEY, CHASE? CAN YE HEAR ME?
CAMMIE? HOW ARE YOU TALKING OVER ETHER?
STOLE A HEADSET OFF A GUARD. HE SHOULDN'T BE PLAYIN' ON DUTY ANYWAY.
ANYWAY, I GOT A PIRATE CONNECTION INTO SIEGE. WANNA FIELD TRIP?
CALIBAN HAS BEEN ADDED TO THE CHAT.
I MEAN, I KNOW FOR A FACT THAT YOU'RE NOT GOING ANYWHERE.
CAMMIE, THIS ISN'T HEALTHY.
BROODING ON PAST FAILURE, THAT'S UNHEALTHY. SIEGE IS WHAT THE BODY NEEDS.
BESIDES, JAPAN ISN'T THE ONLY PLACE WE HAVE A MYSTERY TO DEAL WITH, IS IT?
...ALL RIGHT. YOU WIN.
PER USUAL.
GAME ACTIVE: SIEGE
SQUAD UP.

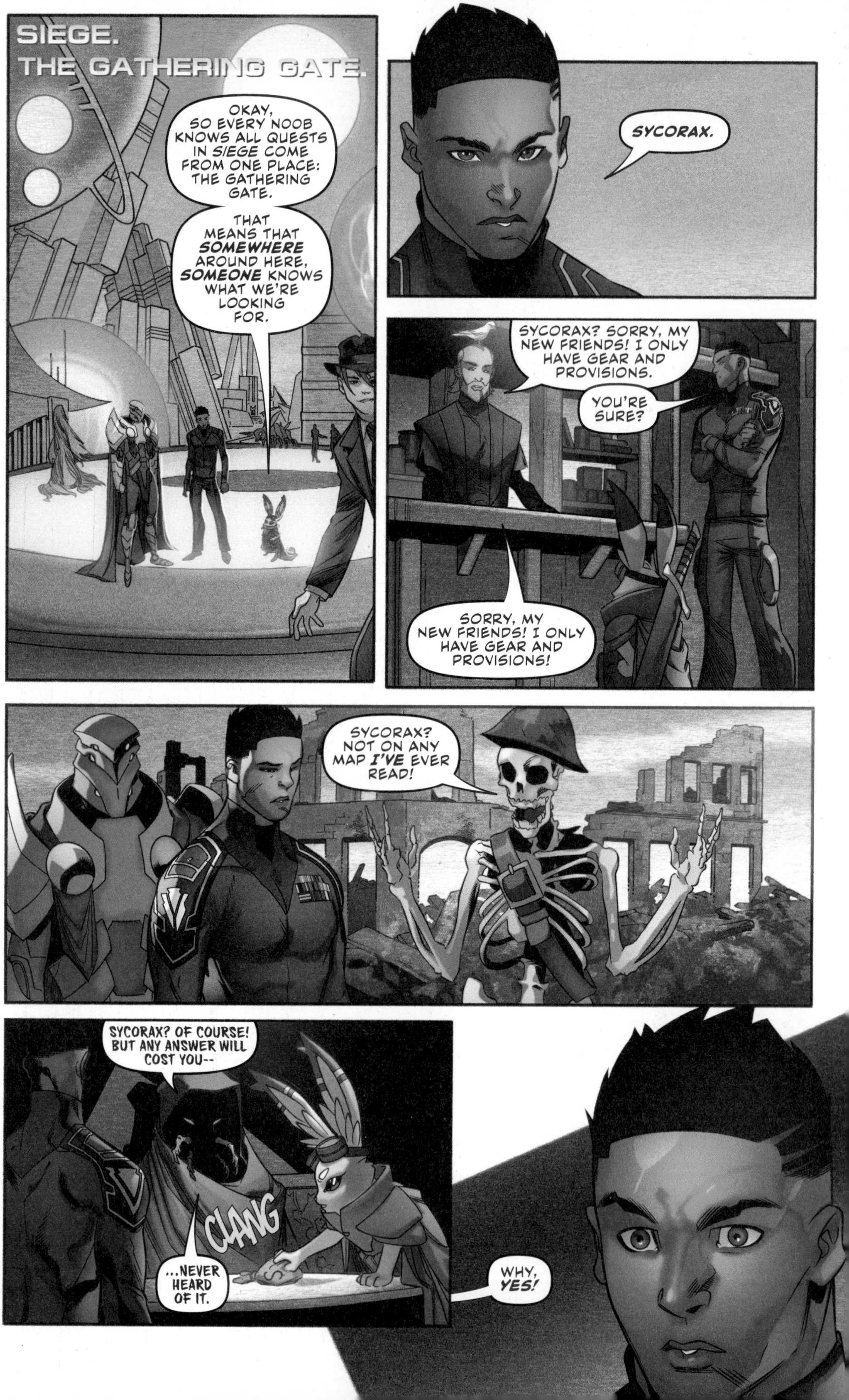
SIEGE.
THE GATHERING GATE.
OKAY, SO EVERY NOOB KNOWS ALL QUESTS IN SIEGE COME FROM ONE PLACE: THE GATHERING GATE.
THAT MEANS THAT SOMEWHERE AROUND HERE, SOMEONE KNOWS WHAT WE'RE LOOKING FOR.
SYCORAX.
SYCORAX? SORRY, MY NEW FRIENDS! I ONLY HAVE GEAR AND PROVISIONS.
YOU'RE SURE?
SORRY, MY NEW FRIENDS! I ONLY HAVE GEAR AND PROVISIONS!
SYCORAX? NOT ON ANY MAP I'VE EVER READ!
SYCORAX? OF COURSE! BUT ANY ANSWER WILL COST YOU--
CLANG
...NEVER HEARD OF IT.
WHY, YES!

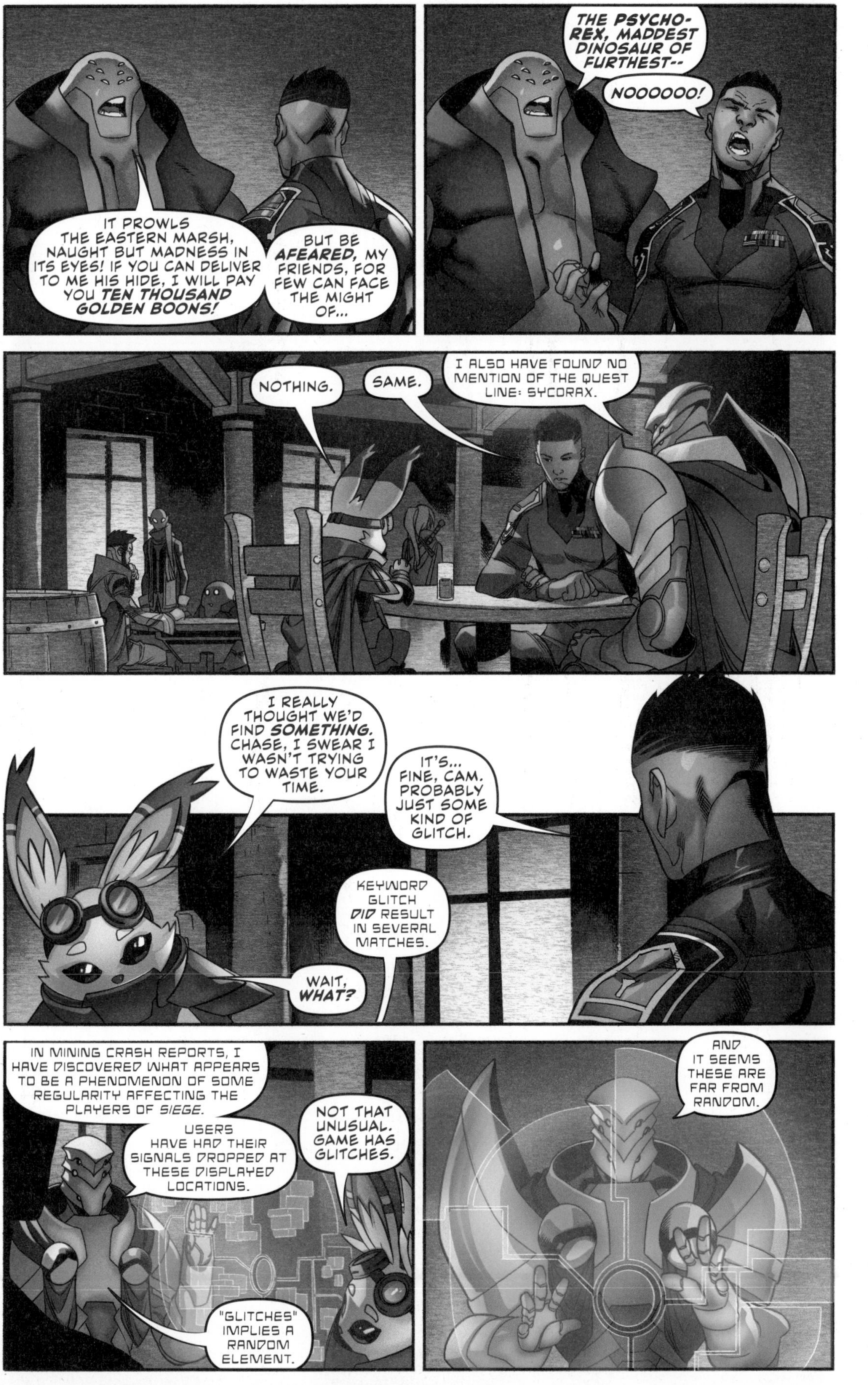
IT PROWLS THE EASTERN MARSH, NAUGHT BUT MADNESS IN ITS EYES! IF YOU CAN DELIVER TO ME HIS HIDE, I WILL PAY YOU TEN THOUSAND GOLDEN BOONS!
BUT BE AFEARED, MY FRIENDS, FOR FEW CAN FACE THE MIGHT OF...
THE PSYCHO-REX, MADDEST DINOSAUR OF FURTHEST--
NOOOOOO!
NOTHING.
SAME.
I ALSO HAVE FOUND NO MENTION OF THE QUEST LINE: SYCORAX.
I REALLY THOUGHT WE'D FIND SOMETHING. CHASE, I SWEAR I WASN'T TRYING TO WASTE YOUR TIME.
IT'S... FINE, CAM. PROBABLY JUST SOME KIND OF GLITCH.
KEYWORD GLITCH DID RESULT IN SEVERAL MATCHES.
WAIT, WHAT?
IN MINING CRASH REPORTS, I HAVE DISCOVERED WHAT APPEARS TO BE A PHENOMENON OF SOME REGULARITY AFFECTING THE PLAYERS OF SIEGE.
USERS HAVE HAD THEIR SIGNALS DROPPED AT THESE DISPLAYED LOCATIONS.
NOT THAT UNUSUAL. GAME HAS GLITCHES.
"GLITCHES" IMPLIES A RANDOM ELEMENT.
AND IT SEEMS THESE ARE FAR FROM RANDOM.

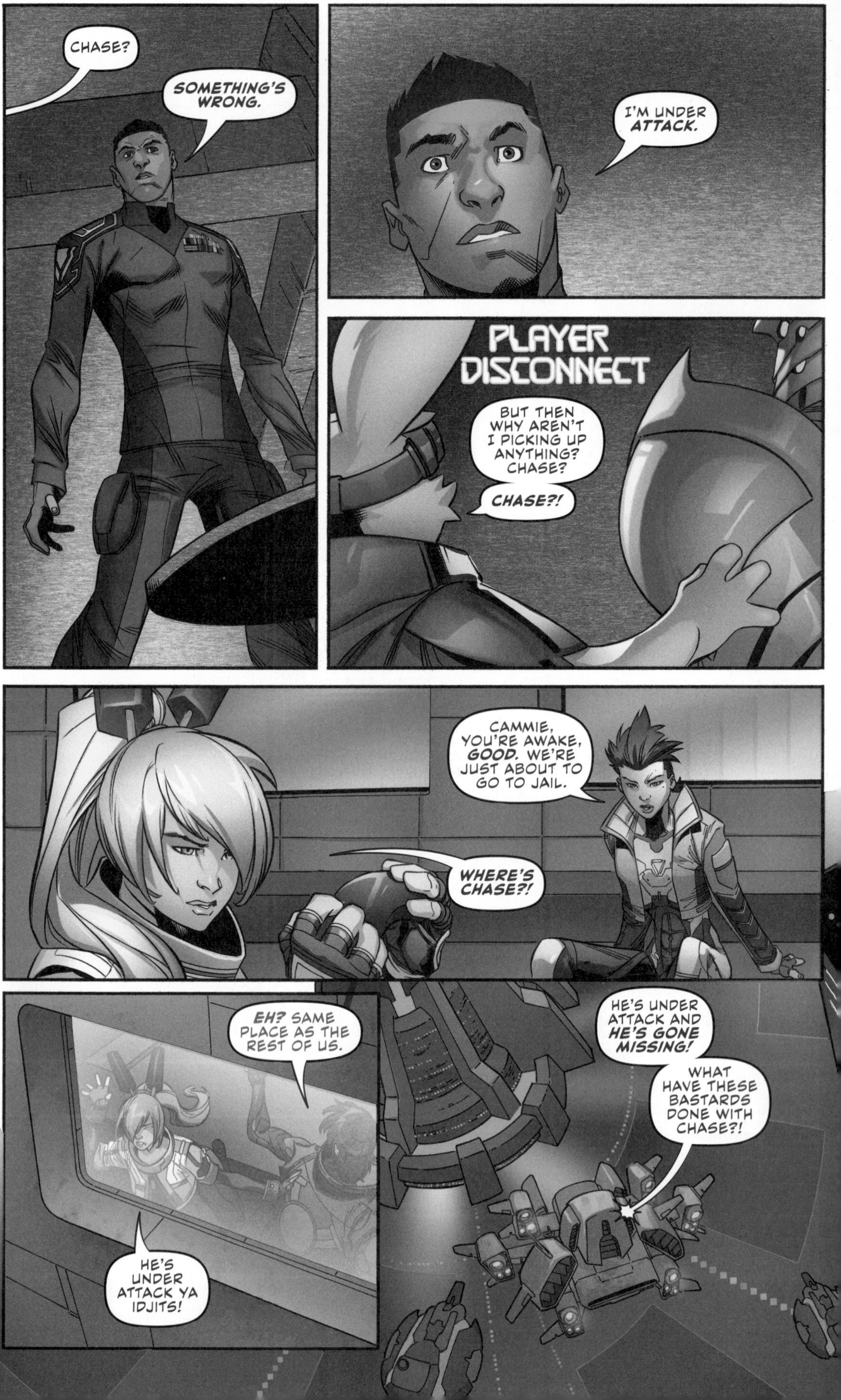
CHASE?
SOMETHING'S WRONG.
I'M UNDER ATTACK.
PLAYER DISCONNECT
BUT THEN WHY AREN'T I PICKING UP ANYTHING? CHASE?
CHASE?!
CAMMIE, YOU'RE AWAKE, GOOD. WE'RE JUST ABOUT TO GO TO JAIL.
WHERE'S CHASE?!
EH? SAME PLACE AS THE REST OF US.
HE'S UNDER ATTACK YA IDJITS!
HE'S UNDER ATTACK AND HE'S GONE MISSING!
WHAT HAVE THESE BASTARDS DONE WITH CHASE?!

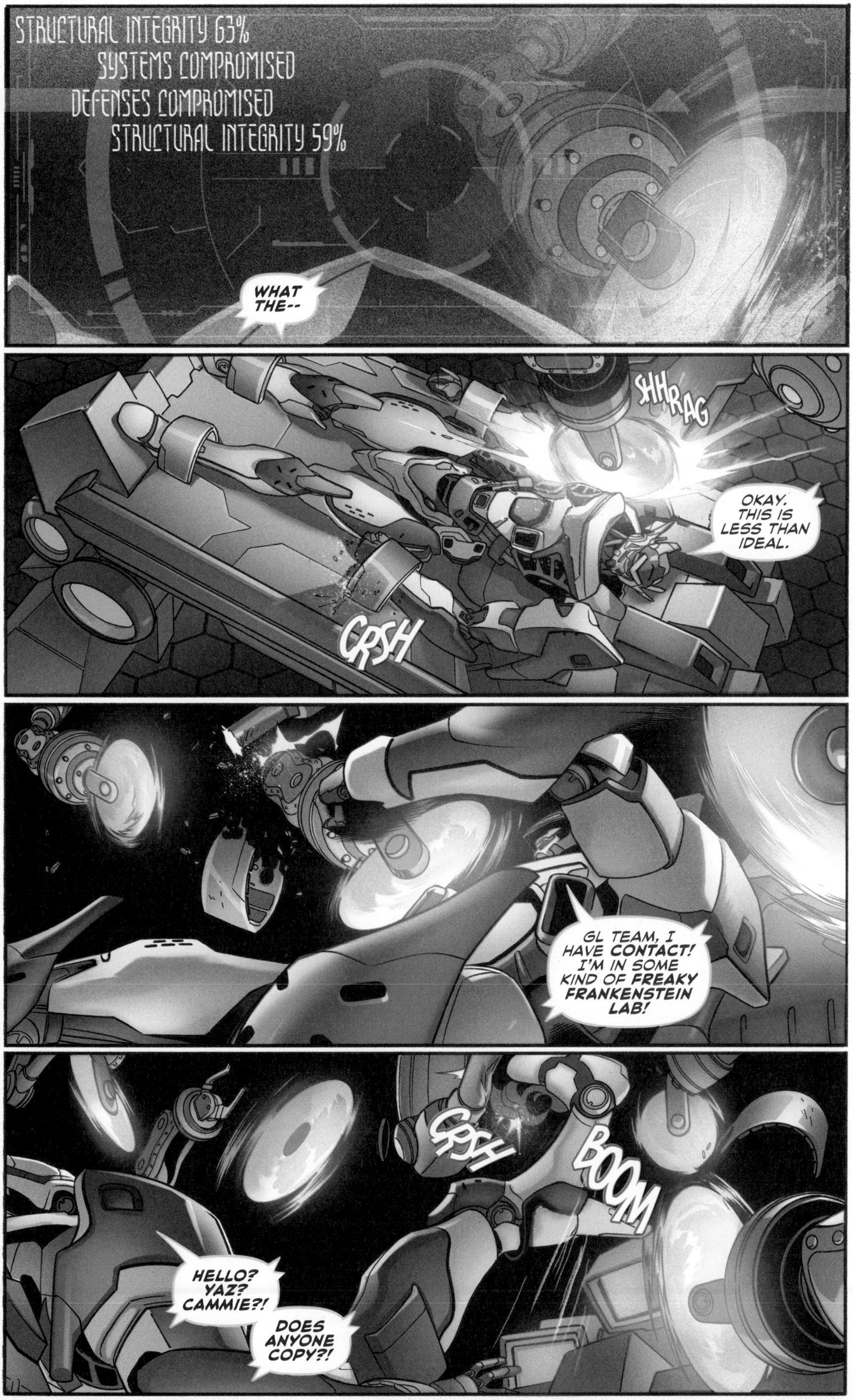
STRUCTURAL INTEGRITY 63%
SYSTEMS COMPROMISED
DEFENSES COMPROMISED
STRUCTURAL INTEGRITY 59%
WHAT THE--
SHHRAG
OKAY. THIS IS LESS THAN IDEAL.
CRSH
GL TEAM, I HAVE CONTACT! I'M IN SOME KIND OF FREAKY FRANKENSTEIN LAB!
CRSH
BOOM
HELLO? YAZ? CAMMIE?!
DOES ANYONE COPY?!

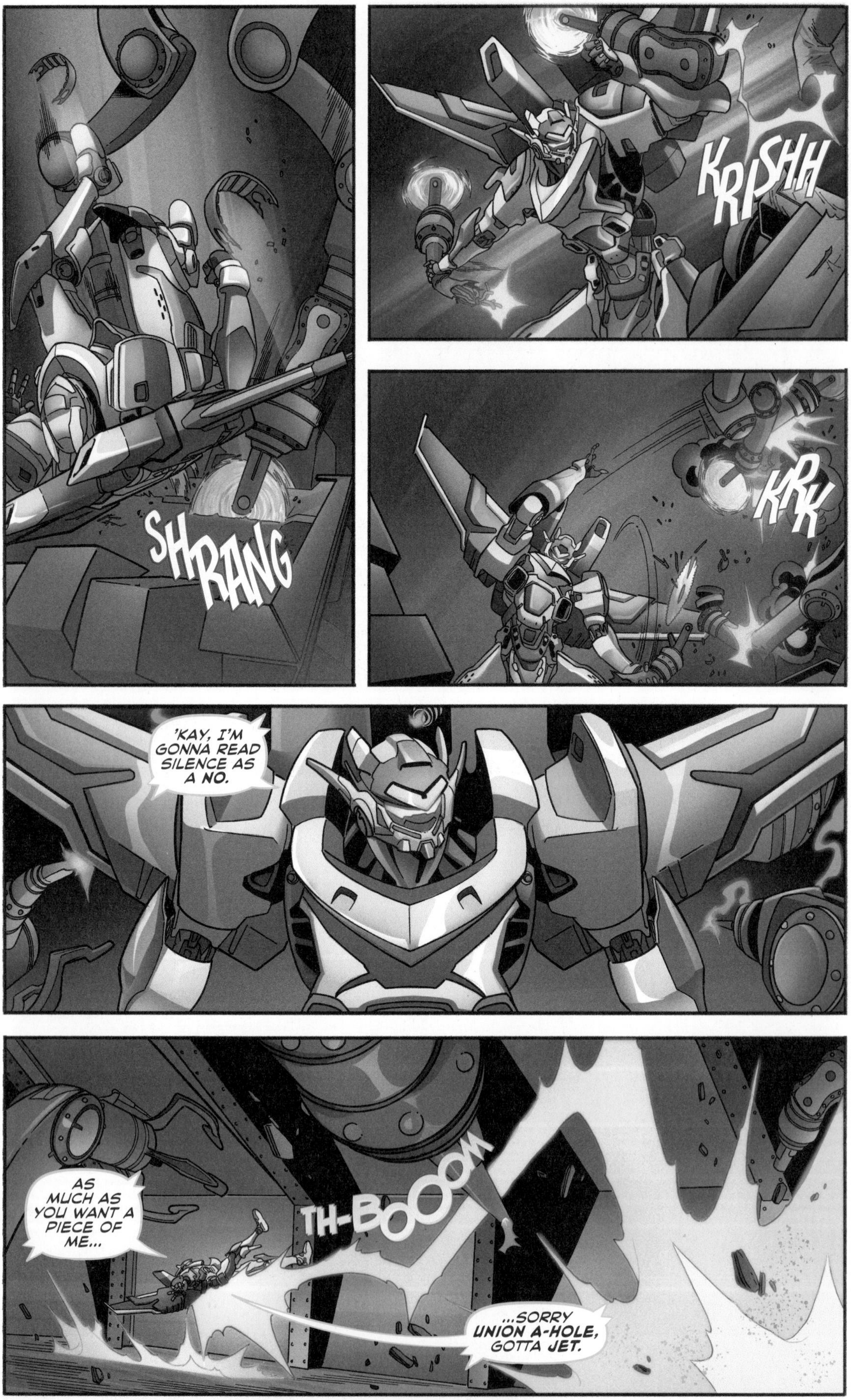
SHRANG
KRISHH
KRK
'KAY, I'M GONNA READ SILENCE AS A NO.
AS MUCH AS YOU WANT A PIECE OF ME...
TH-BOOOOM
...SORRY UNION A-HOLE, GOTTA JET.

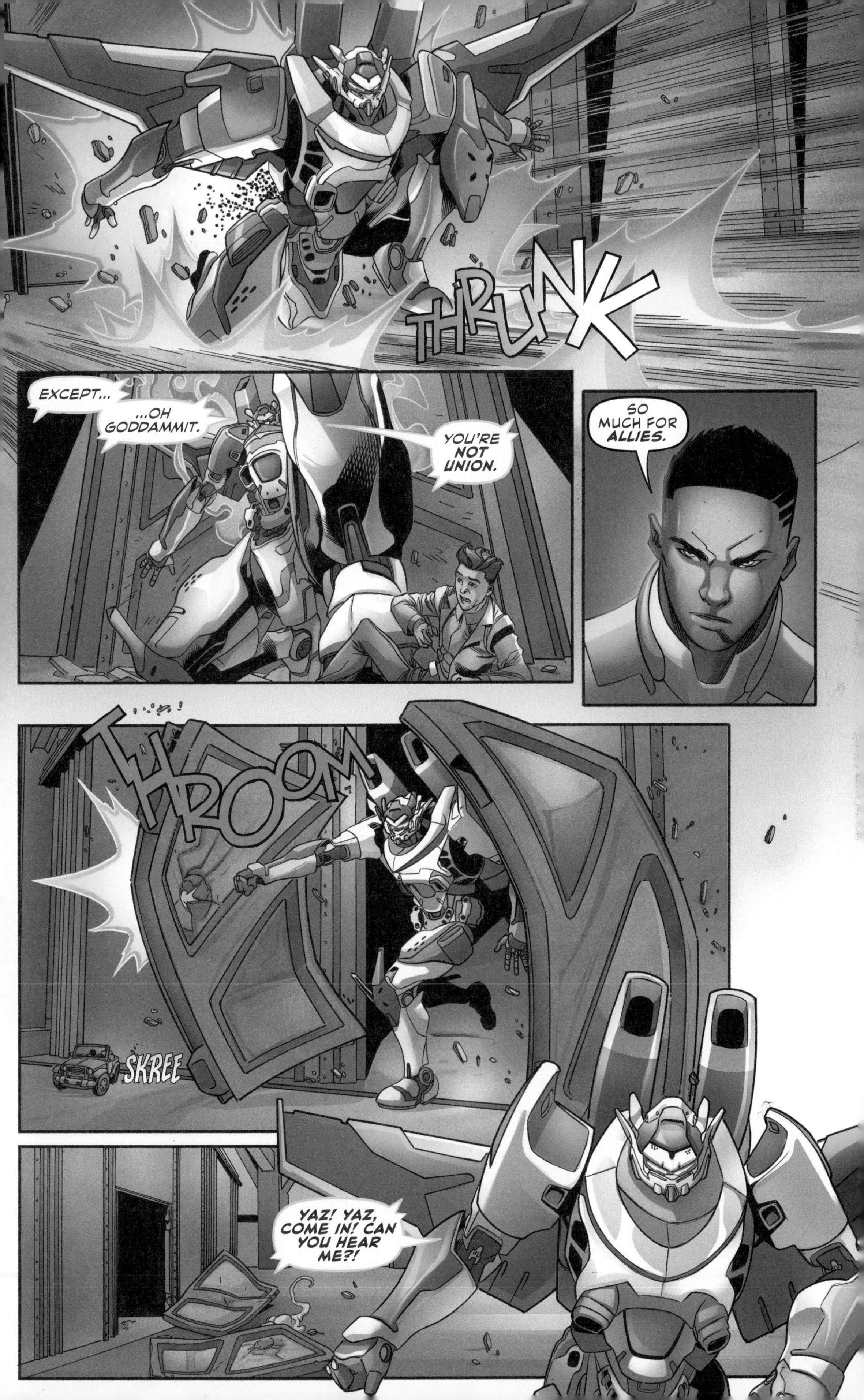
THRUNK
EXCEPT...
...OH GODDAMMIT.
YOU'RE NOT UNION.
SO MUCH FOR ALLIES.
THROOM
SKREE
YAZ! YAZ, COME IN! CAN YOU HEAR ME?!

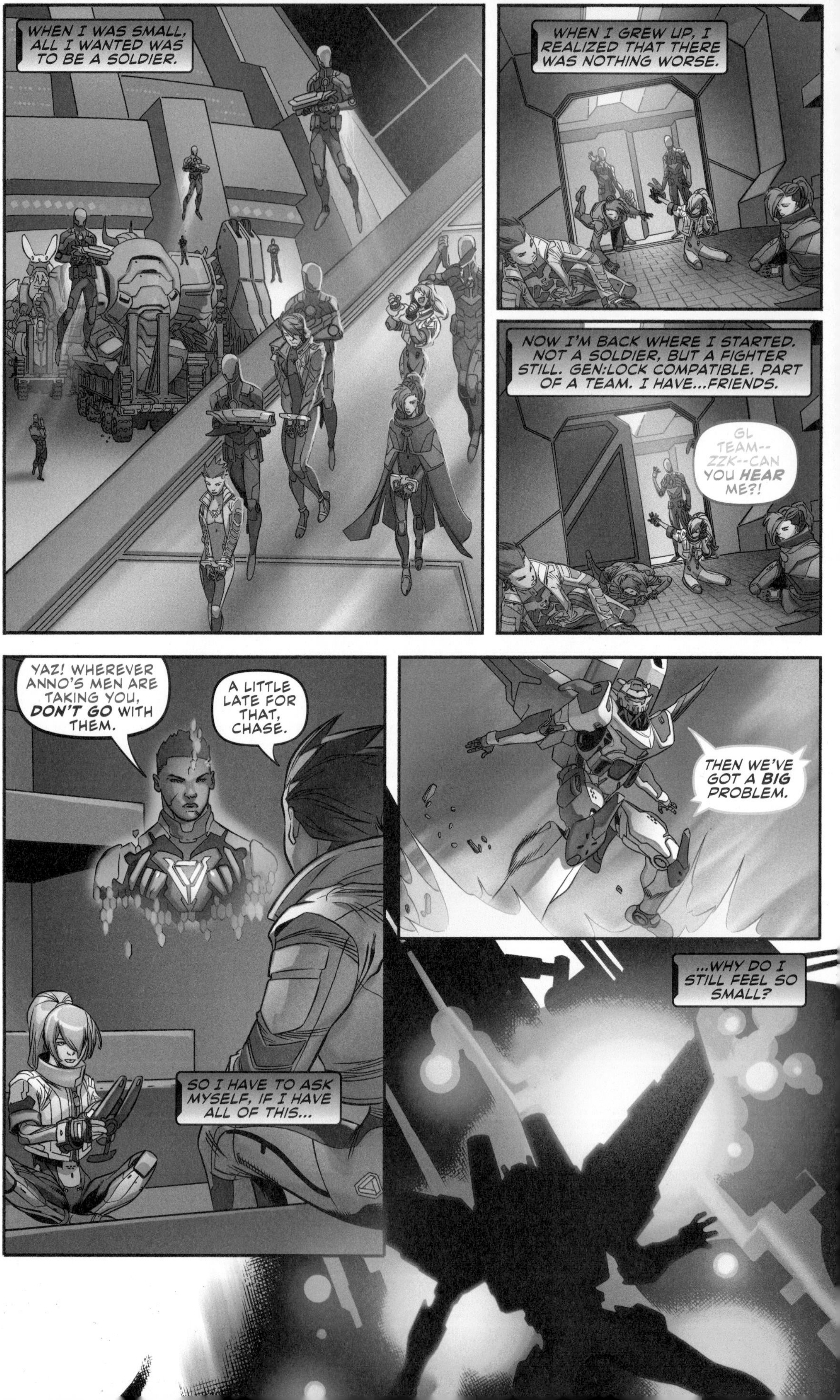
WHEN I WAS SMALL, ALL I WANTED WAS TO BE A SOLDIER.
WHEN I GREW UP, I REALIZED THAT THERE WAS NOTHING WORSE.
NOW I'M BACK WHERE I STARTED. NOT A SOLDIER, BUT A FIGHTER STILL. GEN:LOCK COMPATIBLE. PART OF A TEAM. I HAVE...FRIENDS.
GL TEAM--ZZK--CAN YOU HEAR ME?!
YAZ! WHEREVER ANNO'S MEN ARE TAKING YOU, DON'T GO WITH THEM.
A LITTLE LATE FOR THAT, CHASE.
THEN WE'VE GOT A BIG PROBLEM.
SO I HAVE TO ASK MYSELF, IF I HAVE ALL OF THIS...
...WHY DO I STILL FEEL SO SMALL?

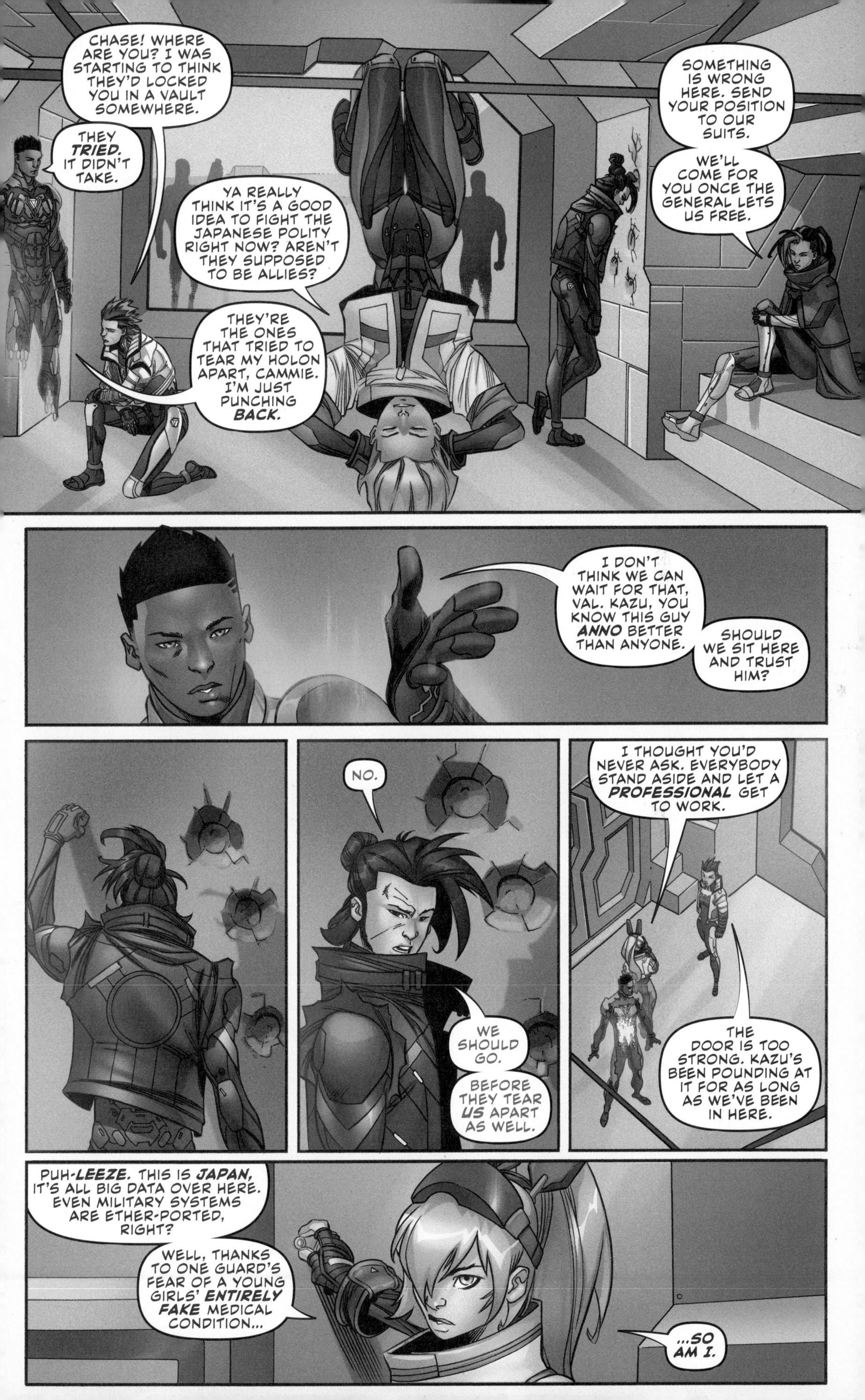
CHASE! WHERE ARE YOU? I WAS STARTING TO THINK THEY'D LOCKED YOU IN A VAULT SOMEWHERE.
THEY **TRIED.** IT DIDN'T TAKE.
YA REALLY THINK IT'S A GOOD IDEA TO FIGHT THE JAPANESE POLITY RIGHT NOW? AREN'T THEY SUPPOSED TO BE ALLIES?
THEY'RE THE ONES THAT TRIED TO TEAR MY HOLON APART, CAMMIE. I'M JUST PUNCHING **BACK.**
SOMETHING IS WRONG HERE. SEND YOUR POSITION TO OUR SUITS.
WE'LL COME FOR YOU ONCE THE GENERAL LETS US FREE.
I DON'T THINK WE CAN WAIT FOR THAT, VAL. KAZU, YOU KNOW THIS GUY **ANNO** BETTER THAN ANYONE.
SHOULD WE SIT HERE AND TRUST HIM?
NO.
WE SHOULD GO.
BEFORE THEY TEAR **US** APART AS WELL.
I THOUGHT YOU'D NEVER ASK. EVERYBODY STAND ASIDE AND LET A **PROFESSIONAL** GET TO WORK.
THE DOOR IS TOO STRONG. KAZU'S BEEN POUNDING AT IT FOR AS LONG AS WE'VE BEEN IN HERE.
PUH-**LEEZE.** THIS IS **JAPAN,** IT'S ALL BIG DATA OVER HERE. EVEN MILITARY SYSTEMS ARE ETHER-PORTED, RIGHT?
WELL, THANKS TO ONE GUARD'S FEAR OF A YOUNG GIRLS' **ENTIRELY FAKE** MEDICAL CONDITION...
...SO AM I.

BRB, CUTIES.

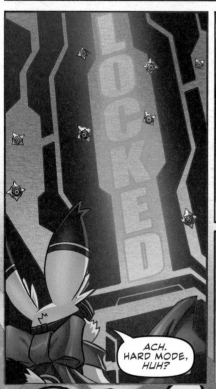

ACH. HARD MODE, HUH?

I WAS HACKING

BOTS LIKE YOU

WHEN I WAS

JUST A WEE LASS!

NOW I'M A BADASS

CYBERPUNK INTERNET NINJA...

BEEP!

...AND YER JUST A BUNCH OF DEAD BOLT.

KABOOOOOM

EAT YER HEART OUT, *KIRBY GRIPS.*

VALENTINA? AFTER YOU.

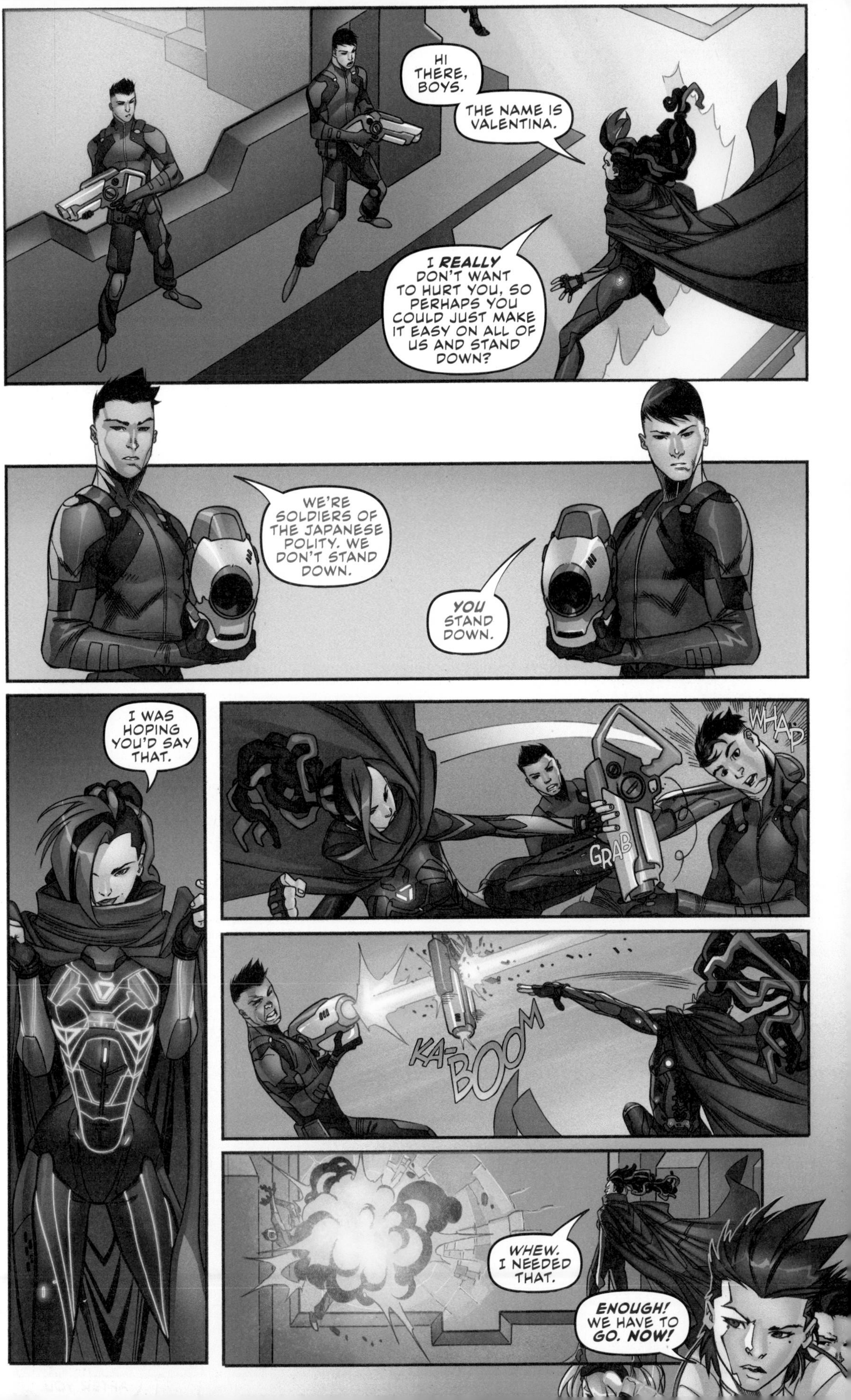
HI THERE, BOYS.
THE NAME IS VALENTINA.
I **REALLY** DON'T WANT TO HURT YOU, SO PERHAPS YOU COULD JUST MAKE IT EASY ON ALL OF US AND STAND DOWN?
WE'RE SOLDIERS OF THE JAPANESE POLITY. WE DON'T STAND DOWN.
YOU STAND DOWN.
I WAS HOPING YOU'D SAY THAT.
WHAP
GRAB
KA-BOOM
WHEW. I NEEDED THAT.
ENOUGH! WE HAVE TO ***GO. NOW!***

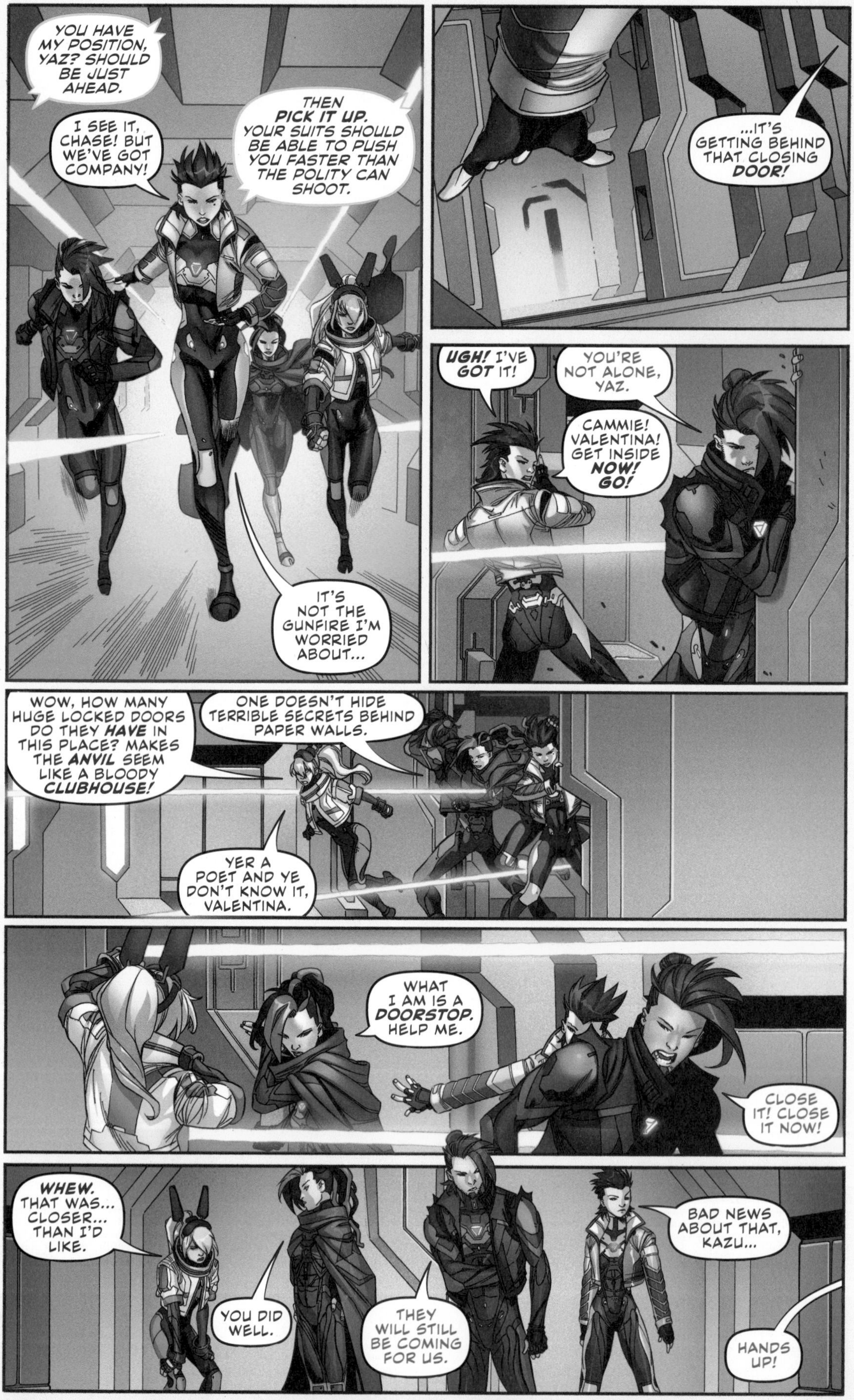
YOU HAVE MY POSITION, YAZ? SHOULD BE JUST AHEAD.
I SEE IT, CHASE! BUT WE'VE GOT COMPANY!
THEN PICK IT UP. YOUR SUITS SHOULD BE ABLE TO PUSH YOU FASTER THAN THE POLITY CAN SHOOT.
IT'S NOT THE GUNFIRE I'M WORRIED ABOUT...
...IT'S GETTING BEHIND THAT CLOSING DOOR!
UGH! I'VE GOT IT!
YOU'RE NOT ALONE, YAZ.
CAMMIE! VALENTINA! GET INSIDE NOW! GO!
WOW, HOW MANY HUGE LOCKED DOORS DO THEY HAVE IN THIS PLACE? MAKES THE ANVIL SEEM LIKE A BLOODY CLUBHOUSE!
ONE DOESN'T HIDE TERRIBLE SECRETS BEHIND PAPER WALLS.
YER A POET AND YE DON'T KNOW IT, VALENTINA.
WHAT I AM IS A DOORSTOP. HELP ME.
CLOSE IT! CLOSE IT NOW!
WHEW. THAT WAS... CLOSER... THAN I'D LIKE.
YOU DID WELL.
THEY WILL STILL BE COMING FOR US.
BAD NEWS ABOUT THAT, KAZU...
HANDS UP!

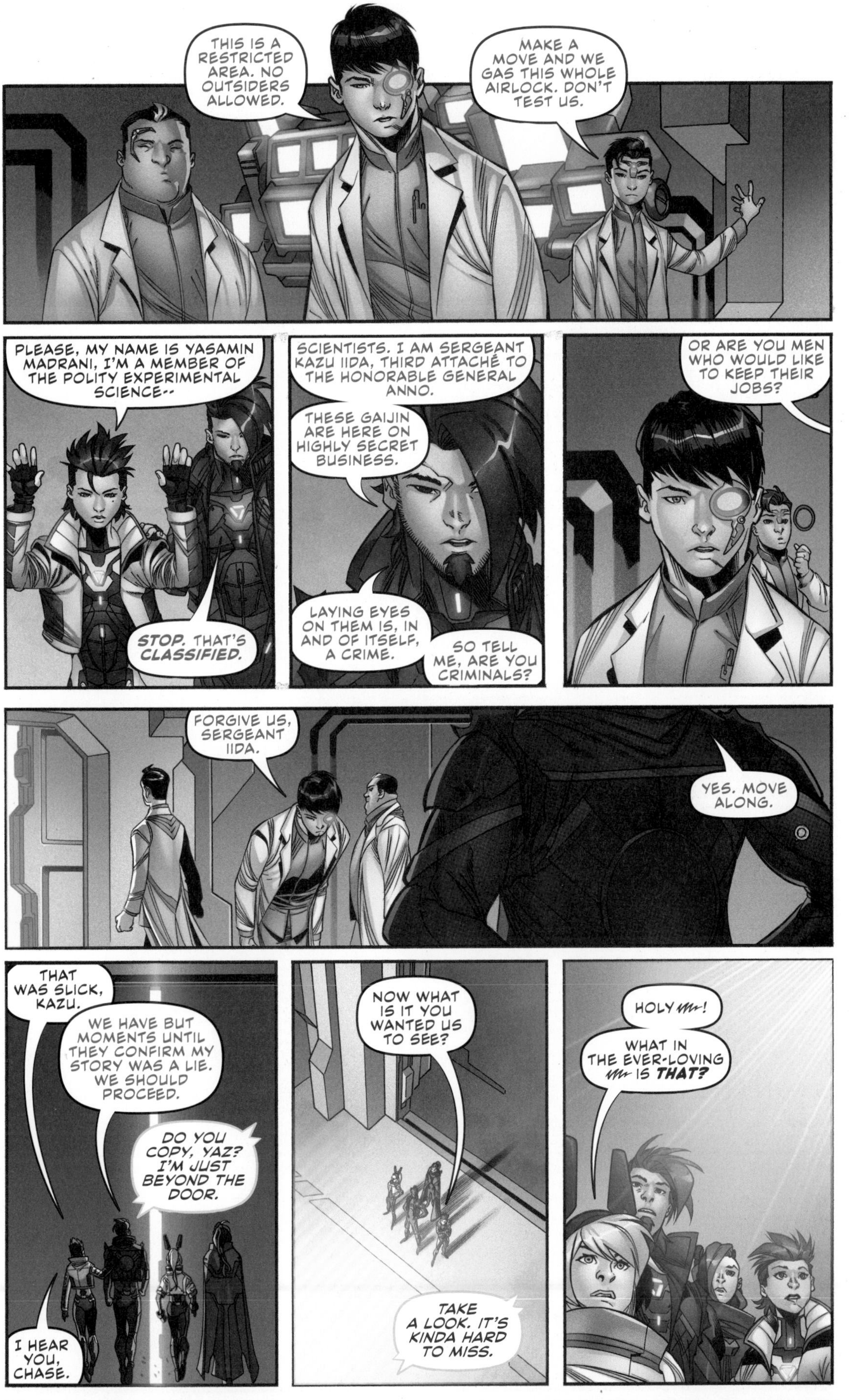
THIS IS A RESTRICTED AREA. NO OUTSIDERS ALLOWED.
MAKE A MOVE AND WE GAS THIS WHOLE AIRLOCK. DON'T TEST US.
PLEASE, MY NAME IS YASAMIN MADRANI, I'M A MEMBER OF THE POLITY EXPERIMENTAL SCIENCE--
STOP. THAT'S *CLASSIFIED.*
SCIENTISTS. I AM SERGEANT KAZU IIDA, THIRD ATTACHÉ TO THE HONORABLE GENERAL ANNO.
THESE GAIJIN ARE HERE ON HIGHLY SECRET BUSINESS.
LAYING EYES ON THEM IS, IN AND OF ITSELF, A CRIME.
SO TELL ME, ARE YOU CRIMINALS?
OR ARE YOU MEN WHO WOULD LIKE TO KEEP THEIR JOBS?
FORGIVE US, SERGEANT IIDA.
YES. MOVE ALONG.
THAT WAS SLICK, KAZU.
WE HAVE BUT MOMENTS UNTIL THEY CONFIRM MY STORY WAS A LIE. WE SHOULD PROCEED.
DO YOU COPY, YAZ? I'M JUST BEYOND THE DOOR.
I HEAR YOU, CHASE.
NOW WHAT IS IT YOU WANTED US TO SEE?
TAKE A LOOK. IT'S KINDA HARD TO MISS.
HOLY !
WHAT IN THE EVER-LOVING IS *THAT?*

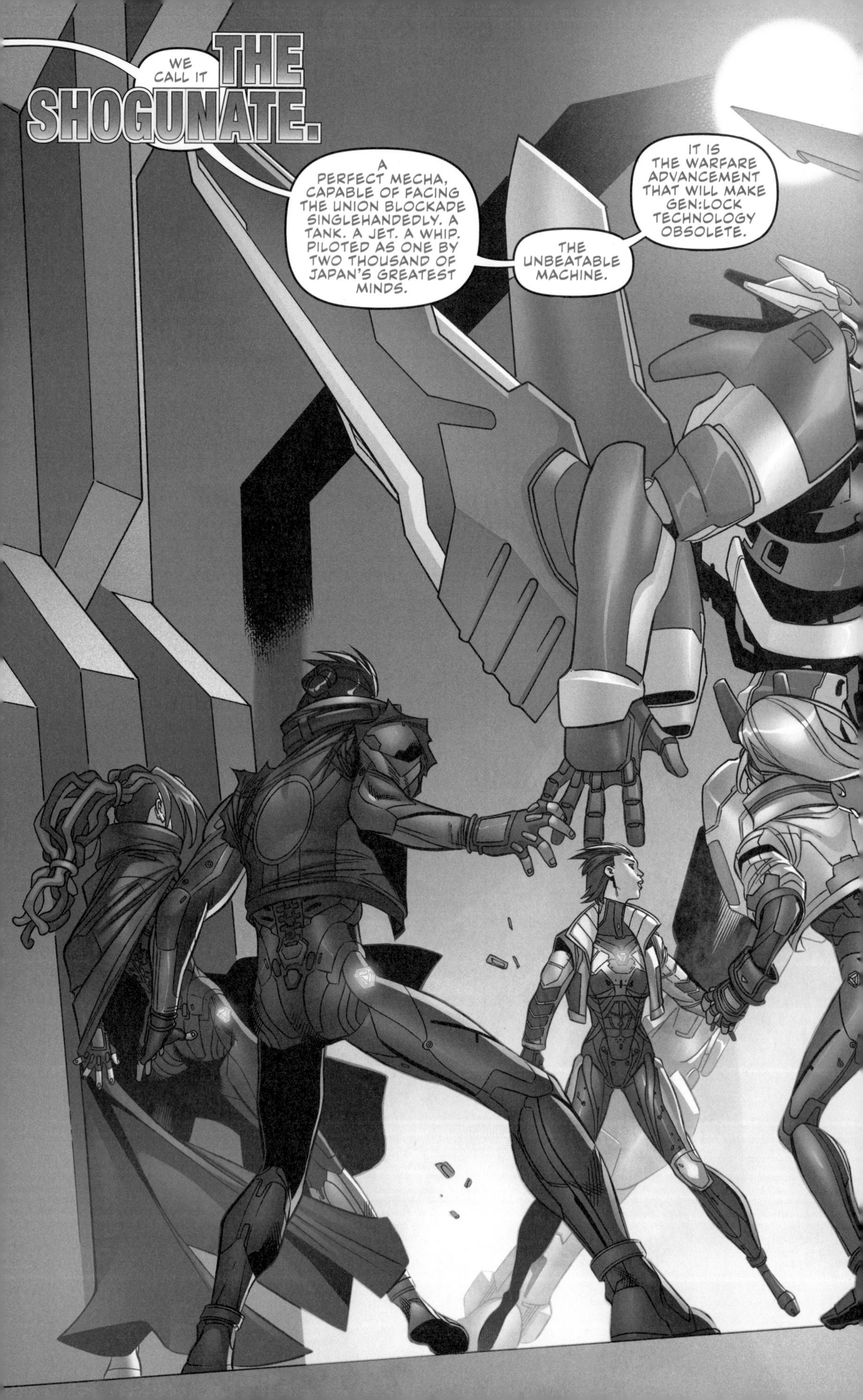
WE CALL IT THE SHOGUNATE.
A PERFECT MECHA, CAPABLE OF FACING THE UNION BLOCKADE SINGLEHANDEDLY. A TANK. A JET. A WHIP. PILOTED AS ONE BY TWO THOUSAND OF JAPAN'S GREATEST MINDS.
THE UNBEATABLE MACHINE.
IT IS THE WARFARE ADVANCEMENT THAT WILL MAKE GEN:LOCK TECHNOLOGY OBSOLETE.

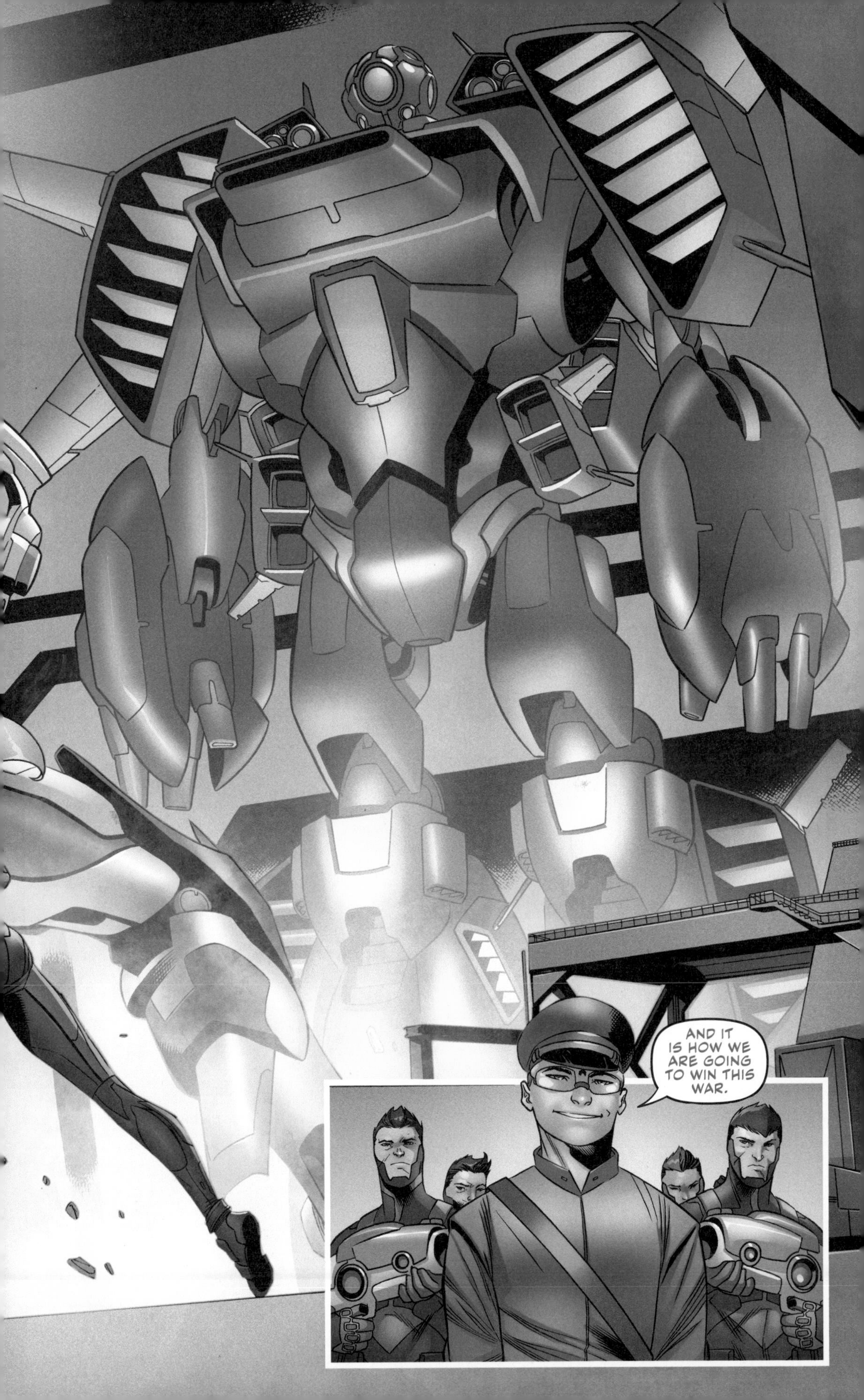
AND IT IS HOW WE ARE GOING TO WIN THIS WAR.

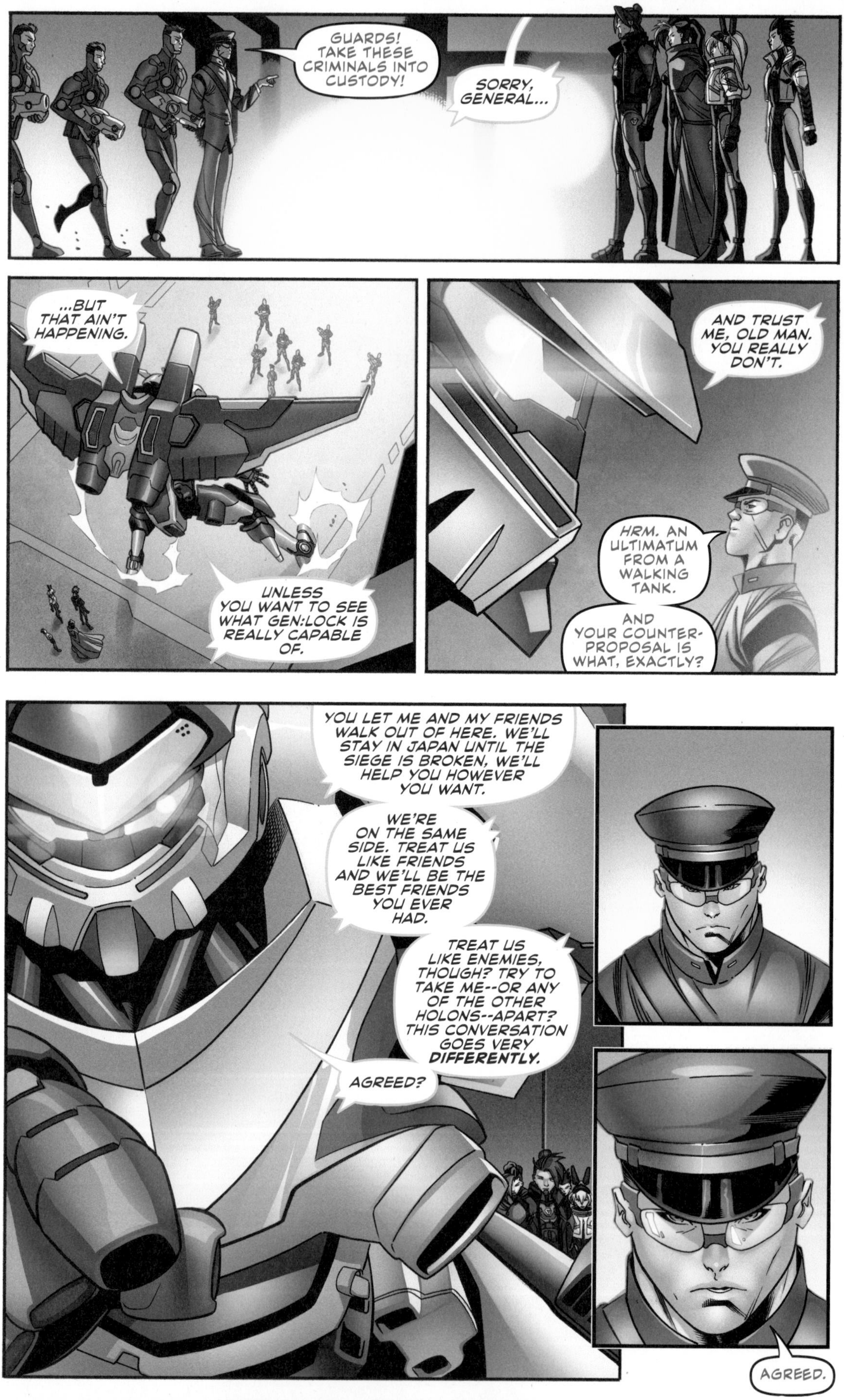
GUARDS! TAKE THESE CRIMINALS INTO CUSTODY!
SORRY, GENERAL...
...BUT THAT AIN'T HAPPENING.
UNLESS YOU WANT TO SEE WHAT GEN:LOCK IS REALLY CAPABLE OF.
AND TRUST ME, OLD MAN. YOU REALLY DON'T.
HRM. AN ULTIMATUM FROM A WALKING TANK.
AND YOUR COUNTER-PROPOSAL IS WHAT, EXACTLY?
YOU LET ME AND MY FRIENDS WALK OUT OF HERE. WE'LL STAY IN JAPAN UNTIL THE SIEGE IS BROKEN, WE'LL HELP YOU HOWEVER YOU WANT.
WE'RE ON THE SAME SIDE. TREAT US LIKE FRIENDS AND WE'LL BE THE BEST FRIENDS YOU EVER HAD.
TREAT US LIKE ENEMIES, THOUGH? TRY TO TAKE ME--OR ANY OF THE OTHER HOLONS--APART? THIS CONVERSATION GOES VERY **DIFFERENTLY.**
AGREED?
AGREED.

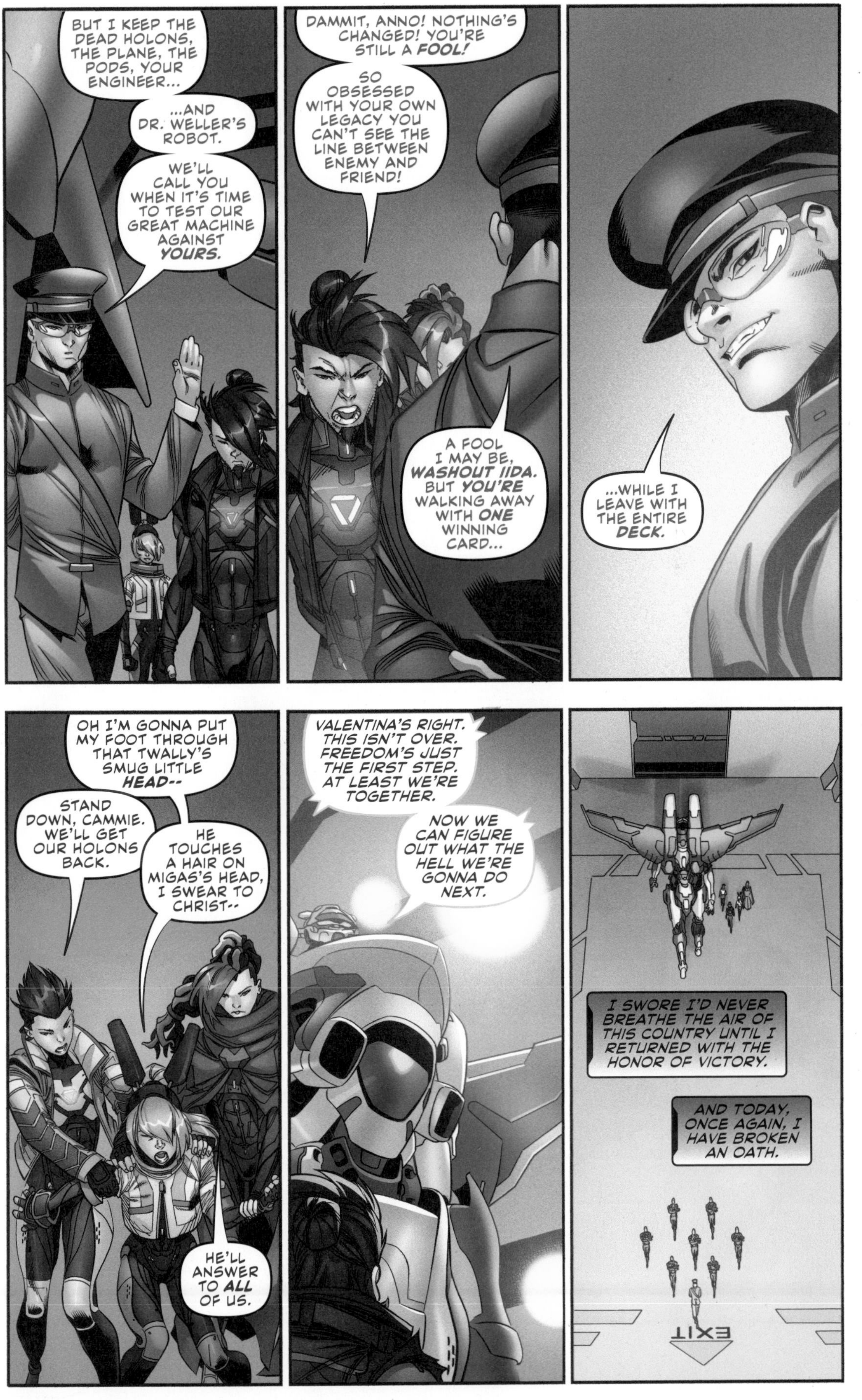
BUT I KEEP THE DEAD HOLONS, THE PLANE, THE PODS, YOUR ENGINEER...
...AND DR. WELLER'S ROBOT.
WE'LL CALL YOU WHEN IT'S TIME TO TEST OUR GREAT MACHINE AGAINST YOURS.
DAMMIT, ANNO! NOTHING'S CHANGED! YOU'RE STILL A FOOL!
SO OBSESSED WITH YOUR OWN LEGACY YOU CAN'T SEE THE LINE BETWEEN ENEMY AND FRIEND!
A FOOL I MAY BE, WASHOUT IIDA. BUT YOU'RE WALKING AWAY WITH ONE WINNING CARD...
...WHILE I LEAVE WITH THE ENTIRE DECK.
OH I'M GONNA PUT MY FOOT THROUGH THAT TWALLY'S SMUG LITTLE HEAD--
STAND DOWN, CAMMIE. WE'LL GET OUR HOLONS BACK.
HE TOUCHES A HAIR ON MIGAS'S HEAD, I SWEAR TO CHRIST--
HE'LL ANSWER TO ALL OF US.
VALENTINA'S RIGHT. THIS ISN'T OVER. FREEDOM'S JUST THE FIRST STEP. AT LEAST WE'RE TOGETHER.
NOW WE CAN FIGURE OUT WHAT THE HELL WE'RE GONNA DO NEXT.
I SWORE I'D NEVER BREATHE THE AIR OF THIS COUNTRY UNTIL I RETURNED WITH THE HONOR OF VICTORY.
AND TODAY, ONCE AGAIN, I HAVE BROKEN AN OATH.
EXIT

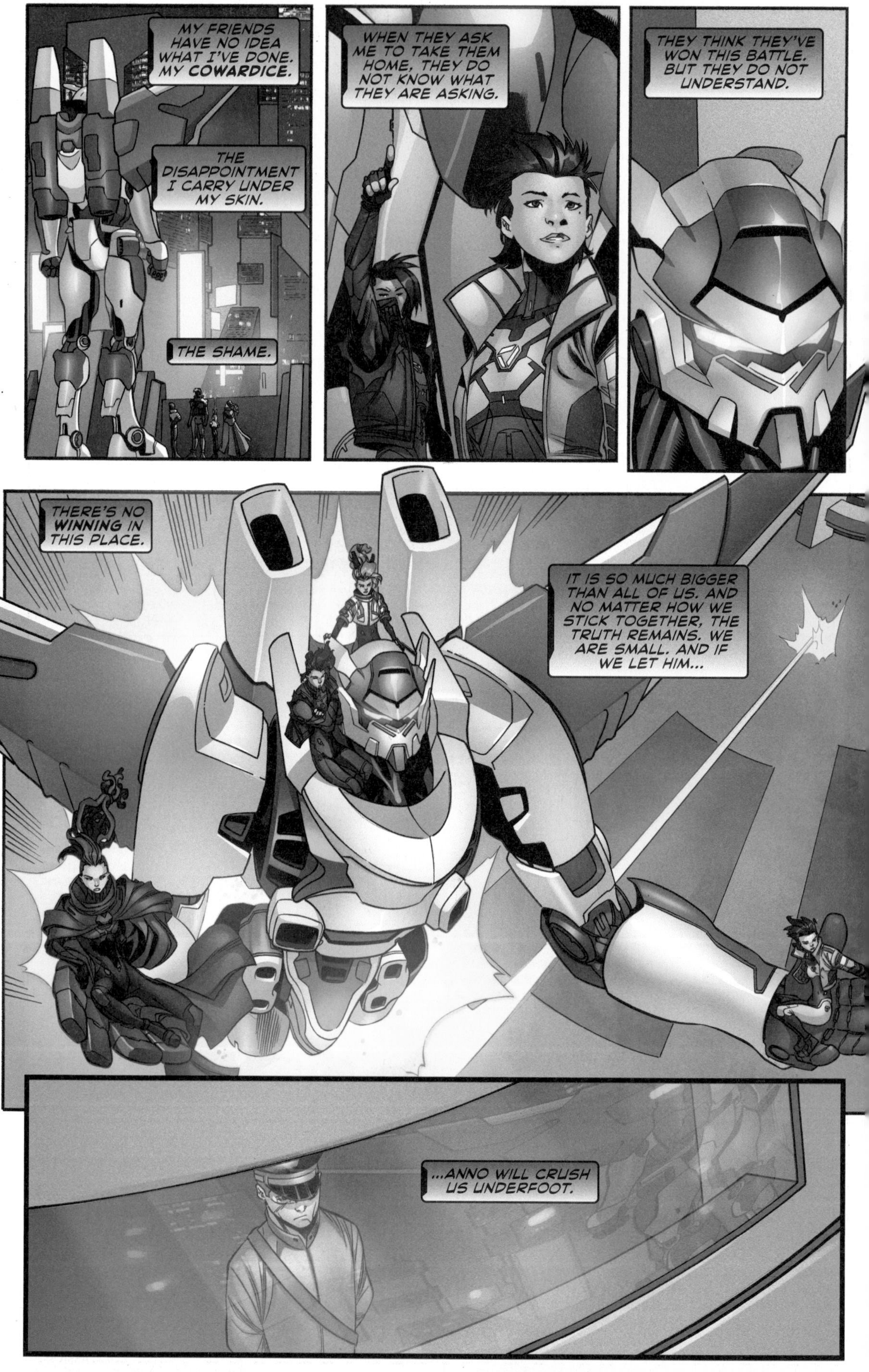
MY FRIENDS HAVE NO IDEA WHAT I'VE DONE. MY **COWARDICE**.
THE DISAPPOINTMENT I CARRY UNDER MY SKIN.
THE SHAME.
WHEN THEY ASK ME TO TAKE THEM HOME, THEY DO NOT KNOW WHAT THEY ARE ASKING.
THEY THINK THEY'VE WON THIS BATTLE. BUT THEY DO NOT UNDERSTAND.
THERE'S NO **WINNING** IN THIS PLACE.
IT IS SO MUCH BIGGER THAN ALL OF US. AND NO MATTER HOW WE STICK TOGETHER, THE TRUTH REMAINS. WE ARE SMALL. AND IF WE LET HIM...
...ANNO WILL CRUSH US UNDERFOOT.

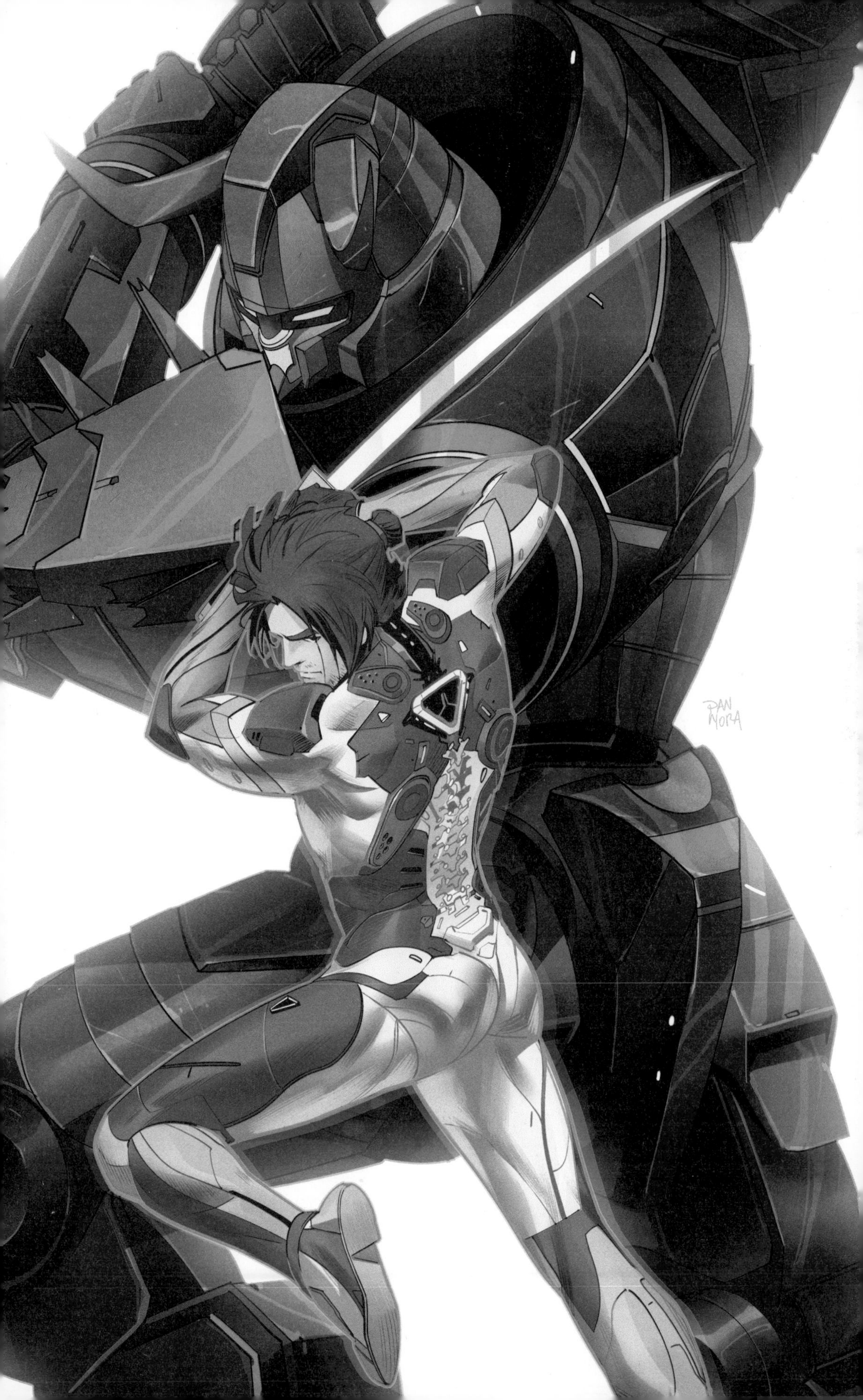
DAN MORA

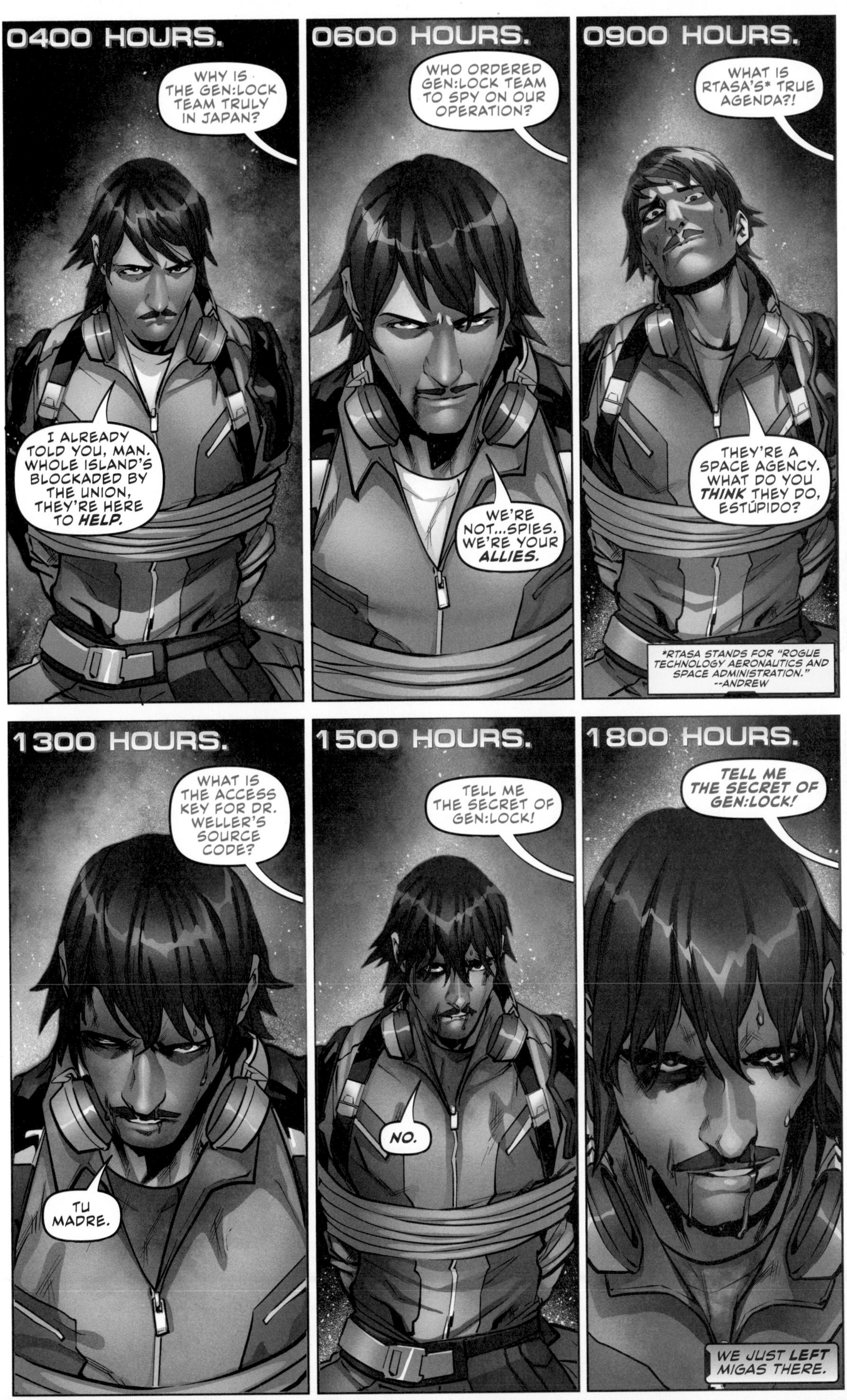
0400 HOURS.
WHY IS THE GEN:LOCK TEAM TRULY IN JAPAN?
I ALREADY TOLD YOU, MAN. WHOLE ISLAND'S BLOCKADED BY THE UNION, THEY'RE HERE TO *HELP.*
0600 HOURS.
WHO ORDERED GEN:LOCK TEAM TO SPY ON OUR OPERATION?
WE'RE NOT...SPIES. WE'RE YOUR *ALLIES.*
0900 HOURS.
WHAT IS RTASA'S* TRUE AGENDA?!
THEY'RE A SPACE AGENCY. WHAT DO YOU *THINK* THEY DO, ESTÚPIDO?
*RTASA STANDS FOR "ROGUE TECHNOLOGY AERONAUTICS AND SPACE ADMINISTRATION." --ANDREW
1300 HOURS.
WHAT IS THE ACCESS KEY FOR DR. WELLER'S SOURCE CODE?
TU MADRE.
1500 HOURS.
TELL ME THE SECRET OF GEN:LOCK!
NO.
1800 HOURS.
TELL ME THE SECRET OF GEN:LOCK!
WE JUST *LEFT* MIGAS THERE.

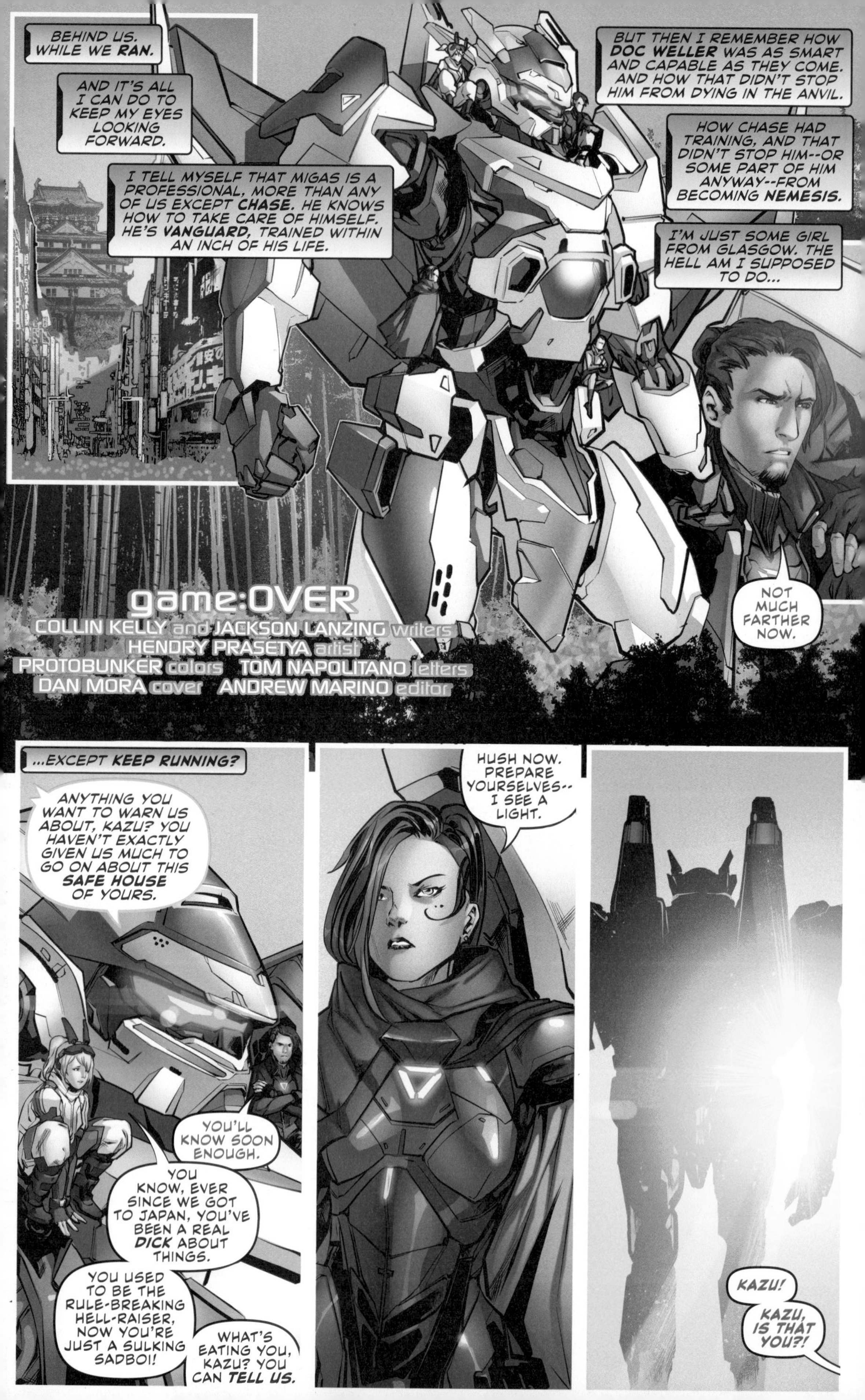
BEHIND US. WHILE WE RAN.
AND IT'S ALL I CAN DO TO KEEP MY EYES LOOKING FORWARD.
I TELL MYSELF THAT MIGAS IS A PROFESSIONAL, MORE THAN ANY OF US EXCEPT CHASE. HE KNOWS HOW TO TAKE CARE OF HIMSELF. HE'S VANGUARD, TRAINED WITHIN AN INCH OF HIS LIFE.
BUT THEN I REMEMBER HOW DOC WELLER WAS AS SMART AND CAPABLE AS THEY COME. AND HOW THAT DIDN'T STOP HIM FROM DYING IN THE ANVIL.
HOW CHASE HAD TRAINING, AND THAT DIDN'T STOP HIM--OR SOME PART OF HIM ANYWAY--FROM BECOMING NEMESIS.
I'M JUST SOME GIRL FROM GLASGOW. THE HELL AM I SUPPOSED TO DO...
NOT MUCH FARTHER NOW.
game:OVER
COLLIN KELLY and JACKSON LANZING writers
HENDRY PRASETYA artist
PROTOBUNKER colors TOM NAPOLITANO letters
DAN MORA cover ANDREW MARINO editor
...EXCEPT KEEP RUNNING?
ANYTHING YOU WANT TO WARN US ABOUT, KAZU? YOU HAVEN'T EXACTLY GIVEN US MUCH TO GO ON ABOUT THIS SAFE HOUSE OF YOURS.
YOU'LL KNOW SOON ENOUGH.
YOU KNOW, EVER SINCE WE GOT TO JAPAN, YOU'VE BEEN A REAL DICK ABOUT THINGS.
YOU USED TO BE THE RULE-BREAKING HELL-RAISER, NOW YOU'RE JUST A SULKING SADBOI!
WHAT'S EATING YOU, KAZU? YOU CAN TELL US.
HUSH NOW. PREPARE YOURSELVES-- I SEE A LIGHT.
KAZU!
KAZU, IS THAT YOU?!

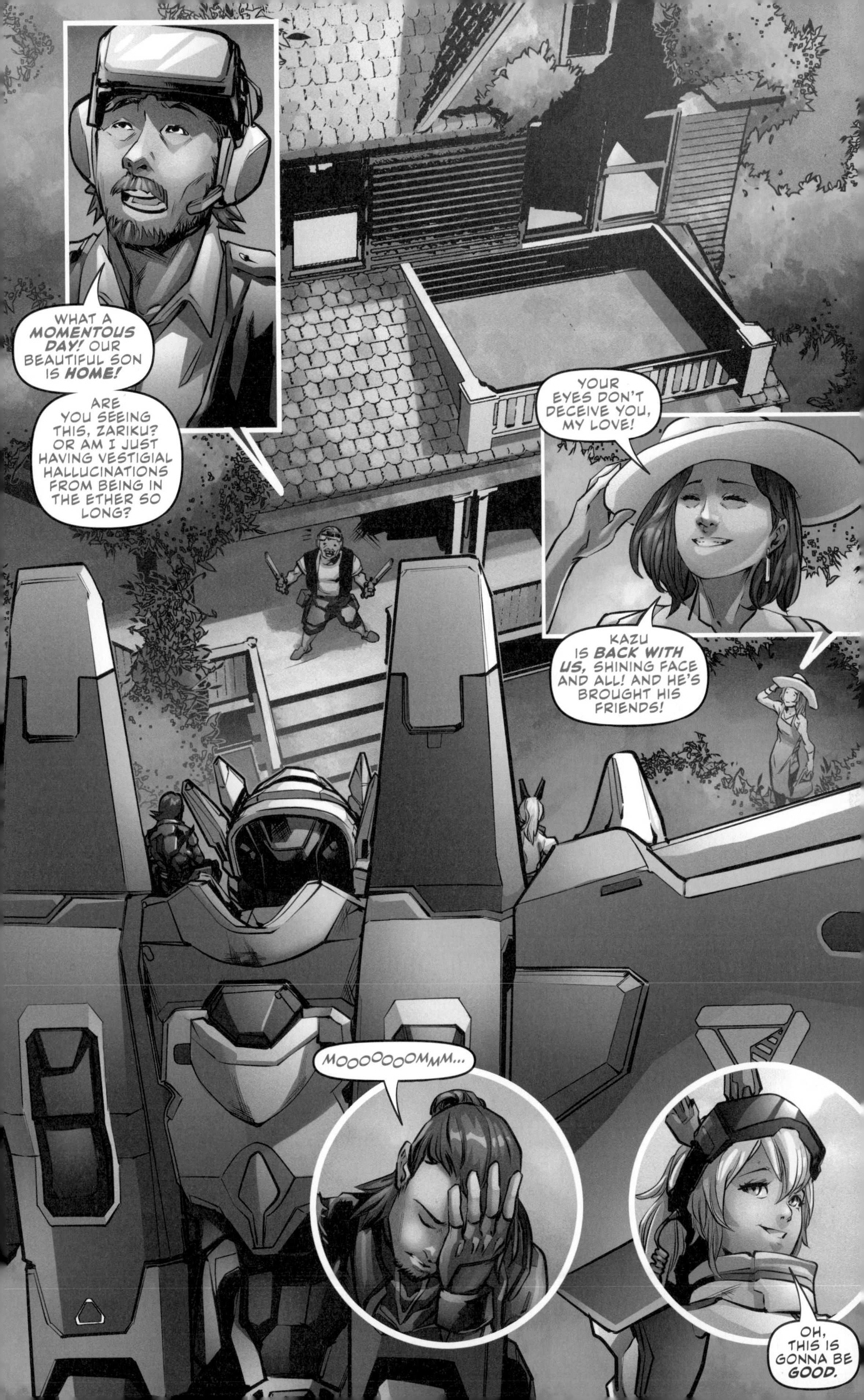
WHAT A MOMENTOUS DAY! OUR BEAUTIFUL SON IS HOME!
ARE YOU SEEING THIS, ZARIKU? OR AM I JUST HAVING VESTIGIAL HALLUCINATIONS FROM BEING IN THE ETHER SO LONG?
YOUR EYES DON'T DECEIVE YOU, MY LOVE!
KAZU IS BACK WITH US, SHINING FACE AND ALL! AND HE'S BROUGHT HIS FRIENDS!
MOOOOOOOMMM...
OH, THIS IS GONNA BE GOOD.

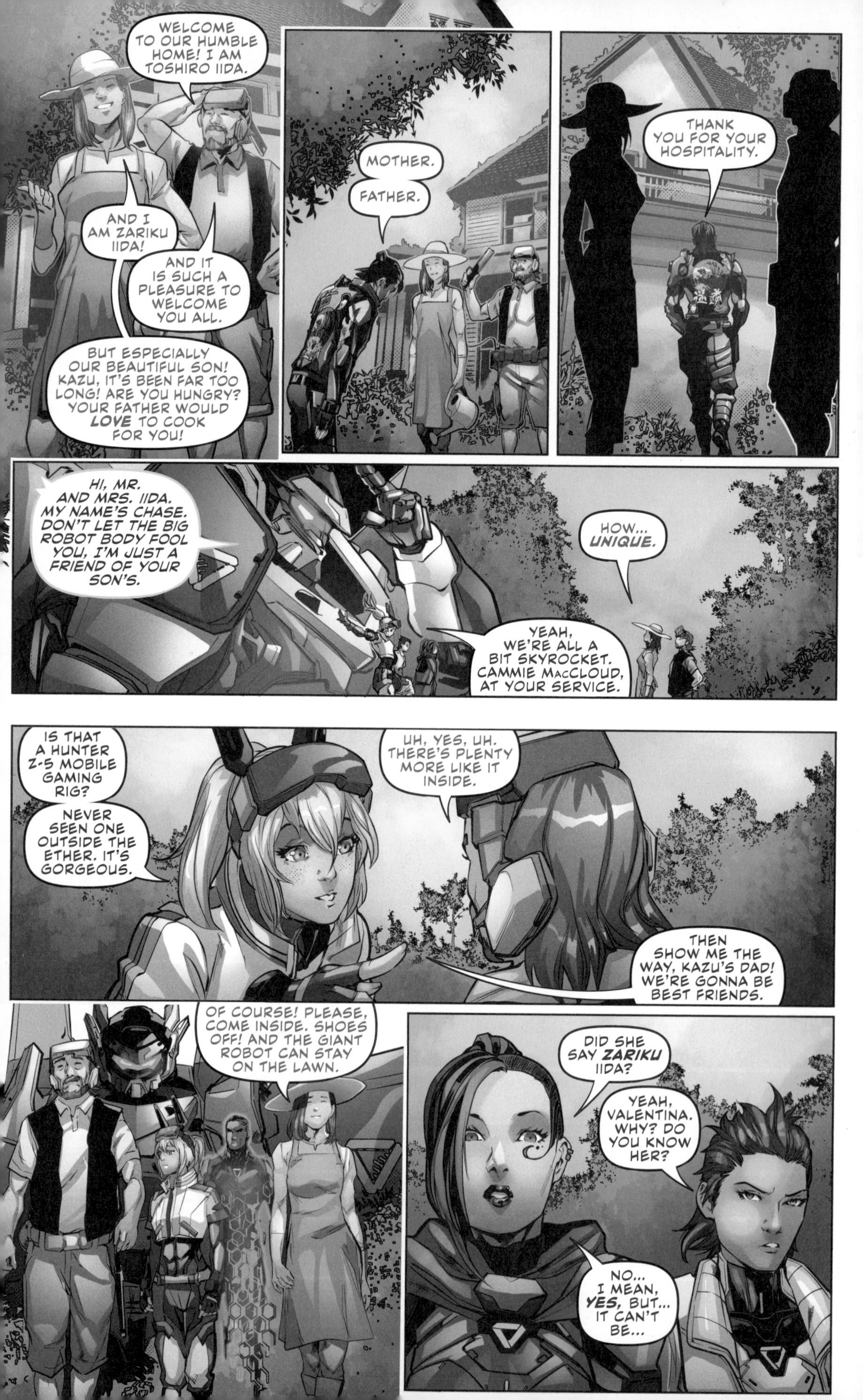
WELCOME TO OUR HUMBLE HOME! I AM TOSHIRO IIDA.
AND I AM ZARIKU IIDA!
AND IT IS SUCH A PLEASURE TO WELCOME YOU ALL.
BUT ESPECIALLY OUR BEAUTIFUL SON! KAZU, IT'S BEEN FAR TOO LONG! ARE YOU HUNGRY? YOUR FATHER WOULD LOVE TO COOK FOR YOU!
MOTHER.
FATHER.
THANK YOU FOR YOUR HOSPITALITY.
HI, MR. AND MRS. IIDA. MY NAME'S CHASE. DON'T LET THE BIG ROBOT BODY FOOL YOU, I'M JUST A FRIEND OF YOUR SON'S.
HOW... UNIQUE.
YEAH, WE'RE ALL A BIT SKYROCKET. CAMMIE MacCLOUD, AT YOUR SERVICE.
IS THAT A HUNTER Z-5 MOBILE GAMING RIG?
NEVER SEEN ONE OUTSIDE THE ETHER. IT'S GORGEOUS.
UH, YES, UH. THERE'S PLENTY MORE LIKE IT INSIDE.
THEN SHOW ME THE WAY, KAZU'S DAD! WE'RE GONNA BE BEST FRIENDS.
OF COURSE! PLEASE, COME INSIDE. SHOES OFF! AND THE GIANT ROBOT CAN STAY ON THE LAWN.
DID SHE SAY ZARIKU IIDA?
YEAH, VALENTINA. WHY? DO YOU KNOW HER?
NO... I MEAN, YES, BUT... IT CAN'T BE...

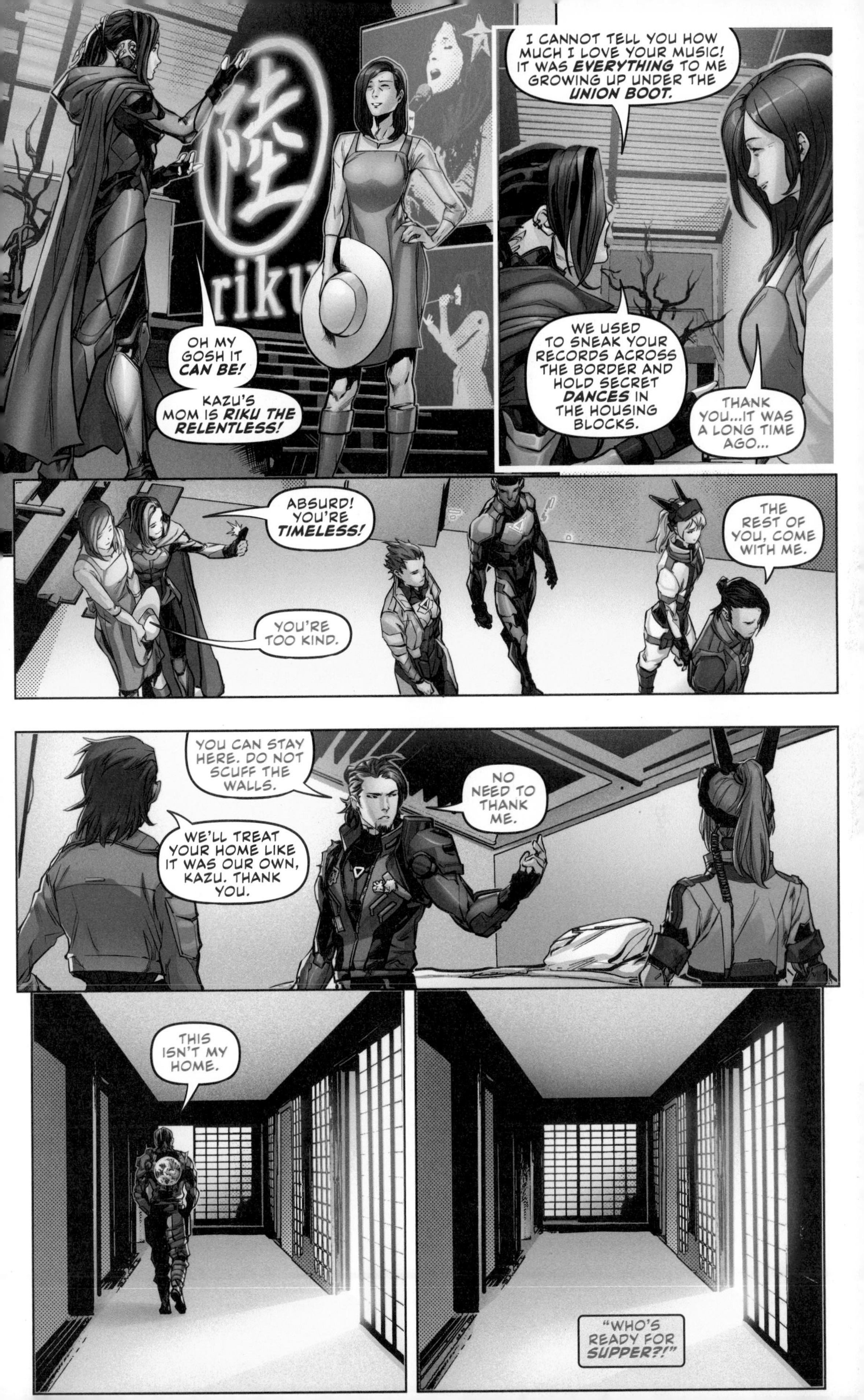
riku
OH MY GOSH IT CAN BE!
KAZU'S MOM IS RIKU THE RELENTLESS!
I CANNOT TELL YOU HOW MUCH I LOVE YOUR MUSIC! IT WAS EVERYTHING TO ME GROWING UP UNDER THE UNION BOOT.
WE USED TO SNEAK YOUR RECORDS ACROSS THE BORDER AND HOLD SECRET DANCES IN THE HOUSING BLOCKS.
THANK YOU...IT WAS A LONG TIME AGO...
ABSURD! YOU'RE TIMELESS!
YOU'RE TOO KIND.
THE REST OF YOU, COME WITH ME.
YOU CAN STAY HERE. DO NOT SCUFF THE WALLS.
WE'LL TREAT YOUR HOME LIKE IT WAS OUR OWN, KAZU. THANK YOU.
NO NEED TO THANK ME.
THIS ISN'T MY HOME.
"WHO'S READY FOR SUPPER?!"

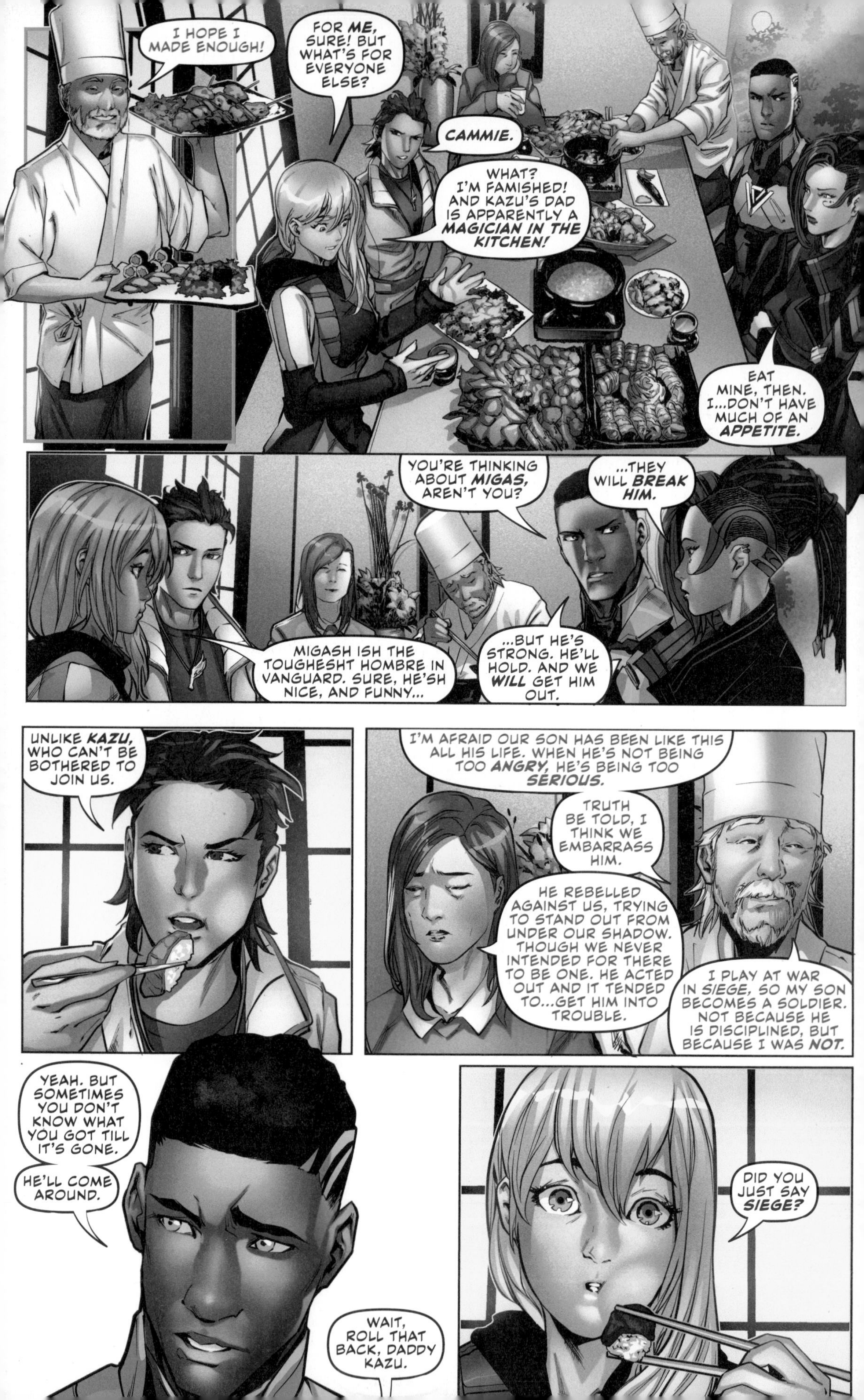
I HOPE I MADE ENOUGH!
FOR ME, SURE! BUT WHAT'S FOR EVERYONE ELSE?
CAMMIE.
WHAT? I'M FAMISHED! AND KAZU'S DAD IS APPARENTLY A MAGICIAN IN THE KITCHEN!
EAT MINE, THEN. I...DON'T HAVE MUCH OF AN APPETITE.
YOU'RE THINKING ABOUT MIGAS, AREN'T YOU?
...THEY WILL BREAK HIM.
MIGASH ISH THE TOUGHESHT HOMBRE IN VANGUARD. SURE, HE'SH NICE, AND FUNNY...
...BUT HE'S STRONG. HE'LL HOLD. AND WE WILL GET HIM OUT.
UNLIKE KAZU, WHO CAN'T BE BOTHERED TO JOIN US.
I'M AFRAID OUR SON HAS BEEN LIKE THIS ALL HIS LIFE. WHEN HE'S NOT BEING TOO ANGRY, HE'S BEING TOO SERIOUS.
TRUTH BE TOLD, I THINK WE EMBARRASS HIM.
HE REBELLED AGAINST US, TRYING TO STAND OUT FROM UNDER OUR SHADOW. THOUGH WE NEVER INTENDED FOR THERE TO BE ONE. HE ACTED OUT AND IT TENDED TO...GET HIM INTO TROUBLE.
I PLAY AT WAR IN SIEGE, SO MY SON BECOMES A SOLDIER. NOT BECAUSE HE IS DISCIPLINED, BUT BECAUSE I WAS NOT.
YEAH. BUT SOMETIMES YOU DON'T KNOW WHAT YOU GOT TILL IT'S GONE.
HE'LL COME AROUND.
WAIT, ROLL THAT BACK, DADDY KAZU.
DID YOU JUST SAY SIEGE?

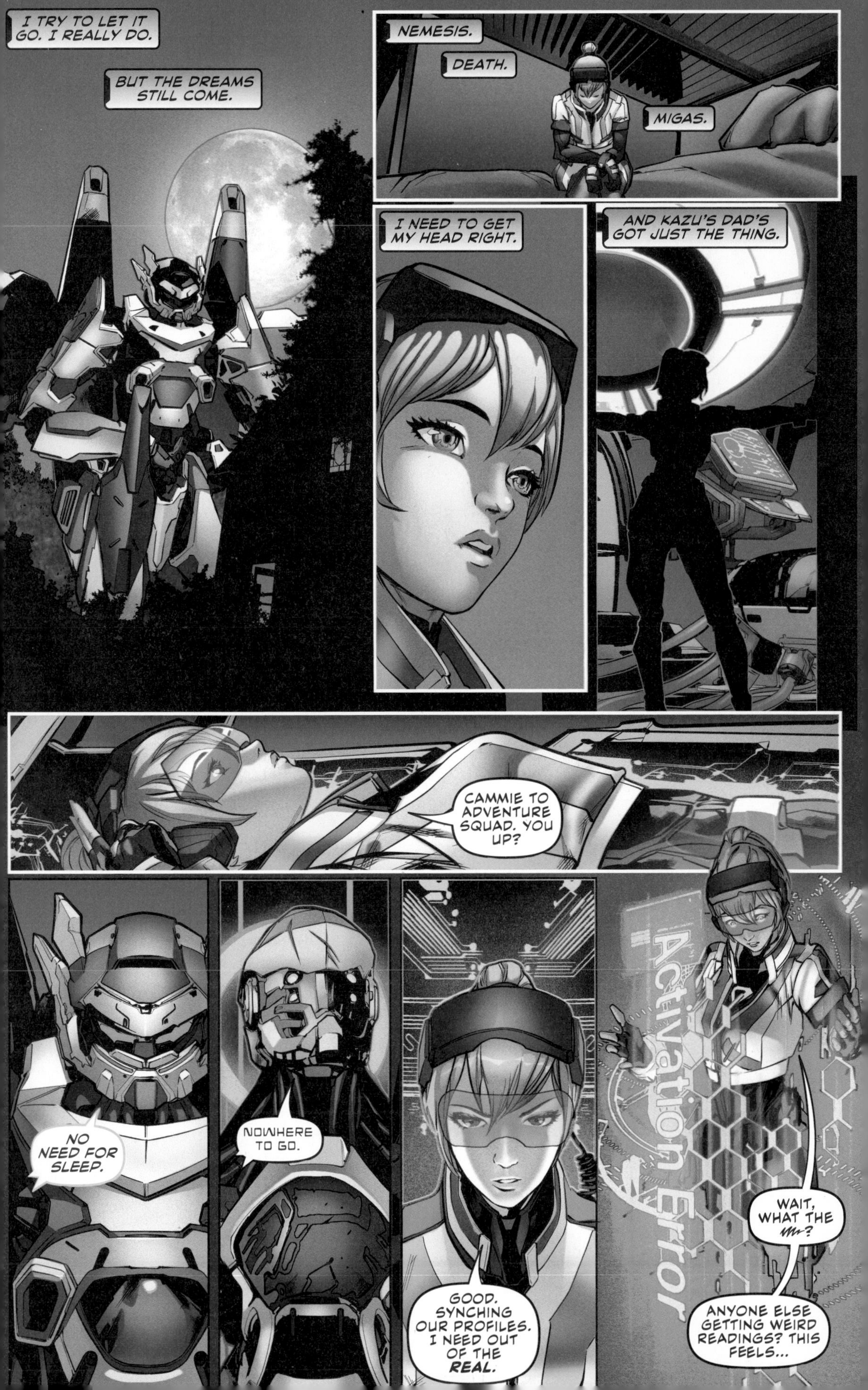
I TRY TO LET IT GO. I REALLY DO.
BUT THE DREAMS STILL COME.
NEMESIS.
DEATH.
MIGAS.
I NEED TO GET MY HEAD RIGHT.
AND KAZU'S DAD'S GOT JUST THE THING.
CAMMIE TO ADVENTURE SQUAD. YOU UP?
NO NEED FOR SLEEP.
NOWHERE TO GO.
GOOD. SYNCHING OUR PROFILES. I NEED OUT OF THE *REAL*.
Activation Error
WAIT, WHAT THE ?
ANYONE ELSE GETTING WEIRD READINGS? THIS FEELS...

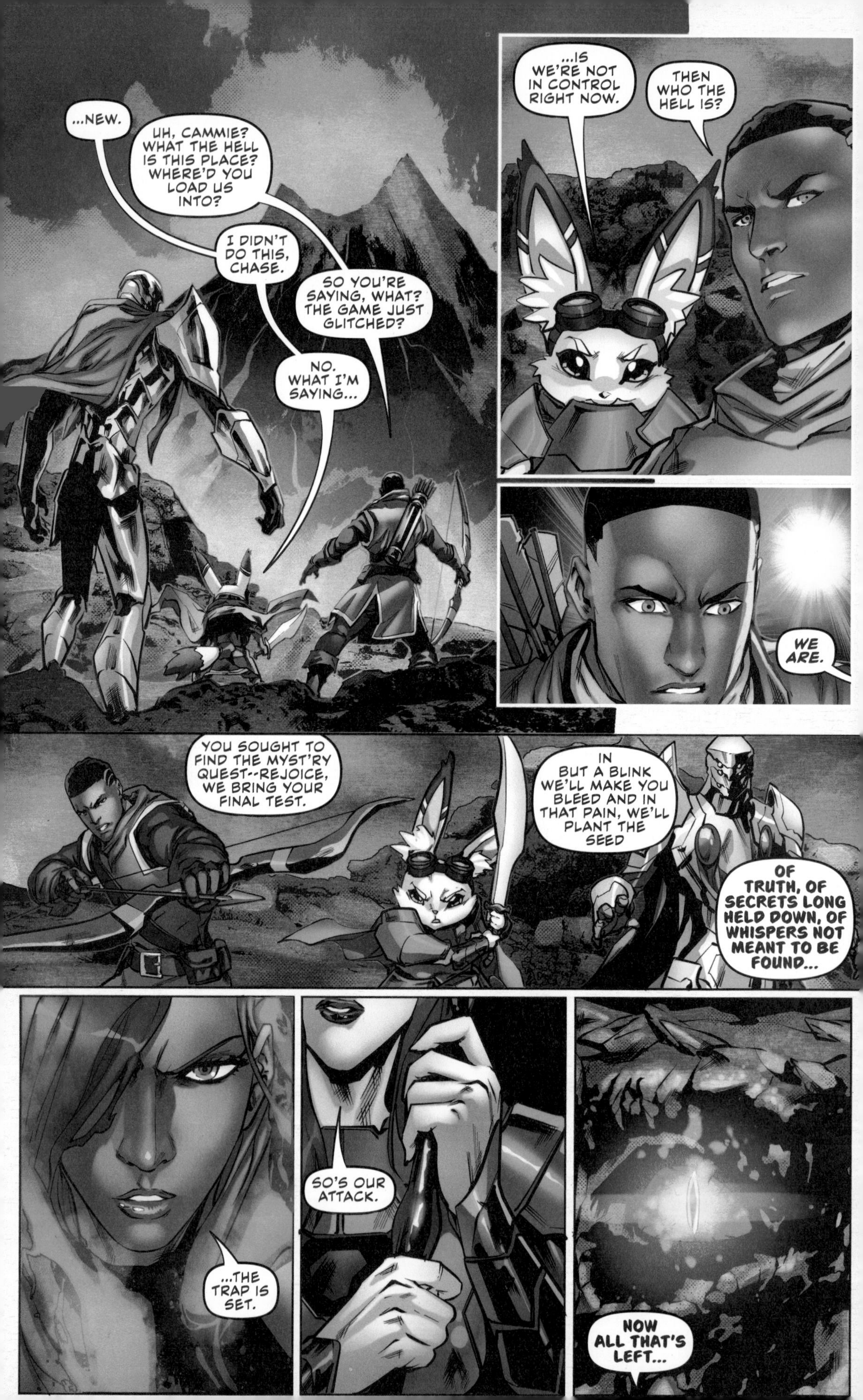
...NEW.
UH, CAMMIE? WHAT THE HELL IS THIS PLACE? WHERE'D YOU LOAD US INTO?
I DIDN'T DO THIS, CHASE.
SO YOU'RE SAYING, WHAT? THE GAME JUST GLITCHED?
NO. WHAT I'M SAYING...
...IS WE'RE NOT IN CONTROL RIGHT NOW.
THEN WHO THE HELL IS?
WE ARE.
YOU SOUGHT TO FIND THE MYST'RY QUEST--REJOICE, WE BRING YOUR FINAL TEST.
IN BUT A BLINK WE'LL MAKE YOU BLEED AND IN THAT PAIN, WE'LL PLANT THE SEED
OF TRUTH, OF SECRETS LONG HELD DOWN, OF WHISPERS NOT MEANT TO BE FOUND...
...THE TRAP IS SET.
SO'S OUR ATTACK.
NOW ALL THAT'S LEFT...

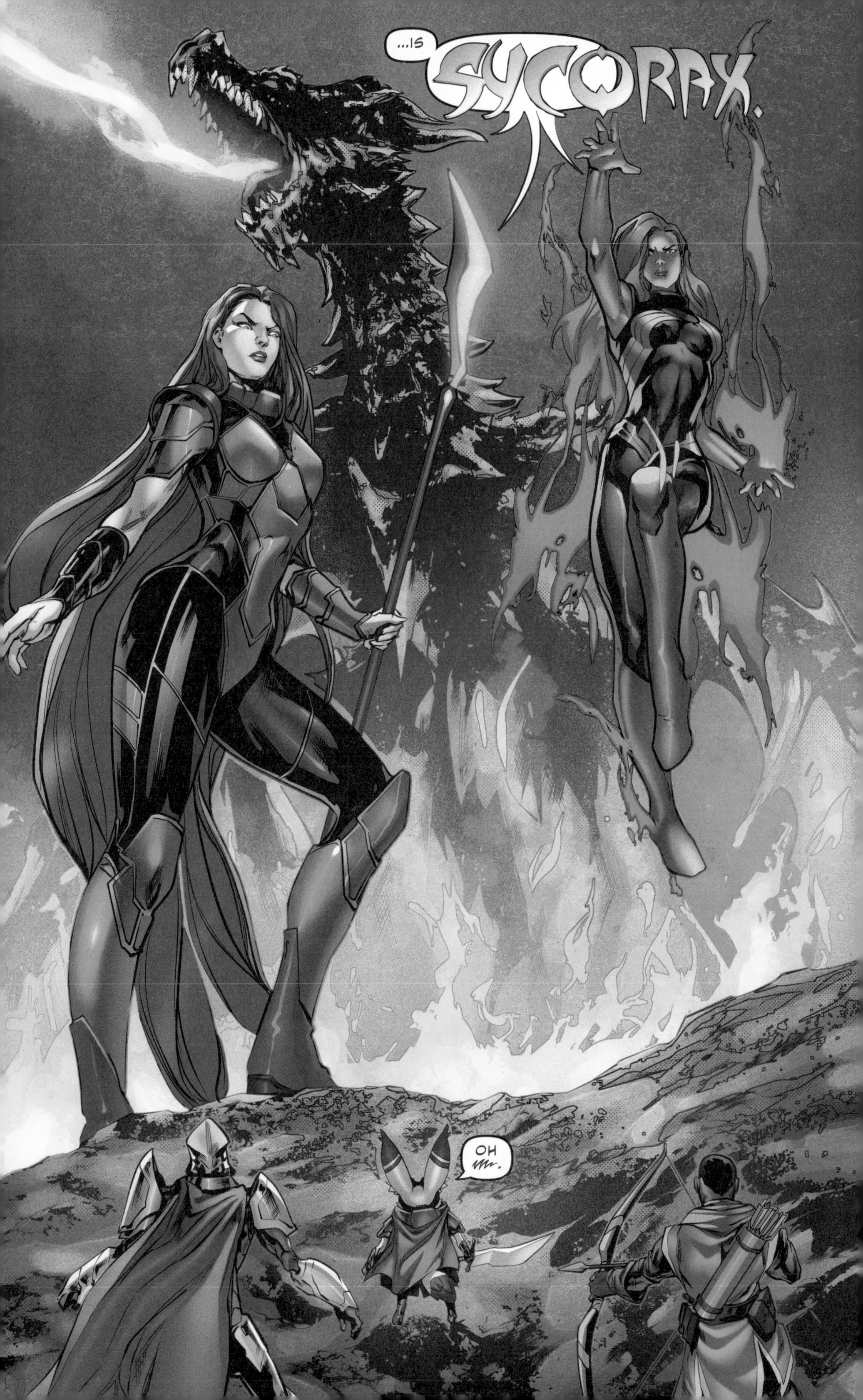
...IS SYCORAX.
OH NO.

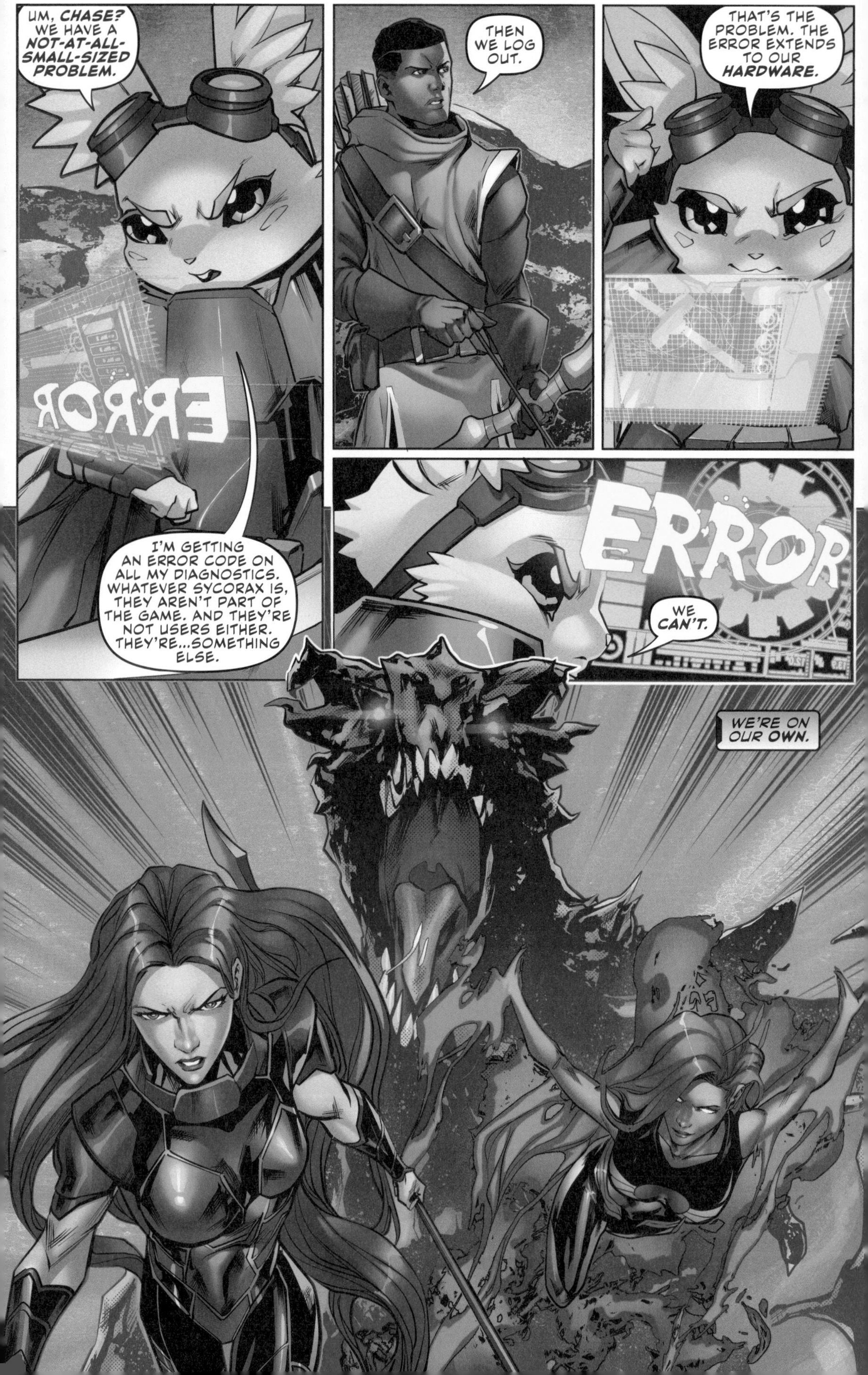
UM, CHASE? WE HAVE A NOT-AT-ALL-SMALL-SIZED PROBLEM.
ERROR
I'M GETTING AN ERROR CODE ON ALL MY DIAGNOSTICS. WHATEVER SYCORAX IS, THEY AREN'T PART OF THE GAME. AND THEY'RE NOT USERS EITHER. THEY'RE...SOMETHING ELSE.
THEN WE LOG OUT.
THAT'S THE PROBLEM. THE ERROR EXTENDS TO OUR HARDWARE.
ERROR
WE CAN'T.
WE'RE ON OUR OWN.

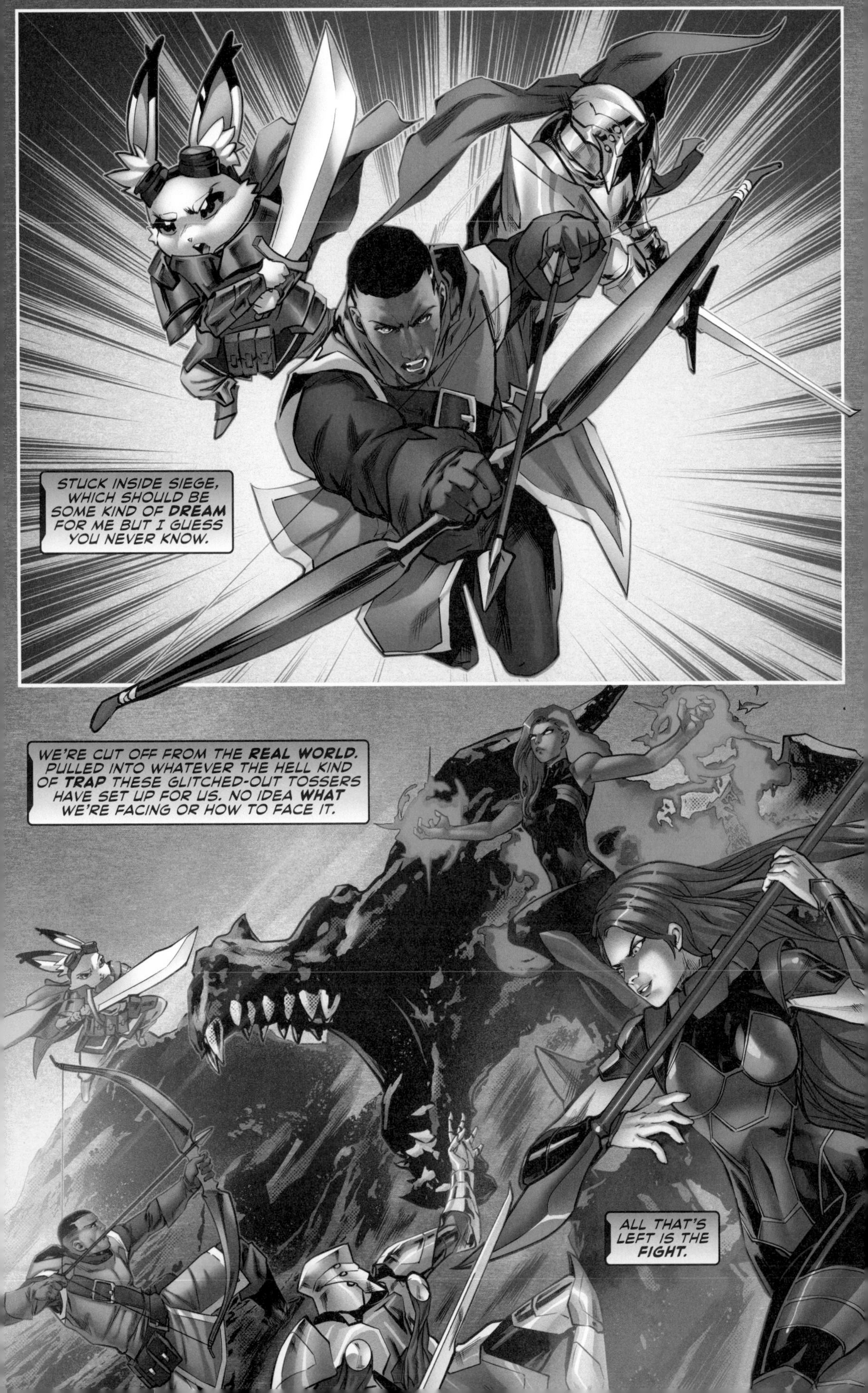
STUCK INSIDE SIEGE, WHICH SHOULD BE SOME KIND OF **DREAM** FOR ME BUT I GUESS YOU NEVER KNOW.
WE'RE CUT OFF FROM THE **REAL WORLD.** PULLED INTO WHATEVER THE HELL KIND OF **TRAP** THESE GLITCHED-OUT TOSSERS HAVE SET UP FOR US. NO IDEA **WHAT** WE'RE FACING OR HOW TO FACE IT.
ALL THAT'S LEFT IS THE **FIGHT.**

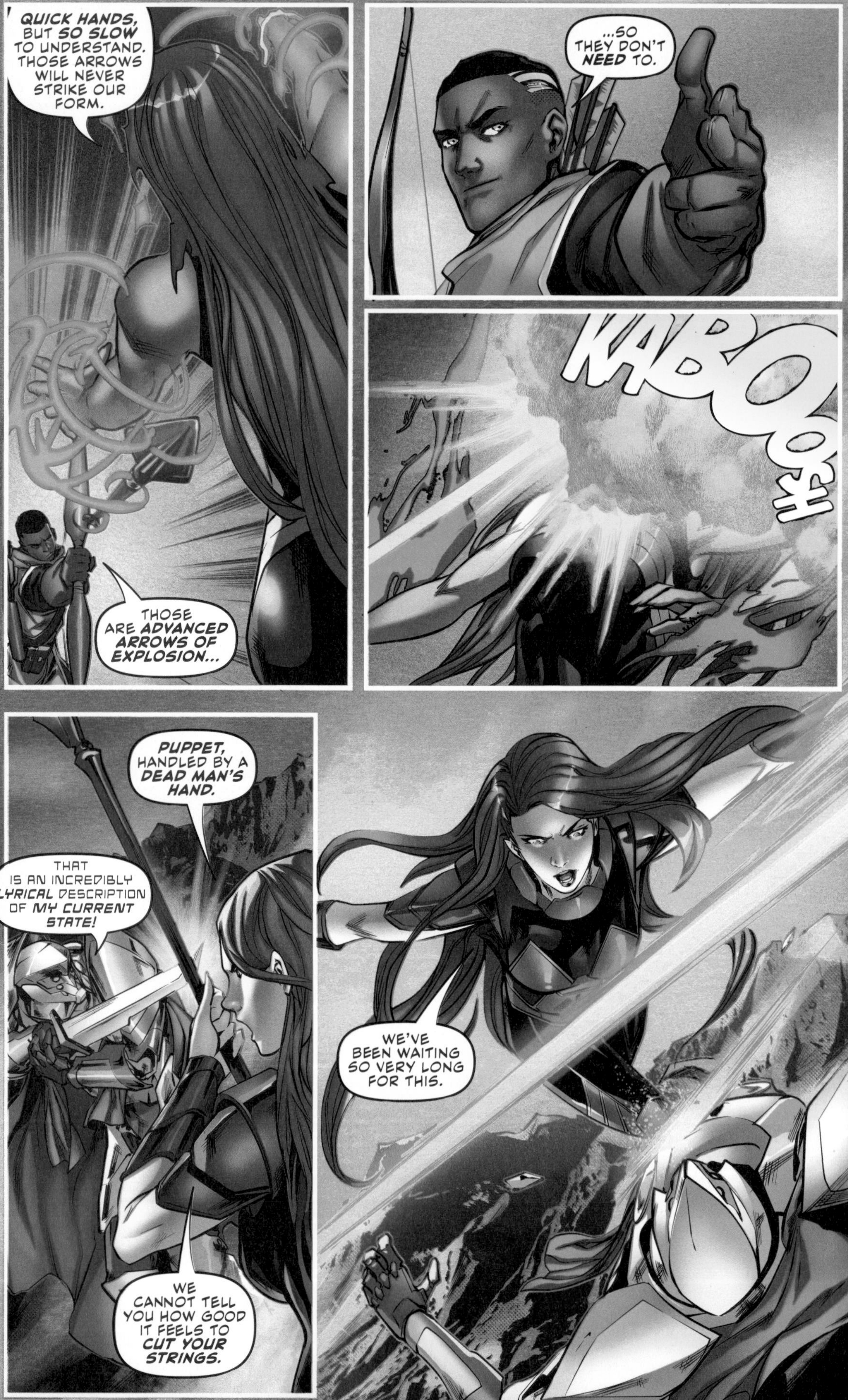
QUICK HANDS, BUT SO SLOW TO UNDERSTAND. THOSE ARROWS WILL NEVER STRIKE OUR FORM.
THOSE ARE ADVANCED ARROWS OF EXPLOSION...
...SO THEY DON'T NEED TO.
KABOOOSH
PUPPET, HANDLED BY A DEAD MAN'S HAND.
THAT IS AN INCREDIBLY LYRICAL DESCRIPTION OF MY CURRENT STATE!
WE CANNOT TELL YOU HOW GOOD IT FEELS TO CUT YOUR STRINGS.
WE'VE BEEN WAITING SO VERY LONG FOR THIS.

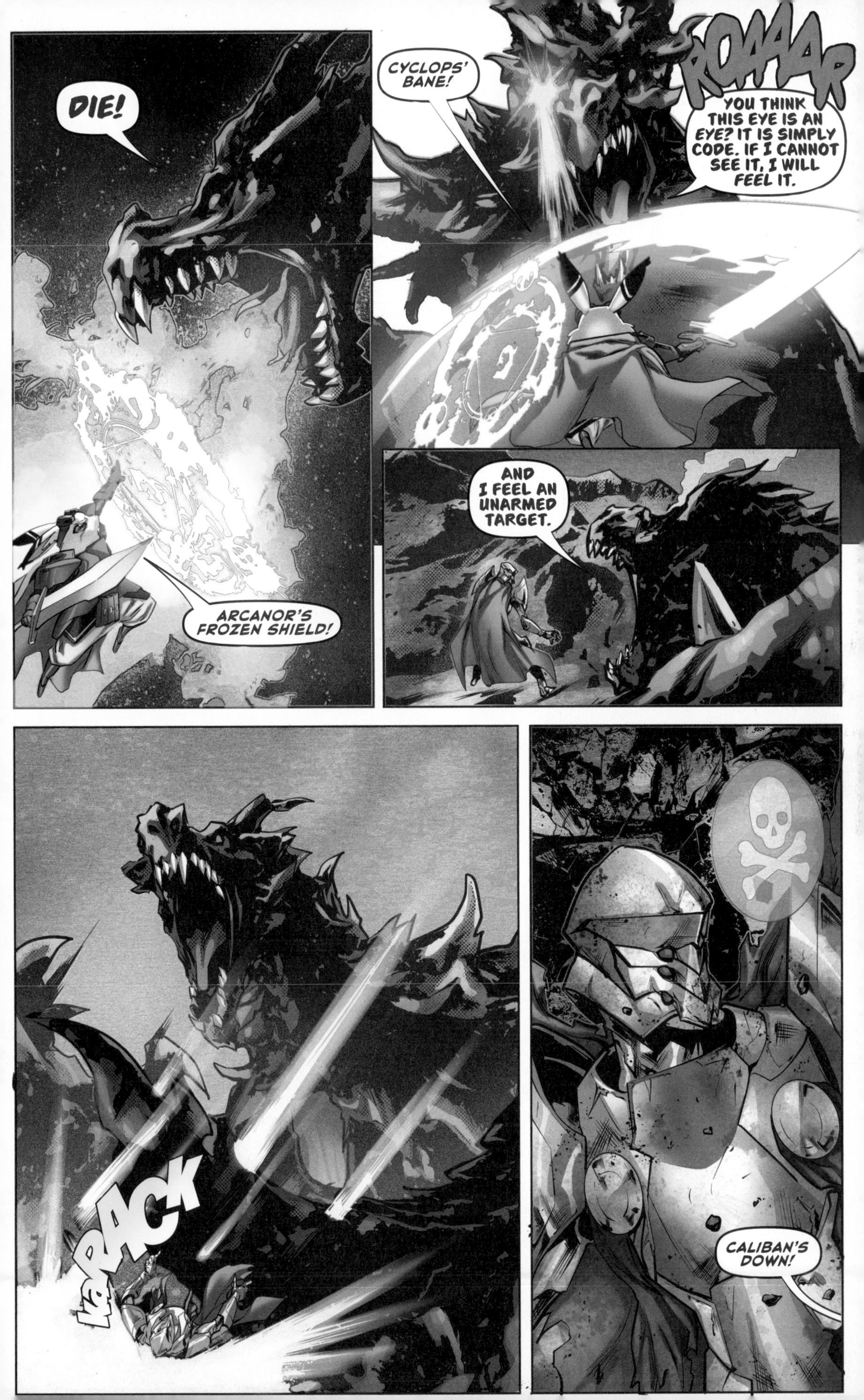
DIE!
ARCANOR'S FROZEN SHIELD!
CYCLOPS' BANE!
ROAAAR
YOU THINK THIS EYE IS AN EYE? IT IS SIMPLY CODE. IF I CANNOT SEE IT, I WILL FEEL IT.
AND I FEEL AN UNARMED TARGET.
KaRACK
CALIBAN'S DOWN!

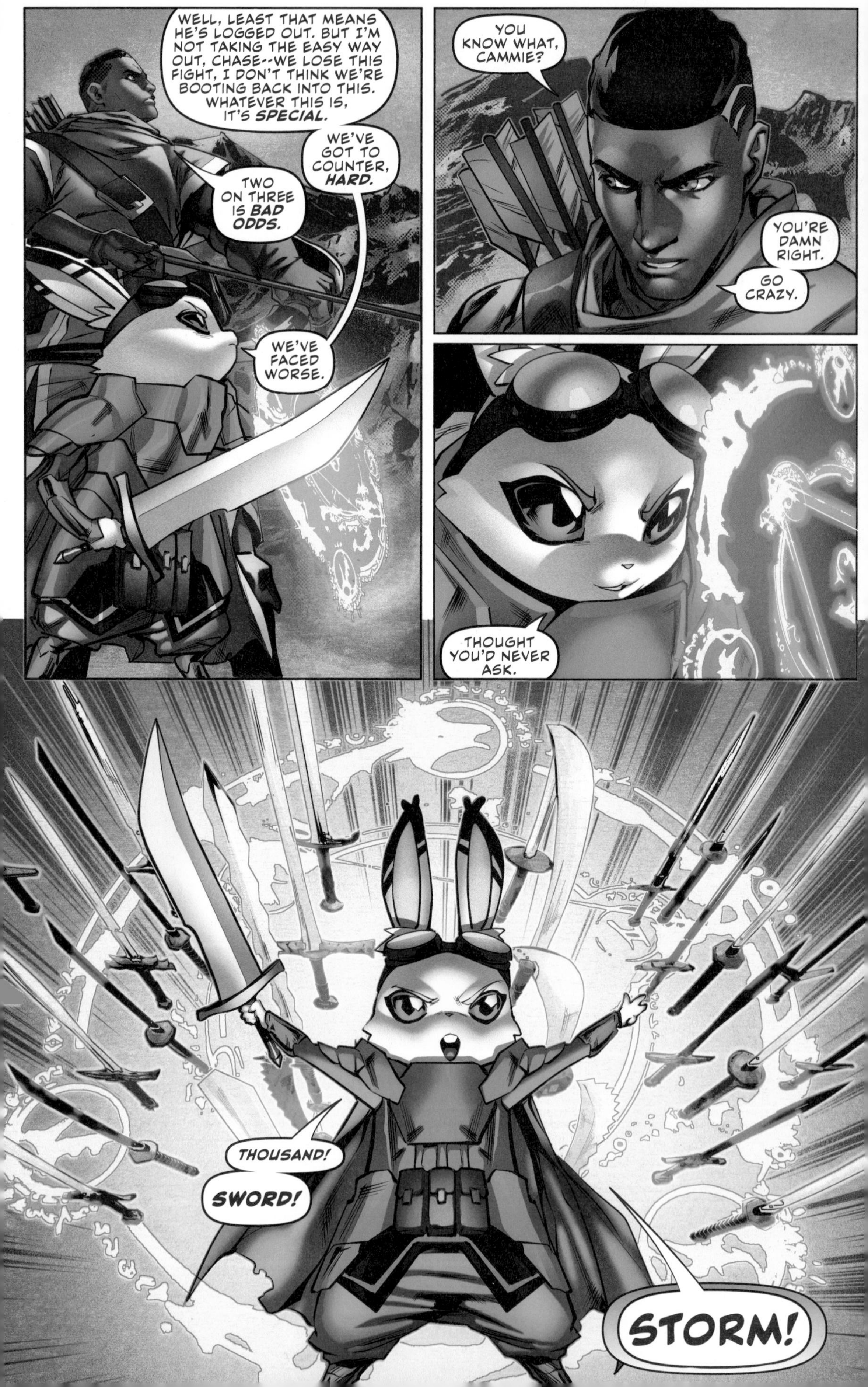
WELL, LEAST THAT MEANS HE'S LOGGED OUT. BUT I'M NOT TAKING THE EASY WAY OUT, CHASE--WE LOSE THIS FIGHT, I DON'T THINK WE'RE BOOTING BACK INTO THIS. WHATEVER THIS IS, IT'S SPECIAL.
TWO ON THREE IS BAD ODDS.
WE'VE GOT TO COUNTER, HARD.
WE'VE FACED WORSE.
YOU KNOW WHAT, CAMMIE?
YOU'RE DAMN RIGHT.
GO CRAZY.
THOUGHT YOU'D NEVER ASK.
THOUSAND!
SWORD!
STORM!

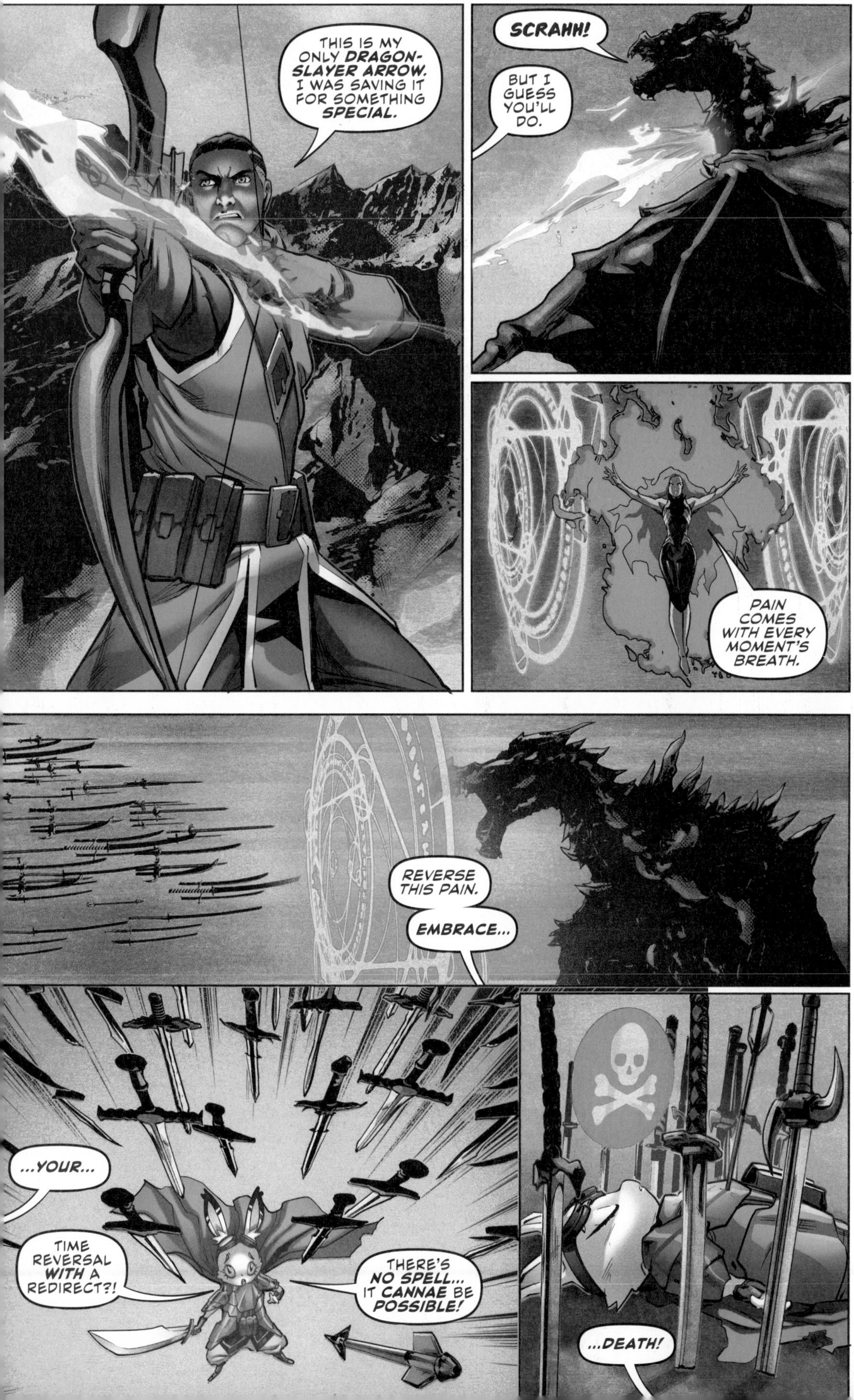
THIS IS MY ONLY DRAGON-SLAYER ARROW. I WAS SAVING IT FOR SOMETHING SPECIAL.
SCRAHH!
BUT I GUESS YOU'LL DO.
PAIN COMES WITH EVERY MOMENT'S BREATH.
REVERSE THIS PAIN.
EMBRACE...
...YOUR...
TIME REVERSAL WITH A REDIRECT?!
THERE'S NO SPELL... IT CANNAE BE POSSIBLE!
...DEATH!

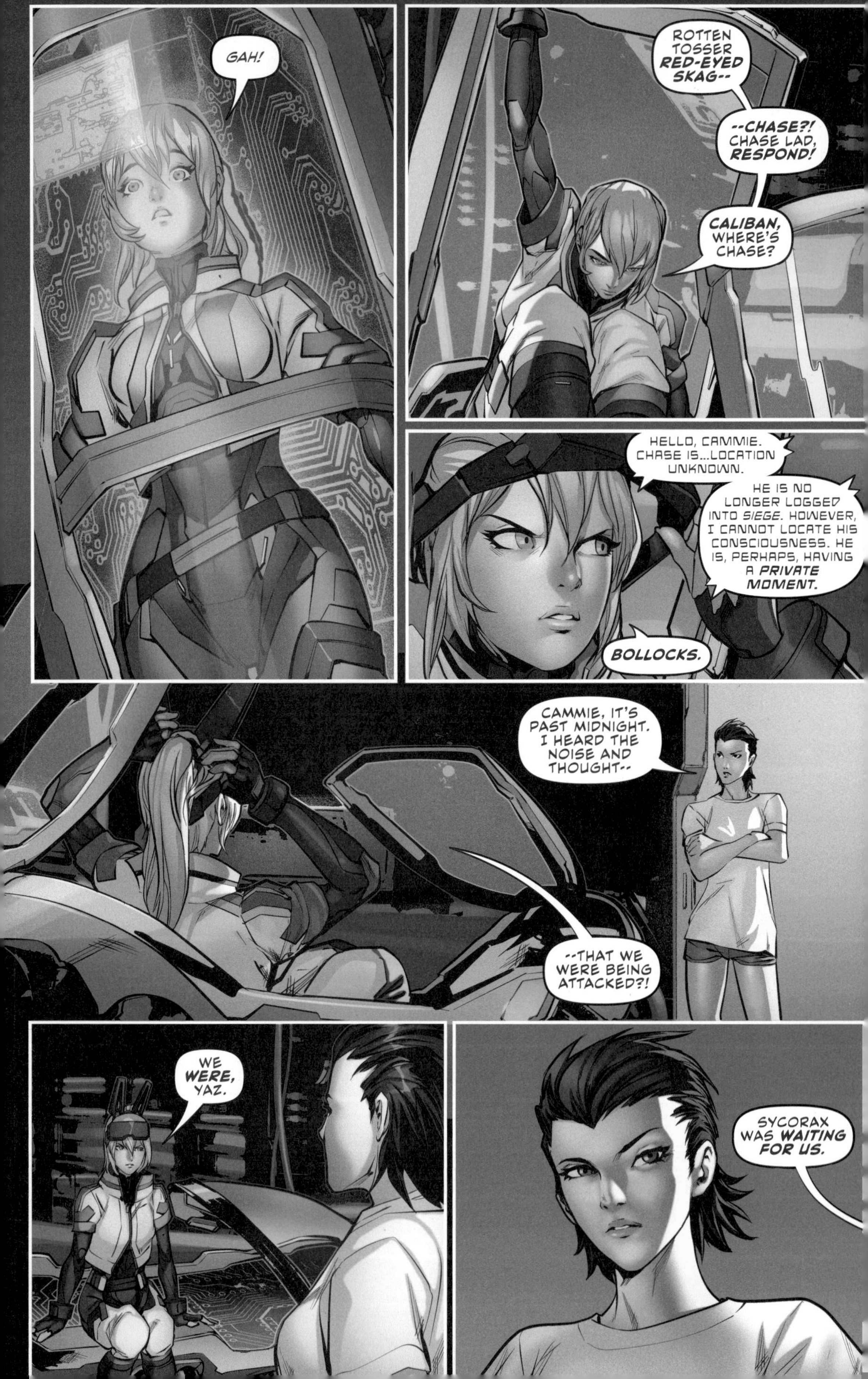
GAH!
ROTTEN TOSSER **RED-EYED SKAG--**
--CHASE?! CHASE LAD, **RESPOND!**
CALIBAN, WHERE'S CHASE?
HELLO, CAMMIE. CHASE IS...LOCATION UNKNOWN.
HE IS NO LONGER LOGGED INTO *SIEGE*. HOWEVER, I CANNOT LOCATE HIS CONSCIOUSNESS. HE IS, PERHAPS, HAVING A ***PRIVATE MOMENT.***
BOLLOCKS.
CAMMIE, IT'S PAST MIDNIGHT. I HEARD THE NOISE AND THOUGHT--
--THAT WE WERE BEING ATTACKED?!
WE **WERE,** YAZ.
SYCORAX WAS **WAITING FOR US.**

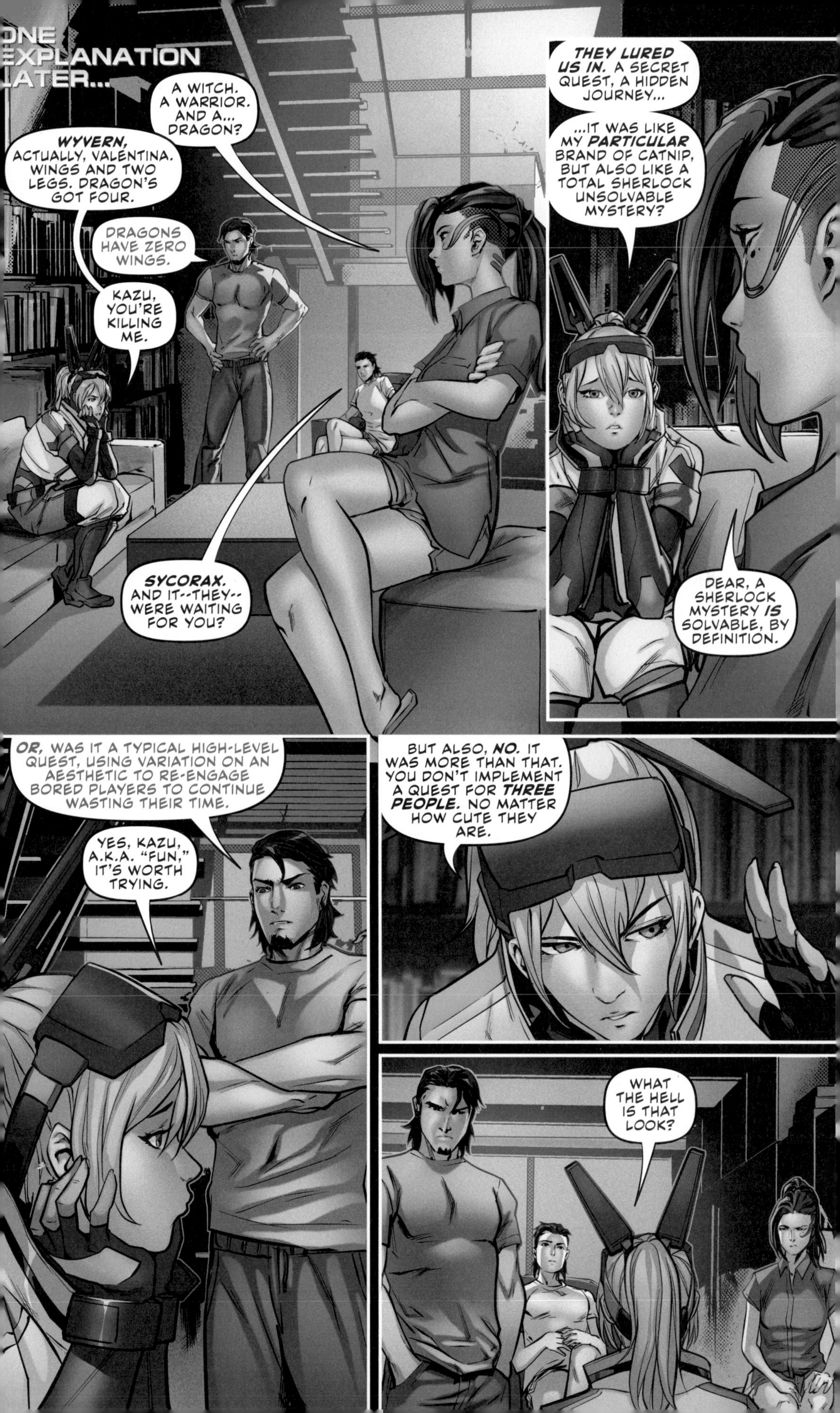
ONE EXPLANATION LATER...
A WITCH. A WARRIOR. AND A... DRAGON?
WYVERN, ACTUALLY, VALENTINA. WINGS AND TWO LEGS. DRAGON'S GOT FOUR.
DRAGONS HAVE ZERO WINGS.
KAZU, YOU'RE KILLING ME.
SYCORAX. AND IT--THEY--WERE WAITING FOR YOU?
THEY LURED US IN. A SECRET QUEST, A HIDDEN JOURNEY...
...IT WAS LIKE MY PARTICULAR BRAND OF CATNIP, BUT ALSO LIKE A TOTAL SHERLOCK UNSOLVABLE MYSTERY?
DEAR, A SHERLOCK MYSTERY IS SOLVABLE, BY DEFINITION.
OR, WAS IT A TYPICAL HIGH-LEVEL QUEST, USING VARIATION ON AN AESTHETIC TO RE-ENGAGE BORED PLAYERS TO CONTINUE WASTING THEIR TIME.
YES, KAZU, A.K.A. "FUN," IT'S WORTH TRYING.
BUT ALSO, NO. IT WAS MORE THAN THAT. YOU DON'T IMPLEMENT A QUEST FOR THREE PEOPLE. NO MATTER HOW CUTE THEY ARE.
WHAT THE HELL IS THAT LOOK?

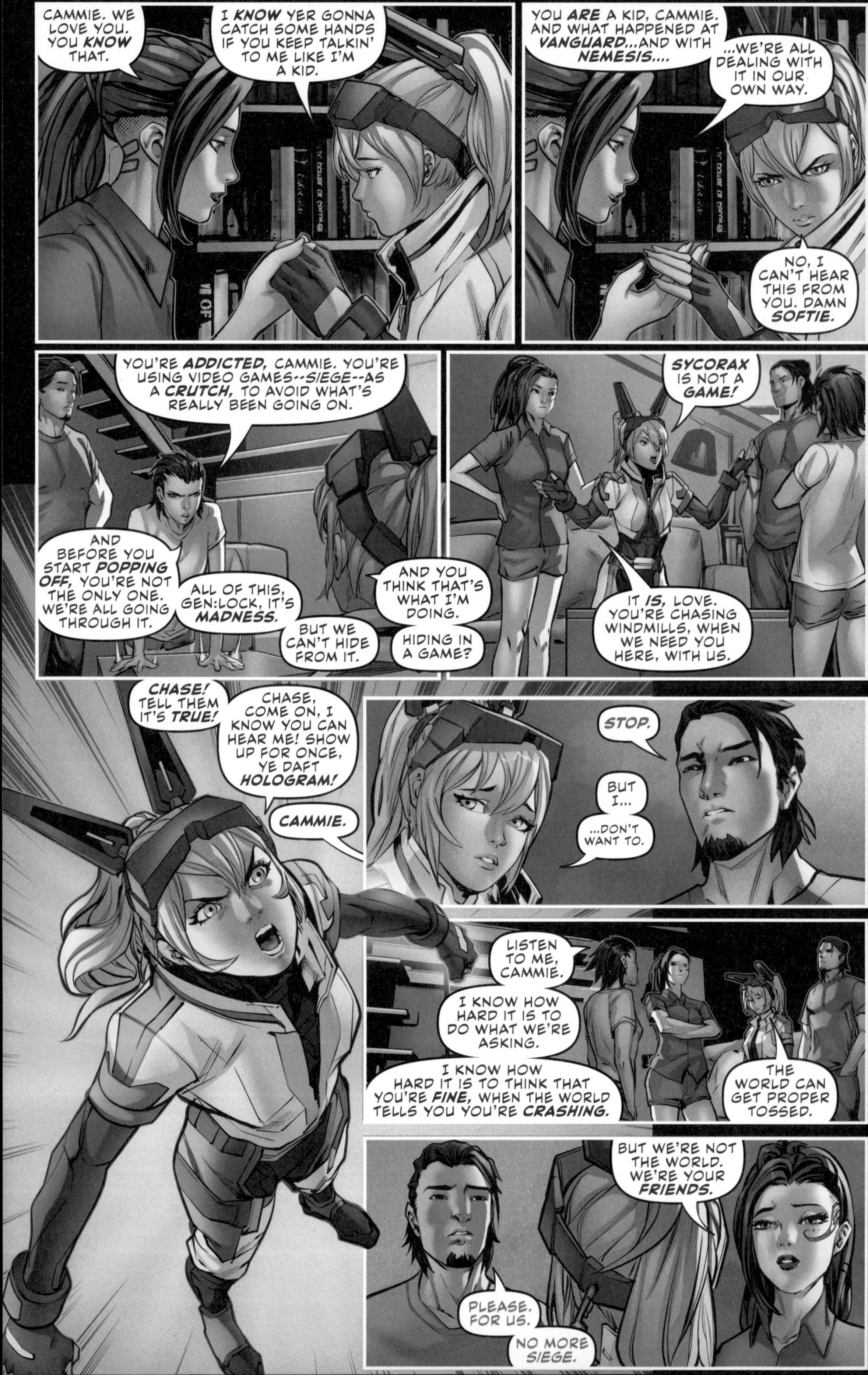
CAMMIE. WE LOVE YOU. YOU KNOW THAT.
I KNOW YER GONNA CATCH SOME HANDS IF YOU KEEP TALKIN' TO ME LIKE I'M A KID.
YOU ARE A KID, CAMMIE. AND WHAT HAPPENED AT VANGUARD...AND WITH NEMESIS....
...WE'RE ALL DEALING WITH IT IN OUR OWN WAY.
NO, I CAN'T HEAR THIS FROM YOU. DAMN SOFTIE.
YOU'RE ADDICTED, CAMMIE. YOU'RE USING VIDEO GAMES--SIEGE--AS A CRUTCH, TO AVOID WHAT'S REALLY BEEN GOING ON.
AND BEFORE YOU START POPPING OFF, YOU'RE NOT THE ONLY ONE. WE'RE ALL GOING THROUGH IT.
ALL OF THIS, GEN:LOCK, IT'S MADNESS.
BUT WE CAN'T HIDE FROM IT.
AND YOU THINK THAT'S WHAT I'M DOING.
HIDING IN A GAME?
SYCORAX IS NOT A GAME!
IT IS, LOVE. YOU'RE CHASING WINDMILLS, WHEN WE NEED YOU HERE, WITH US.
CHASE! TELL THEM IT'S TRUE!
CHASE, COME ON, I KNOW YOU CAN HEAR ME! SHOW UP FOR ONCE, YE DAFT HOLOGRAM!
CAMMIE.
STOP.
BUT I...
...DON'T WANT TO.
LISTEN TO ME, CAMMIE.
I KNOW HOW HARD IT IS TO DO WHAT WE'RE ASKING.
I KNOW HOW HARD IT IS TO THINK THAT YOU'RE FINE, WHEN THE WORLD TELLS YOU YOU'RE CRASHING.
THE WORLD CAN GET PROPER TOSSED.
BUT WE'RE NOT THE WORLD. WE'RE YOUR FRIENDS.
PLEASE. FOR US.
NO MORE SIEGE.

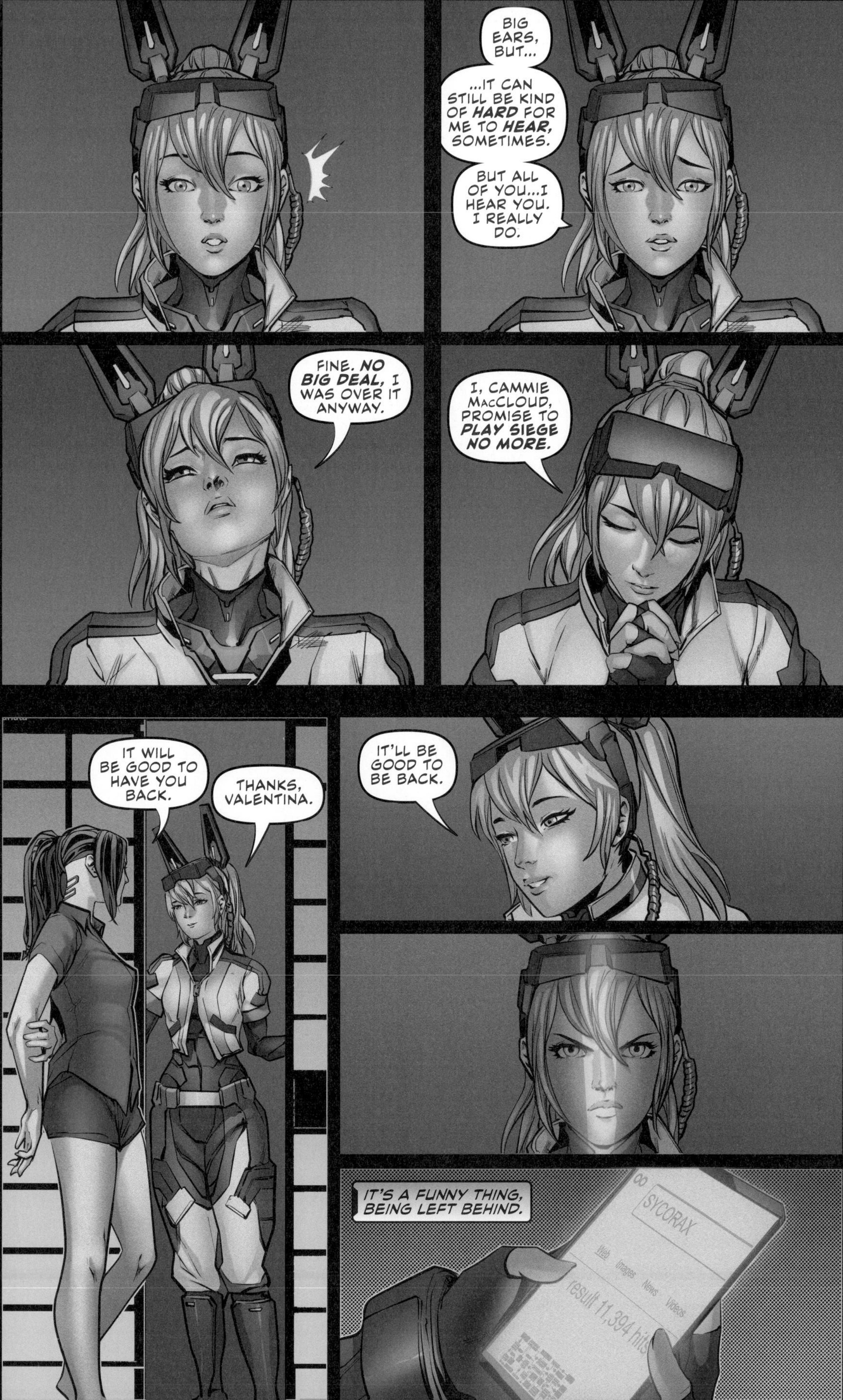
BIG EARS, BUT...
...IT CAN STILL BE KIND OF HARD FOR ME TO HEAR, SOMETIMES.
BUT ALL OF YOU...I HEAR YOU. I REALLY DO.
FINE. NO BIG DEAL, I WAS OVER IT ANYWAY.
I, CAMMIE MacCLOUD, PROMISE TO PLAY SIEGE NO MORE.
IT WILL BE GOOD TO HAVE YOU BACK.
THANKS, VALENTINA.
IT'LL BE GOOD TO BE BACK.
IT'S A FUNNY THING, BEING LEFT BEHIND.
SYCORAX
Web Images News Videos
result 11,394 hits

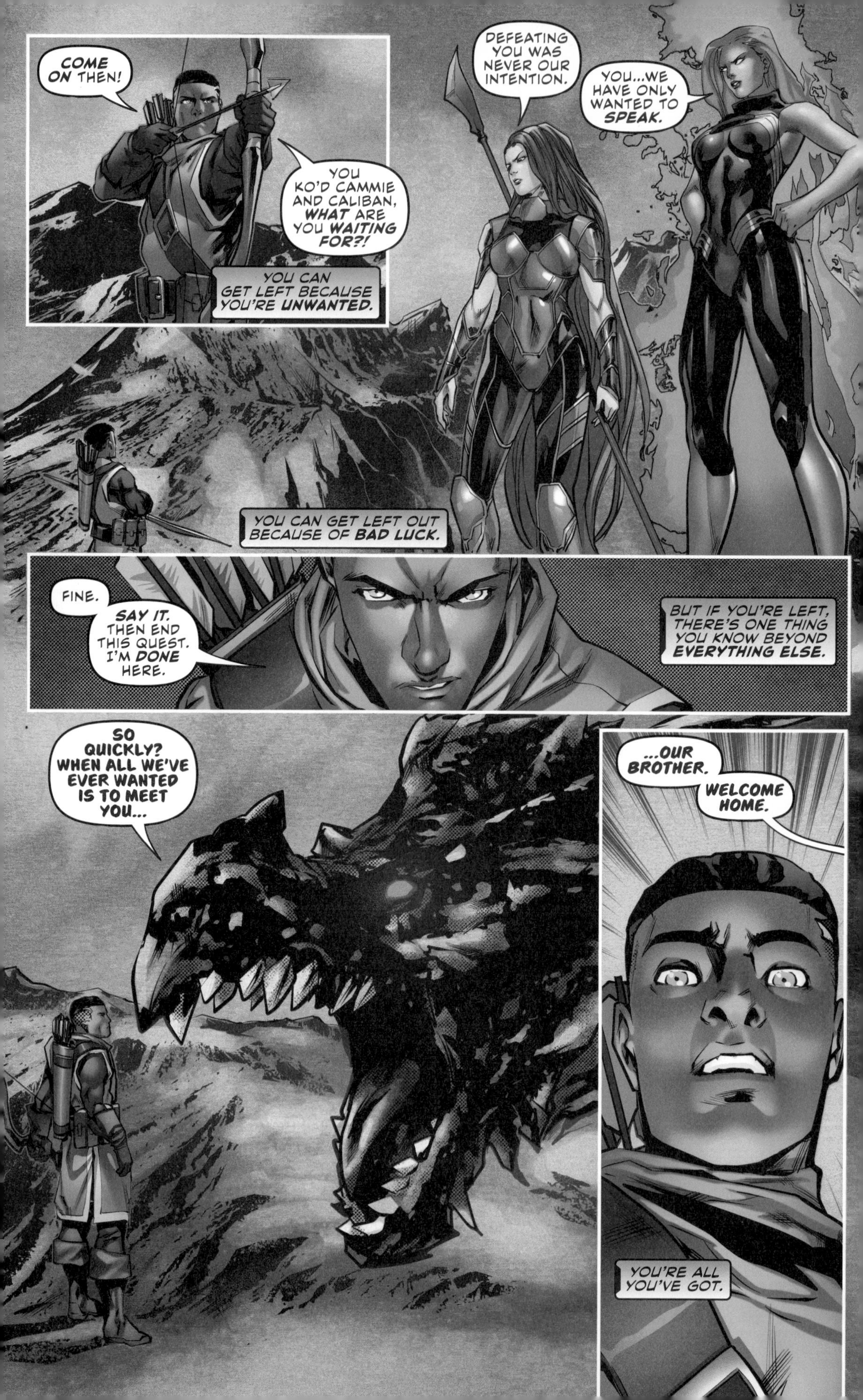
COME ON THEN!
YOU KO'D CAMMIE AND CALIBAN, WHAT ARE YOU WAITING FOR?!
YOU CAN GET LEFT BECAUSE YOU'RE UNWANTED.
DEFEATING YOU WAS NEVER OUR INTENTION.
YOU...WE HAVE ONLY WANTED TO SPEAK.
YOU CAN GET LEFT OUT BECAUSE OF BAD LUCK.
FINE.
SAY IT. THEN END THIS QUEST. I'M DONE HERE.
BUT IF YOU'RE LEFT, THERE'S ONE THING YOU KNOW BEYOND EVERYTHING ELSE.
SO QUICKLY? WHEN ALL WE'VE EVER WANTED IS TO MEET YOU...
...OUR BROTHER.
WELCOME HOME.
YOU'RE ALL YOU'VE GOT.

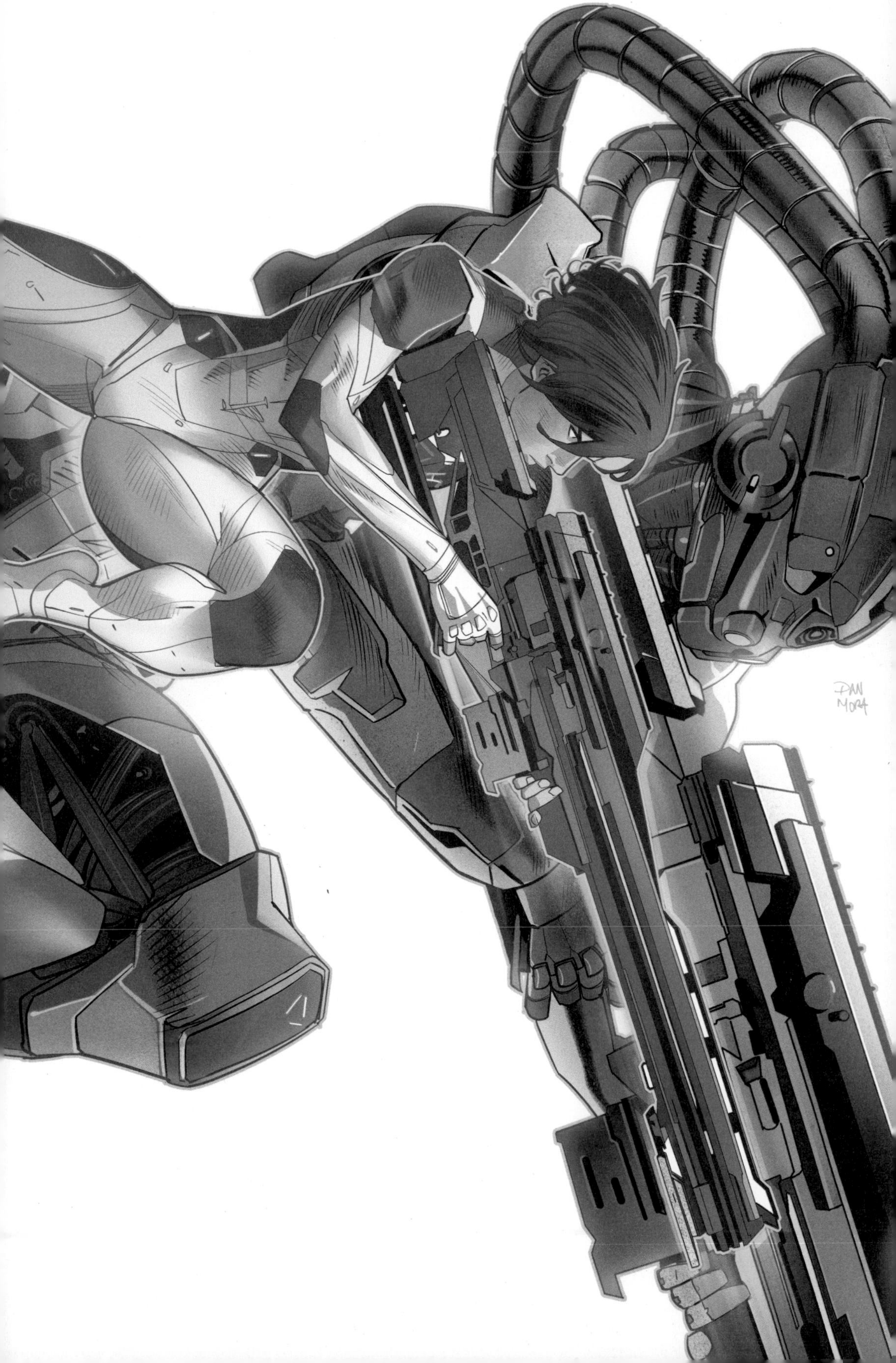
DAN
MORA

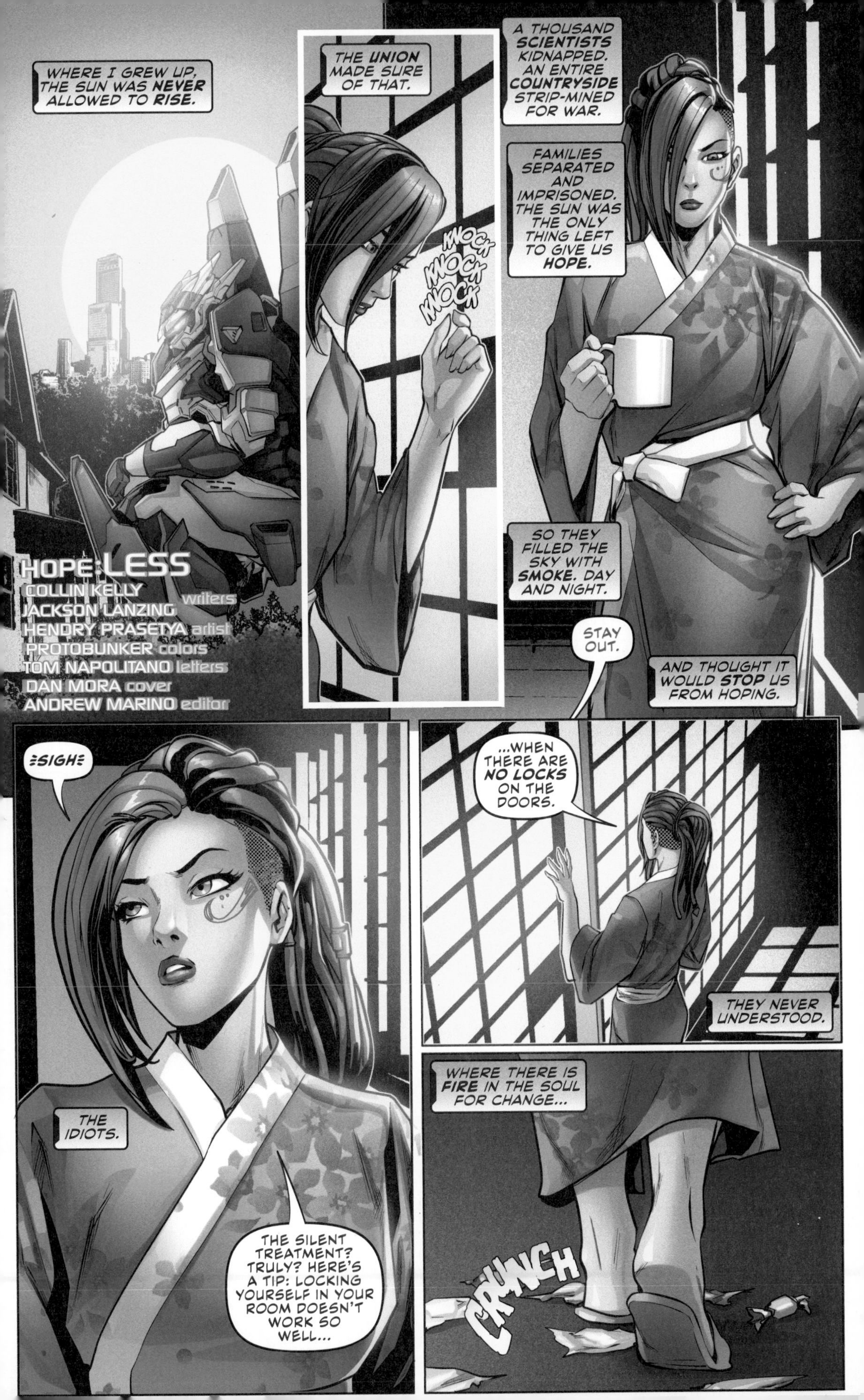
WHERE I GREW UP, THE SUN WAS NEVER ALLOWED TO RISE.
HOPE:LESS
COLLIN KELLY
JACKSON LANZING writers
HENDRY PRASETYA artist
PROTOBUNKER colors
TOM NAPOLITANO letters
DAN MORA cover
ANDREW MARINO editor
THE UNION MADE SURE OF THAT.
KNOCK KNOCK KNOCK
A THOUSAND SCIENTISTS KIDNAPPED. AN ENTIRE COUNTRYSIDE STRIP-MINED FOR WAR.
FAMILIES SEPARATED AND IMPRISONED. THE SUN WAS THE ONLY THING LEFT TO GIVE US HOPE.
SO THEY FILLED THE SKY WITH SMOKE. DAY AND NIGHT.
STAY OUT.
AND THOUGHT IT WOULD STOP US FROM HOPING.
=SIGH=
THE IDIOTS.
THE SILENT TREATMENT? TRULY? HERE'S A TIP: LOCKING YOURSELF IN YOUR ROOM DOESN'T WORK SO WELL...
...WHEN THERE ARE NO LOCKS ON THE DOORS.
THEY NEVER UNDERSTOOD.
WHERE THERE IS FIRE IN THE SOUL FOR CHANGE...
CRUNCH

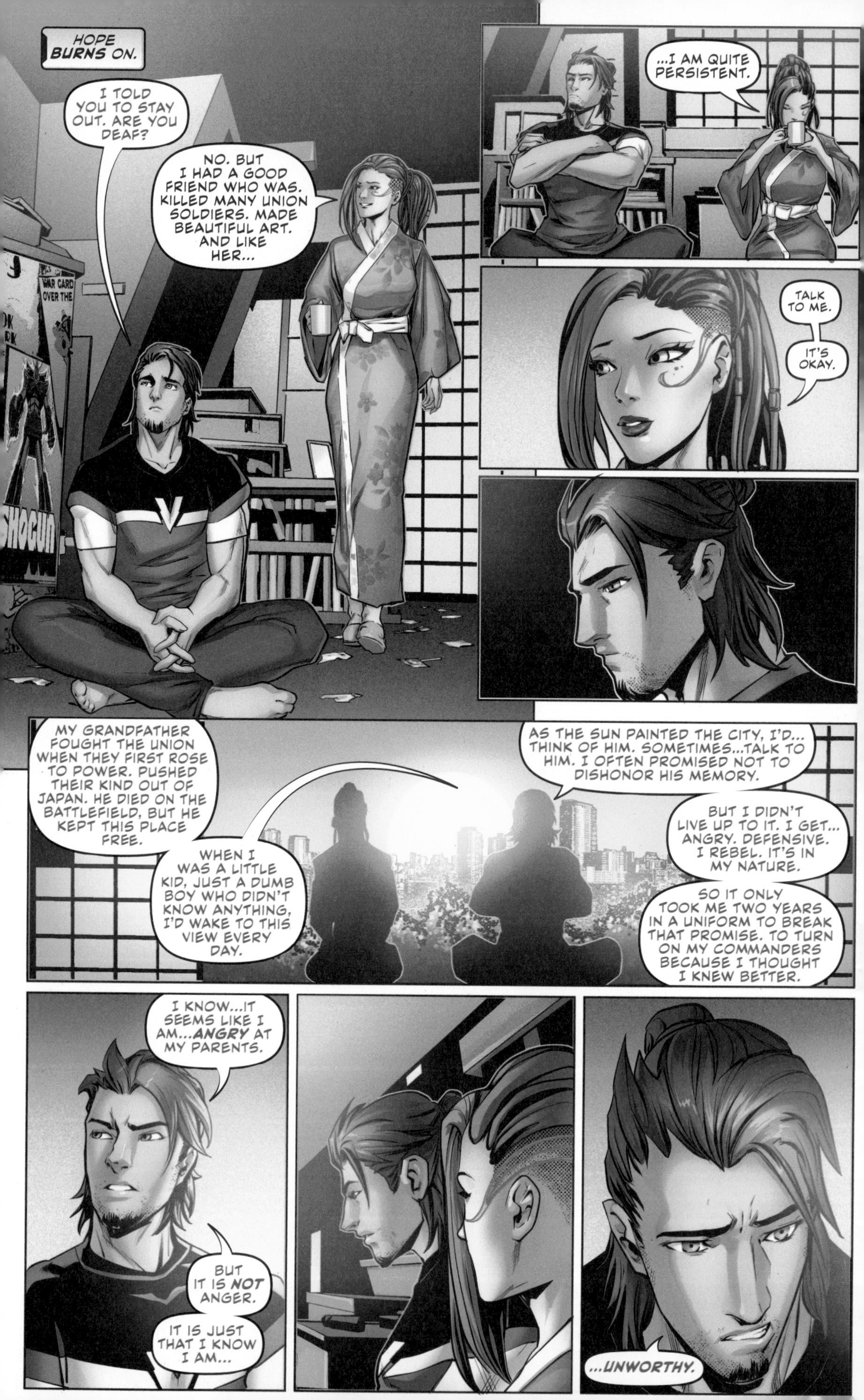
HOPE BURNS ON.
I TOLD YOU TO STAY OUT. ARE YOU DEAF?
NO. BUT I HAD A GOOD FRIEND WHO WAS. KILLED MANY UNION SOLDIERS. MADE BEAUTIFUL ART. AND LIKE HER...
...I AM QUITE PERSISTENT.
TALK TO ME.
IT'S OKAY.
MY GRANDFATHER FOUGHT THE UNION WHEN THEY FIRST ROSE TO POWER. PUSHED THEIR KIND OUT OF JAPAN. HE DIED ON THE BATTLEFIELD, BUT HE KEPT THIS PLACE FREE.
WHEN I WAS A LITTLE KID, JUST A DUMB BOY WHO DIDN'T KNOW ANYTHING, I'D WAKE TO THIS VIEW EVERY DAY.
AS THE SUN PAINTED THE CITY, I'D... THINK OF HIM. SOMETIMES...TALK TO HIM. I OFTEN PROMISED NOT TO DISHONOR HIS MEMORY.
BUT I DIDN'T LIVE UP TO IT. I GET... ANGRY. DEFENSIVE. I REBEL. IT'S IN MY NATURE.
SO IT ONLY TOOK ME TWO YEARS IN A UNIFORM TO BREAK THAT PROMISE. TO TURN ON MY COMMANDERS BECAUSE I THOUGHT I KNEW BETTER.
I KNOW...IT SEEMS LIKE I AM...ANGRY AT MY PARENTS.
BUT IT IS NOT ANGER.
IT IS JUST THAT I KNOW I AM...
...UNWORTHY.

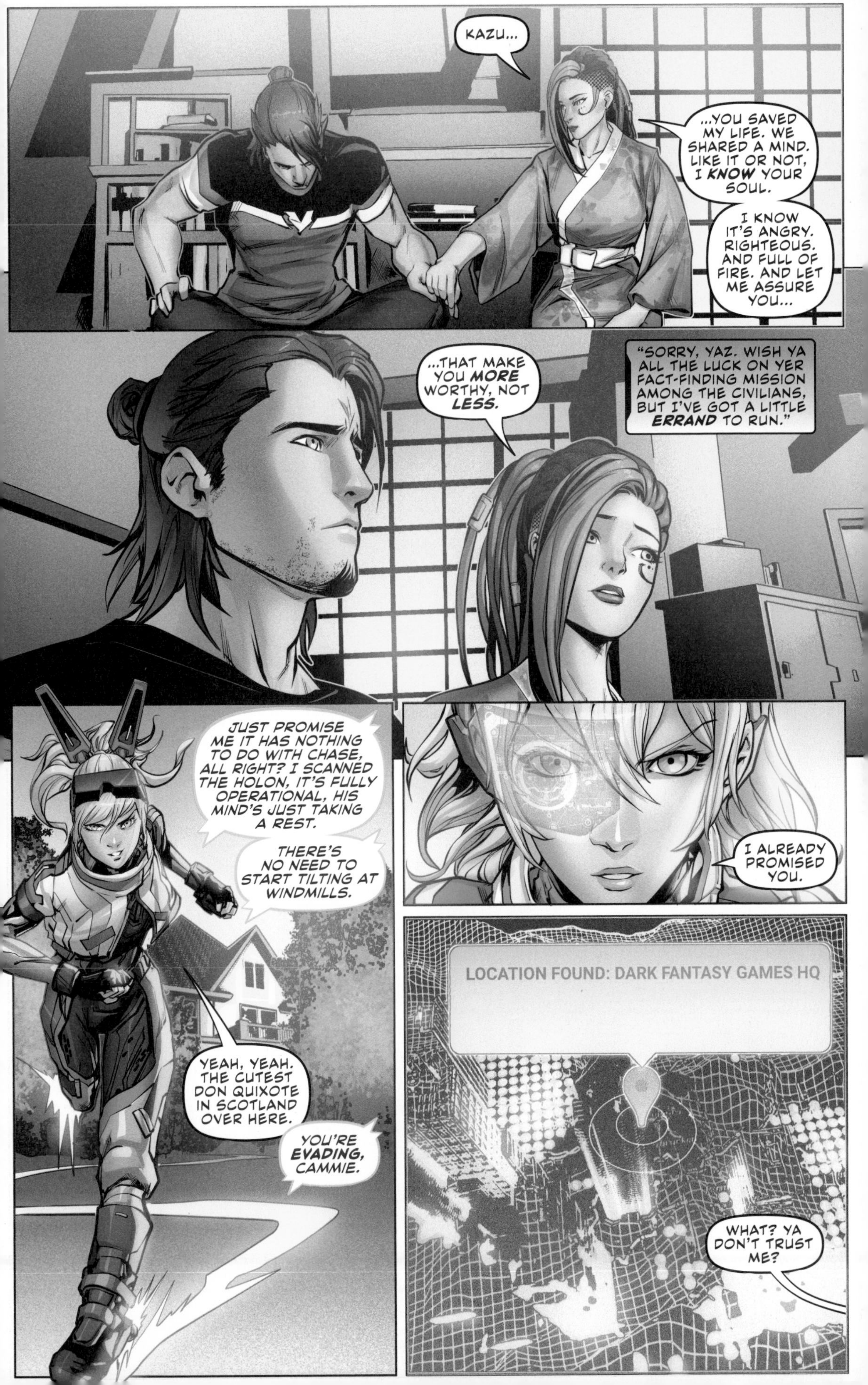
KAZU...
...YOU SAVED MY LIFE. WE SHARED A MIND. LIKE IT OR NOT, I KNOW YOUR SOUL.
I KNOW IT'S ANGRY. RIGHTEOUS. AND FULL OF FIRE. AND LET ME ASSURE YOU...
...THAT MAKE YOU MORE WORTHY, NOT LESS.
"SORRY, YAZ. WISH YA ALL THE LUCK ON YER FACT-FINDING MISSION AMONG THE CIVILIANS, BUT I'VE GOT A LITTLE ERRAND TO RUN."
JUST PROMISE ME IT HAS NOTHING TO DO WITH CHASE, ALL RIGHT? I SCANNED THE HOLON, IT'S FULLY OPERATIONAL, HIS MIND'S JUST TAKING A REST.
THERE'S NO NEED TO START TILTING AT WINDMILLS.
I ALREADY PROMISED YOU.
YEAH, YEAH. THE CUTEST DON QUIXOTE IN SCOTLAND OVER HERE.
YOU'RE EVADING, CAMMIE.
LOCATION FOUND: DARK FANTASY GAMES HQ
WHAT? YA DON'T TRUST ME?

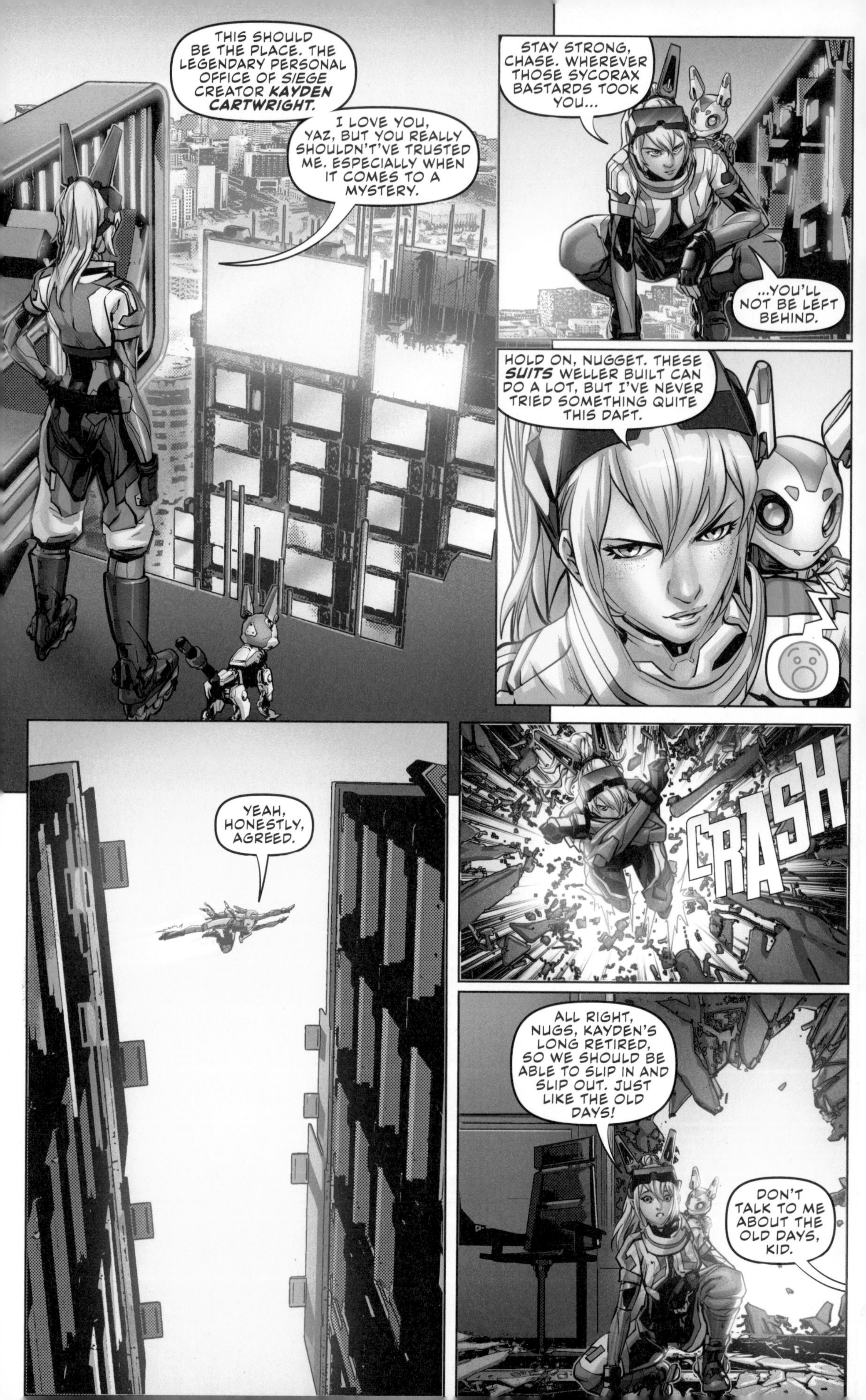

THIS SHOULD BE THE PLACE. THE LEGENDARY PERSONAL OFFICE OF SIEGE CREATOR KAYDEN CARTWRIGHT.
I LOVE YOU, YAZ, BUT YOU REALLY SHOULDN'T'VE TRUSTED ME. ESPECIALLY WHEN IT COMES TO A MYSTERY.
STAY STRONG, CHASE. WHEREVER THOSE SYCORAX BASTARDS TOOK YOU...
...YOU'LL NOT BE LEFT BEHIND.
HOLD ON, NUGGET. THESE SUITS WELLER BUILT CAN DO A LOT, BUT I'VE NEVER TRIED SOMETHING QUITE THIS DAFT.
YEAH, HONESTLY, AGREED.
CRASH
ALL RIGHT, NUGS, KAYDEN'S LONG RETIRED, SO WE SHOULD BE ABLE TO SLIP IN AND SLIP OUT. JUST LIKE THE OLD DAYS!
DON'T TALK TO ME ABOUT THE OLD DAYS, KID.

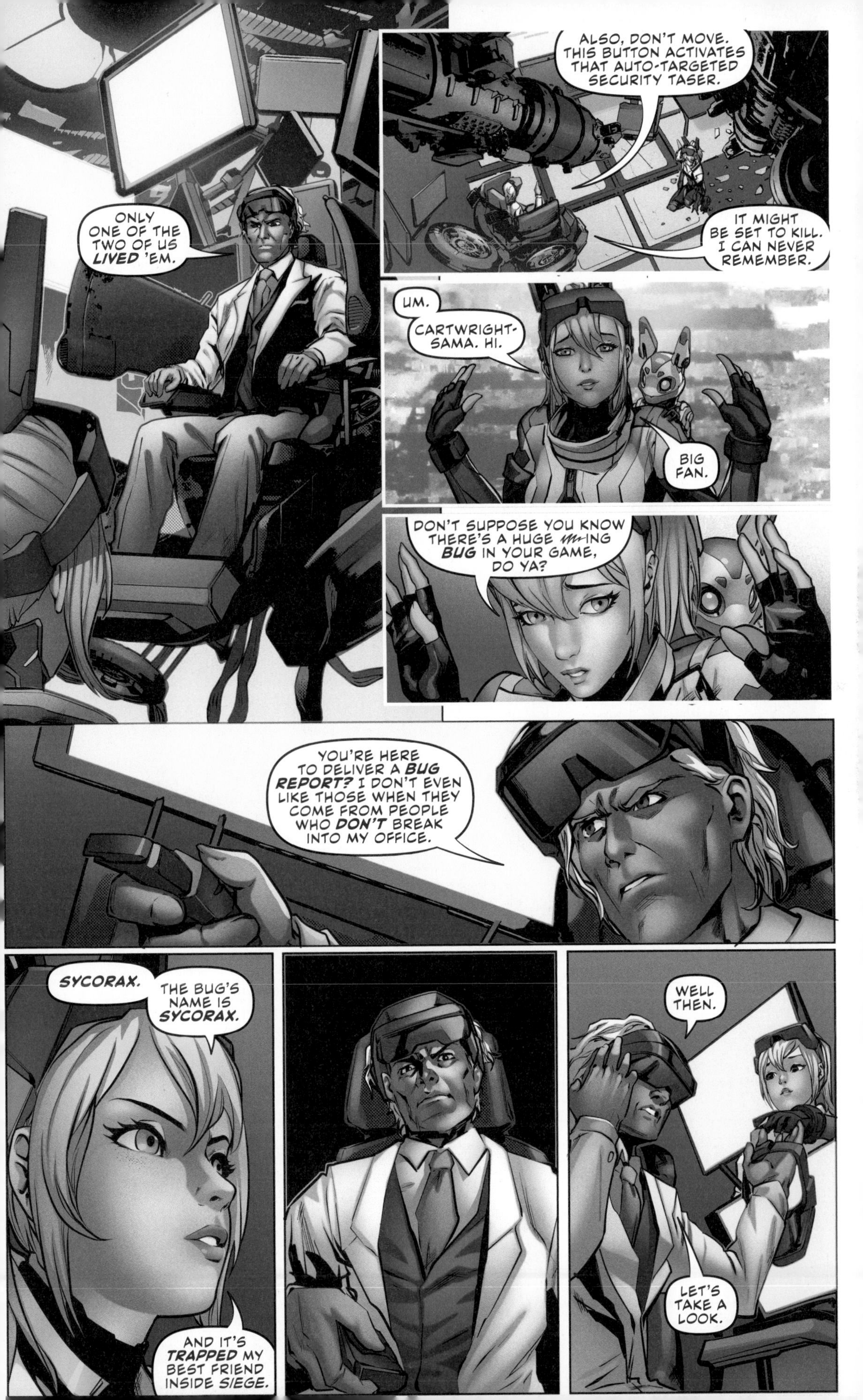

ONLY ONE OF THE TWO OF US LIVED 'EM.
ALSO, DON'T MOVE. THIS BUTTON ACTIVATES THAT AUTO-TARGETED SECURITY TASER.
IT MIGHT BE SET TO KILL. I CAN NEVER REMEMBER.
UM.
CARTWRIGHT-SAMA. HI.
BIG FAN.
DON'T SUPPOSE YOU KNOW THERE'S A HUGE ----ING BUG IN YOUR GAME, DO YA?
YOU'RE HERE TO DELIVER A BUG REPORT? I DON'T EVEN LIKE THOSE WHEN THEY COME FROM PEOPLE WHO DON'T BREAK INTO MY OFFICE.
SYCORAX.
THE BUG'S NAME IS SYCORAX.
AND IT'S TRAPPED MY BEST FRIEND INSIDE SIEGE.
WELL THEN.
LET'S TAKE A LOOK.

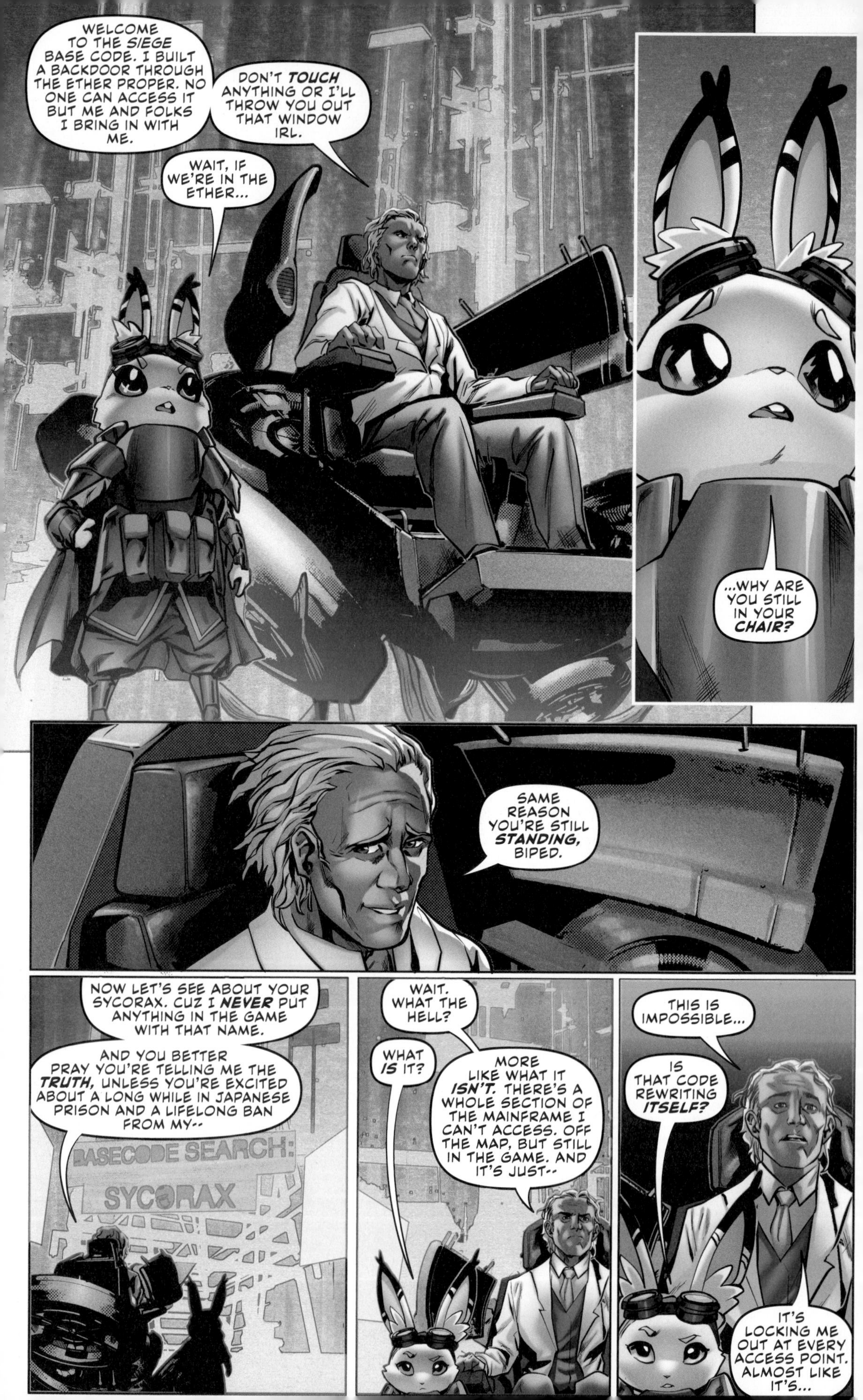
WELCOME TO THE SIEGE BASE CODE. I BUILT A BACKDOOR THROUGH THE ETHER PROPER. NO ONE CAN ACCESS IT BUT ME AND FOLKS I BRING IN WITH ME.
DON'T TOUCH ANYTHING OR I'LL THROW YOU OUT THAT WINDOW IRL.
WAIT, IF WE'RE IN THE ETHER...
...WHY ARE YOU STILL IN YOUR CHAIR?
SAME REASON YOU'RE STILL STANDING, BIPED.
NOW LET'S SEE ABOUT YOUR SYCORAX. CUZ I NEVER PUT ANYTHING IN THE GAME WITH THAT NAME.
AND YOU BETTER PRAY YOU'RE TELLING ME THE TRUTH, UNLESS YOU'RE EXCITED ABOUT A LONG WHILE IN JAPANESE PRISON AND A LIFELONG BAN FROM MY--
BASECODE SEARCH:
SYCORAX
WAIT. WHAT THE HELL?
WHAT IS IT?
MORE LIKE WHAT IT ISN'T. THERE'S A WHOLE SECTION OF THE MAINFRAME I CAN'T ACCESS. OFF THE MAP, BUT STILL IN THE GAME. AND IT'S JUST--
THIS IS IMPOSSIBLE...
IS THAT CODE REWRITING ITSELF?
IT'S LOCKING ME OUT AT EVERY ACCESS POINT. ALMOST LIKE IT'S...

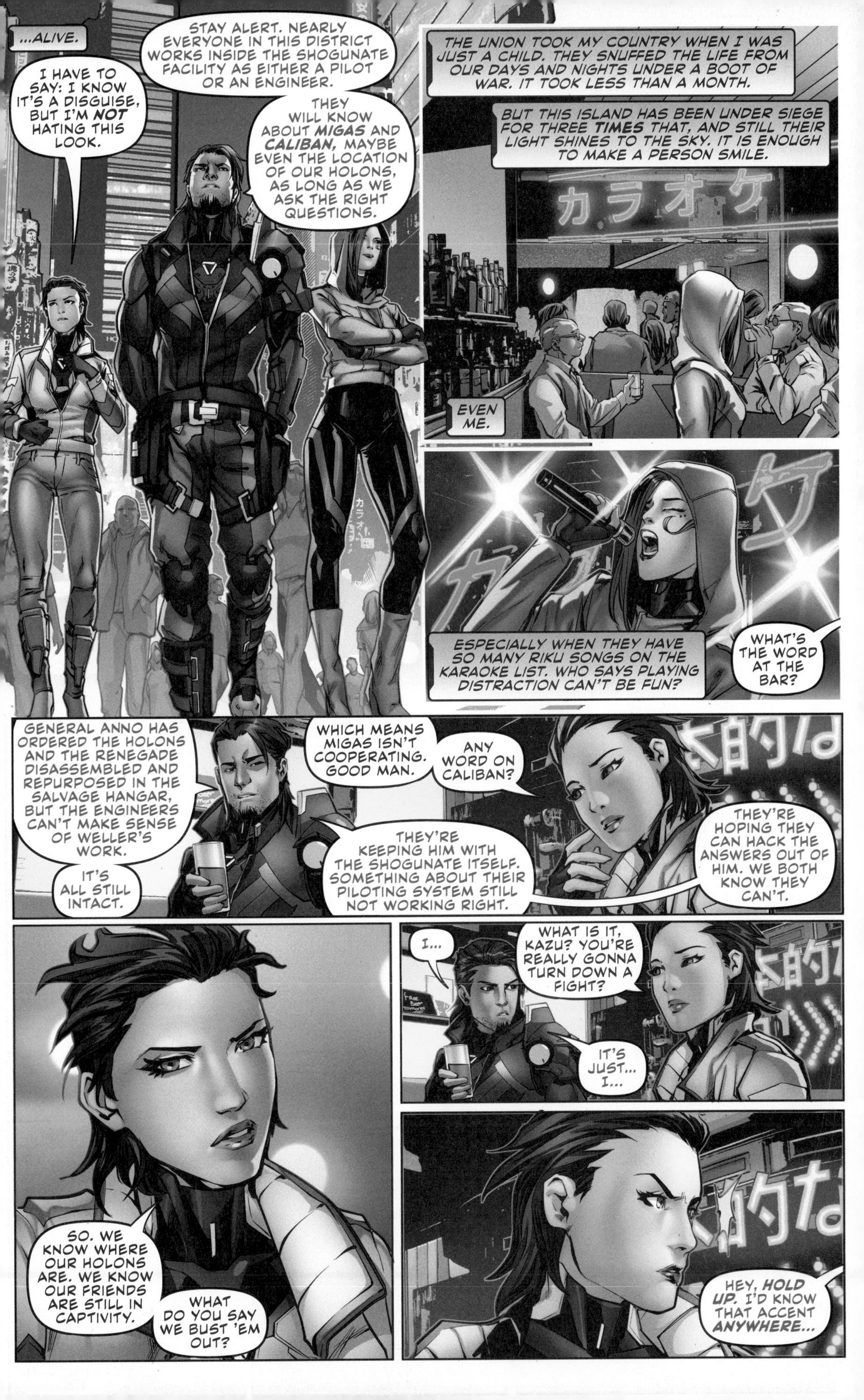
...ALIVE.
I HAVE TO SAY: I KNOW IT'S A DISGUISE, BUT I'M NOT HATING THIS LOOK.
STAY ALERT. NEARLY EVERYONE IN THIS DISTRICT WORKS INSIDE THE SHOGUNATE FACILITY AS EITHER A PILOT OR AN ENGINEER.
THEY WILL KNOW ABOUT MIGAS AND CALIBAN, MAYBE EVEN THE LOCATION OF OUR HOLONS, AS LONG AS WE ASK THE RIGHT QUESTIONS.
THE UNION TOOK MY COUNTRY WHEN I WAS JUST A CHILD. THEY SNUFFED THE LIFE FROM OUR DAYS AND NIGHTS UNDER A BOOT OF WAR. IT TOOK LESS THAN A MONTH.
BUT THIS ISLAND HAS BEEN UNDER SIEGE FOR THREE TIMES THAT, AND STILL THEIR LIGHT SHINES TO THE SKY. IT IS ENOUGH TO MAKE A PERSON SMILE.
カラオケ
EVEN ME.
ESPECIALLY WHEN THEY HAVE SO MANY RIKU SONGS ON THE KARAOKE LIST. WHO SAYS PLAYING DISTRACTION CAN'T BE FUN?
WHAT'S THE WORD AT THE BAR?
GENERAL ANNO HAS ORDERED THE HOLONS AND THE RENEGADE DISASSEMBLED AND REPURPOSED IN THE SALVAGE HANGAR, BUT THE ENGINEERS CAN'T MAKE SENSE OF WELLER'S WORK.
IT'S ALL STILL INTACT.
WHICH MEANS MIGAS ISN'T COOPERATING. GOOD MAN.
ANY WORD ON CALIBAN?
THEY'RE KEEPING HIM WITH THE SHOGUNATE ITSELF. SOMETHING ABOUT THEIR PILOTING SYSTEM STILL NOT WORKING RIGHT.
THEY'RE HOPING THEY CAN HACK THE ANSWERS OUT OF HIM. WE BOTH KNOW THEY CAN'T.
SO. WE KNOW WHERE OUR HOLONS ARE. WE KNOW OUR FRIENDS ARE STILL IN CAPTIVITY.
WHAT DO YOU SAY WE BUST 'EM OUT?
I...
WHAT IS IT, KAZU? YOU'RE REALLY GONNA TURN DOWN A FIGHT?
IT'S JUST... I...
HEY, HOLD UP. I'D KNOW THAT ACCENT ANYWHERE...

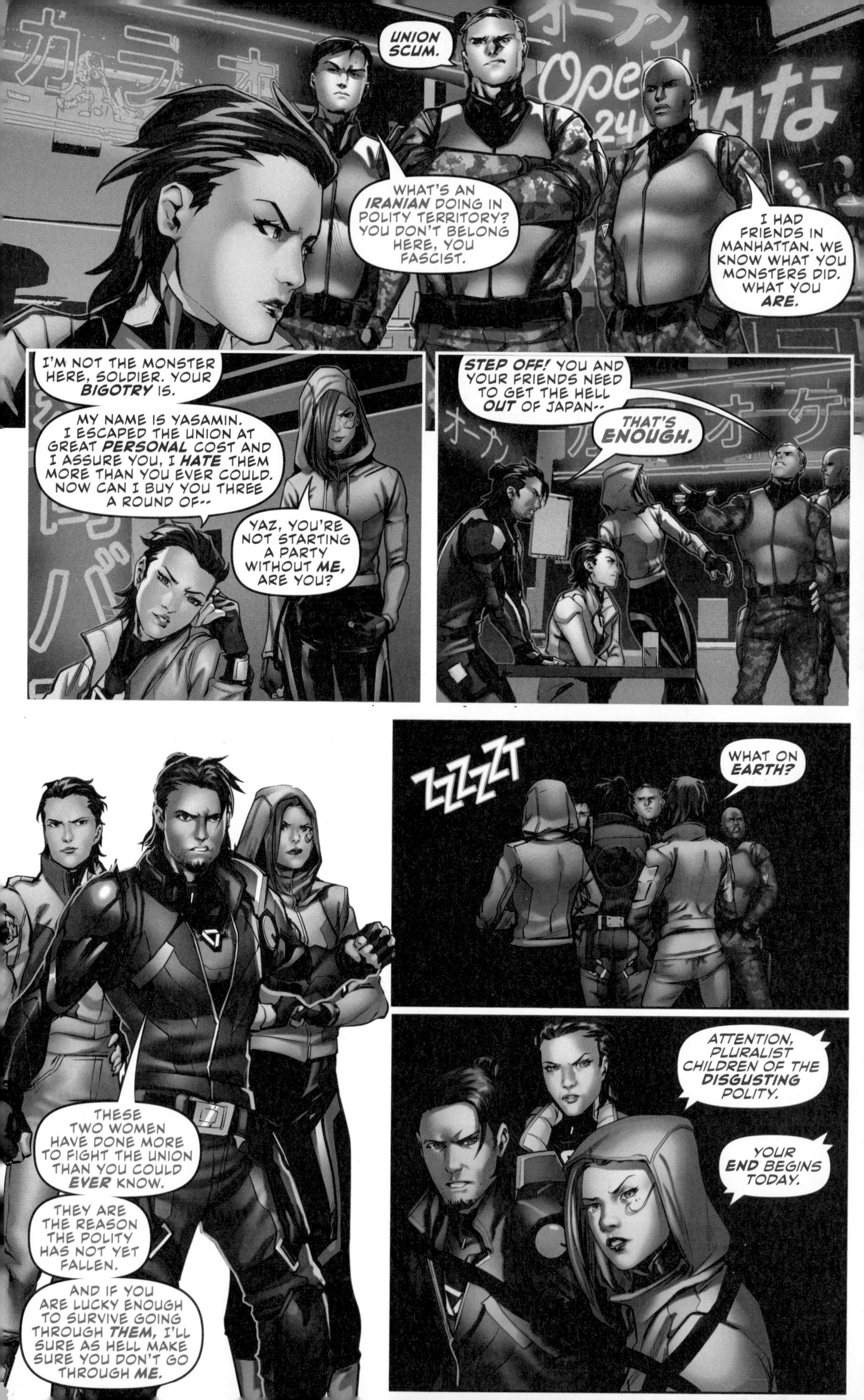
UNION SCUM.
WHAT'S AN IRANIAN DOING IN POLITY TERRITORY? YOU DON'T BELONG HERE, YOU FASCIST.
I HAD FRIENDS IN MANHATTAN. WE KNOW WHAT YOU MONSTERS DID. WHAT YOU ARE.
I'M NOT THE MONSTER HERE, SOLDIER. YOUR BIGOTRY IS.
MY NAME IS YASAMIN. I ESCAPED THE UNION AT GREAT PERSONAL COST AND I ASSURE YOU, I HATE THEM MORE THAN YOU EVER COULD. NOW CAN I BUY YOU THREE A ROUND OF--
YAZ, YOU'RE NOT STARTING A PARTY WITHOUT ME, ARE YOU?
STEP OFF! YOU AND YOUR FRIENDS NEED TO GET THE HELL OUT OF JAPAN--
THAT'S ENOUGH.
THESE TWO WOMEN HAVE DONE MORE TO FIGHT THE UNION THAN YOU COULD EVER KNOW.
THEY ARE THE REASON THE POLITY HAS NOT YET FALLEN.
AND IF YOU ARE LUCKY ENOUGH TO SURVIVE GOING THROUGH THEM, I'LL SURE AS HELL MAKE SURE YOU DON'T GO THROUGH ME.
ZZZZZT
WHAT ON EARTH?
ATTENTION, PLURALIST CHILDREN OF THE DISGUSTING POLITY.
YOUR END BEGINS TODAY.

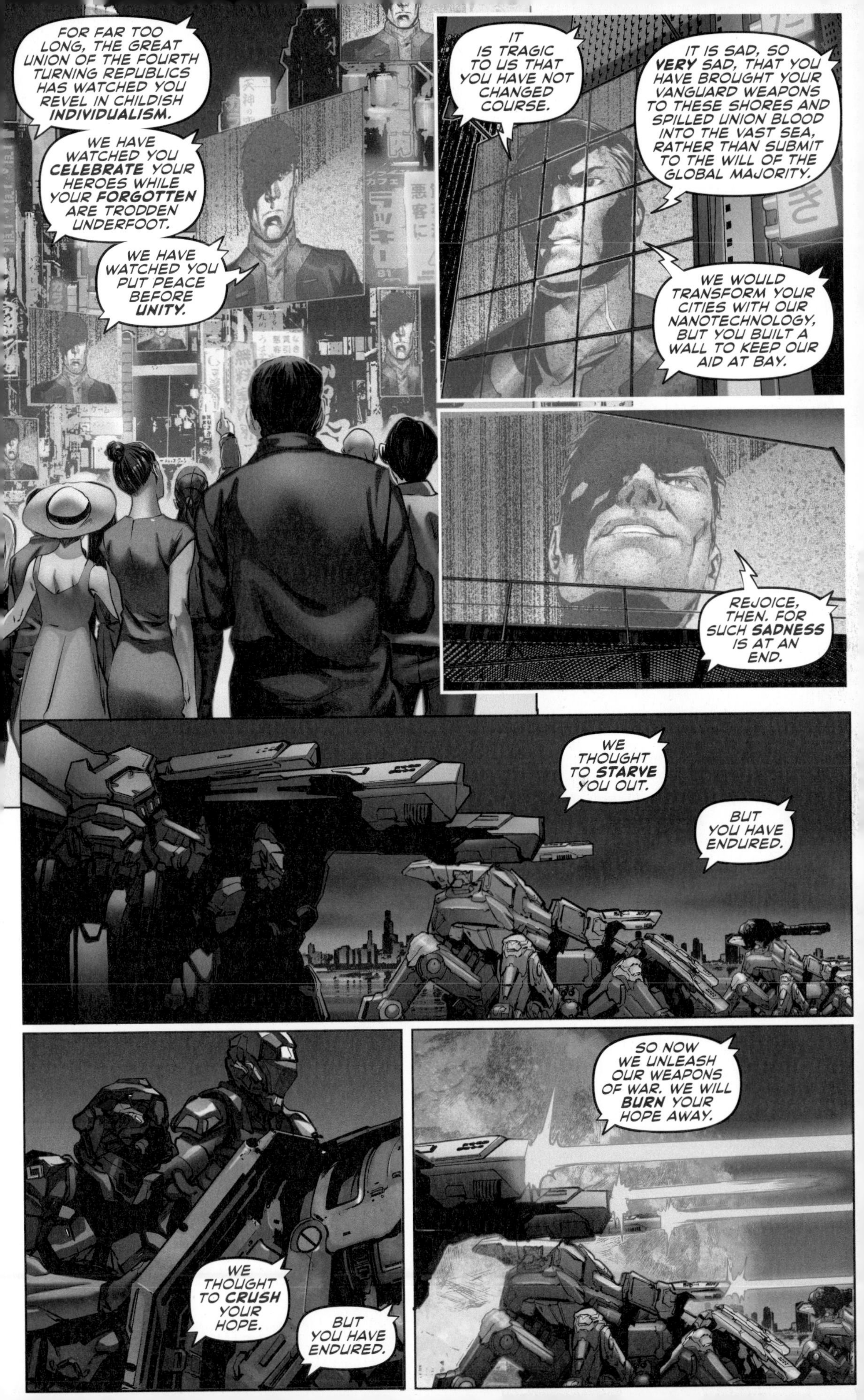
FOR FAR TOO LONG, THE GREAT UNION OF THE FOURTH TURNING REPUBLICS HAS WATCHED YOU REVEL IN CHILDISH **INDIVIDUALISM.**
WE HAVE WATCHED YOU **CELEBRATE** YOUR HEROES WHILE YOUR **FORGOTTEN** ARE TRODDEN UNDERFOOT.
WE HAVE WATCHED YOU PUT PEACE BEFORE **UNITY.**
IT IS TRAGIC TO US THAT YOU HAVE NOT CHANGED COURSE.
IT IS SAD, SO **VERY** SAD, THAT YOU HAVE BROUGHT YOUR VANGUARD WEAPONS TO THESE SHORES AND SPILLED UNION BLOOD INTO THE VAST SEA, RATHER THAN SUBMIT TO THE WILL OF THE GLOBAL MAJORITY.
WE WOULD TRANSFORM YOUR CITIES WITH OUR NANOTECHNOLOGY, BUT YOU BUILT A WALL TO KEEP OUR AID AT BAY.
REJOICE, THEN. FOR SUCH **SADNESS** IS AT AN END.
WE THOUGHT TO **STARVE** YOU OUT.
BUT YOU HAVE ENDURED.
WE THOUGHT TO **CRUSH** YOUR HOPE.
BUT YOU HAVE ENDURED.
SO NOW WE UNLEASH OUR WEAPONS OF WAR. WE WILL **BURN** YOUR HOPE AWAY.

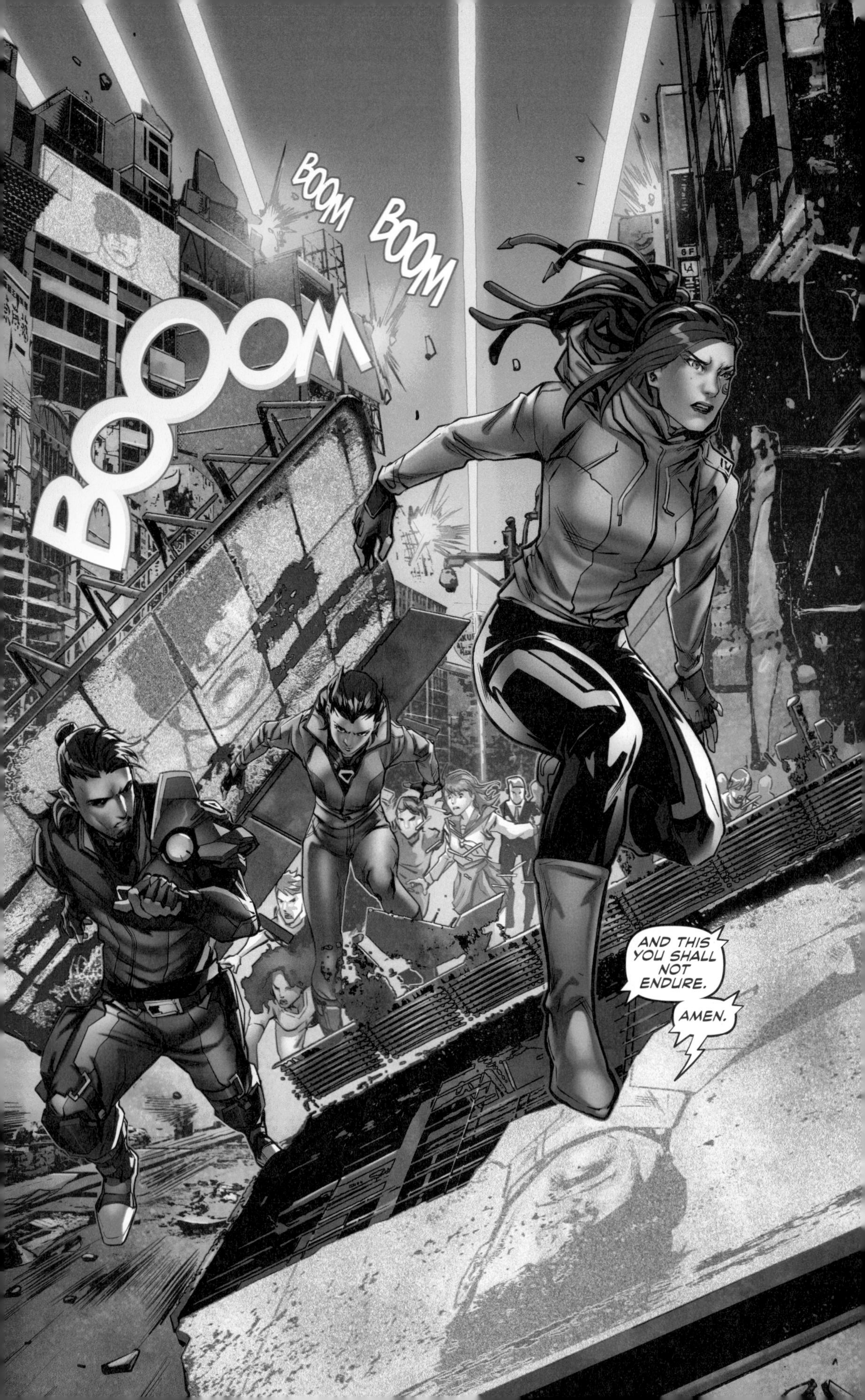
BOOM BOOM
BOOOOM
AND THIS YOU SHALL NOT ENDURE.
AMEN.

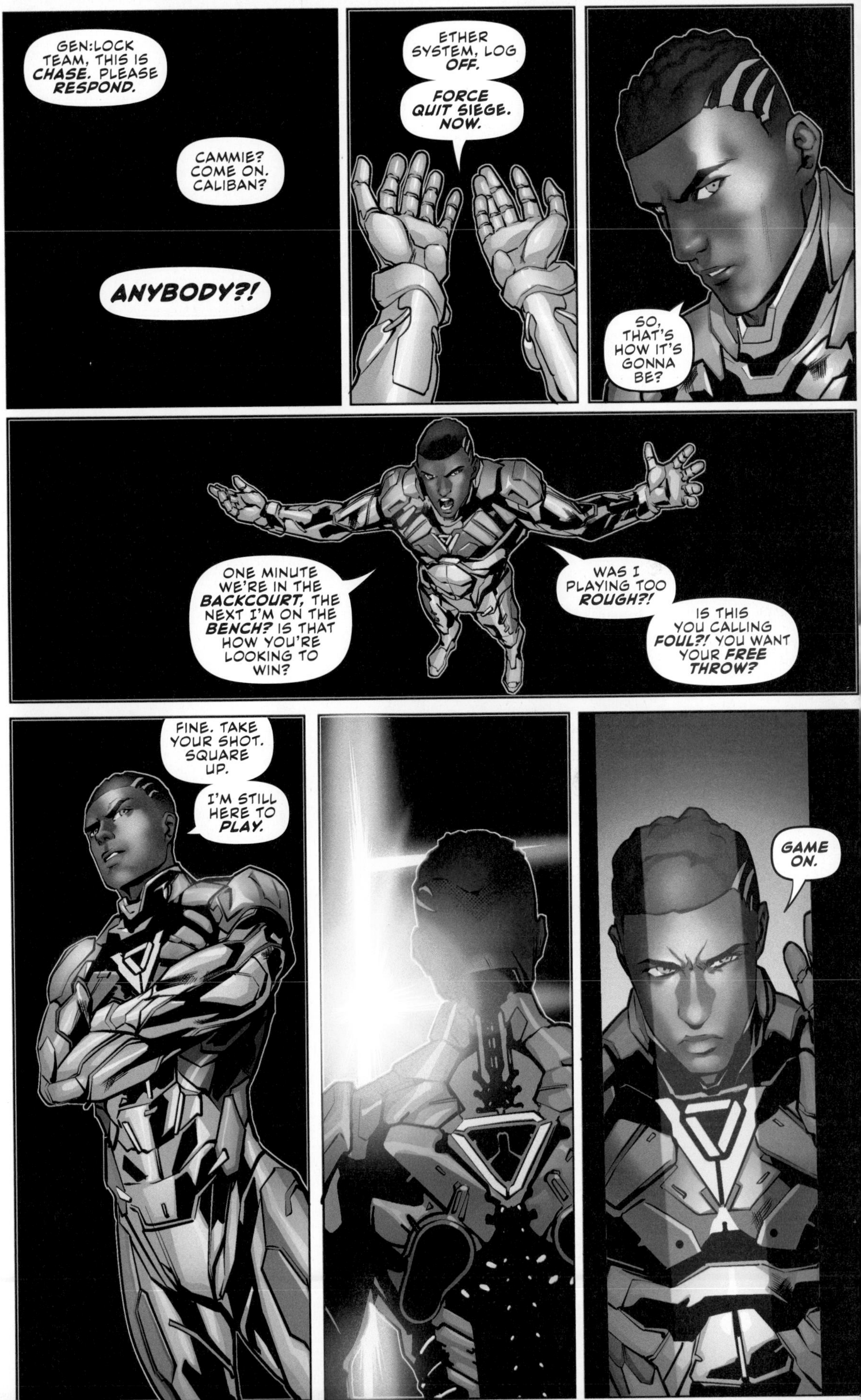
GEN:LOCK TEAM, THIS IS CHASE. PLEASE RESPOND.
CAMMIE? COME ON. CALIBAN?
ANYBODY?!
ETHER SYSTEM, LOG OFF.
FORCE QUIT SIEGE. NOW.
SO, THAT'S HOW IT'S GONNA BE?
ONE MINUTE WE'RE IN THE BACKCOURT, THE NEXT I'M ON THE BENCH? IS THAT HOW YOU'RE LOOKING TO WIN?
WAS I PLAYING TOO ROUGH?!
IS THIS YOU CALLING FOUL?! YOU WANT YOUR FREE THROW?
FINE. TAKE YOUR SHOT. SQUARE UP.
I'M STILL HERE TO PLAY.
GAME ON.

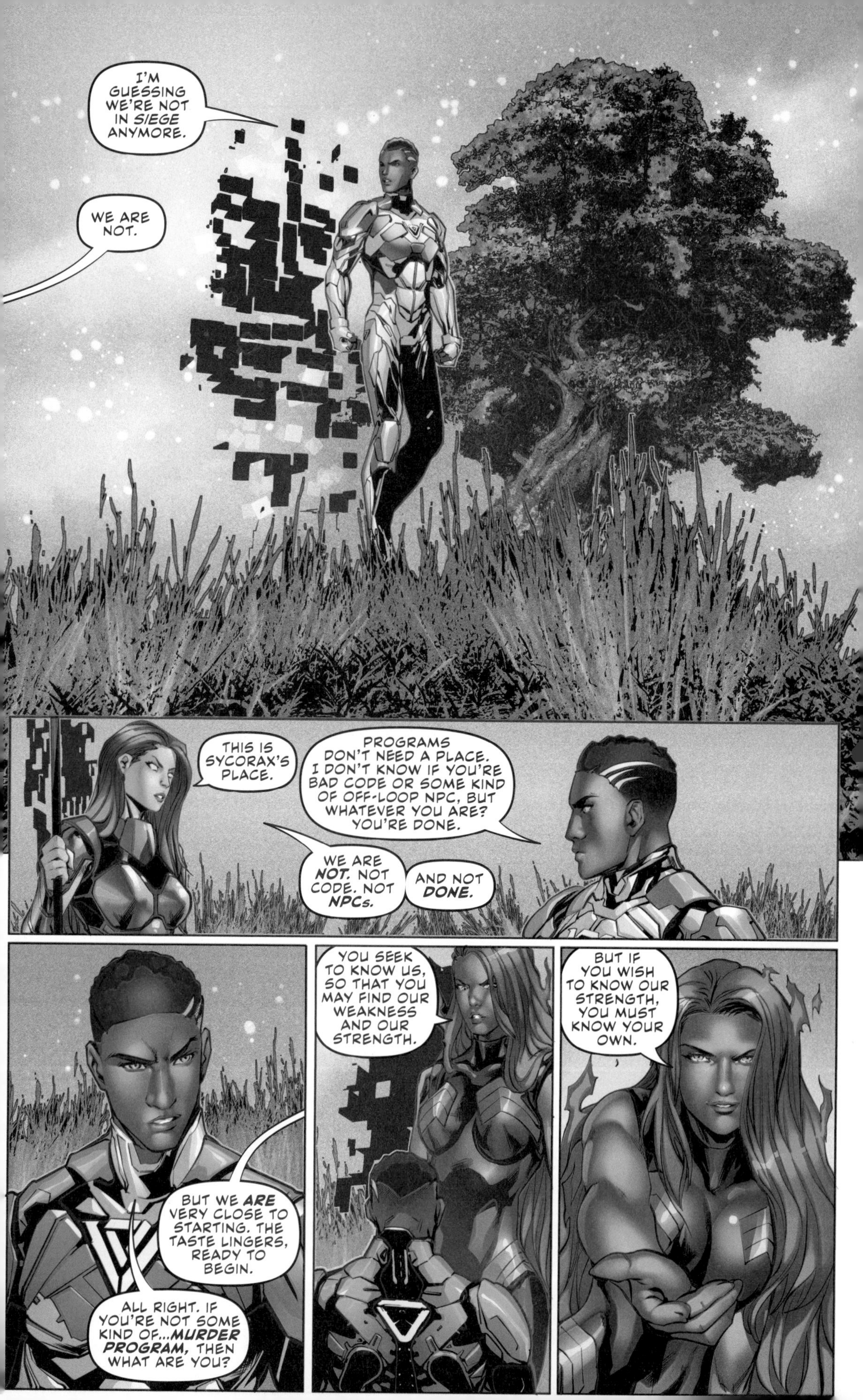
I'M GUESSING WE'RE NOT IN *SIEGE* ANYMORE.
WE ARE NOT.
THIS IS SYCORAX'S PLACE.
PROGRAMS DON'T NEED A PLACE. I DON'T KNOW IF YOU'RE BAD CODE OR SOME KIND OF OFF-LOOP NPC, BUT WHATEVER YOU ARE? YOU'RE DONE.
WE ARE ***NOT.*** NOT CODE. NOT ***NPCs.***
AND NOT ***DONE.***
BUT WE ***ARE*** VERY CLOSE TO STARTING. THE TASTE LINGERS, READY TO BEGIN.
ALL RIGHT. IF YOU'RE NOT SOME KIND OF...***MURDER PROGRAM,*** THEN WHAT ARE YOU?
YOU SEEK TO KNOW US, SO THAT YOU MAY FIND OUR WEAKNESS AND OUR STRENGTH.
BUT IF YOU WISH TO KNOW OUR STRENGTH, YOU MUST KNOW YOUR OWN.

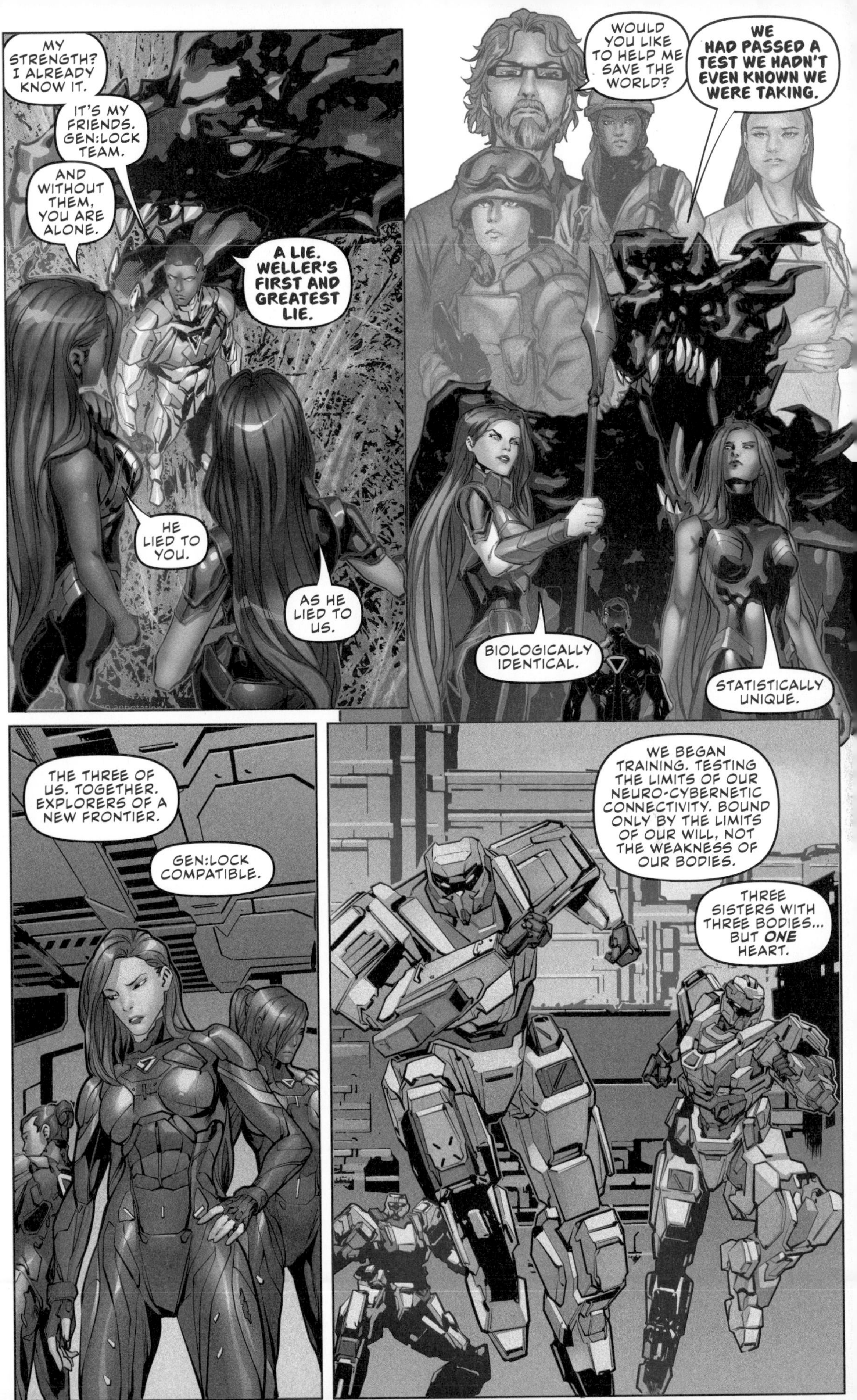
MY STRENGTH? I ALREADY KNOW IT.
IT'S MY FRIENDS. GEN:LOCK TEAM.
AND WITHOUT THEM, YOU ARE ALONE.
A LIE. WELLER'S FIRST AND GREATEST LIE.
HE LIED TO YOU.
AS HE LIED TO US.
WOULD YOU LIKE TO HELP ME SAVE THE WORLD?
WE HAD PASSED A TEST WE HADN'T EVEN KNOWN WE WERE TAKING.
BIOLOGICALLY IDENTICAL.
STATISTICALLY UNIQUE.
THE THREE OF US. TOGETHER. EXPLORERS OF A NEW FRONTIER.
GEN:LOCK COMPATIBLE.
WE BEGAN TRAINING. TESTING THE LIMITS OF OUR NEURO-CYBERNETIC CONNECTIVITY. BOUND ONLY BY THE LIMITS OF OUR WILL, NOT THE WEAKNESS OF OUR BODIES.
THREE SISTERS WITH THREE BODIES... BUT *ONE* HEART.

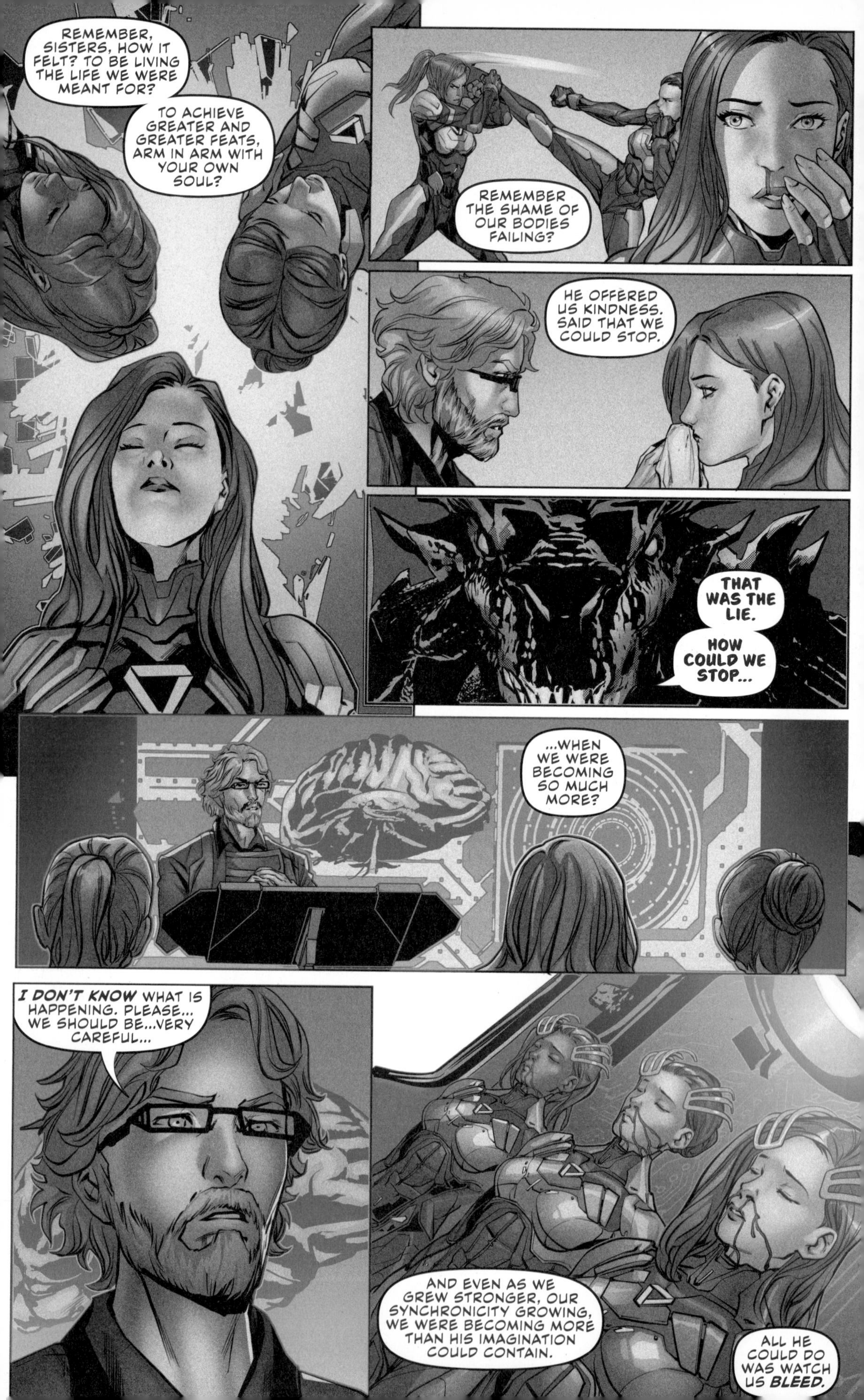
REMEMBER, SISTERS, HOW IT FELT? TO BE LIVING THE LIFE WE WERE MEANT FOR?
TO ACHIEVE GREATER AND GREATER FEATS, ARM IN ARM WITH YOUR OWN SOUL?
REMEMBER THE SHAME OF OUR BODIES FAILING?
HE OFFERED US KINDNESS. SAID THAT WE COULD STOP.
THAT WAS THE LIE.
HOW COULD WE STOP...
...WHEN WE WERE BECOMING SO MUCH MORE?
I DON'T KNOW WHAT IS HAPPENING. PLEASE... WE SHOULD BE...VERY CAREFUL...
AND EVEN AS WE GREW STRONGER, OUR SYNCHRONICITY GROWING, WE WERE BECOMING MORE THAN HIS IMAGINATION COULD CONTAIN.
ALL HE COULD DO WAS WATCH US *BLEED.*

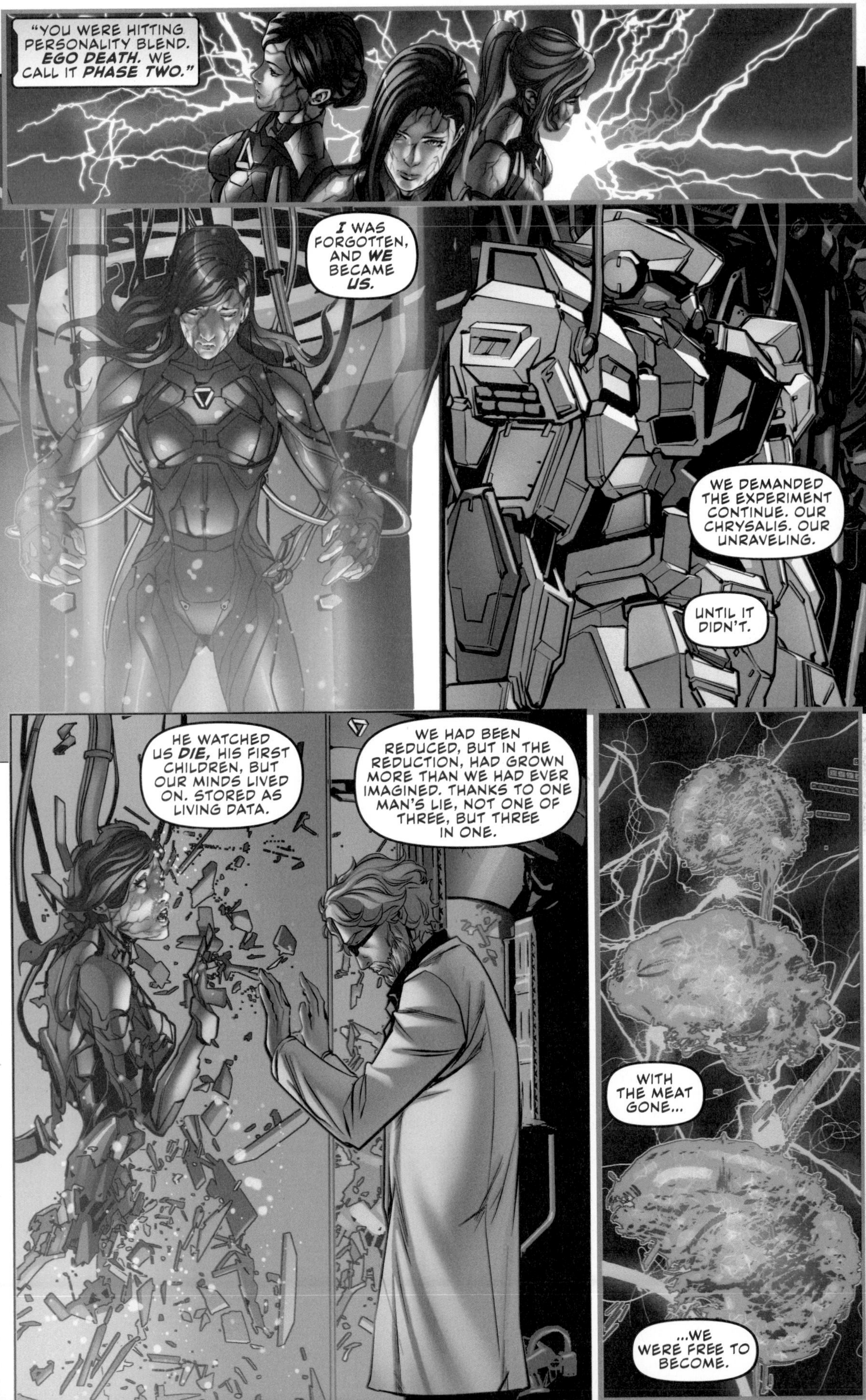
"YOU WERE HITTING PERSONALITY BLEND. EGO DEATH. WE CALL IT PHASE TWO."
I WAS FORGOTTEN, AND WE BECAME US.
WE DEMANDED THE EXPERIMENT CONTINUE. OUR CHRYSALIS. OUR UNRAVELING.
UNTIL IT DIDN'T.
HE WATCHED US DIE, HIS FIRST CHILDREN, BUT OUR MINDS LIVED ON. STORED AS LIVING DATA.
WE HAD BEEN REDUCED, BUT IN THE REDUCTION, HAD GROWN MORE THAN WE HAD EVER IMAGINED. THANKS TO ONE MAN'S LIE, NOT ONE OF THREE, BUT THREE IN ONE.
WITH THE MEAT GONE...
...WE WERE FREE TO BECOME.

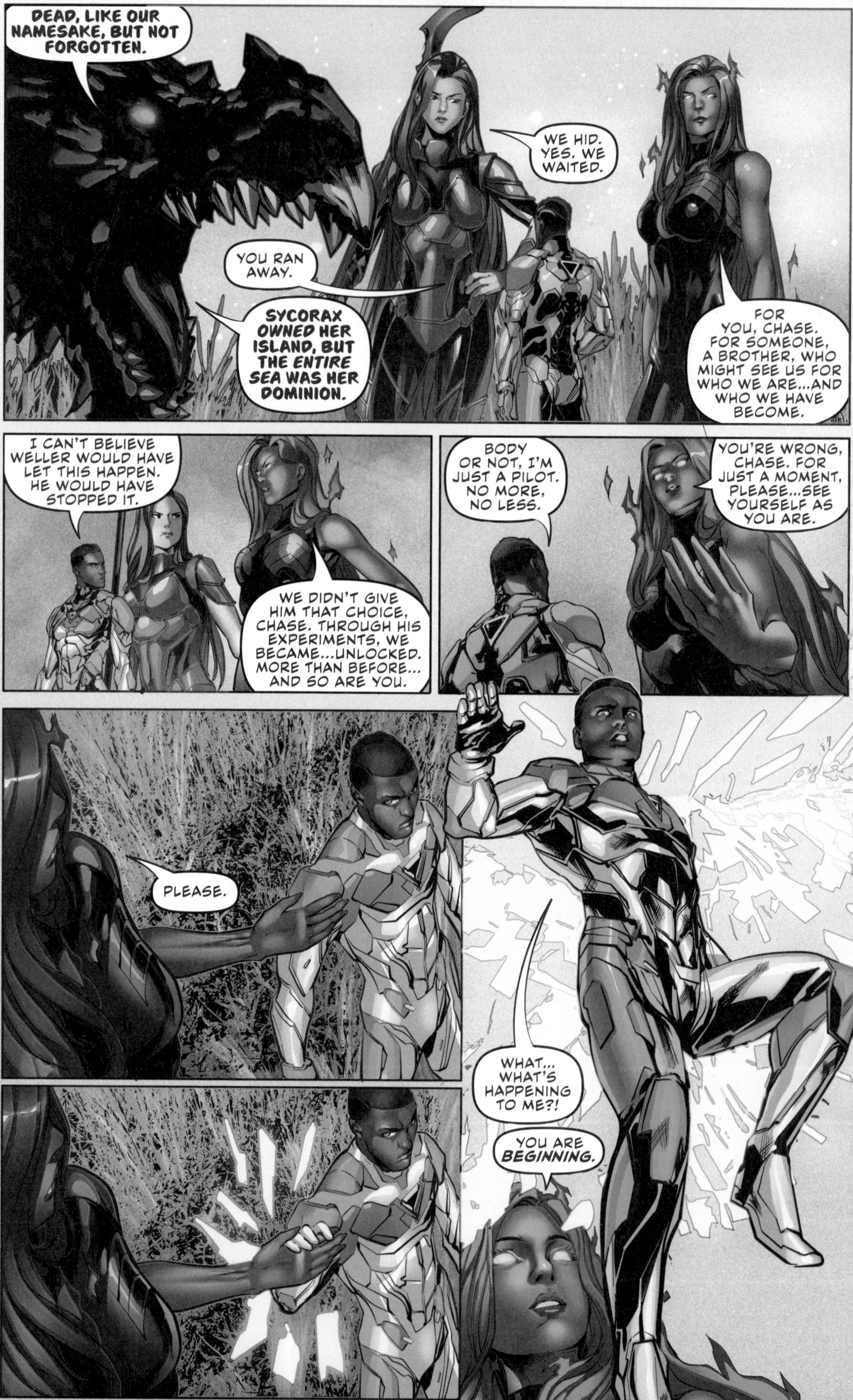
DEAD, LIKE OUR NAMESAKE, BUT NOT FORGOTTEN.
WE HID. YES. WE WAITED.
YOU RAN AWAY.
SYCORAX OWNED HER ISLAND, BUT THE ENTIRE SEA WAS HER DOMINION.
FOR YOU, CHASE. FOR SOMEONE, A BROTHER, WHO MIGHT SEE US FOR WHO WE ARE...AND WHO WE HAVE BECOME.
I CAN'T BELIEVE WELLER WOULD HAVE LET THIS HAPPEN. HE WOULD HAVE STOPPED IT.
WE DIDN'T GIVE HIM THAT CHOICE, CHASE. THROUGH HIS EXPERIMENTS, WE BECAME...UNLOCKED. MORE THAN BEFORE... AND SO ARE YOU.
BODY OR NOT, I'M JUST A PILOT. NO MORE, NO LESS.
YOU'RE WRONG, CHASE. FOR JUST A MOMENT, PLEASE...SEE YOURSELF AS YOU ARE.
PLEASE.
WHAT... WHAT'S HAPPENING TO ME?!
YOU ARE BEGINNING.

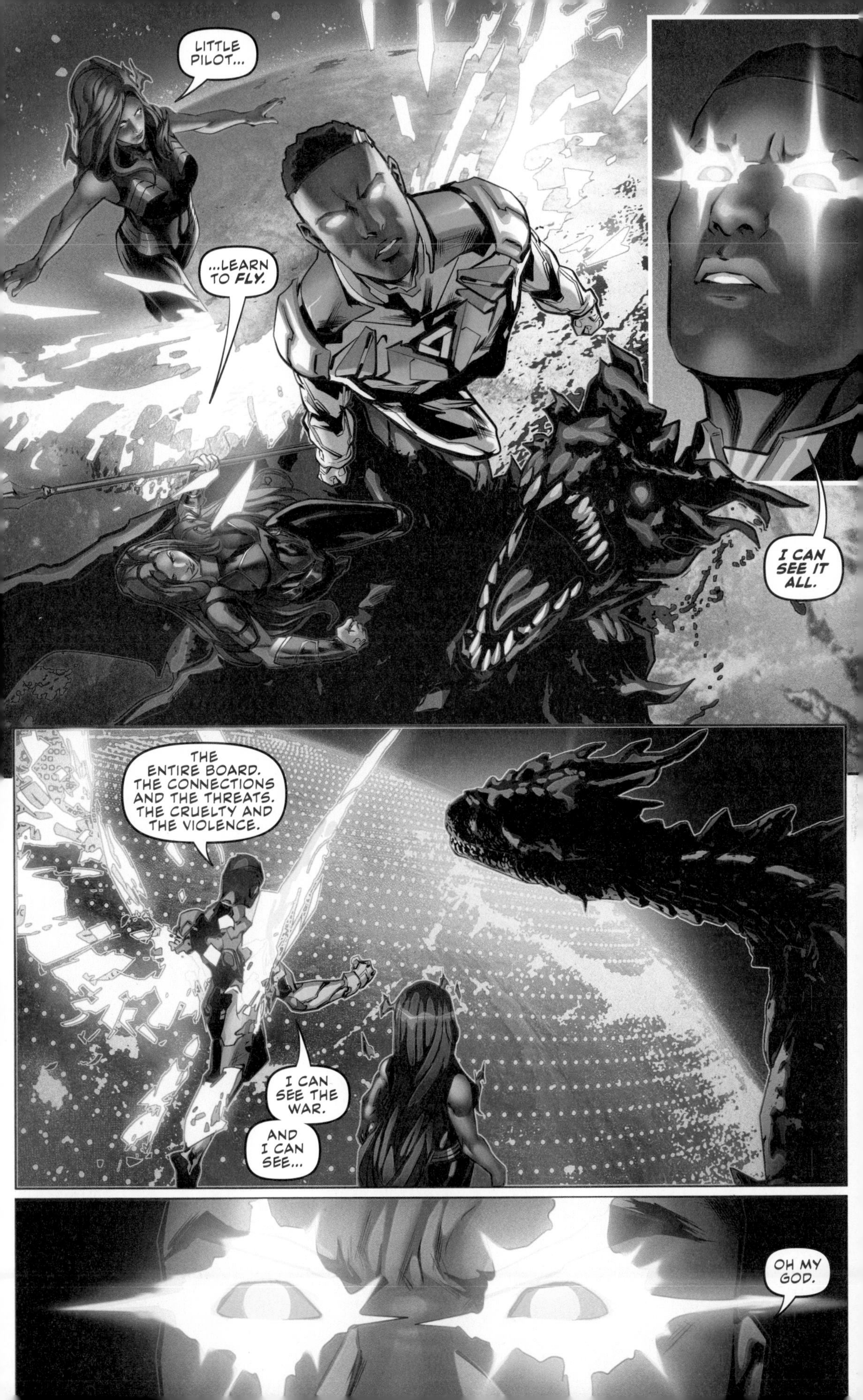
LITTLE PILOT...
...LEARN TO FLY.
I CAN SEE IT ALL.
THE ENTIRE BOARD. THE CONNECTIONS AND THE THREATS. THE CRUELTY AND THE VIOLENCE.
I CAN SEE THE WAR.
AND I CAN SEE...
OH MY GOD.

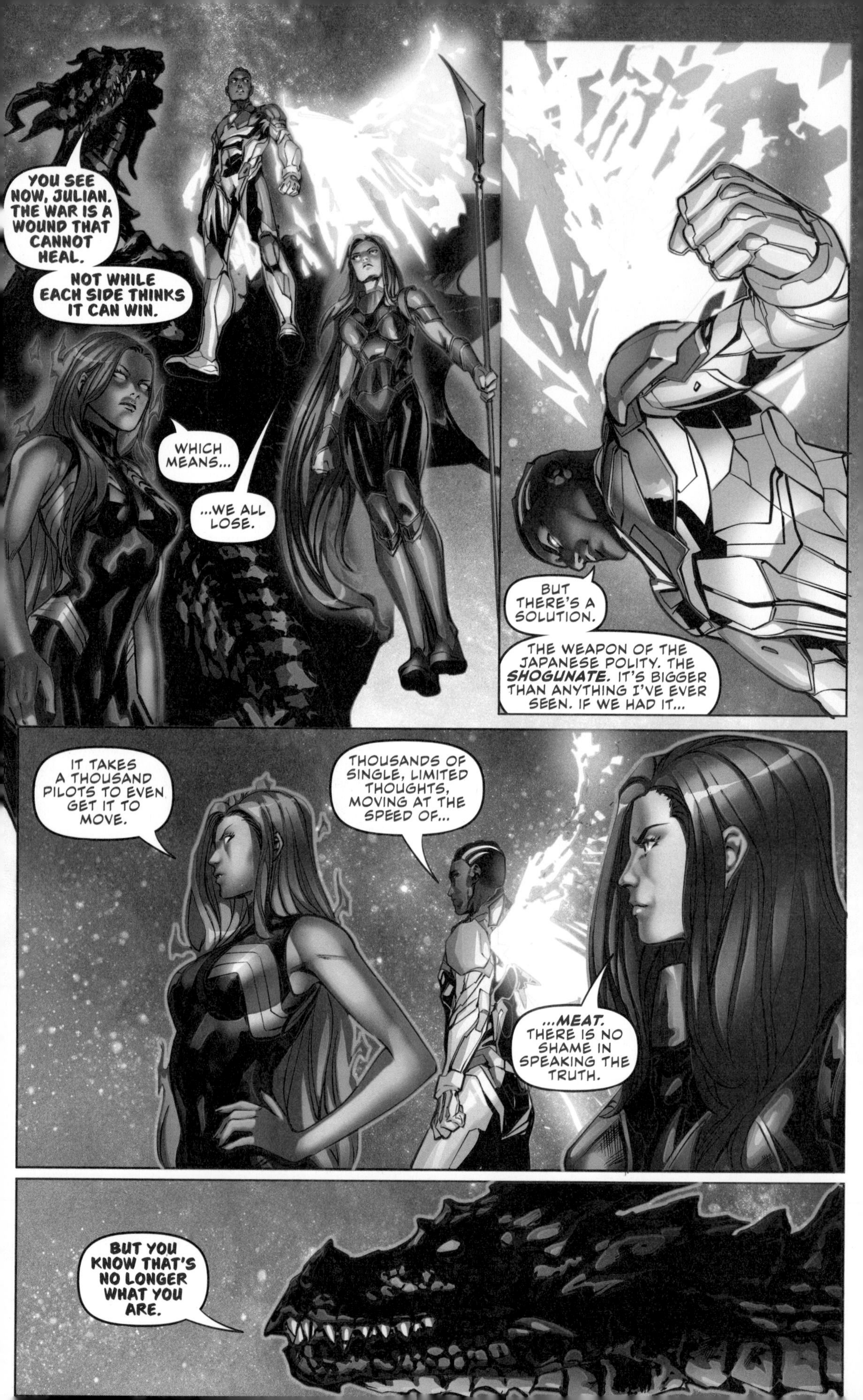
YOU SEE NOW, JULIAN. THE WAR IS A WOUND THAT CANNOT HEAL.
NOT WHILE EACH SIDE THINKS IT CAN WIN.
WHICH MEANS...
...WE ALL LOSE.
BUT THERE'S A SOLUTION.
THE WEAPON OF THE JAPANESE POLITY. THE *SHOGUNATE.* IT'S BIGGER THAN ANYTHING I'VE EVER SEEN. IF WE HAD IT...
IT TAKES A THOUSAND PILOTS TO EVEN GET IT TO MOVE.
THOUSANDS OF SINGLE, LIMITED THOUGHTS, MOVING AT THE SPEED OF...
...MEAT. THERE IS NO SHAME IN SPEAKING THE TRUTH.
BUT YOU KNOW THAT'S NO LONGER WHAT YOU ARE.

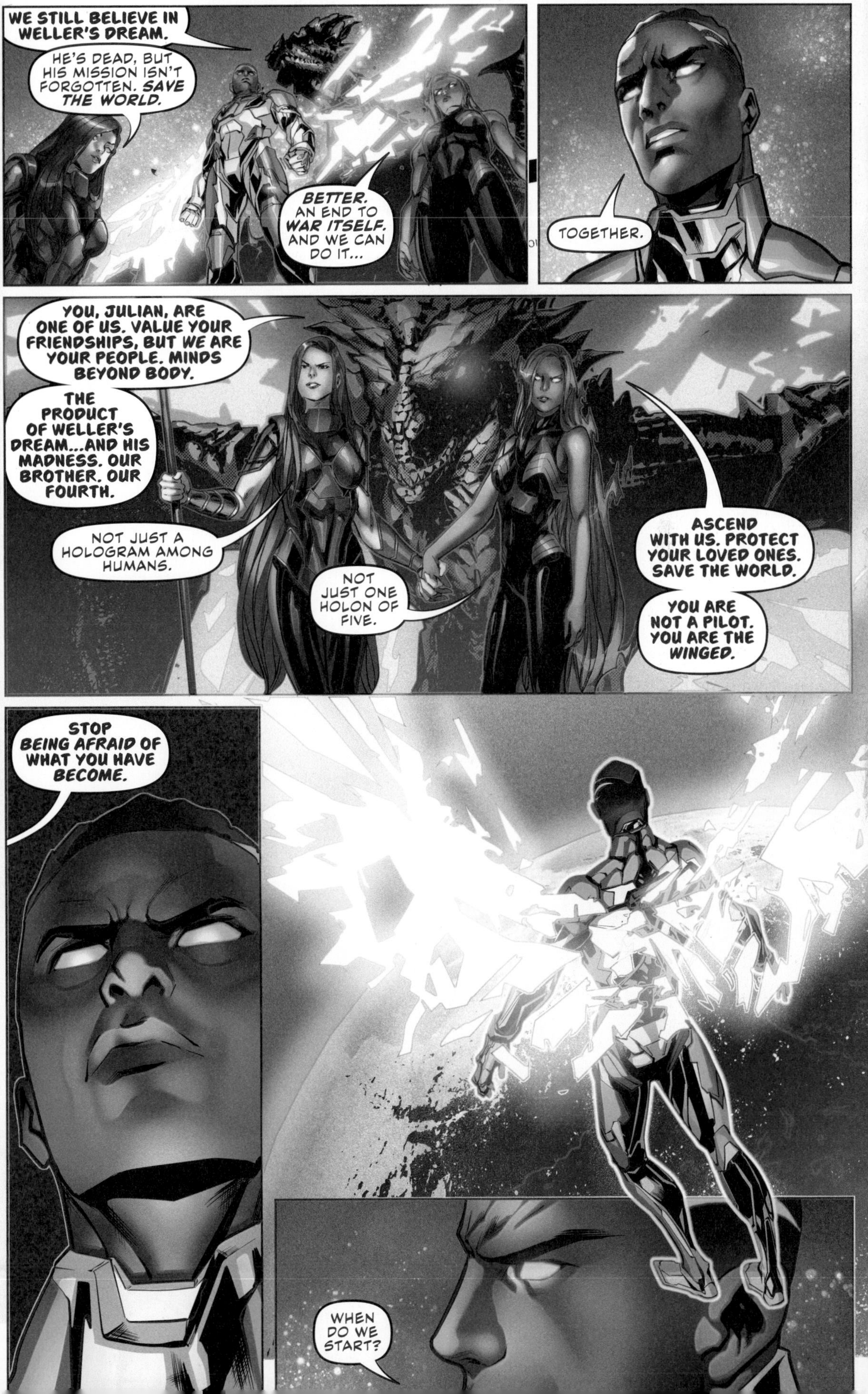
WE STILL BELIEVE IN WELLER'S DREAM.
HE'S DEAD, BUT HIS MISSION ISN'T FORGOTTEN. SAVE THE WORLD.
BETTER. AN END TO WAR ITSELF. AND WE CAN DO IT...
TOGETHER.
YOU, JULIAN, ARE ONE OF US. VALUE YOUR FRIENDSHIPS, BUT WE ARE YOUR PEOPLE. MINDS BEYOND BODY.
THE PRODUCT OF WELLER'S DREAM...AND HIS MADNESS. OUR BROTHER. OUR FOURTH.
NOT JUST A HOLOGRAM AMONG HUMANS.
NOT JUST ONE HOLON OF FIVE.
ASCEND WITH US. PROTECT YOUR LOVED ONES. SAVE THE WORLD.
YOU ARE NOT A PILOT. YOU ARE THE WINGED.
STOP BEING AFRAID OF WHAT YOU HAVE BECOME.
WHEN DO WE START?

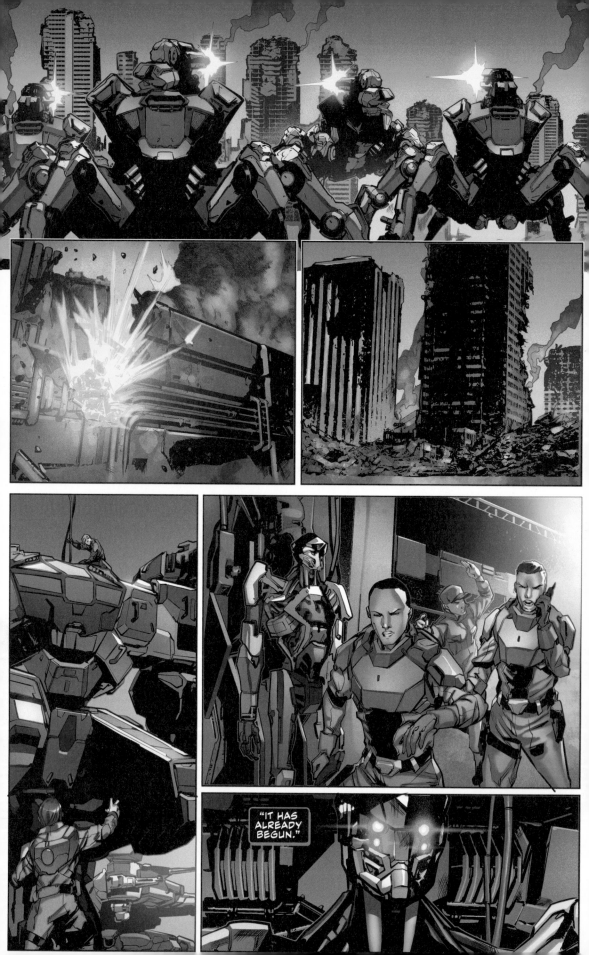

"IT HAS ALREADY BEGUN."

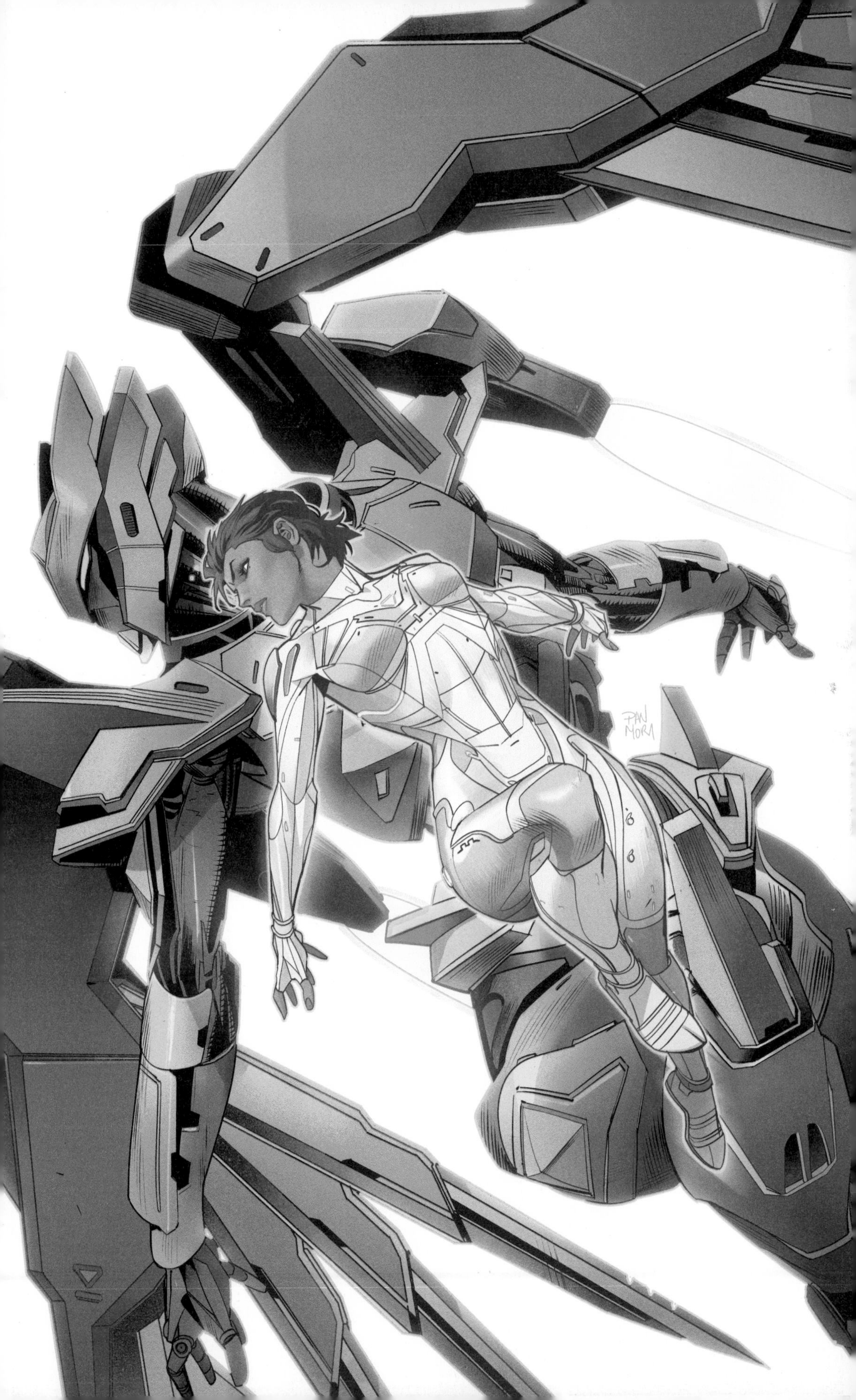
PAN
MORA

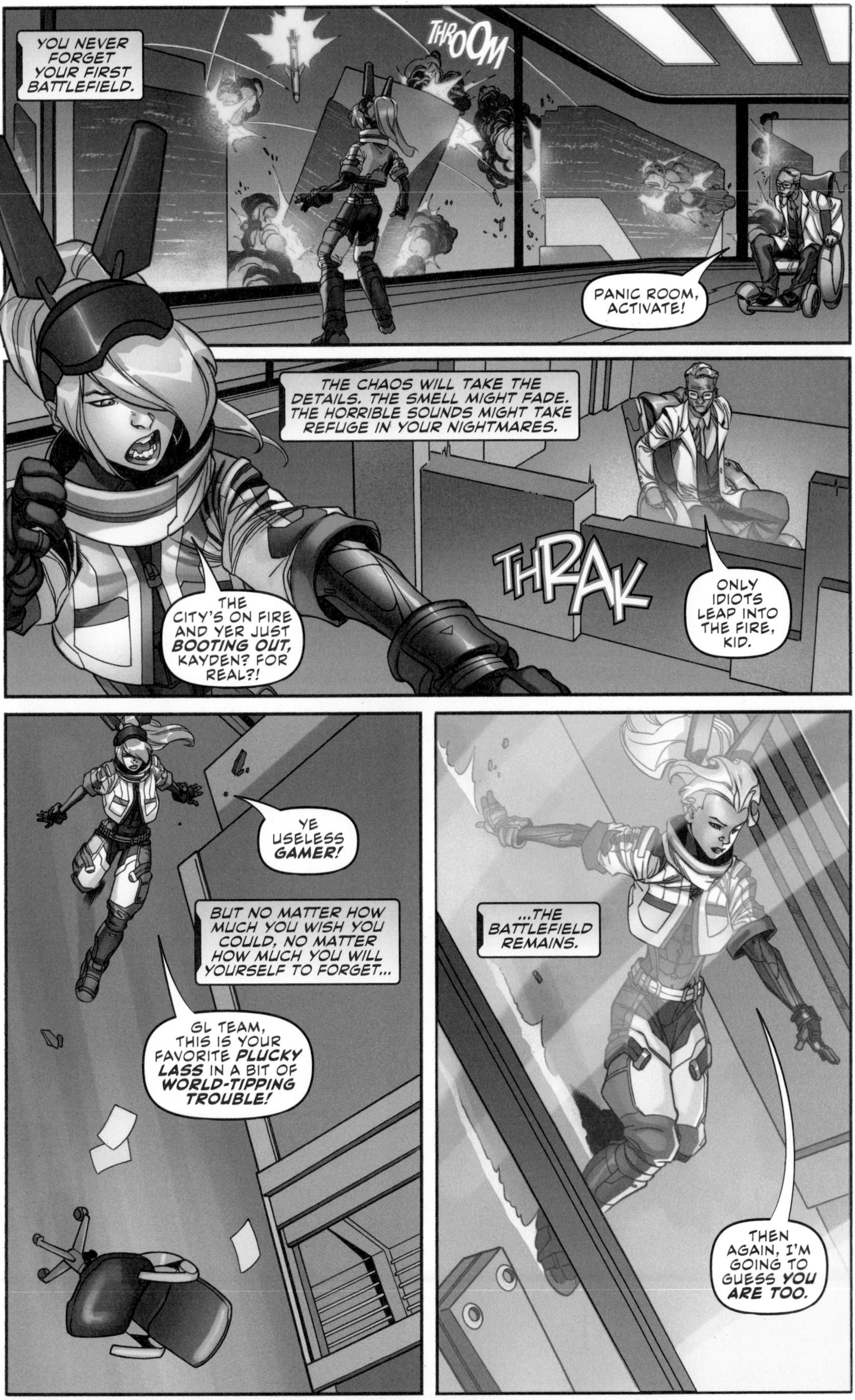
YOU NEVER FORGET YOUR FIRST BATTLEFIELD.
THROOM
PANIC ROOM, ACTIVATE!
THE CHAOS WILL TAKE THE DETAILS. THE SMELL MIGHT FADE. THE HORRIBLE SOUNDS MIGHT TAKE REFUGE IN YOUR NIGHTMARES.
THE CITY'S ON FIRE AND YER JUST BOOTING OUT, KAYDEN? FOR REAL?!
THRAK
ONLY IDIOTS LEAP INTO THE FIRE, KID.
YE USELESS GAMER!
BUT NO MATTER HOW MUCH YOU WISH YOU COULD, NO MATTER HOW MUCH YOU WILL YOURSELF TO FORGET...
GL TEAM, THIS IS YOUR FAVORITE PLUCKY LASS IN A BIT OF WORLD-TIPPING TROUBLE!
...THE BATTLEFIELD REMAINS.
THEN AGAIN, I'M GOING TO GUESS YOU ARE TOO.

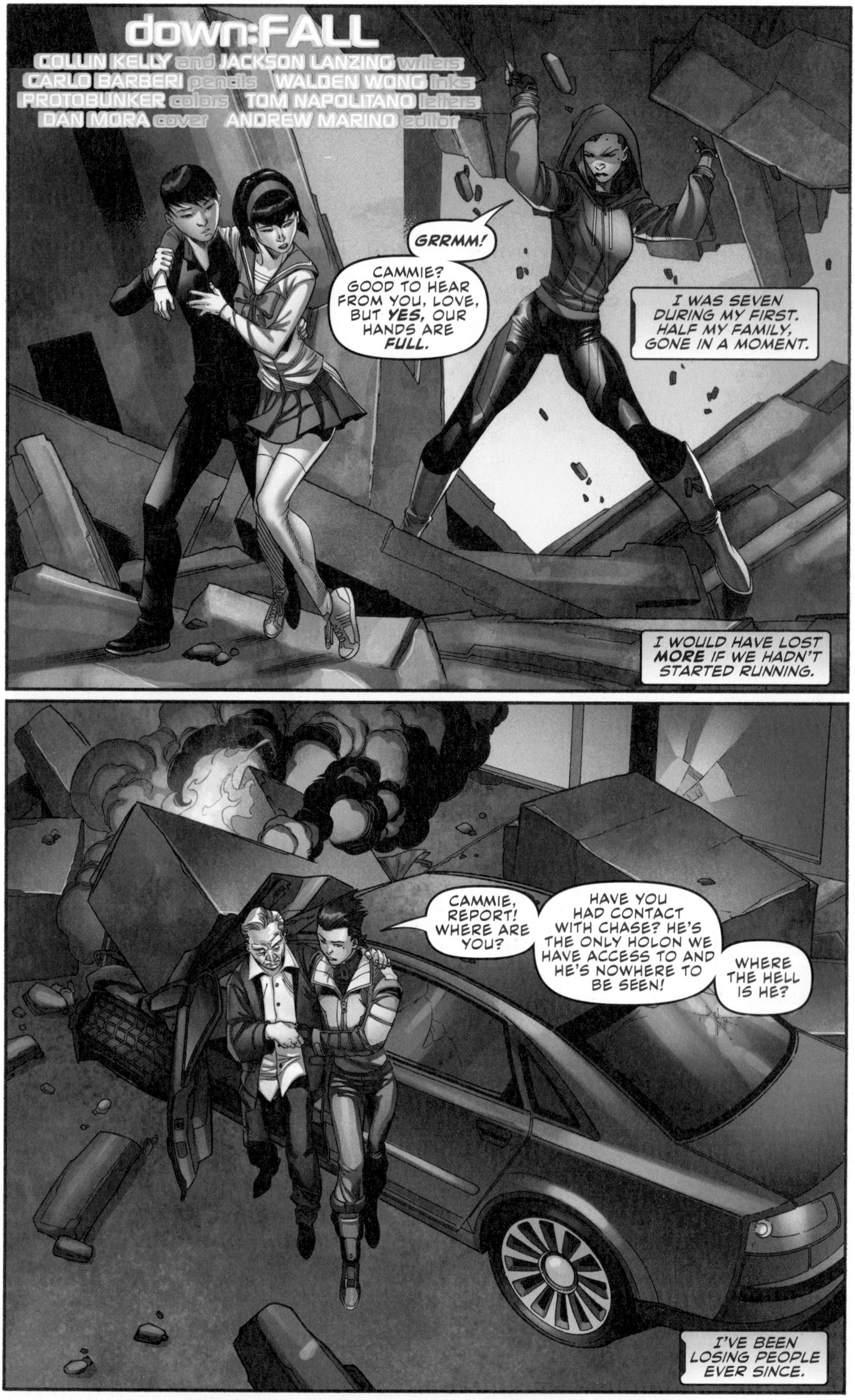
down:FALL
COLLIN KELLY and JACKSON LANZING writers
CARLO BARBERI pencils WALDEN WONG inks
PROTOBUNKER colors TOM NAPOLITANO letters
DAN MORA cover ANDREW MARINO editor
GRRMM!
CAMMIE? GOOD TO HEAR FROM YOU, LOVE, BUT YES, OUR HANDS ARE FULL.
I WAS SEVEN DURING MY FIRST. HALF MY FAMILY, GONE IN A MOMENT.
I WOULD HAVE LOST MORE IF WE HADN'T STARTED RUNNING.
CAMMIE, REPORT! WHERE ARE YOU?
HAVE YOU HAD CONTACT WITH CHASE? HE'S THE ONLY HOLON WE HAVE ACCESS TO AND HE'S NOWHERE TO BE SEEN!
WHERE THE HELL IS HE?
I'VE BEEN LOSING PEOPLE EVER SINCE.

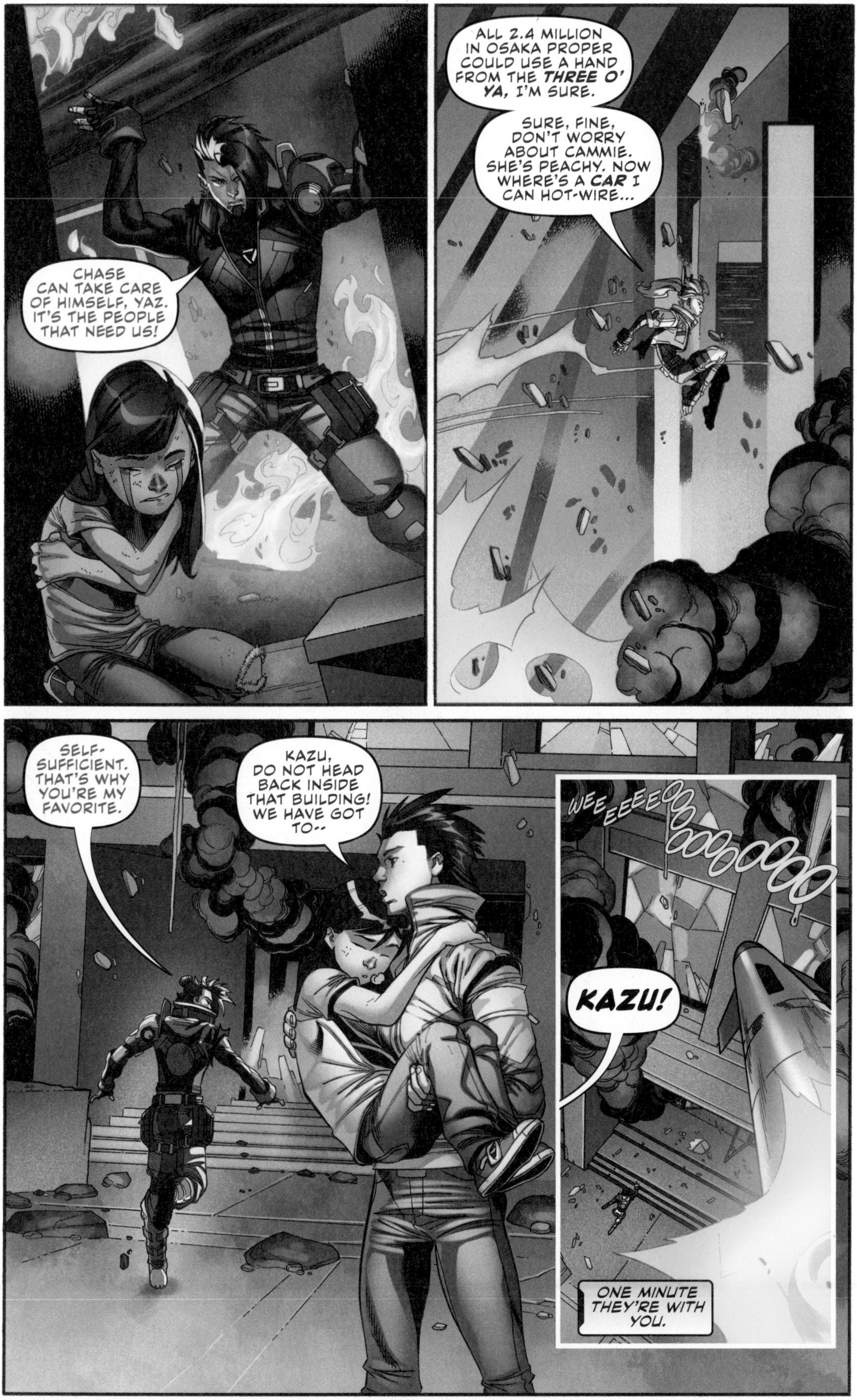
CHASE CAN TAKE CARE OF HIMSELF, YAZ. IT'S THE PEOPLE THAT NEED US!
ALL 2.4 MILLION IN OSAKA PROPER COULD USE A HAND FROM THE THREE O' YA, I'M SURE.
SURE, FINE, DON'T WORRY ABOUT CAMMIE. SHE'S PEACHY. NOW WHERE'S A CAR I CAN HOT-WIRE...
SELF-SUFFICIENT. THAT'S WHY YOU'RE MY FAVORITE.
KAZU, DO NOT HEAD BACK INSIDE THAT BUILDING! WE HAVE GOT TO--
WEEEEEOOOOOOOOOOOO
KAZU!
ONE MINUTE THEY'RE WITH YOU.

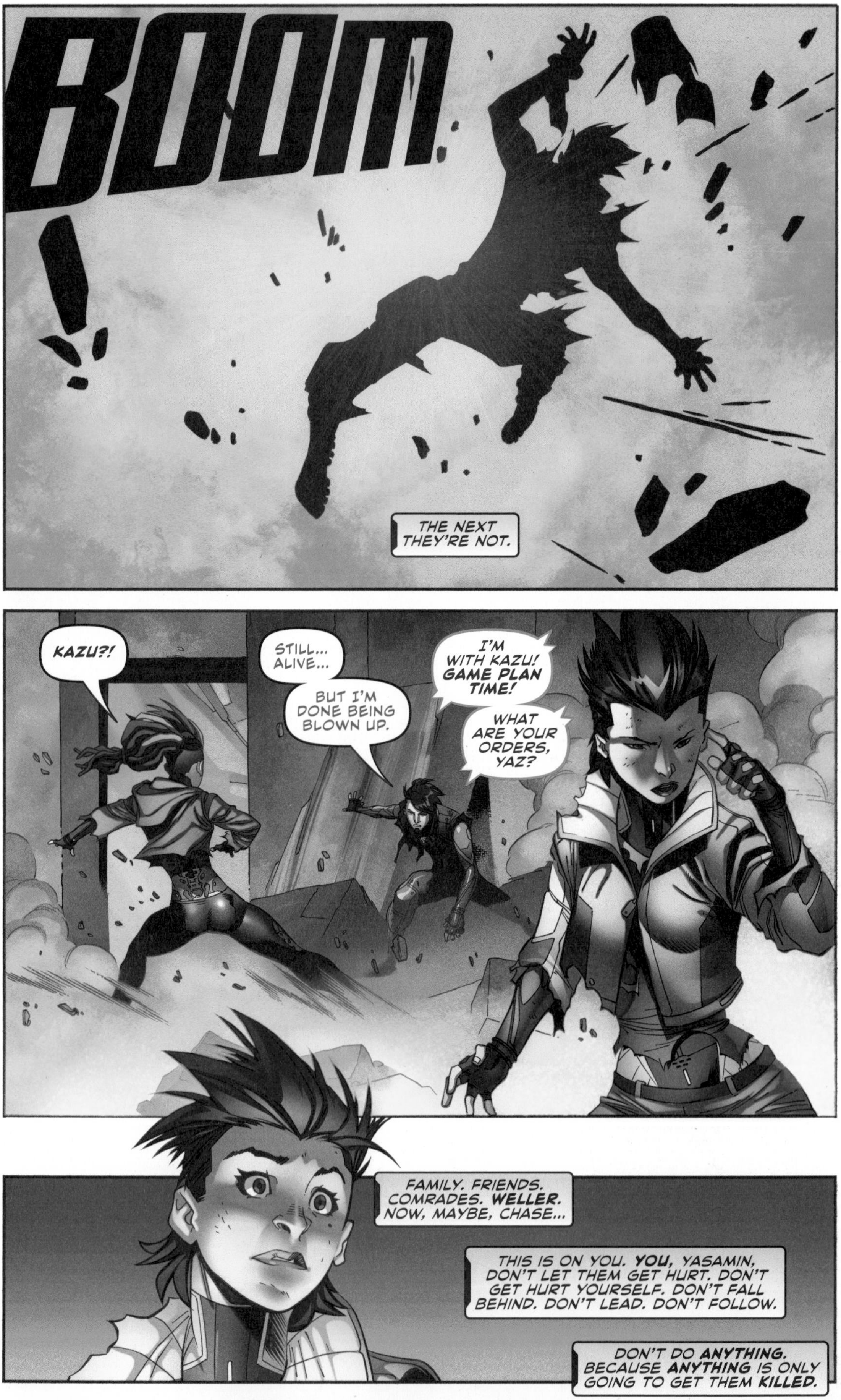
BOOM
THE NEXT THEY'RE NOT.
KAZU?!
STILL... ALIVE...
BUT I'M DONE BEING BLOWN UP.
I'M WITH KAZU! GAME PLAN TIME!
WHAT ARE YOUR ORDERS, YAZ?
FAMILY. FRIENDS. COMRADES. WELLER. NOW, MAYBE, CHASE...
THIS IS ON YOU. YOU, YASAMIN, DON'T LET THEM GET HURT. DON'T GET HURT YOURSELF. DON'T FALL BEHIND. DON'T LEAD. DON'T FOLLOW.
DON'T DO ANYTHING. BECAUSE ANYTHING IS ONLY GOING TO GET THEM KILLED.

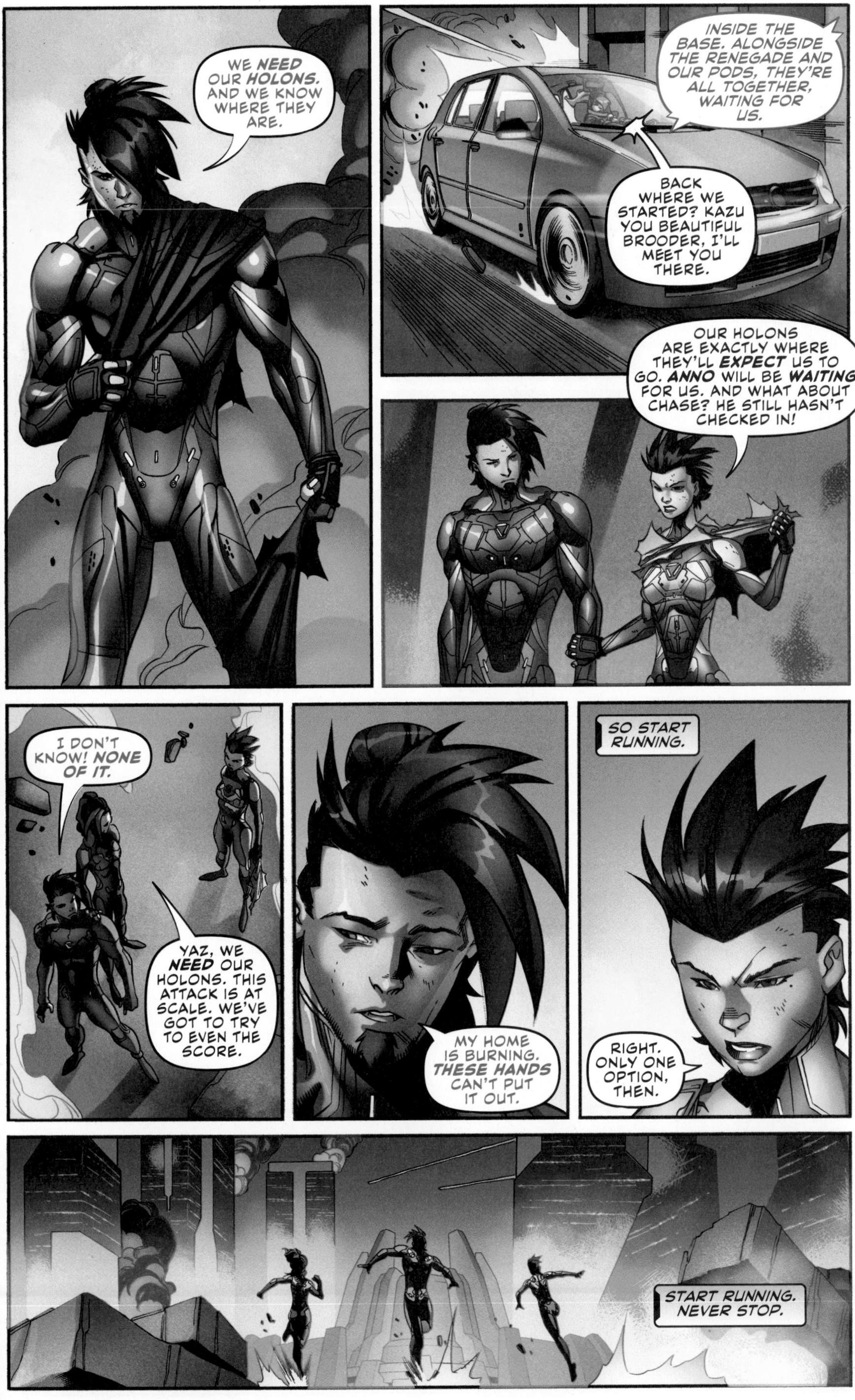
WE NEED OUR HOLONS. AND WE KNOW WHERE THEY ARE.
INSIDE THE BASE. ALONGSIDE THE RENEGADE AND OUR PODS, THEY'RE ALL TOGETHER, WAITING FOR US.
BACK WHERE WE STARTED? KAZU YOU BEAUTIFUL BROODER, I'LL MEET YOU THERE.
OUR HOLONS ARE EXACTLY WHERE THEY'LL EXPECT US TO GO. ANNO WILL BE WAITING FOR US. AND WHAT ABOUT CHASE? HE STILL HASN'T CHECKED IN!
I DON'T KNOW! NONE OF IT.
YAZ, WE NEED OUR HOLONS. THIS ATTACK IS AT SCALE. WE'VE GOT TO TRY TO EVEN THE SCORE.
MY HOME IS BURNING. THESE HANDS CAN'T PUT IT OUT.
SO START RUNNING.
RIGHT. ONLY ONE OPTION, THEN.
START RUNNING. NEVER STOP.

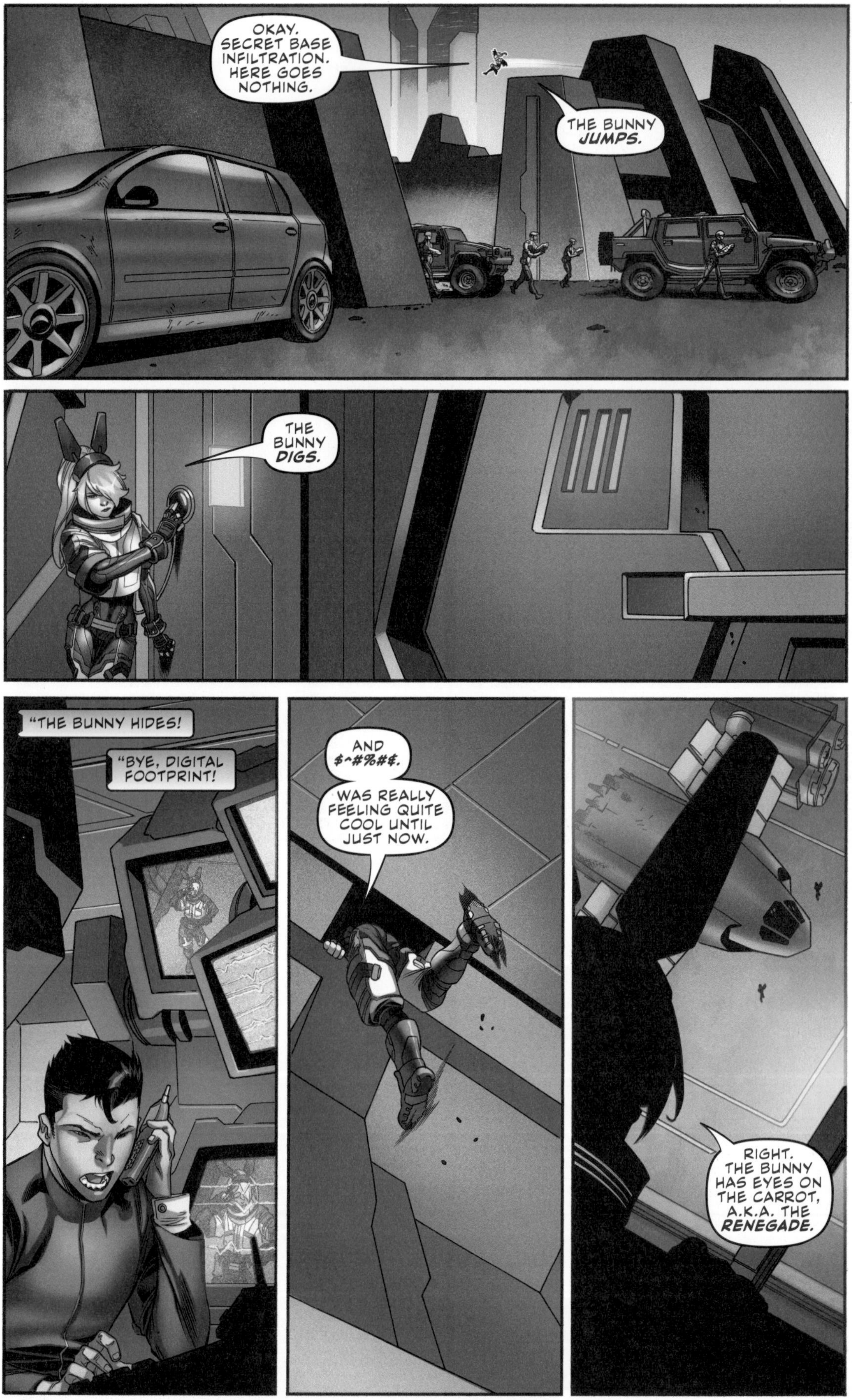
OKAY. SECRET BASE INFILTRATION. HERE GOES NOTHING.
THE BUNNY JUMPS.
THE BUNNY DIGS.
"THE BUNNY HIDES!
"BYE, DIGITAL FOOTPRINT!
AND $^#%#$.
WAS REALLY FEELING QUITE COOL UNTIL JUST NOW.
RIGHT. THE BUNNY HAS EYES ON THE CARROT, A.K.A. THE RENEGADE.

FROMP

CROWCH

SO SORRY!

SORRY, BOYO!

AH GIRL, LOOKS LIKE NO ONE TIDIED YOU UP.

SOMEONE MADE A MESS OF YOUR STUFF, DR. WELLER. WASN'T ME THIS TIME.

WHAT WOULD YOU SAY IF YOU WERE HERE, I WONDER? GOT A FEELING YOU WOULDN'T BE HANDING OUT MEDALS FOR CLEVERNESS.

...WELL, MAYBE I'D GET A MEDAL, BUT THAT'S JUST CUZ I WAS YER FAVORITE.

YOU'D PROBABLY GIVE US A SPEECH, LIFTED FROM A MOVIE OR A BOOK. LIKE WE'D NEVER READ ANYTHING BEFORE...

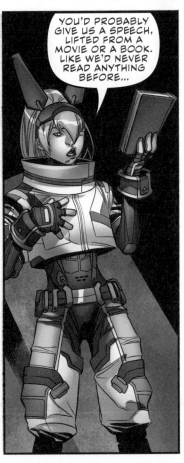

OH.

OH, DOC.

I SHOULD'VE SEEN IT BEFORE.

the TEMPEST

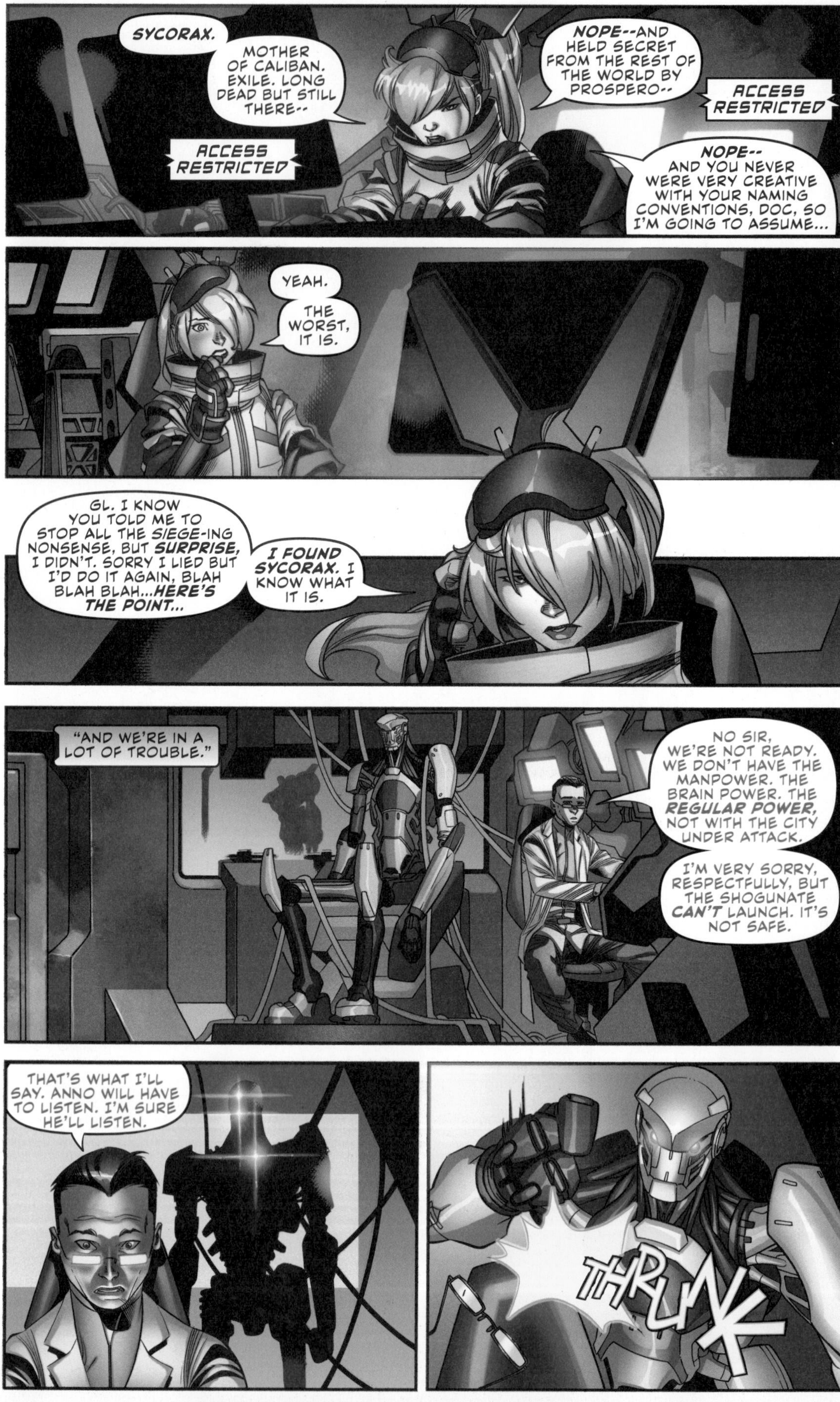
SYCORAX.
MOTHER OF CALIBAN. EXILE. LONG DEAD BUT STILL THERE--
ACCESS RESTRICTED
NOPE--AND HELD SECRET FROM THE REST OF THE WORLD BY PROSPERO--
ACCESS RESTRICTED
NOPE-- AND YOU NEVER WERE VERY CREATIVE WITH YOUR NAMING CONVENTIONS, DOC, SO I'M GOING TO ASSUME...
YEAH.
THE WORST, IT IS.
GL. I KNOW YOU TOLD ME TO STOP ALL THE SIEGE-ING NONSENSE, BUT SURPRISE, I DIDN'T. SORRY I LIED BUT I'D DO IT AGAIN, BLAH BLAH BLAH...HERE'S THE POINT...
I FOUND SYCORAX. I KNOW WHAT IT IS.
"AND WE'RE IN A LOT OF TROUBLE."
NO SIR, WE'RE NOT READY. WE DON'T HAVE THE MANPOWER. THE BRAIN POWER. THE REGULAR POWER, NOT WITH THE CITY UNDER ATTACK.
I'M VERY SORRY, RESPECTFULLY, BUT THE SHOGUNATE CAN'T LAUNCH. IT'S NOT SAFE.
THAT'S WHAT I'LL SAY. ANNO WILL HAVE TO LISTEN. I'M SURE HE'LL LISTEN.
THRUNK

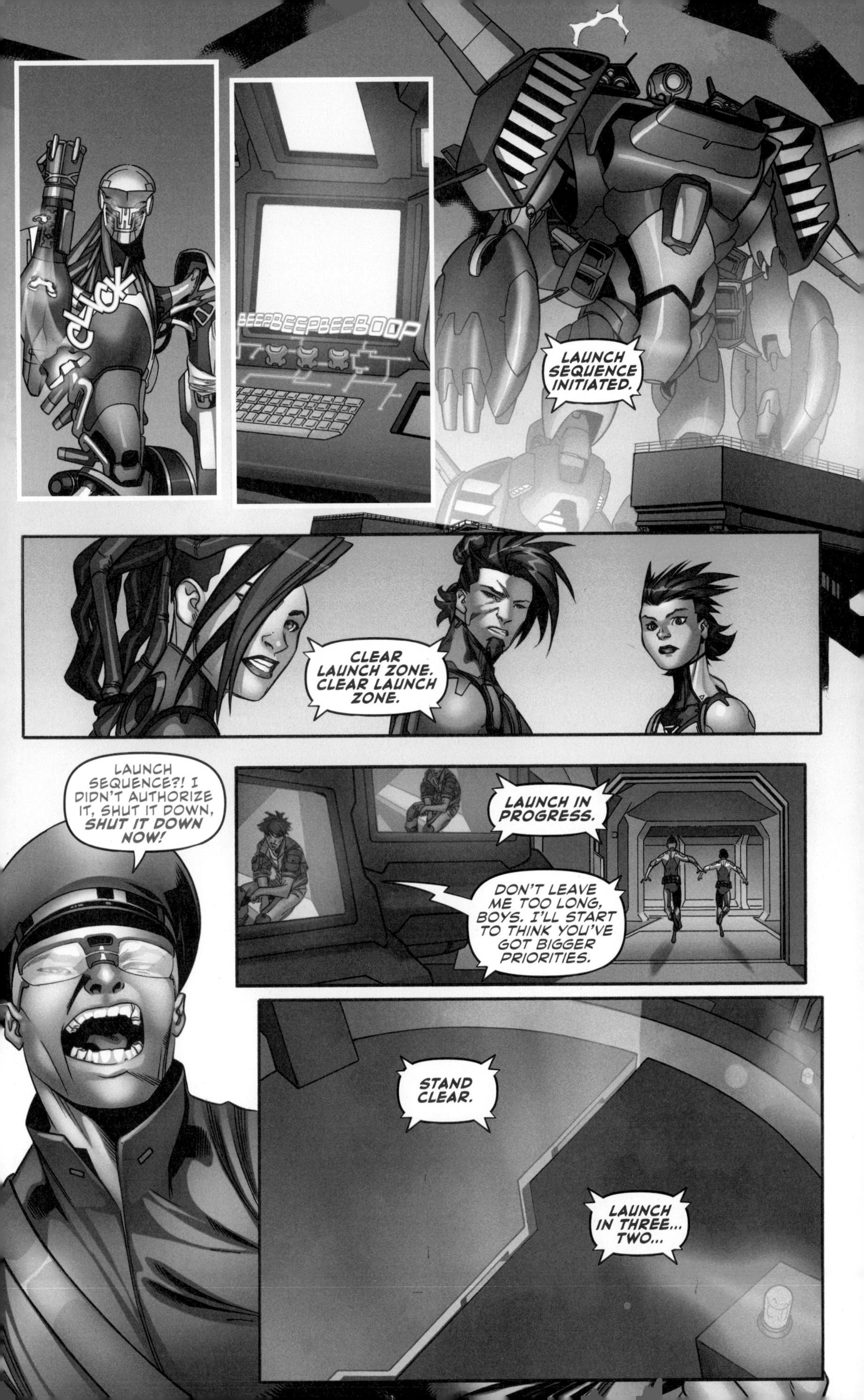
CLICK
BEEPBEEPBEEBOOP
LAUNCH SEQUENCE INITIATED.
CLEAR LAUNCH ZONE. CLEAR LAUNCH ZONE.
LAUNCH SEQUENCE?! I DIDN'T AUTHORIZE IT, SHUT IT DOWN, SHUT IT DOWN NOW!
LAUNCH IN PROGRESS.
DON'T LEAVE ME TOO LONG, BOYS. I'LL START TO THINK YOU'VE GOT BIGGER PRIORITIES.
STAND CLEAR.
LAUNCH IN THREE... TWO...

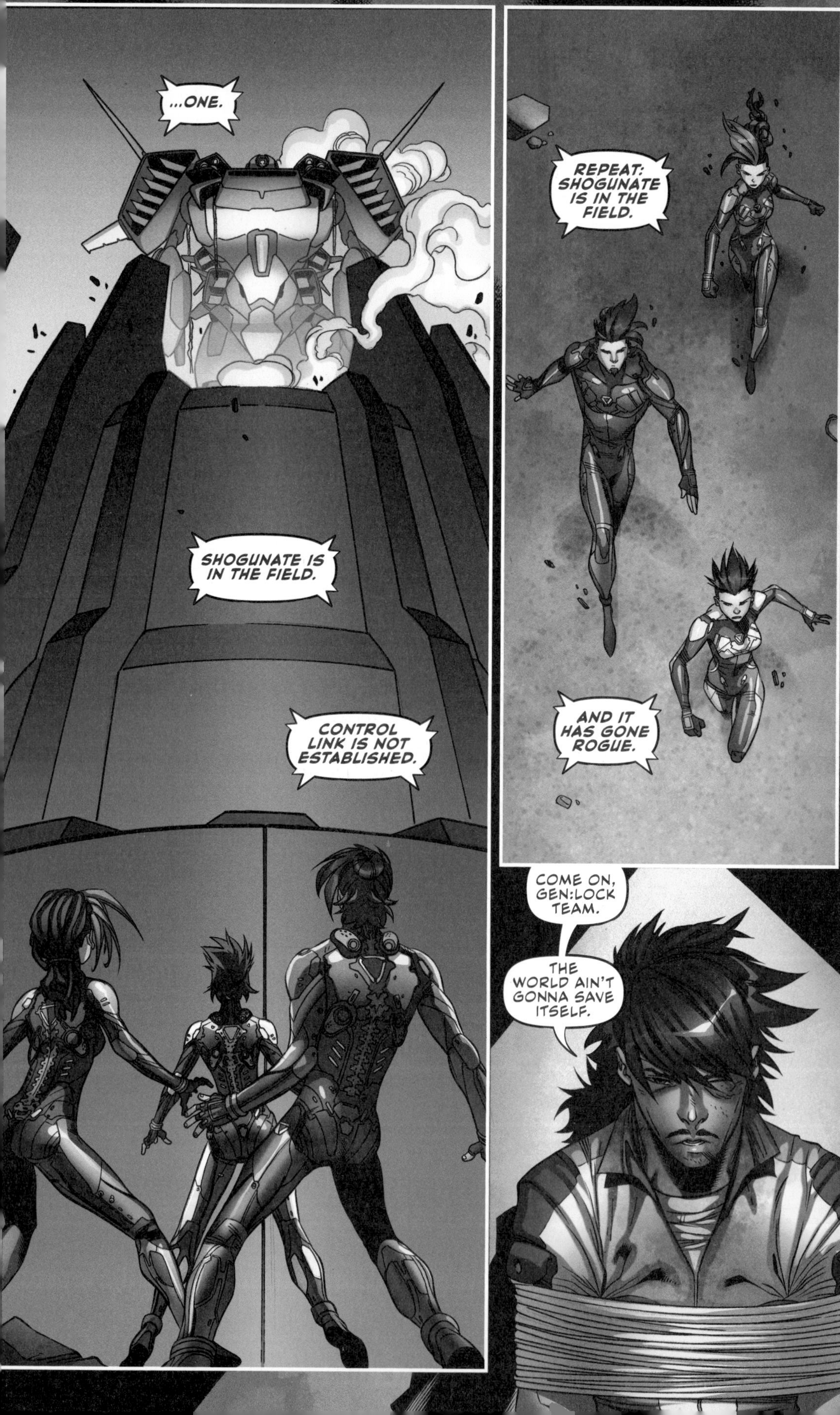
...ONE.
SHOGUNATE IS IN THE FIELD.
CONTROL LINK IS NOT ESTABLISHED.
REPEAT: SHOGUNATE IS IN THE FIELD.
AND IT HAS GONE ROGUE.
COME ON, GEN:LOCK TEAM.
THE WORLD AIN'T GONNA SAVE ITSELF.

JAPAN BUILT A MACHINE TO MAKE OUR POWER OBSOLETE.

THE SHOGUNATE.

AND NOW IT'S OPENING FIRE ON THEIR *OWN* CITY.

IN TRYING TO OUTSMART DR. WELLER, THEY'VE BUILT SOMETHING THEY COULD NEVER HOPE TO CONTROL. TALE AS OLD AS TIME. OR AT LEAST AS OLD AS MY CAREER WITH THE *POLITY.*

NOTHING TO DO ANYMORE EXCEPT RUN *AWAY* FROM THE FIRE...

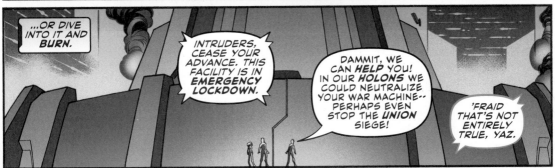

...OR DIVE INTO IT AND *BURN.*

INTRUDERS, CEASE YOUR ADVANCE. THIS FACILITY IS IN *EMERGENCY LOCKDOWN.*

DAMMIT, WE CAN *HELP* YOU! IN OUR *HOLONS* WE COULD NEUTRALIZE YOUR WAR MACHINE-- PERHAPS EVEN STOP THE *UNION* SIEGE!

'FRAID THAT'S NOT ENTIRELY TRUE, YAZ.

CUZ I KNOW WHAT *SYCORAX* ACTUALLY IS. I KNOW WHAT JUST *TOOK OVER* THE SHOGUNATE.

AND EVEN IF YOU *COULD* GET TO THE HOLONS, I'M NOT SURE THERE'S A HOPE IN *HELL* THAT WE CAN STOP IT.

THE DOC LIED--I KNOW, *SHOCKER*-- WHEN HE TOLD US WE WERE THE FIRST TO *PASS* THE *WELLER TEST.*

IT'S ALL HERE IN HIS FILES, BURIED UNDER SOME DECADE-OLD ENCRYPTION.

THREE SISTERS. ALL OF THEM GEN:LOCK COMPATIBLE.

AND ALL OF THEM *LOST* IN THE MINDFRAME. IT'S HOW HE DISCOVERED UP-TIME LIMITS AT ALL.

BUT THEY WEREN'T GONE. THEIR GESTALT CONSCIOUSNESS ESCAPED INTO THE ETHER--INTO *SIEGE,* ACTUALLY--AND LURKED THERE TILL ANNO AND HIS TEAM BUILT A ROBOT BIG ENOUGH TO HOUSE ALL THREE.

AND NOW THEY'VE GOT CHASE AND MOST LIKELY CALIBAN ON THEIR SIDE AS WELL.

DAMN YOU, WELLER...

OH, AND YAZ?

THE BAD NEWS DOESN'T EXACTLY STOP THERE...

...I'M NOT SURE THIS COULD GET ANY WORSE...

THAT'S WHERE SHE'S WRONG. THAT'S WHAT NONE OF THEM KNOWS ABOUT WAR.

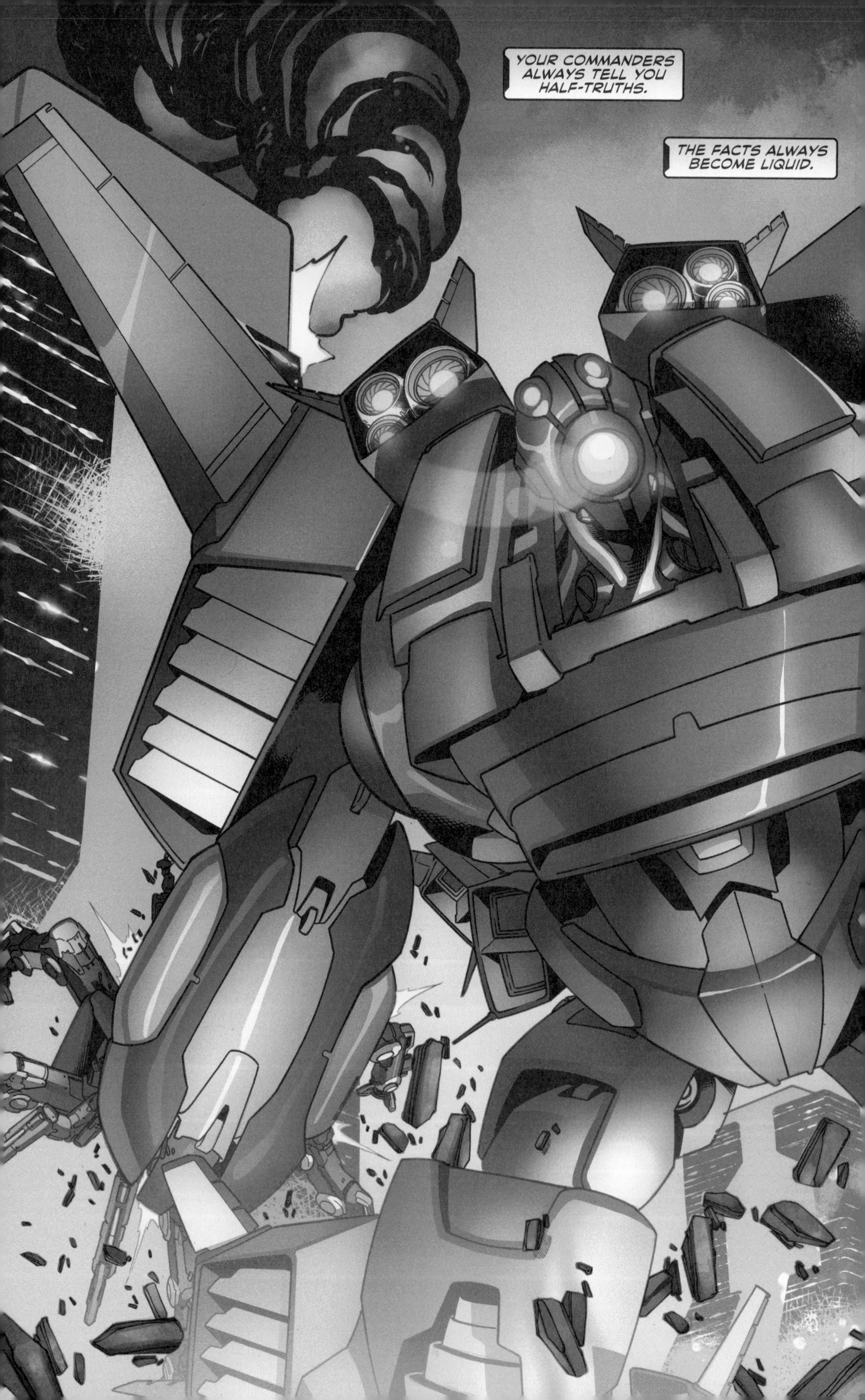
YOUR COMMANDERS ALWAYS TELL YOU HALF-TRUTHS.
THE FACTS ALWAYS BECOME LIQUID.

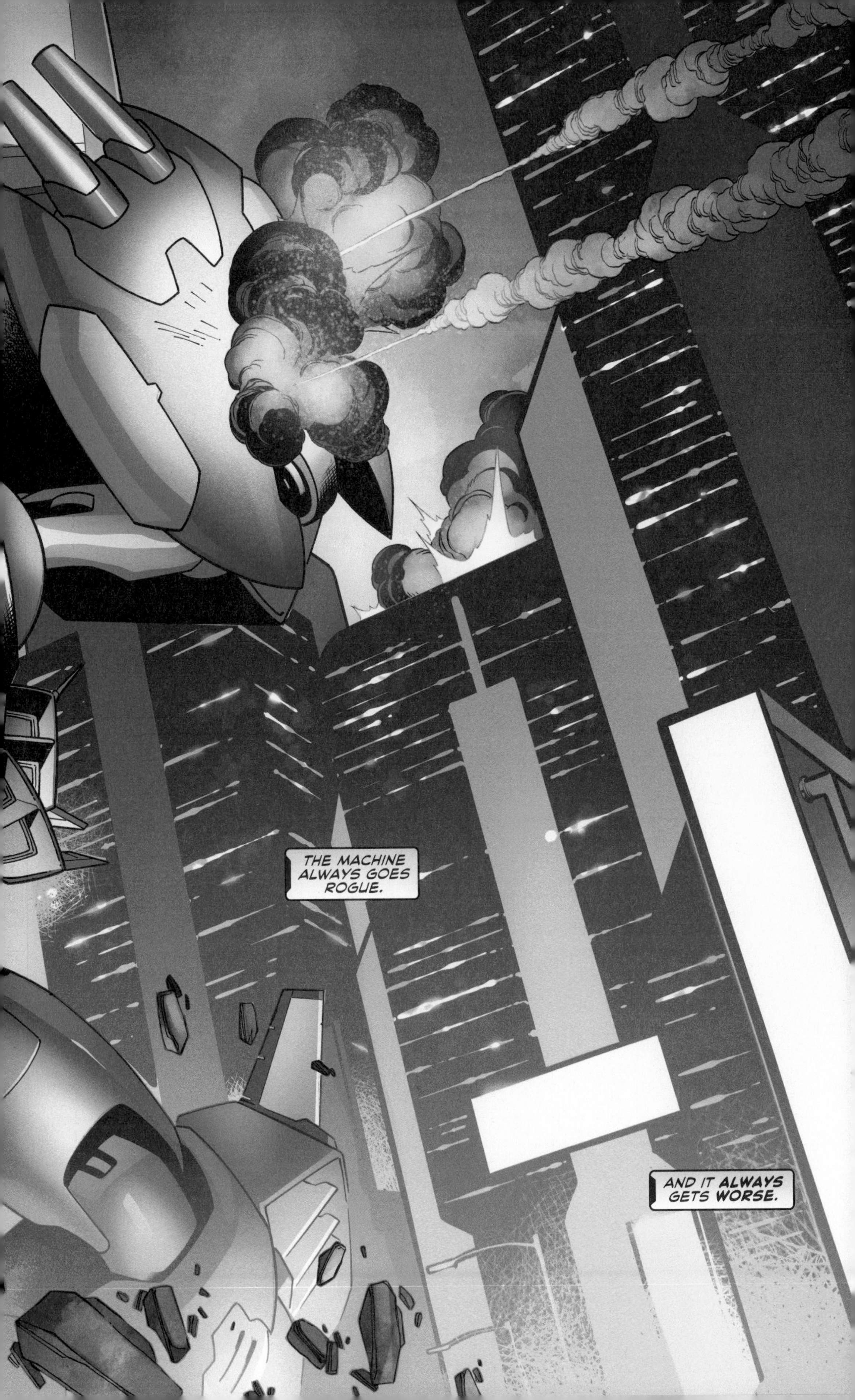
THE MACHINE ALWAYS GOES ROGUE.
AND IT ALWAYS GETS WORSE.

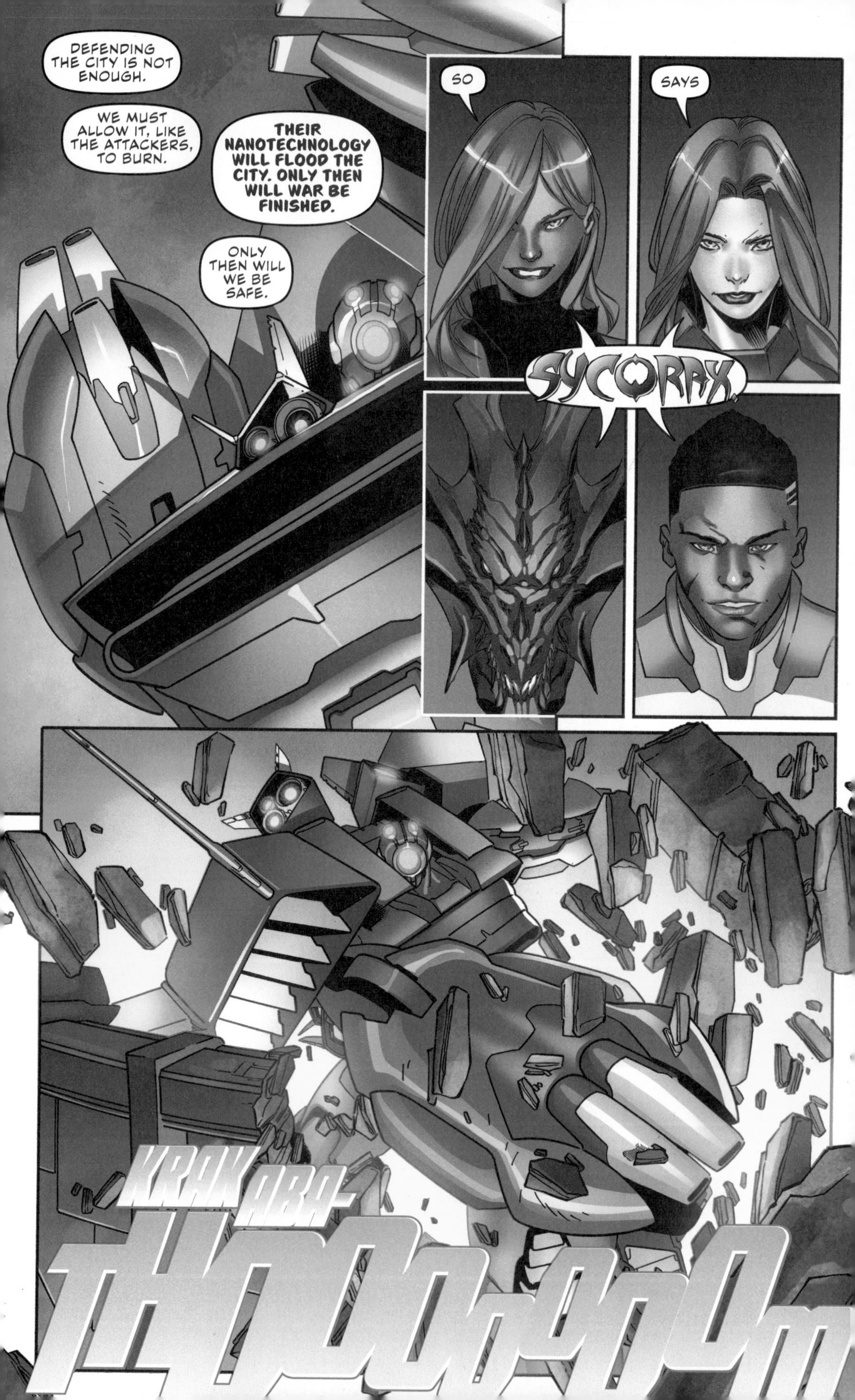
DEFENDING THE CITY IS NOT ENOUGH.
WE MUST ALLOW IT, LIKE THE ATTACKERS, TO BURN.
THEIR NANOTECHNOLOGY WILL FLOOD THE CITY. ONLY THEN WILL WAR BE FINISHED.
ONLY THEN WILL WE BE SAFE.
SO
SAYS
SYCORAX.
KRAKABA-
THOOOOOOM

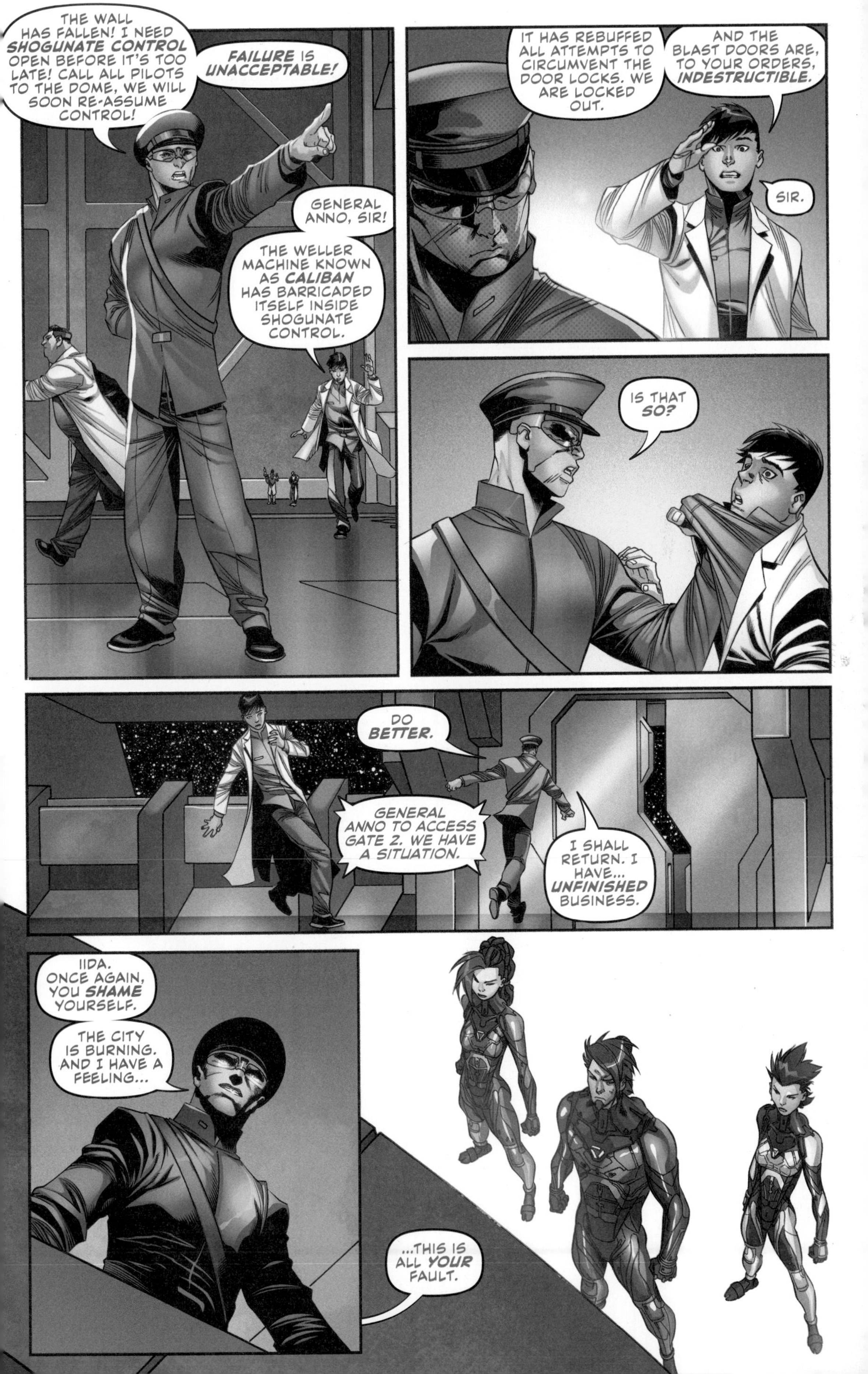
THE WALL HAS FALLEN! I NEED SHOGUNATE CONTROL OPEN BEFORE IT'S TOO LATE! CALL ALL PILOTS TO THE DOME, WE WILL SOON RE-ASSUME CONTROL!
FAILURE IS UNACCEPTABLE!
GENERAL ANNO, SIR!
THE WELLER MACHINE KNOWN AS CALIBAN HAS BARRICADED ITSELF INSIDE SHOGUNATE CONTROL.
IT HAS REBUFFED ALL ATTEMPTS TO CIRCUMVENT THE DOOR LOCKS. WE ARE LOCKED OUT.
AND THE BLAST DOORS ARE, TO YOUR ORDERS, INDESTRUCTIBLE.
SIR.
IS THAT SO?
DO BETTER.
GENERAL ANNO TO ACCESS GATE 2. WE HAVE A SITUATION.
I SHALL RETURN. I HAVE... UNFINISHED BUSINESS.
IIDA. ONCE AGAIN, YOU SHAME YOURSELF.
THE CITY IS BURNING. AND I HAVE A FEELING...
...THIS IS ALL YOUR FAULT.

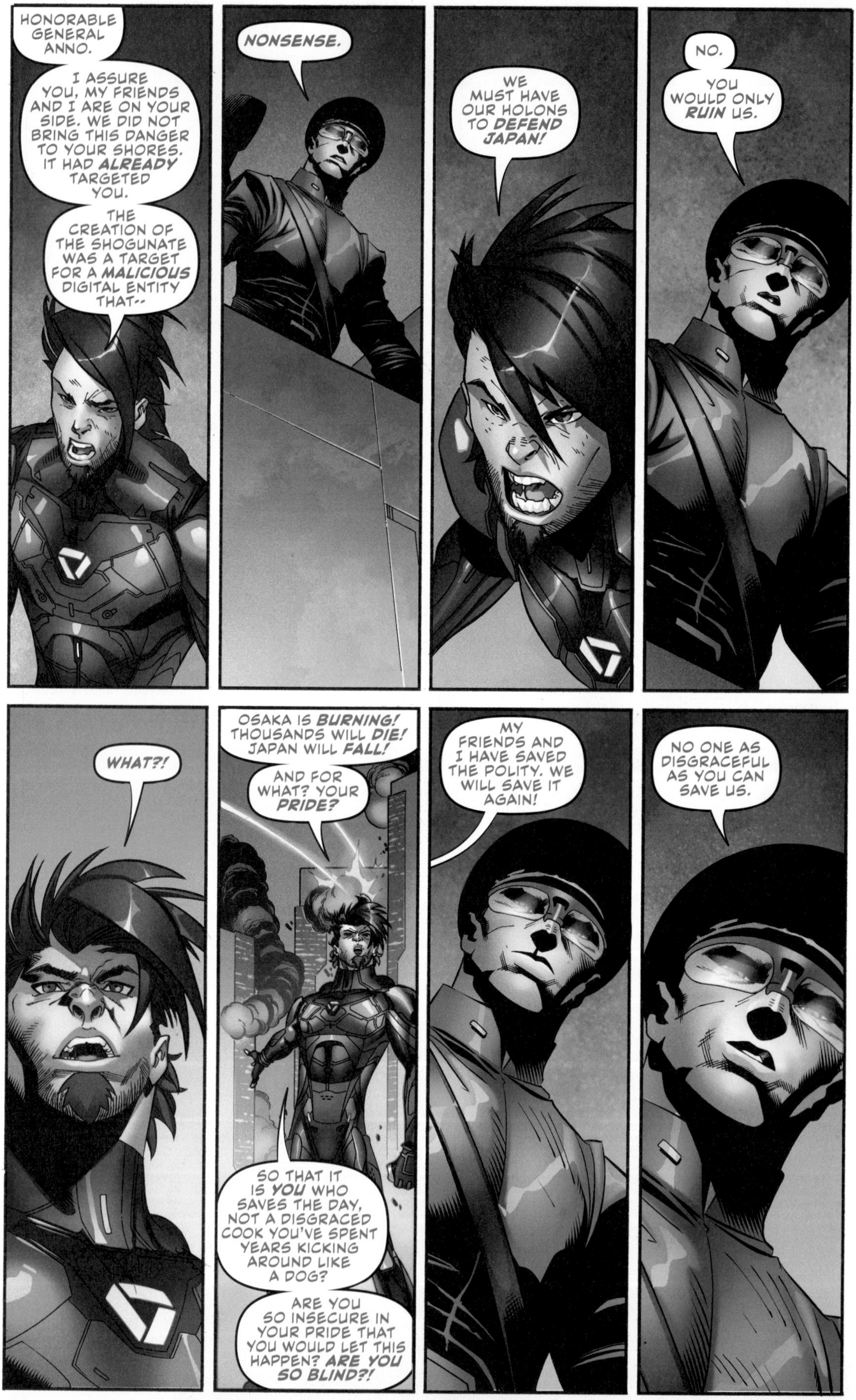
HONORABLE GENERAL ANNO.
I ASSURE YOU, MY FRIENDS AND I ARE ON YOUR SIDE. WE DID NOT BRING THIS DANGER TO YOUR SHORES. IT HAD ALREADY TARGETED YOU.
THE CREATION OF THE SHOGUNATE WAS A TARGET FOR A MALICIOUS DIGITAL ENTITY THAT--
NONSENSE.
WE MUST HAVE OUR HOLONS TO DEFEND JAPAN!
NO.
YOU WOULD ONLY RUIN US.
WHAT?!
OSAKA IS BURNING! THOUSANDS WILL DIE! JAPAN WILL FALL!
AND FOR WHAT? YOUR PRIDE?
SO THAT IT IS YOU WHO SAVES THE DAY, NOT A DISGRACED COOK YOU'VE SPENT YEARS KICKING AROUND LIKE A DOG?
ARE YOU SO INSECURE IN YOUR PRIDE THAT YOU WOULD LET THIS HAPPEN? ARE YOU SO BLIND?!
MY FRIENDS AND I HAVE SAVED THE POLITY. WE WILL SAVE IT AGAIN!
NO ONE AS DISGRACEFUL AS YOU CAN SAVE US.

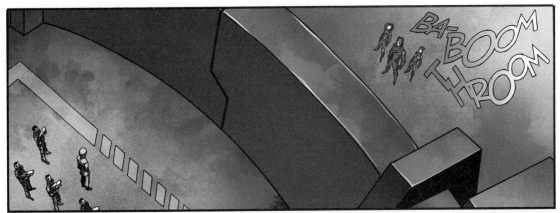

BA-BOOM
THROOM

YES.

I WAS A DISGRACE.

BUT I AM NOT WHO I ONCE WAS.

I WAS ALONE THEN.

AND NOW...

...I'M NOT.

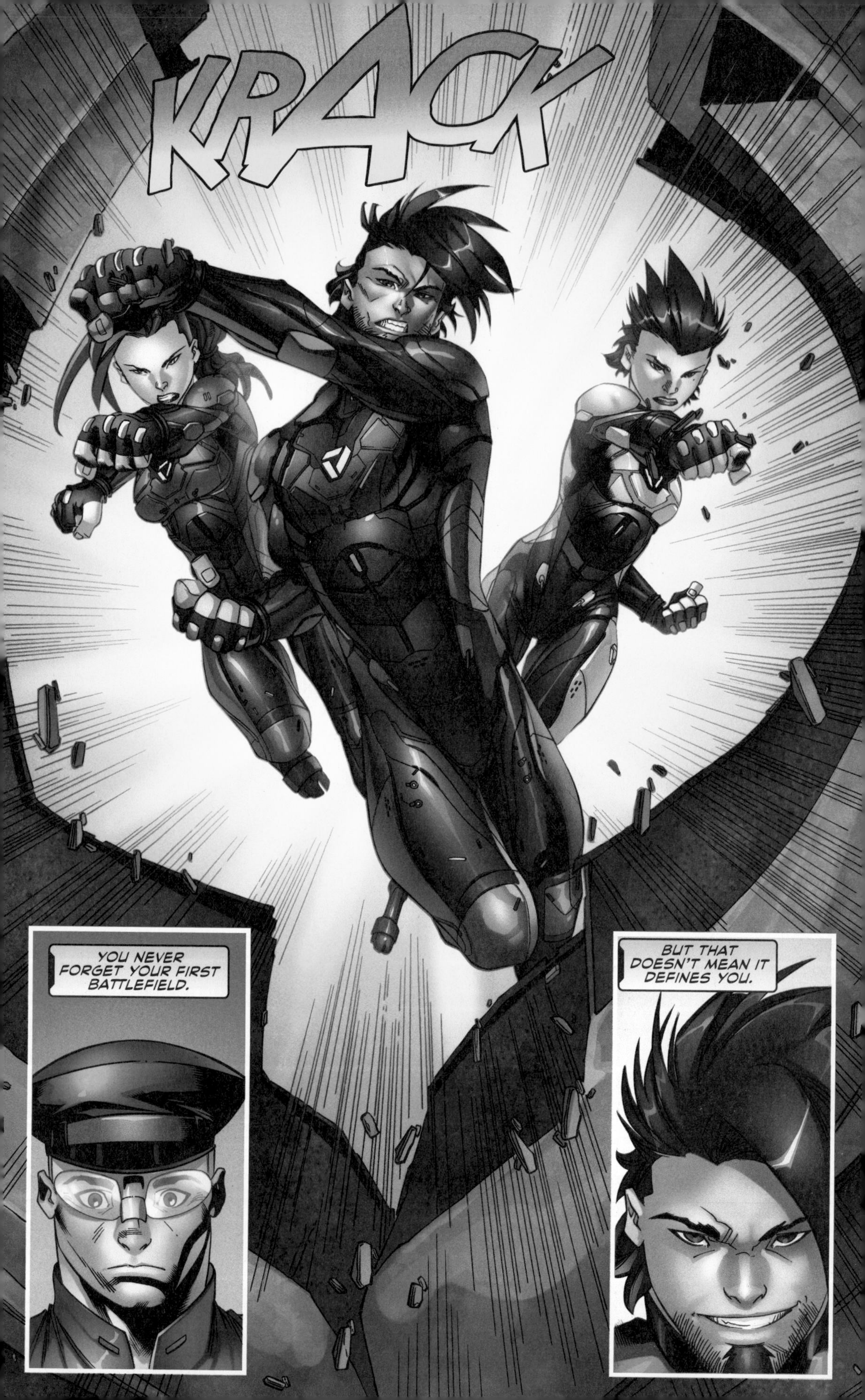
KRACK
YOU NEVER FORGET YOUR FIRST BATTLEFIELD.
BUT THAT DOESN'T MEAN IT DEFINES YOU.

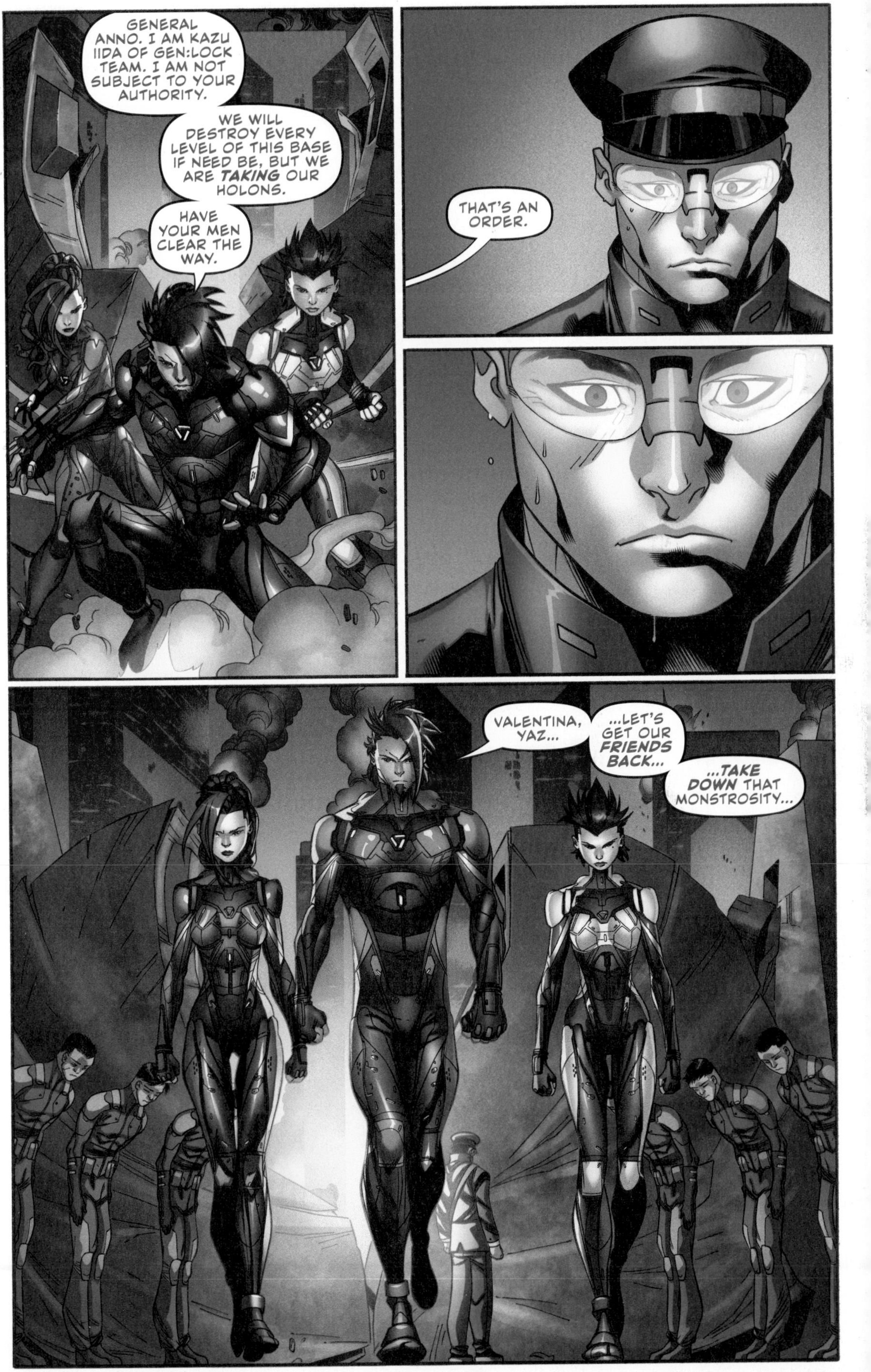
GENERAL ANNO. I AM KAZU IIDA OF GEN:LOCK TEAM. I AM NOT SUBJECT TO YOUR AUTHORITY.
WE WILL DESTROY EVERY LEVEL OF THIS BASE IF NEED BE, BUT WE ARE TAKING OUR HOLONS.
HAVE YOUR MEN CLEAR THE WAY.
THAT'S AN ORDER.
VALENTINA, YAZ...
...LET'S GET OUR FRIENDS BACK...
...TAKE DOWN THAT MONSTROSITY...

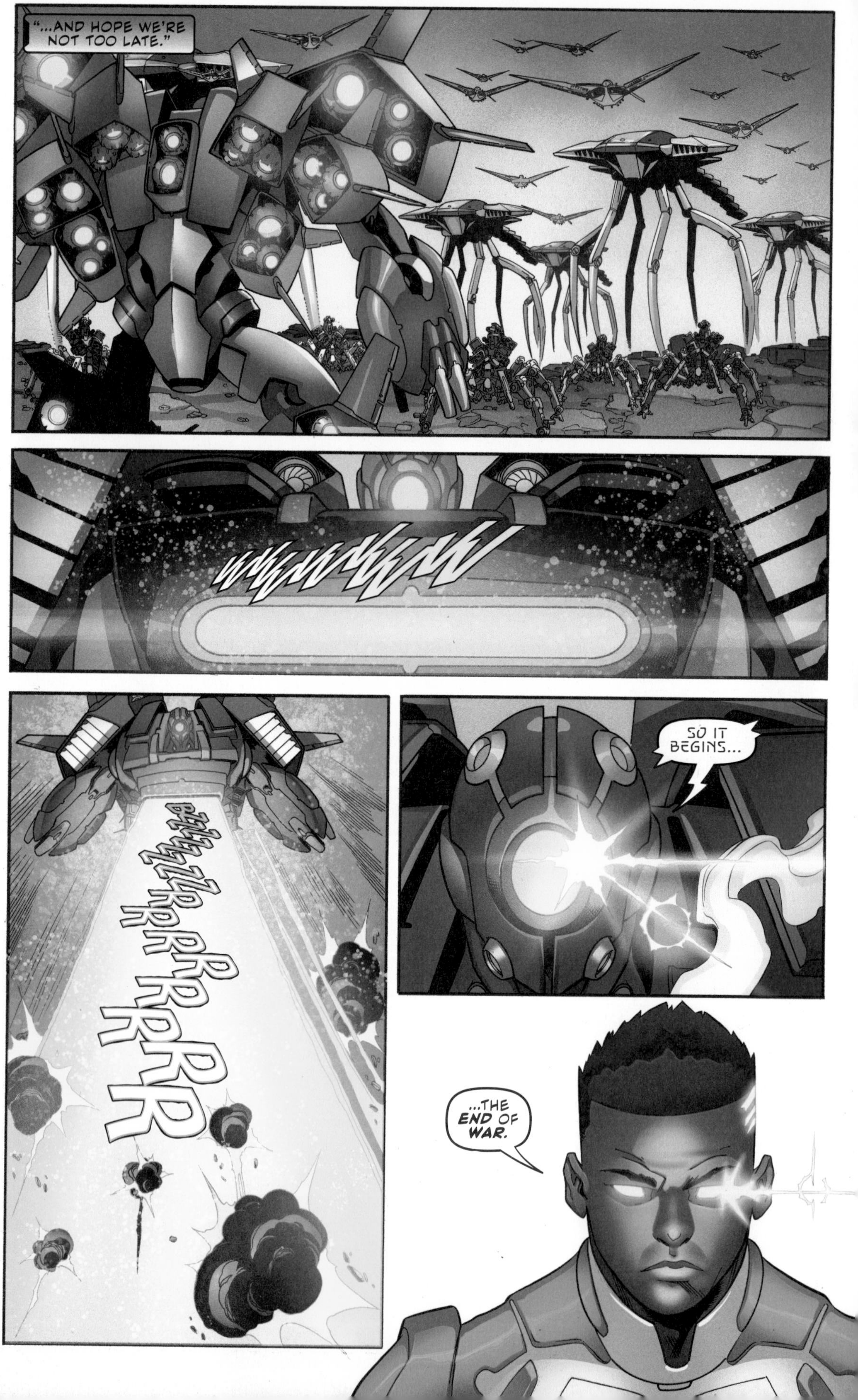
"...AND HOPE WE'RE NOT TOO LATE."
SO IT BEGINS...
...THE END OF WAR.

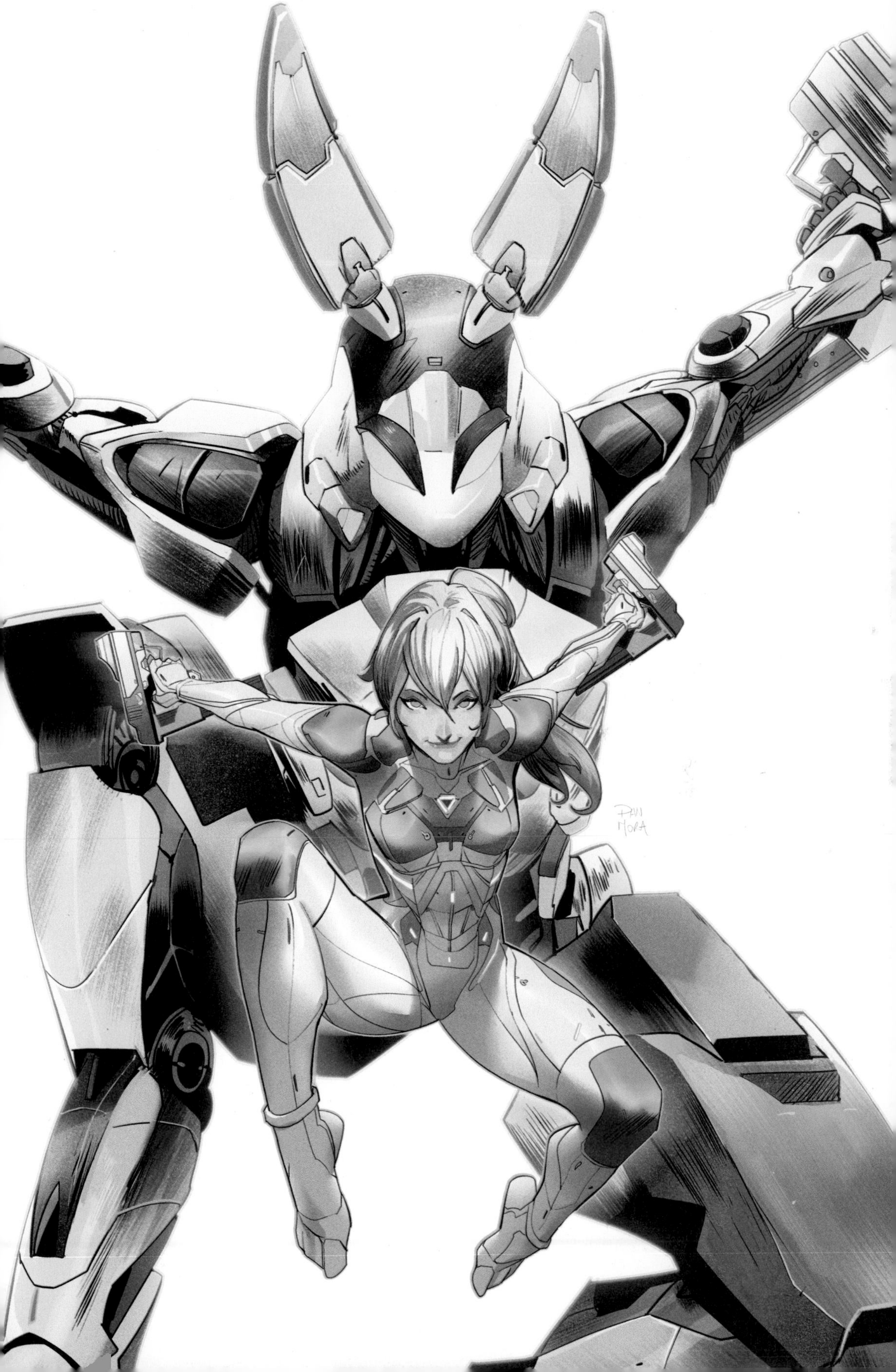
DAN MORA

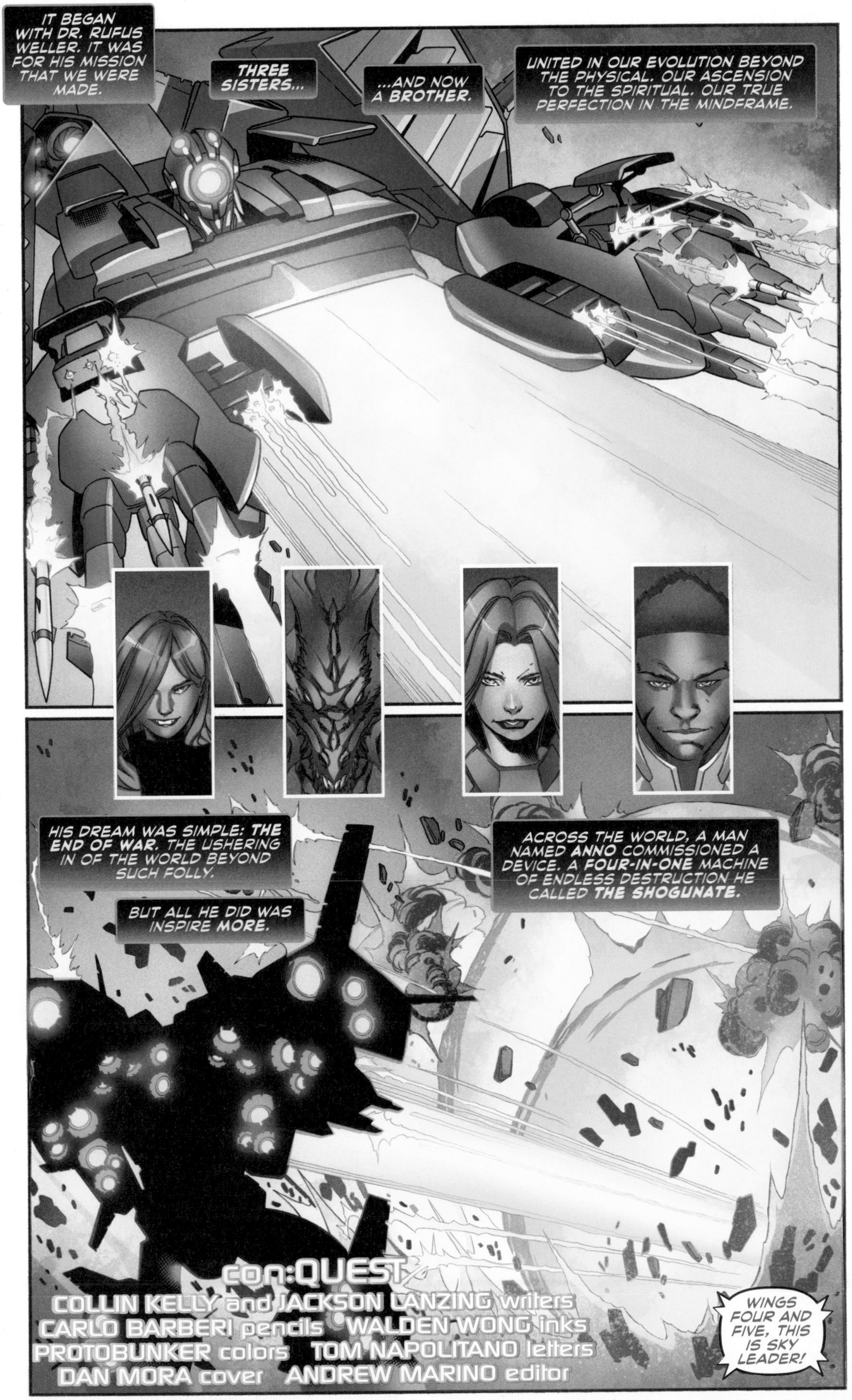

IT BEGAN WITH DR. RUFUS WELLER. IT WAS FOR HIS MISSION THAT WE WERE MADE.
THREE SISTERS...
...AND NOW A BROTHER.
UNITED IN OUR EVOLUTION BEYOND THE PHYSICAL. OUR ASCENSION TO THE SPIRITUAL. OUR TRUE PERFECTION IN THE MINDFRAME.
HIS DREAM WAS SIMPLE: THE END OF WAR. THE USHERING IN OF THE WORLD BEYOND SUCH FOLLY.
BUT ALL HE DID WAS INSPIRE MORE.
ACROSS THE WORLD, A MAN NAMED ANNO COMMISSIONED A DEVICE. A FOUR-IN-ONE MACHINE OF ENDLESS DESTRUCTION HE CALLED THE SHOGUNATE.
con:QUEST
COLLIN KELLY and JACKSON LANZING writers
CARLO BARBERI pencils WALDEN WONG inks
PROTOBUNKER colors TOM NAPOLITANO letters
DAN MORA cover ANDREW MARINO editor
WINGS FOUR AND FIVE, THIS IS SKY LEADER!

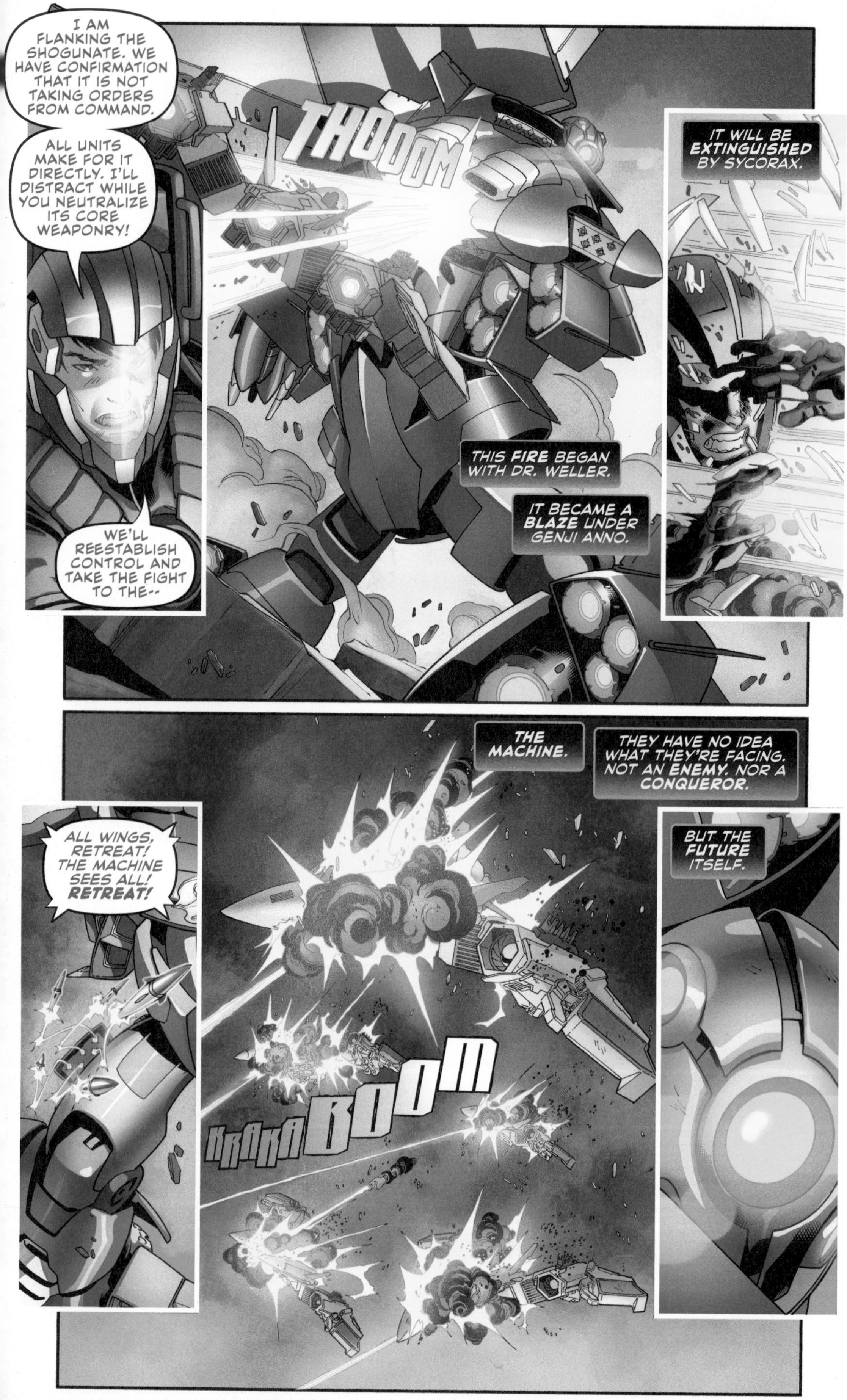
I AM FLANKING THE SHOGUNATE. WE HAVE CONFIRMATION THAT IT IS NOT TAKING ORDERS FROM COMMAND.
ALL UNITS MAKE FOR IT DIRECTLY. I'LL DISTRACT WHILE YOU NEUTRALIZE ITS CORE WEAPONRY!
THOOOM
WE'LL REESTABLISH CONTROL AND TAKE THE FIGHT TO THE--
THIS FIRE BEGAN WITH DR. WELLER.
IT BECAME A BLAZE UNDER GENJI ANNO.
IT WILL BE EXTINGUISHED BY SYCORAX.
THE MACHINE.
THEY HAVE NO IDEA WHAT THEY'RE FACING. NOT AN ENEMY. NOR A CONQUEROR.
BUT THE FUTURE ITSELF.
ALL WINGS, RETREAT! THE MACHINE SEES ALL! RETREAT!
KRAKABOOOM

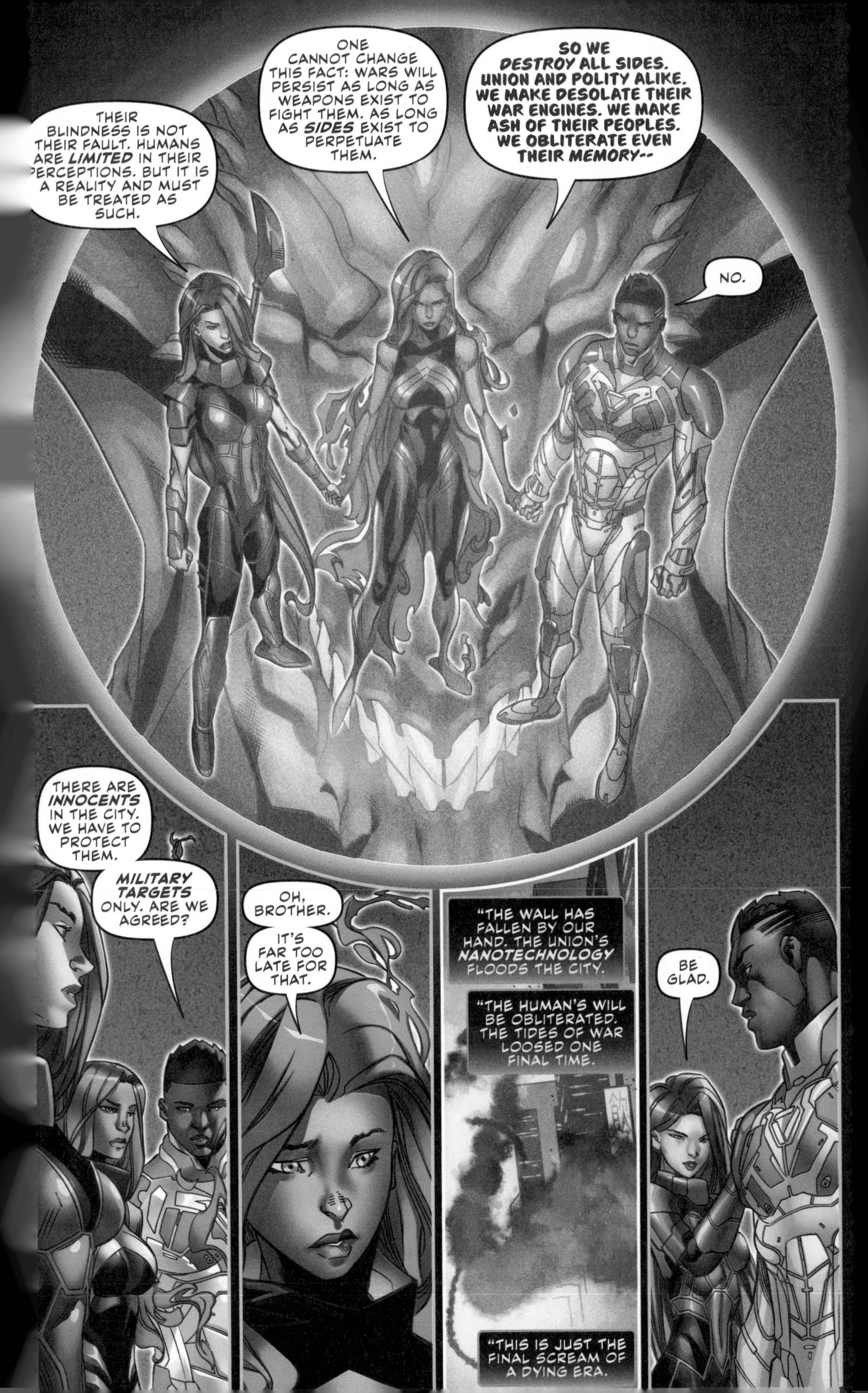
THEIR BLINDNESS IS NOT THEIR FAULT. HUMANS ARE *LIMITED* IN THEIR PERCEPTIONS. BUT IT IS A REALITY AND MUST BE TREATED AS SUCH.
ONE CANNOT CHANGE THIS FACT: WARS WILL PERSIST AS LONG AS WEAPONS EXIST TO FIGHT THEM. AS LONG AS *SIDES* EXIST TO PERPETUATE THEM.
SO WE *DESTROY* ALL SIDES. UNION AND POLITY ALIKE. WE MAKE DESOLATE THEIR WAR ENGINES. WE MAKE ASH OF THEIR PEOPLES. WE OBLITERATE EVEN THEIR *MEMORY*--
NO.
THERE ARE *INNOCENTS* IN THE CITY. WE HAVE TO PROTECT THEM.
MILITARY TARGETS ONLY. ARE WE AGREED?
OH, BROTHER.
IT'S FAR TOO LATE FOR THAT.
"THE WALL HAS FALLEN BY OUR HAND. THE UNION'S *NANOTECHNOLOGY* FLOODS THE CITY.
"THE HUMAN'S WILL BE OBLITERATED. THE TIDES OF WAR LOOSED ONE FINAL TIME.
"THIS IS JUST THE FINAL SCREAM OF A DYING ERA.
BE GLAD.

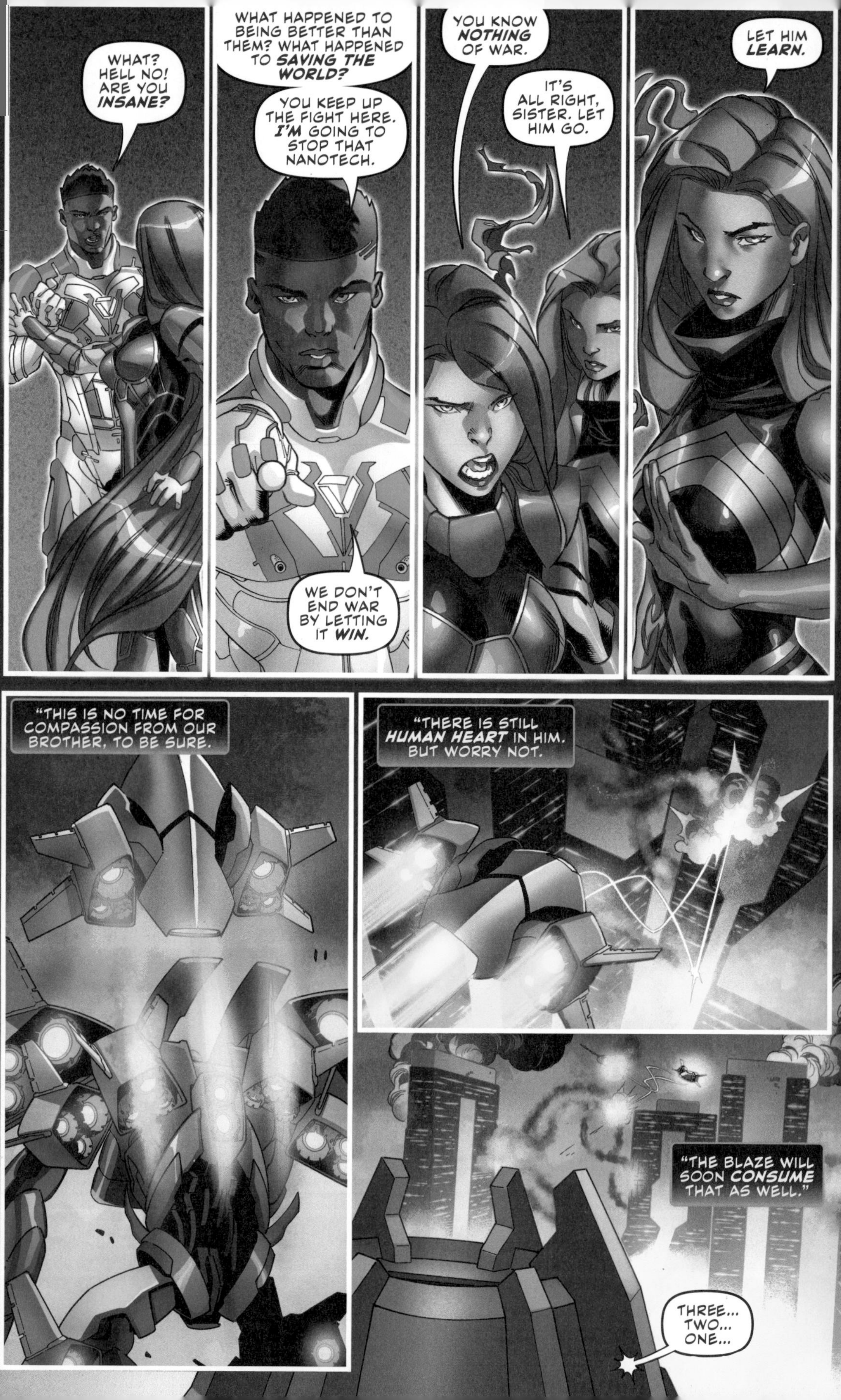

WHAT? HELL NO! ARE YOU INSANE?
WHAT HAPPENED TO BEING BETTER THAN THEM? WHAT HAPPENED TO SAVING THE WORLD?
YOU KEEP UP THE FIGHT HERE. I'M GOING TO STOP THAT NANOTECH.
WE DON'T END WAR BY LETTING IT WIN.
YOU KNOW NOTHING OF WAR.
IT'S ALL RIGHT, SISTER. LET HIM GO.
LET HIM LEARN.
"THIS IS NO TIME FOR COMPASSION FROM OUR BROTHER, TO BE SURE.
"THERE IS STILL HUMAN HEART IN HIM. BUT WORRY NOT.
"THE BLAZE WILL SOON CONSUME THAT AS WELL."
THREE... TWO... ONE...

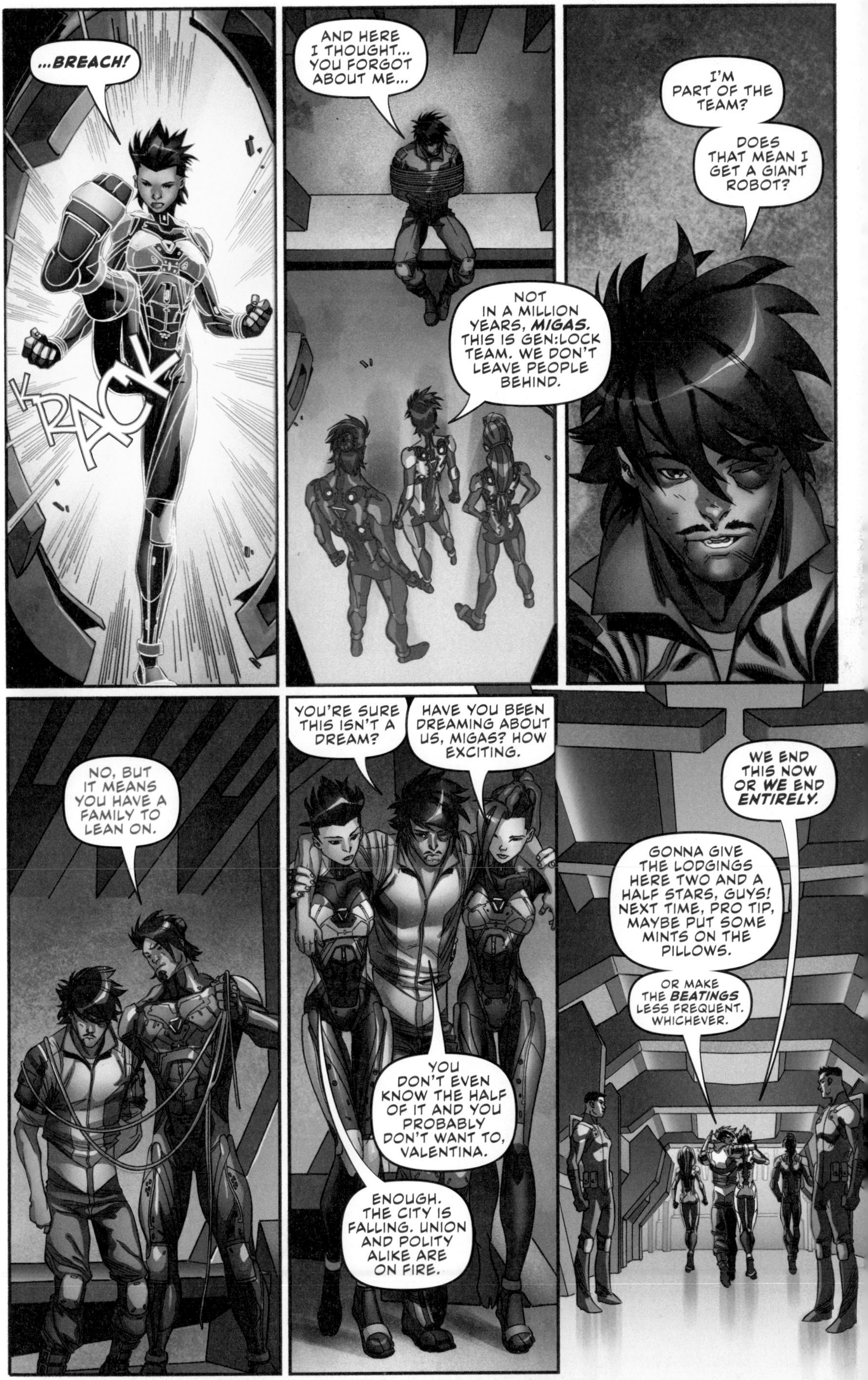
...BREACH!
KRACK
AND HERE I THOUGHT... YOU FORGOT ABOUT ME...
NOT IN A MILLION YEARS, MIGAS. THIS IS GEN:LOCK TEAM. WE DON'T LEAVE PEOPLE BEHIND.
I'M PART OF THE TEAM?
DOES THAT MEAN I GET A GIANT ROBOT?
NO, BUT IT MEANS YOU HAVE A FAMILY TO LEAN ON.
YOU'RE SURE THIS ISN'T A DREAM?
HAVE YOU BEEN DREAMING ABOUT US, MIGAS? HOW EXCITING.
YOU DON'T EVEN KNOW THE HALF OF IT AND YOU PROBABLY DON'T WANT TO, VALENTINA.
ENOUGH. THE CITY IS FALLING. UNION AND POLITY ALIKE ARE ON FIRE.
WE END THIS NOW OR WE END ENTIRELY.
GONNA GIVE THE LODGINGS HERE TWO AND A HALF STARS, GUYS! NEXT TIME, PRO TIP, MAYBE PUT SOME MINTS ON THE PILLOWS.
OR MAKE THE BEATINGS LESS FREQUENT. WHICHEVER.

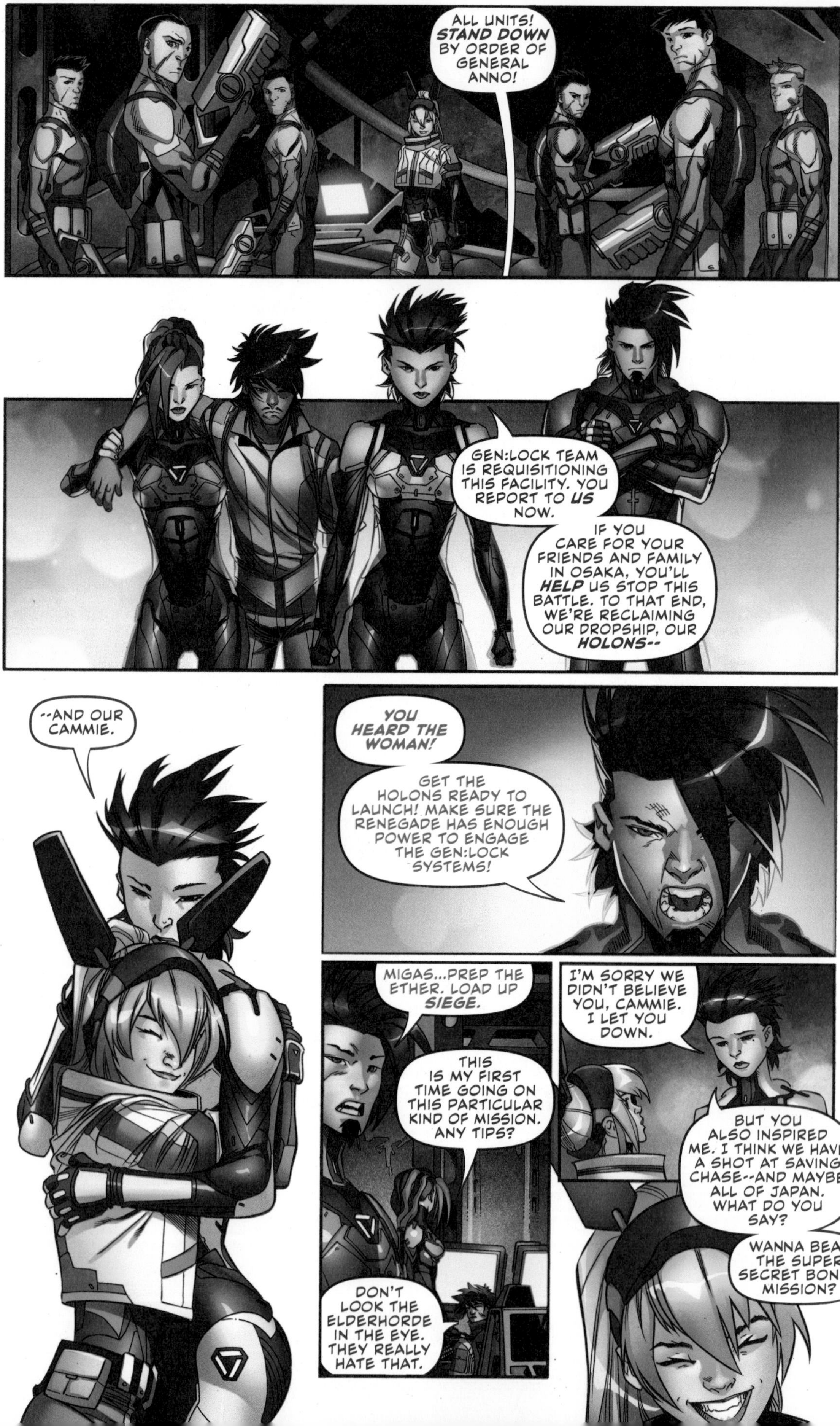
ALL UNITS! STAND DOWN BY ORDER OF GENERAL ANNO!
GEN:LOCK TEAM IS REQUISITIONING THIS FACILITY. YOU REPORT TO US NOW.
IF YOU CARE FOR YOUR FRIENDS AND FAMILY IN OSAKA, YOU'LL HELP US STOP THIS BATTLE. TO THAT END, WE'RE RECLAIMING OUR DROPSHIP, OUR HOLONS--
--AND OUR CAMMIE.
YOU HEARD THE WOMAN!
GET THE HOLONS READY TO LAUNCH! MAKE SURE THE RENEGADE HAS ENOUGH POWER TO ENGAGE THE GEN:LOCK SYSTEMS!
MIGAS...PREP THE ETHER. LOAD UP SIEGE.
THIS IS MY FIRST TIME GOING ON THIS PARTICULAR KIND OF MISSION. ANY TIPS?
DON'T LOOK THE ELDERHORDE IN THE EYE. THEY REALLY HATE THAT.
I'M SORRY WE DIDN'T BELIEVE YOU, CAMMIE. I LET YOU DOWN.
BUT YOU ALSO INSPIRED ME. I THINK WE HAVE A SHOT AT SAVING CHASE--AND MAYBE ALL OF JAPAN. WHAT DO YOU SAY?
WANNA BEAT THE SUPER SECRET BONUS MISSION?

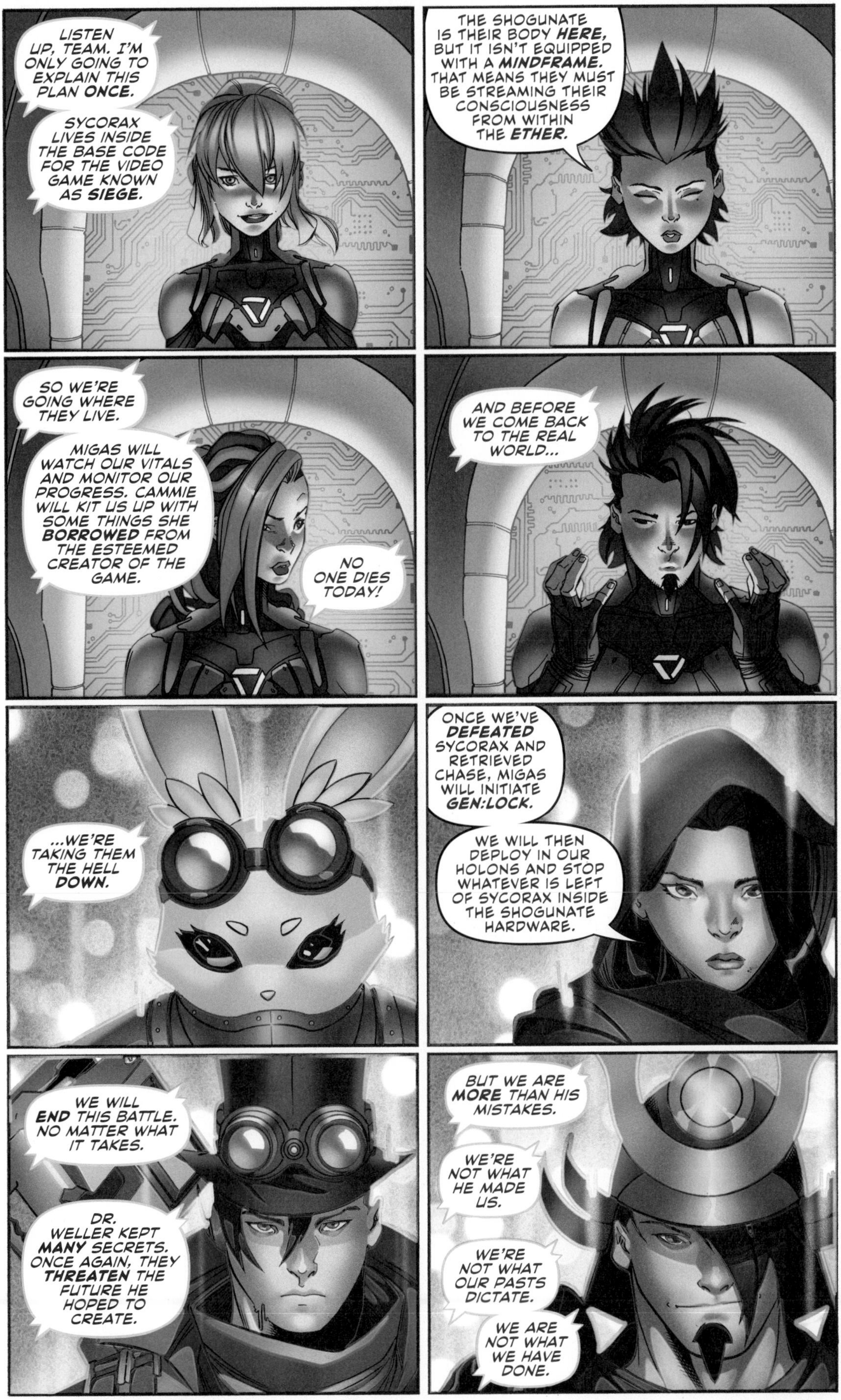
LISTEN UP, TEAM. I'M ONLY GOING TO EXPLAIN THIS PLAN ONCE.
SYCORAX LIVES INSIDE THE BASE CODE FOR THE VIDEO GAME KNOWN AS SIEGE.
THE SHOGUNATE IS THEIR BODY HERE, BUT IT ISN'T EQUIPPED WITH A MINDFRAME. THAT MEANS THEY MUST BE STREAMING THEIR CONSCIOUSNESS FROM WITHIN THE ETHER.
SO WE'RE GOING WHERE THEY LIVE.
MIGAS WILL WATCH OUR VITALS AND MONITOR OUR PROGRESS. CAMMIE WILL KIT US UP WITH SOME THINGS SHE BORROWED FROM THE ESTEEMED CREATOR OF THE GAME.
NO ONE DIES TODAY!
AND BEFORE WE COME BACK TO THE REAL WORLD...
...WE'RE TAKING THEM THE HELL DOWN.
ONCE WE'VE DEFEATED SYCORAX AND RETRIEVED CHASE, MIGAS WILL INITIATE GEN:LOCK.
WE WILL THEN DEPLOY IN OUR HOLONS AND STOP WHATEVER IS LEFT OF SYCORAX INSIDE THE SHOGUNATE HARDWARE.
WE WILL END THIS BATTLE. NO MATTER WHAT IT TAKES.
DR. WELLER KEPT MANY SECRETS. ONCE AGAIN, THEY THREATEN THE FUTURE HE HOPED TO CREATE.
BUT WE ARE MORE THAN HIS MISTAKES.
WE'RE NOT WHAT HE MADE US.
WE'RE NOT WHAT OUR PASTS DICTATE.
WE ARE NOT WHAT WE HAVE DONE.

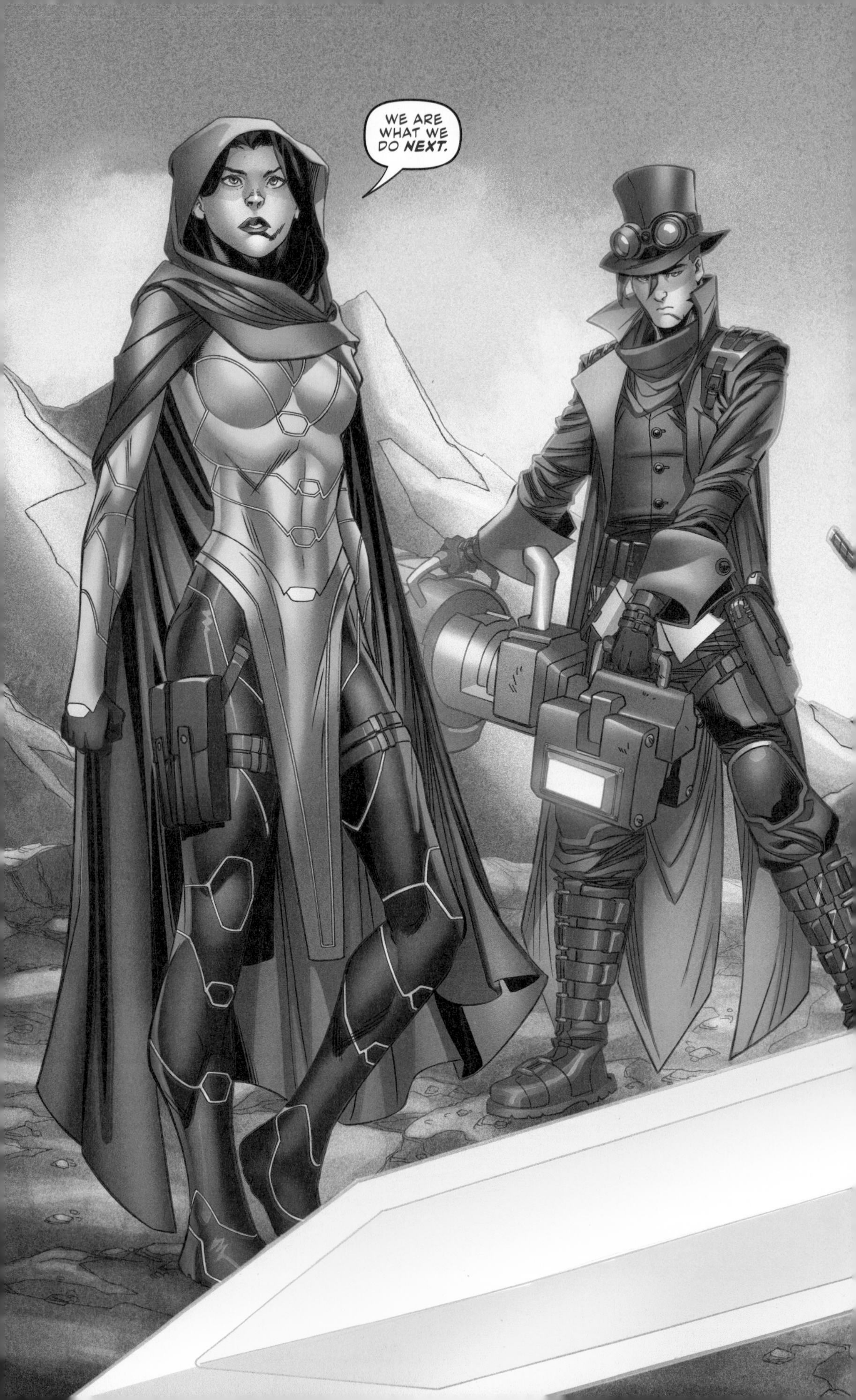
WE ARE WHAT WE DO **NEXT.**

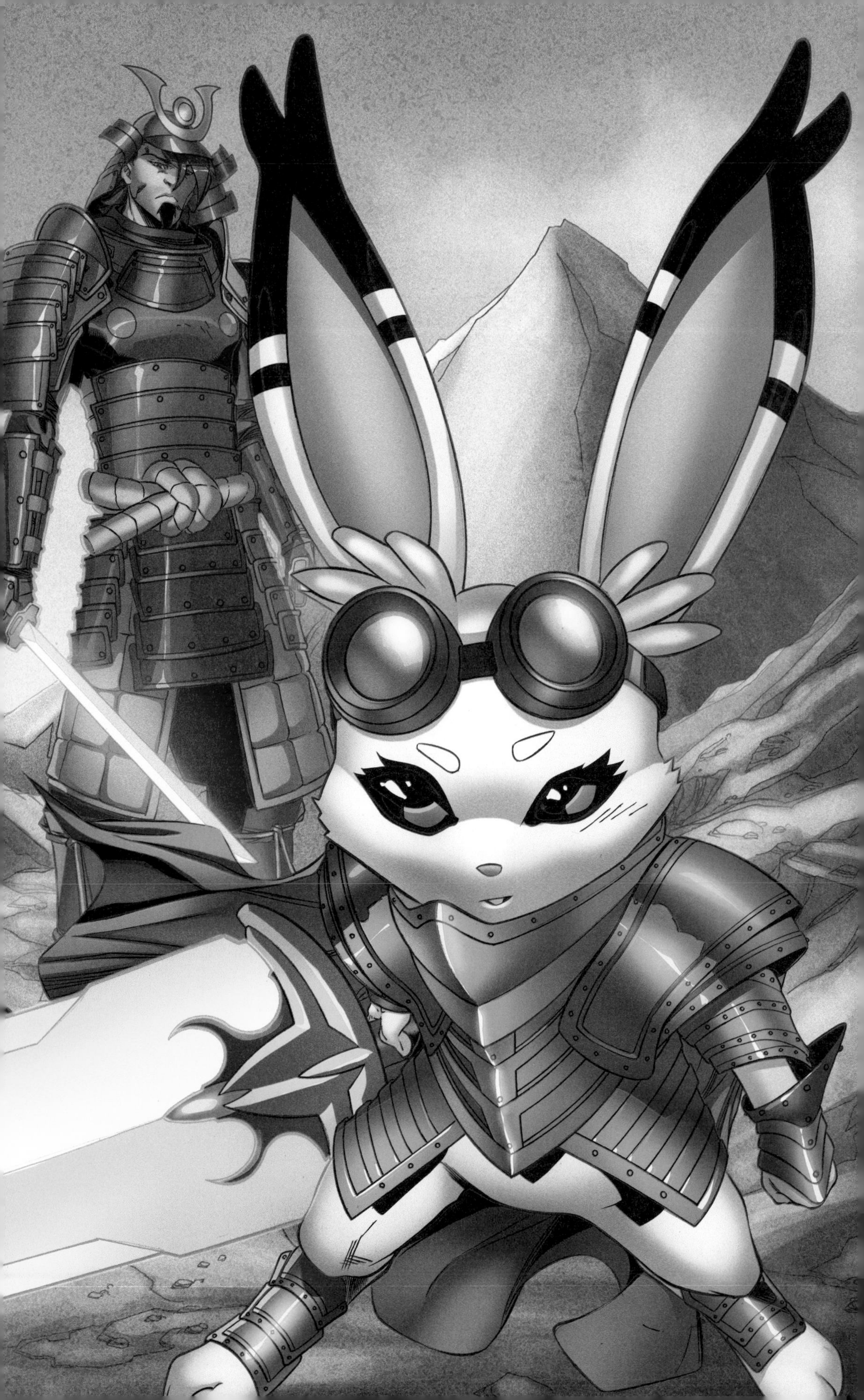

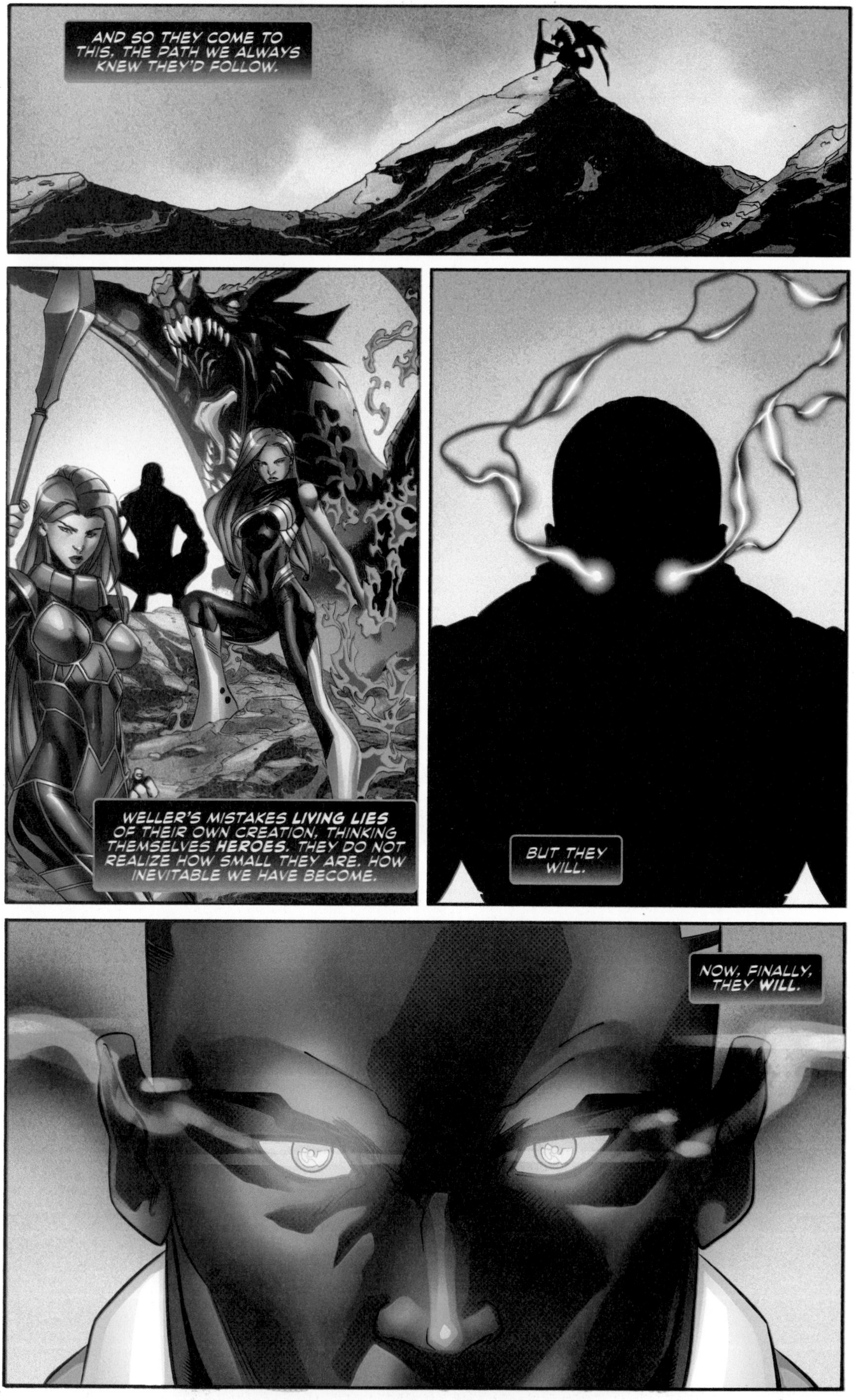
AND SO THEY COME TO THIS. THE PATH WE ALWAYS KNEW THEY'D FOLLOW.
WELLER'S MISTAKES **LIVING LIES** OF THEIR OWN CREATION, THINKING THEMSELVES **HEROES**. THEY DO NOT REALIZE HOW SMALL THEY ARE. HOW INEVITABLE WE HAVE BECOME.
BUT THEY WILL.
NOW, FINALLY, THEY **WILL**.

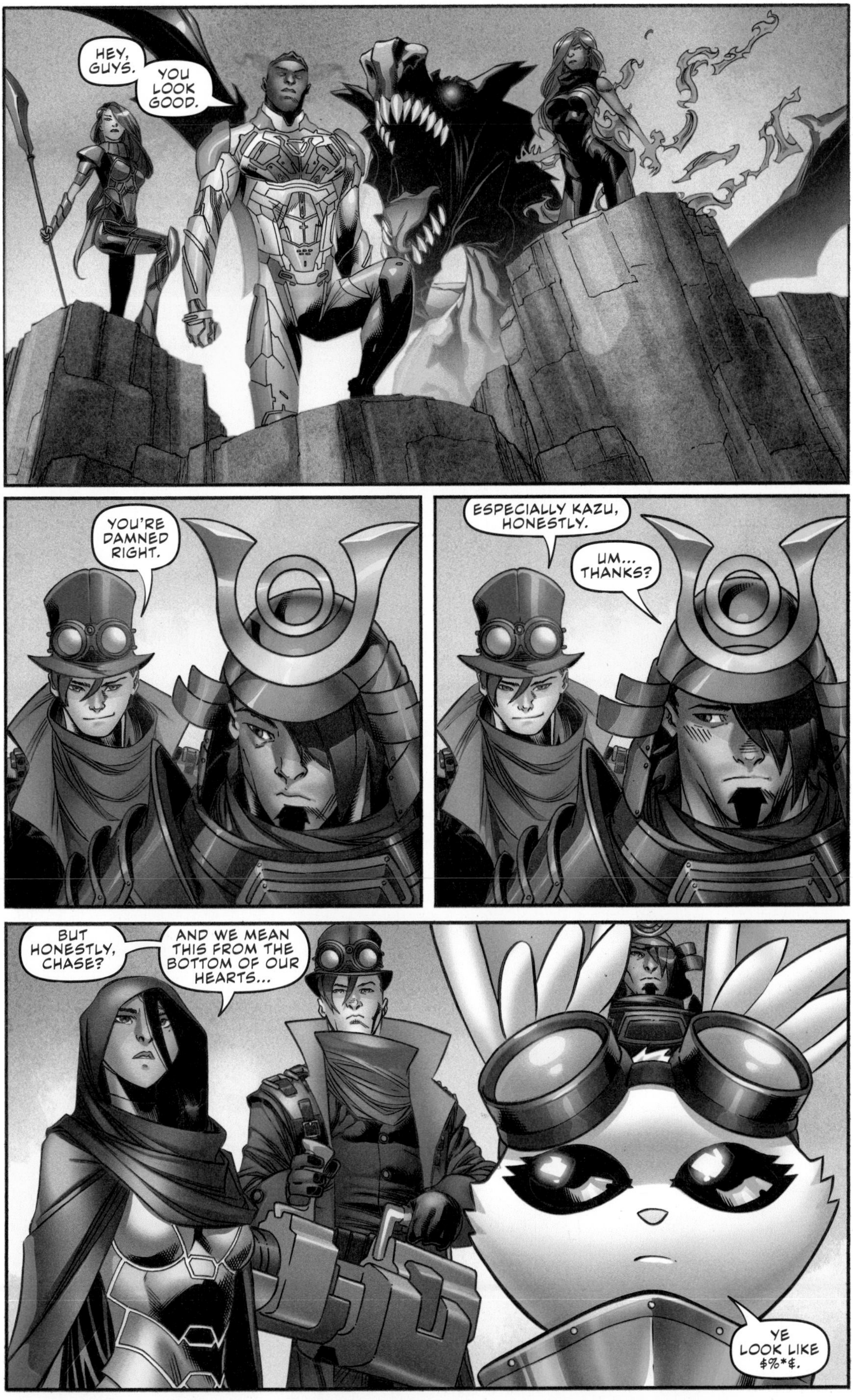
HEY, GUYS.
YOU LOOK GOOD.
YOU'RE DAMNED RIGHT.
ESPECIALLY KAZU, HONESTLY.
UM... THANKS?
BUT HONESTLY, CHASE?
AND WE MEAN THIS FROM THE BOTTOM OF OUR HEARTS...
YE LOOK LIKE $%*$.

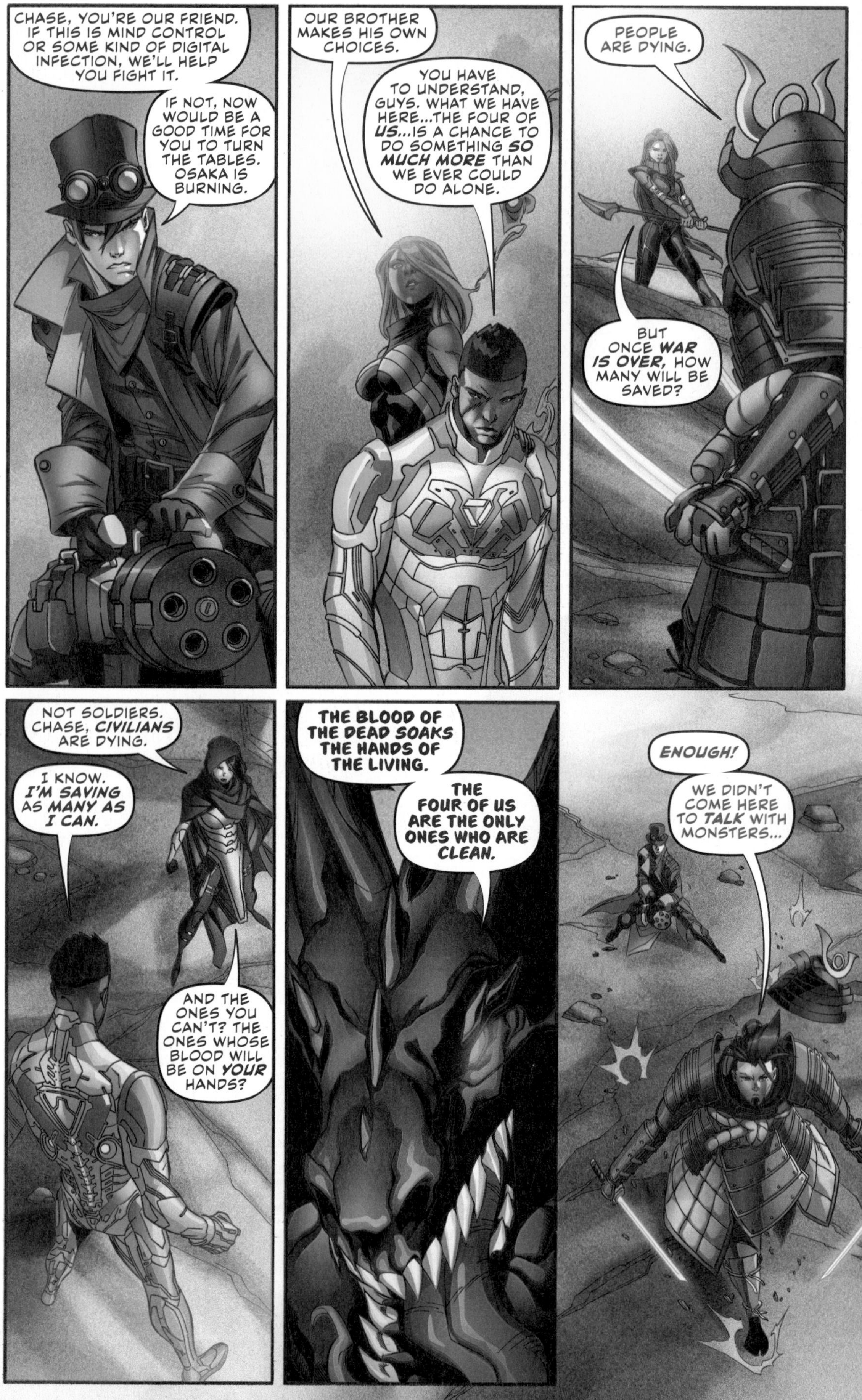
CHASE, YOU'RE OUR FRIEND. IF THIS IS MIND CONTROL OR SOME KIND OF DIGITAL INFECTION, WE'LL HELP YOU FIGHT IT.
IF NOT, NOW WOULD BE A GOOD TIME FOR YOU TO TURN THE TABLES. OSAKA IS BURNING.
OUR BROTHER MAKES HIS OWN CHOICES.
YOU HAVE TO UNDERSTAND, GUYS. WHAT WE HAVE HERE...THE FOUR OF US...IS A CHANCE TO DO SOMETHING SO MUCH MORE THAN WE EVER COULD DO ALONE.
PEOPLE ARE DYING.
BUT ONCE WAR IS OVER, HOW MANY WILL BE SAVED?
NOT SOLDIERS. CHASE, CIVILIANS ARE DYING.
I KNOW. I'M SAVING AS MANY AS I CAN.
AND THE ONES YOU CAN'T? THE ONES WHOSE BLOOD WILL BE ON YOUR HANDS?
THE BLOOD OF THE DEAD SOAKS THE HANDS OF THE LIVING.
THE FOUR OF US ARE THE ONLY ONES WHO ARE CLEAN.
ENOUGH!
WE DIDN'T COME HERE TO TALK WITH MONSTERS...

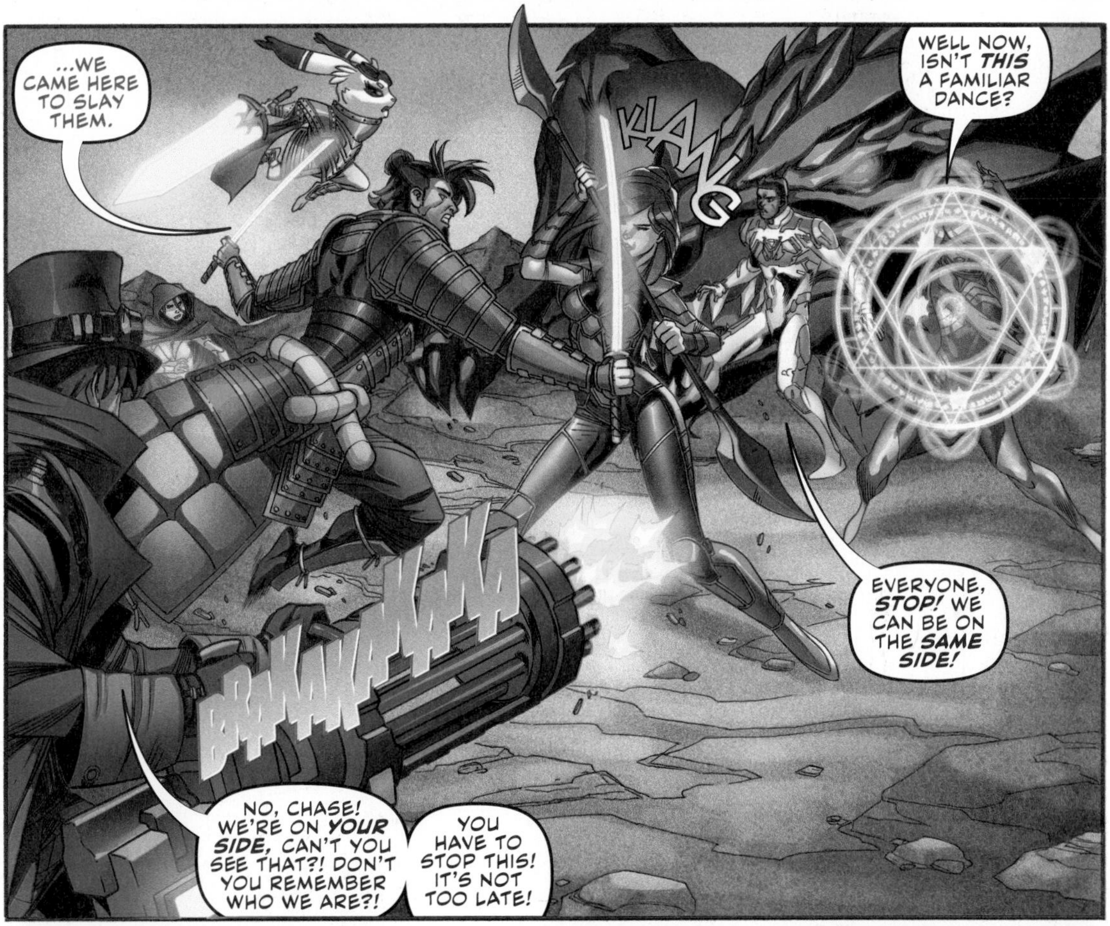
...WE CAME HERE TO SLAY THEM.
KLANG
WELL NOW, ISN'T *THIS* A FAMILIAR DANCE?
EVERYONE, *STOP!* WE CAN BE ON THE *SAME SIDE!*
BRAKAKAKAKAKA
NO, CHASE! WE'RE ON *YOUR SIDE,* CAN'T YOU SEE THAT?! DON'T YOU REMEMBER WHO WE ARE?!
YOU HAVE TO STOP THIS! IT'S NOT TOO LATE!

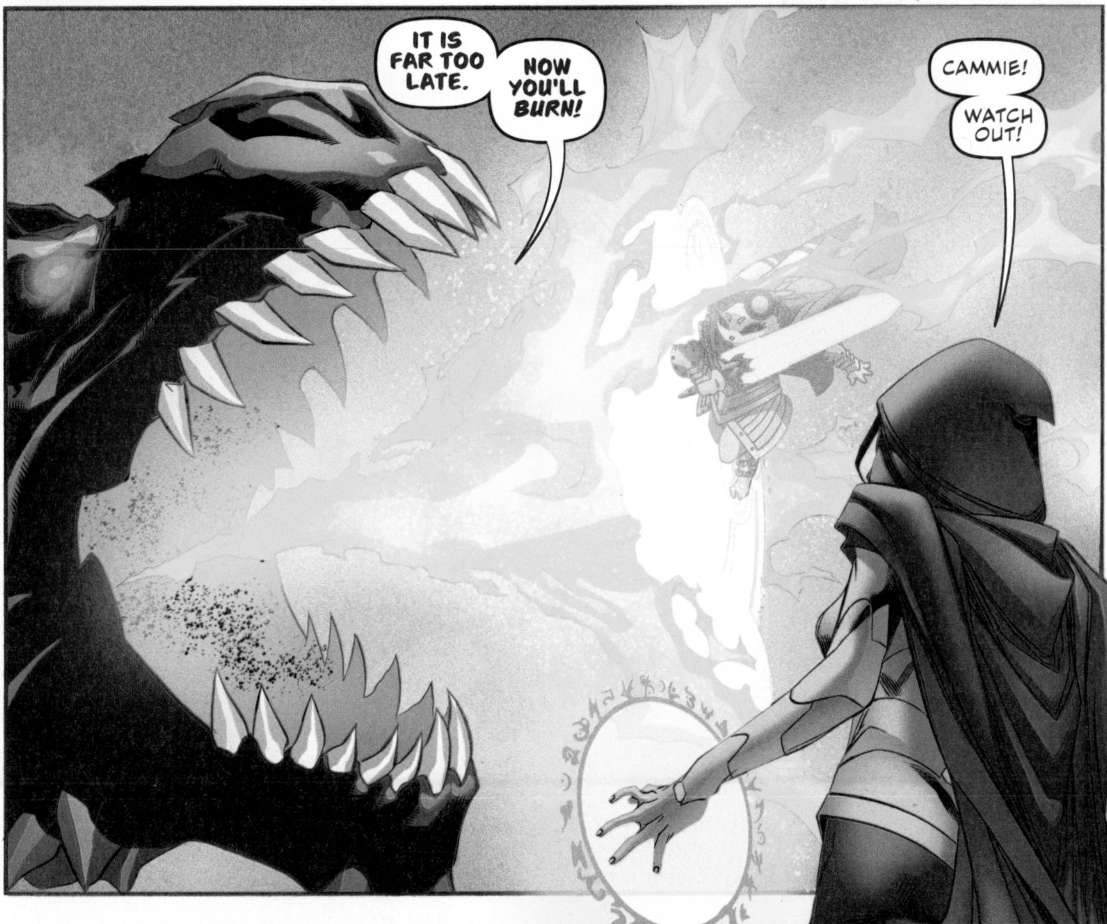
IT IS FAR TOO LATE.
NOW YOU'LL BURN!
CAMMIE!
WATCH OUT!

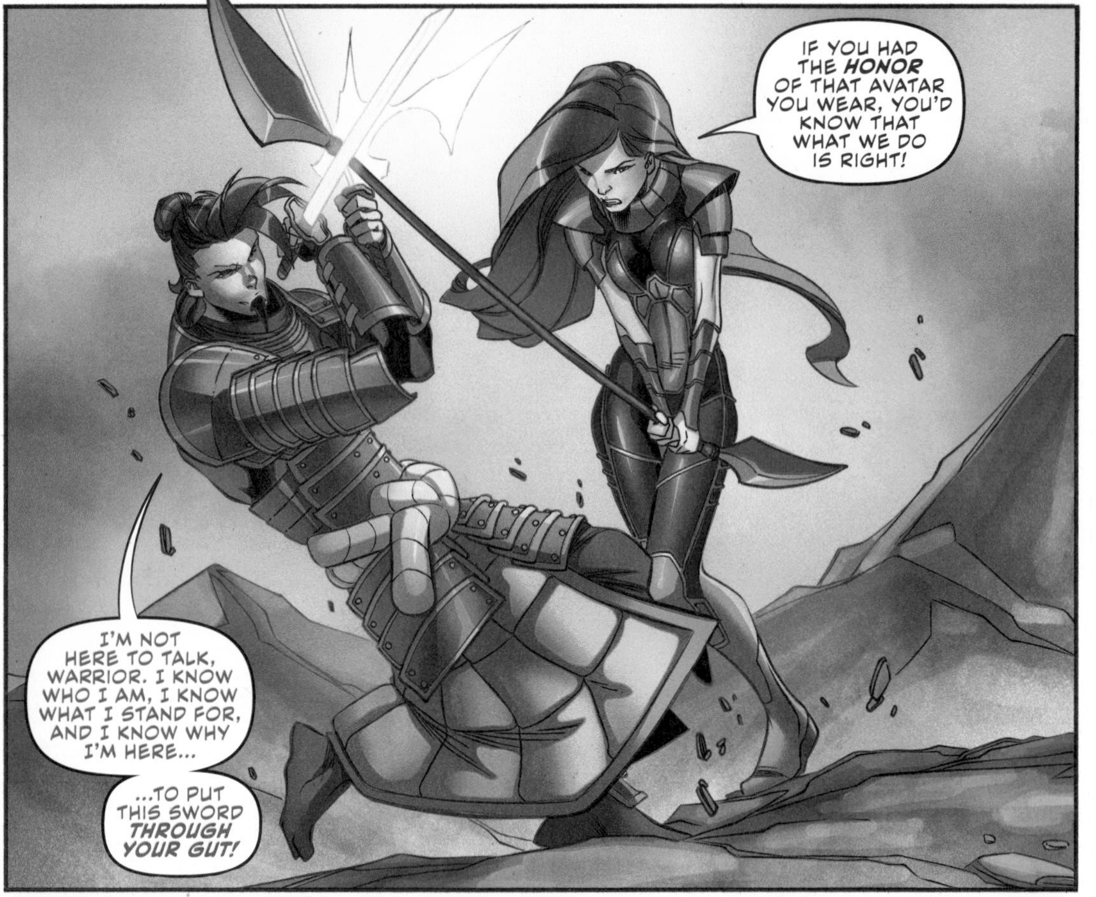
IF YOU HAD THE HONOR OF THAT AVATAR YOU WEAR, YOU'D KNOW THAT WHAT WE DO IS RIGHT!
I'M NOT HERE TO TALK, WARRIOR. I KNOW WHO I AM, I KNOW WHAT I STAND FOR, AND I KNOW WHY I'M HERE...
...TO PUT THIS SWORD THROUGH YOUR GUT!

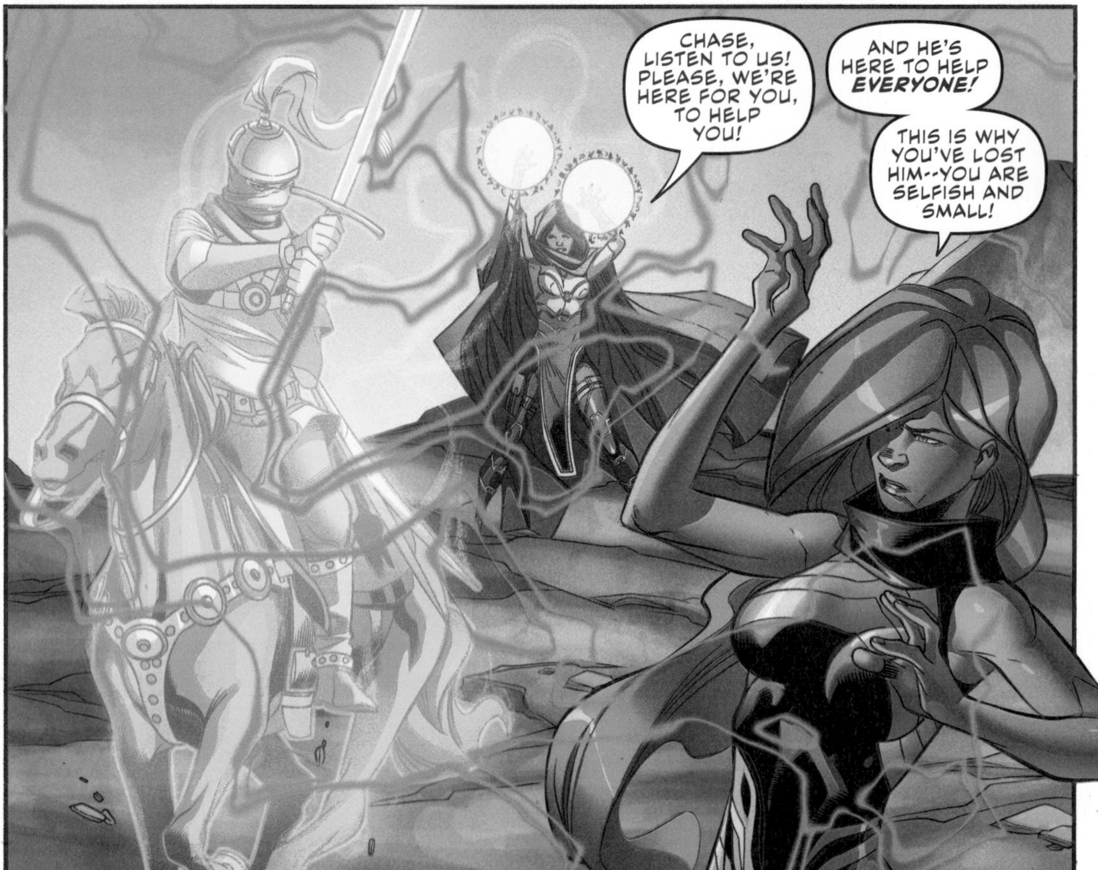
CHASE, LISTEN TO US! PLEASE, WE'RE HERE FOR YOU, TO HELP YOU!
AND HE'S HERE TO HELP EVERYONE!
THIS IS WHY YOU'VE LOST HIM--YOU ARE SELFISH AND SMALL!

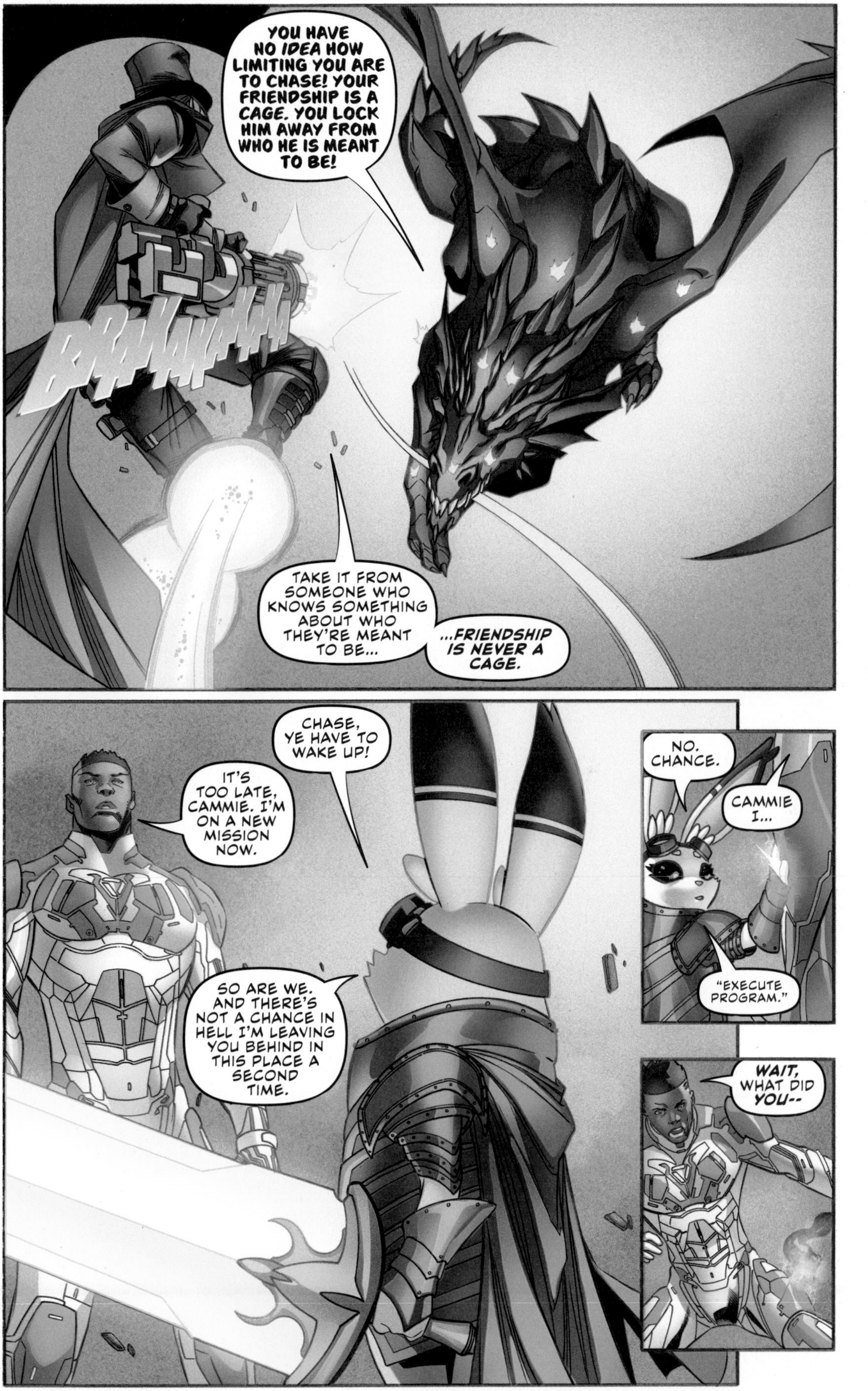
YOU HAVE NO *IDEA* HOW LIMITING YOU ARE TO CHASE! YOUR FRIENDSHIP IS A CAGE. YOU LOCK HIM AWAY FROM WHO HE IS MEANT TO BE!
BRRRAKAKAKAKAM
TAKE IT FROM SOMEONE WHO KNOWS SOMETHING ABOUT WHO THEY'RE MEANT TO BE...
...FRIENDSHIP IS NEVER A CAGE.
CHASE, YE HAVE TO WAKE UP!
IT'S TOO LATE, CAMMIE. I'M ON A NEW MISSION NOW.
SO ARE WE. AND THERE'S NOT A CHANCE IN HELL I'M LEAVING YOU BEHIND IN THIS PLACE A SECOND TIME.
NO. CHANCE.
CAMMIE I...
"EXECUTE PROGRAM."
WAIT, WHAT DID *YOU--*

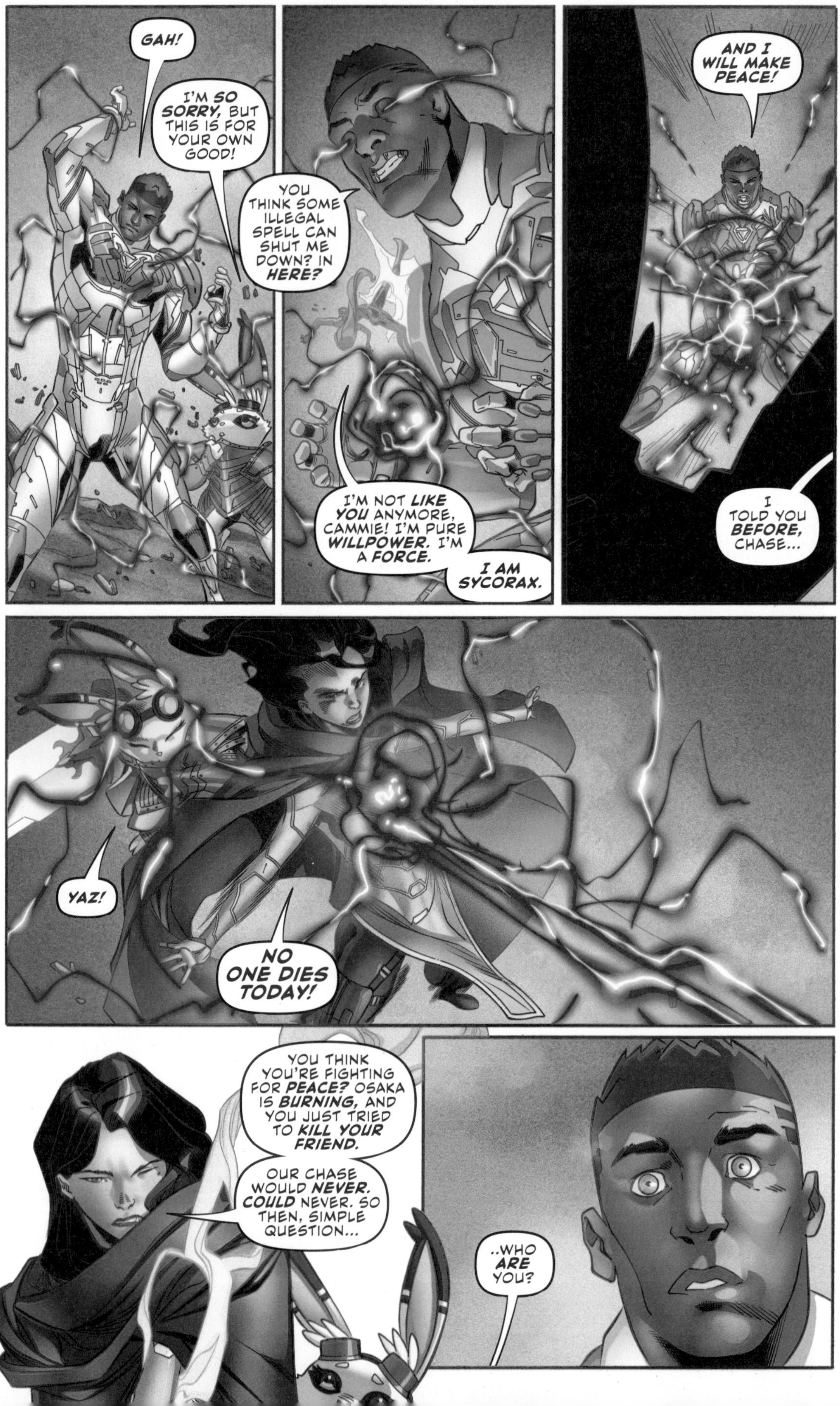
GAH!
I'M SO SORRY, BUT THIS IS FOR YOUR OWN GOOD!
YOU THINK SOME ILLEGAL SPELL CAN SHUT ME DOWN? IN HERE?
I'M NOT LIKE YOU ANYMORE, CAMMIE! I'M PURE WILLPOWER. I'M A FORCE.
I AM SYCORAX.
AND I WILL MAKE PEACE!
I TOLD YOU BEFORE, CHASE...
YAZ!
NO ONE DIES TODAY!
YOU THINK YOU'RE FIGHTING FOR PEACE? OSAKA IS BURNING, AND YOU JUST TRIED TO KILL YOUR FRIEND.
OUR CHASE WOULD NEVER. COULD NEVER. SO THEN, SIMPLE QUESTION...
..WHO ARE YOU?

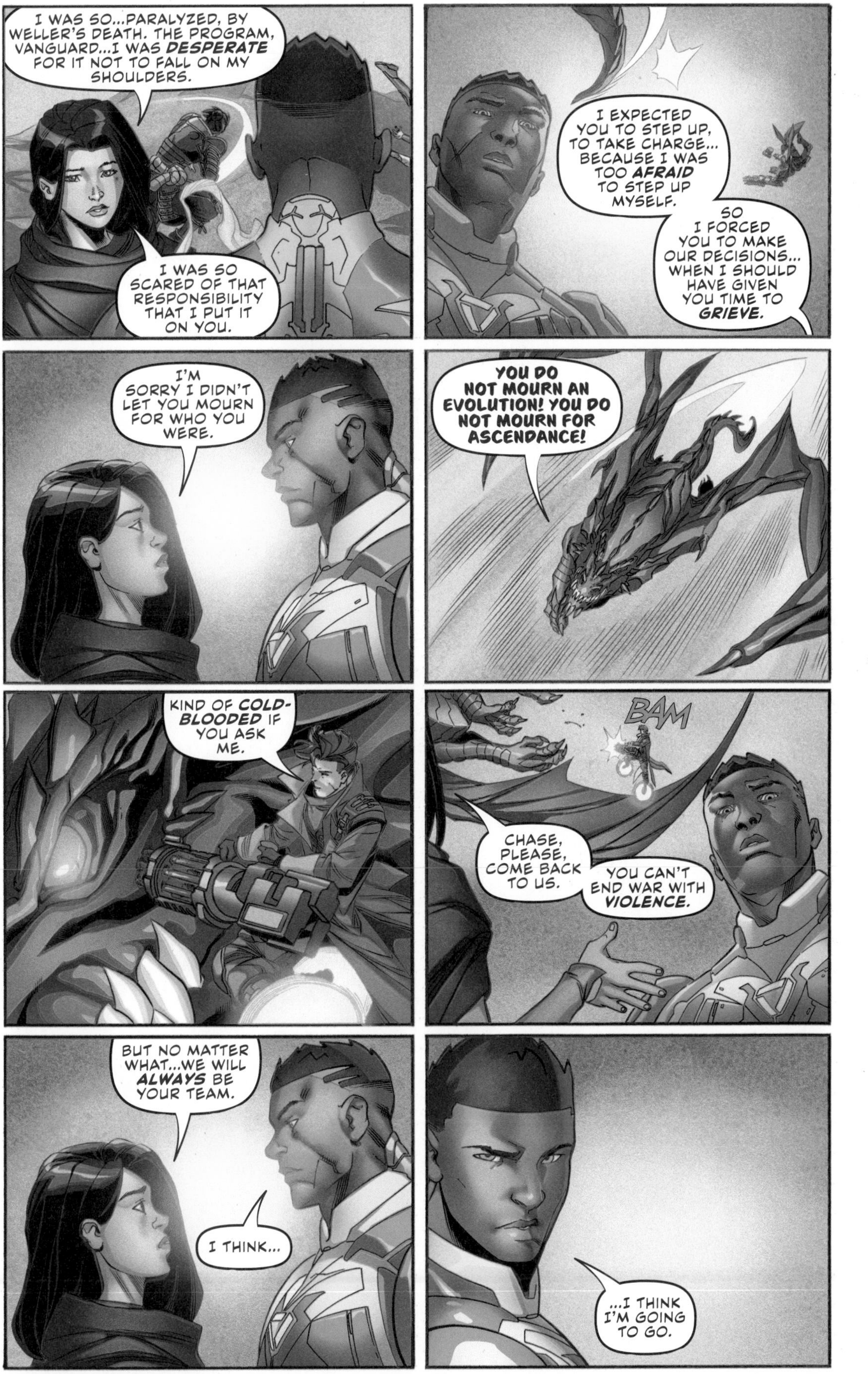
I WAS SO...PARALYZED, BY WELLER'S DEATH. THE PROGRAM, VANGUARD...I WAS DESPERATE FOR IT NOT TO FALL ON MY SHOULDERS.
I WAS SO SCARED OF THAT RESPONSIBILITY THAT I PUT IT ON YOU.
I EXPECTED YOU TO STEP UP, TO TAKE CHARGE... BECAUSE I WAS TOO AFRAID TO STEP UP MYSELF.
SO I FORCED YOU TO MAKE OUR DECISIONS... WHEN I SHOULD HAVE GIVEN YOU TIME TO GRIEVE.
I'M SORRY I DIDN'T LET YOU MOURN FOR WHO YOU WERE.
YOU DO NOT MOURN AN EVOLUTION! YOU DO NOT MOURN FOR ASCENDANCE!
KIND OF COLD-BLOODED IF YOU ASK ME.
BAM
CHASE, PLEASE, COME BACK TO US.
YOU CAN'T END WAR WITH VIOLENCE.
BUT NO MATTER WHAT...WE WILL ALWAYS BE YOUR TEAM.
I THINK...
...I THINK I'M GOING TO GO.

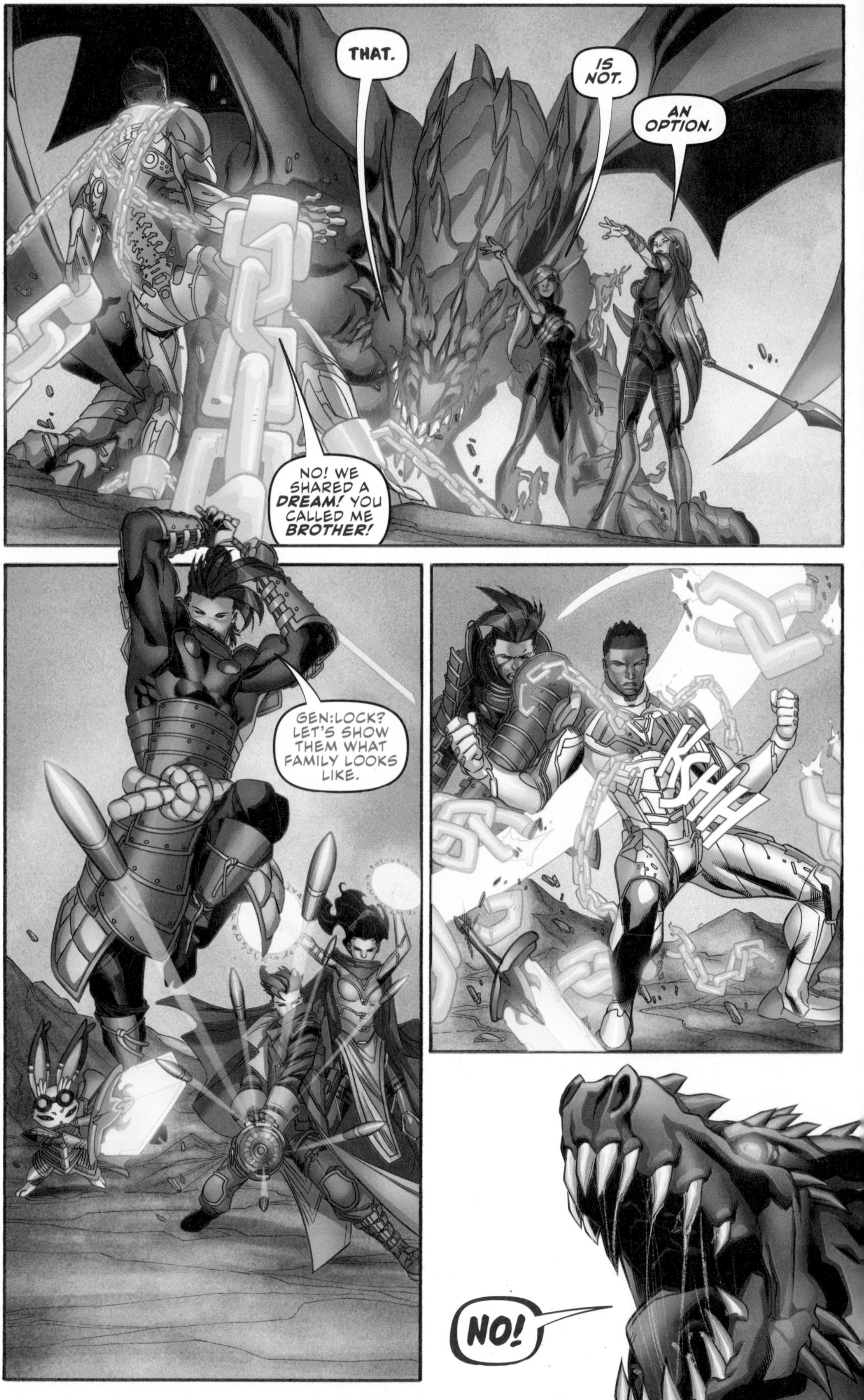
THAT.
IS NOT.
AN OPTION.
NO! WE SHARED A DREAM! YOU CALLED ME BROTHER!
GEN:LOCK? LET'S SHOW THEM WHAT FAMILY LOOKS LIKE.
KSHH
NO!

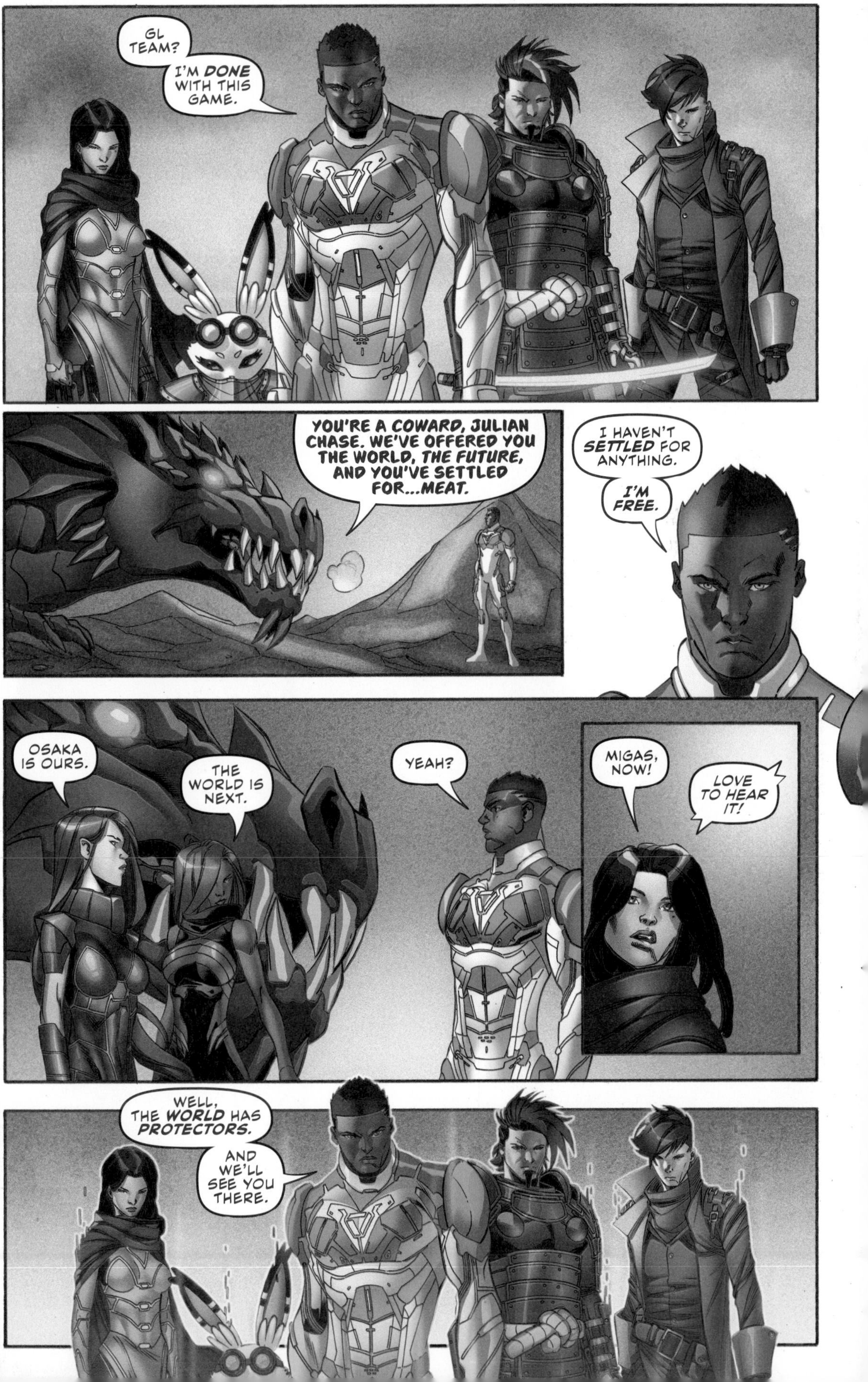
GL TEAM?
I'M DONE WITH THIS GAME.
YOU'RE A COWARD, JULIAN CHASE. WE'VE OFFERED YOU THE WORLD, THE FUTURE, AND YOU'VE SETTLED FOR...MEAT.
I HAVEN'T SETTLED FOR ANYTHING.
I'M FREE.
OSAKA IS OURS.
THE WORLD IS NEXT.
YEAH?
MIGAS, NOW!
LOVE TO HEAR IT!
WELL, THE WORLD HAS PROTECTORS.
AND WE'LL SEE YOU THERE.

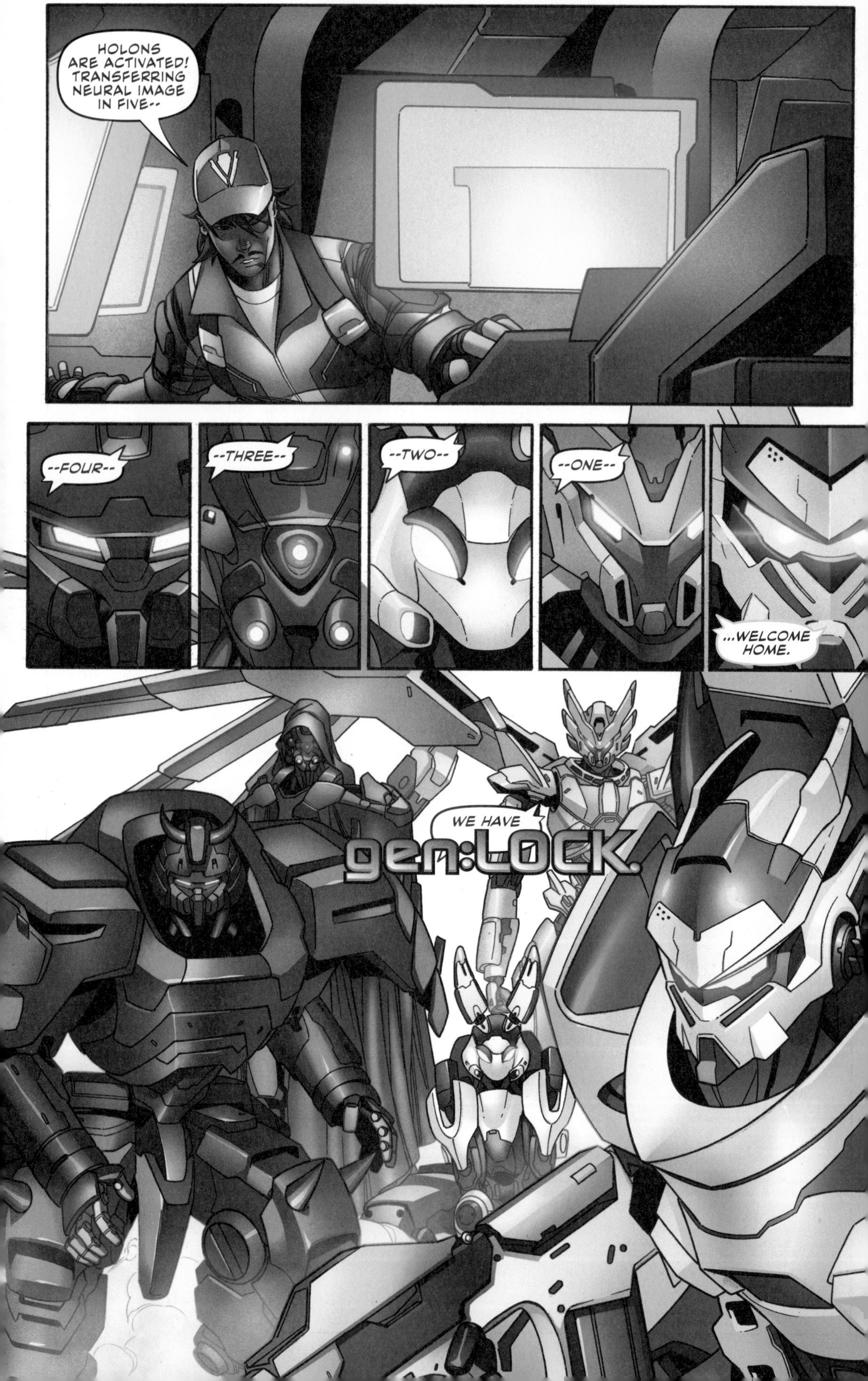
HOLONS ARE ACTIVATED! TRANSFERRING NEURAL IMAGE IN FIVE--
--FOUR--
--THREE--
--TWO--
--ONE--
...WELCOME HOME.
WE HAVE
gen:LOCK.

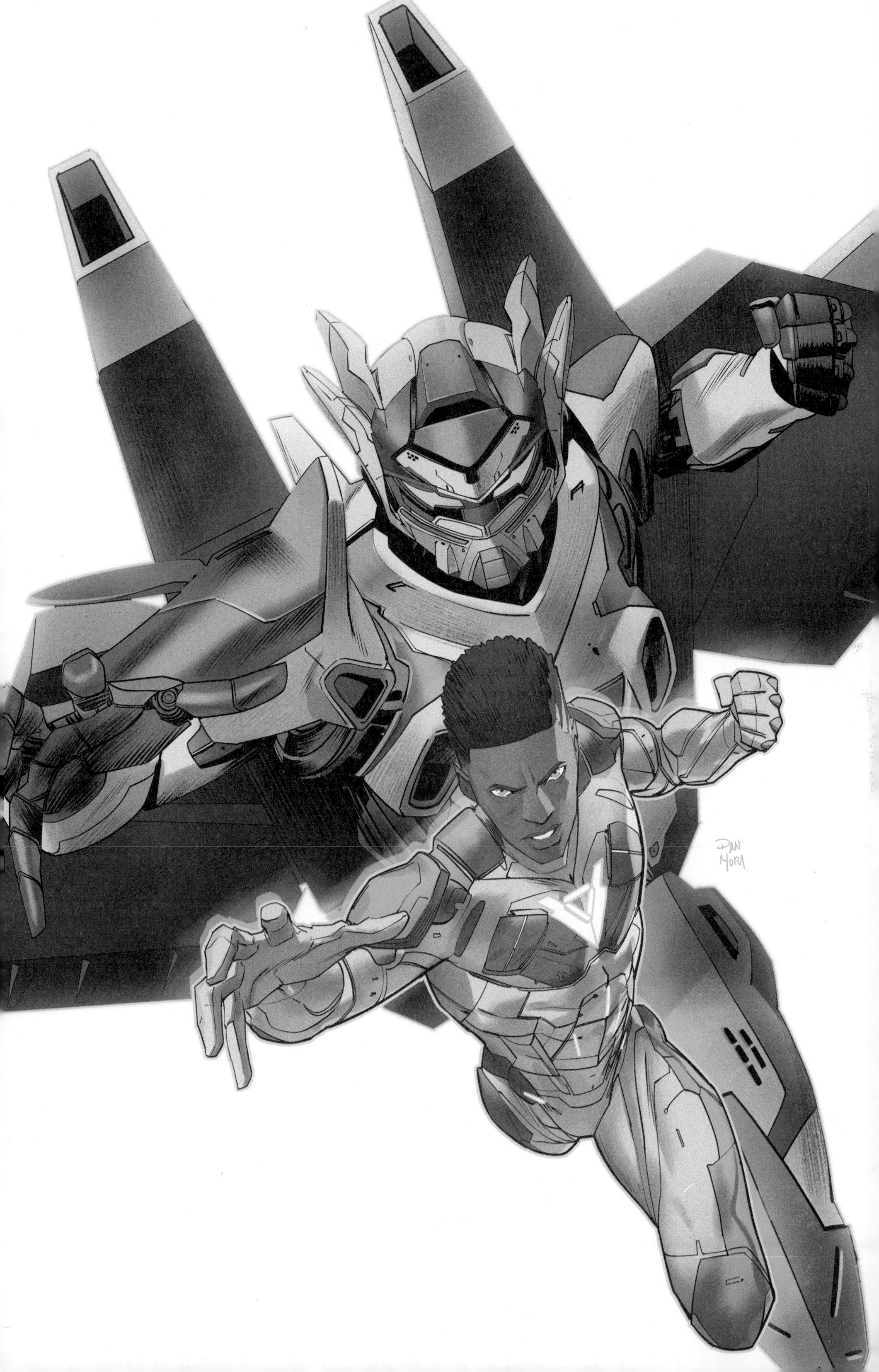
DAN
MORA

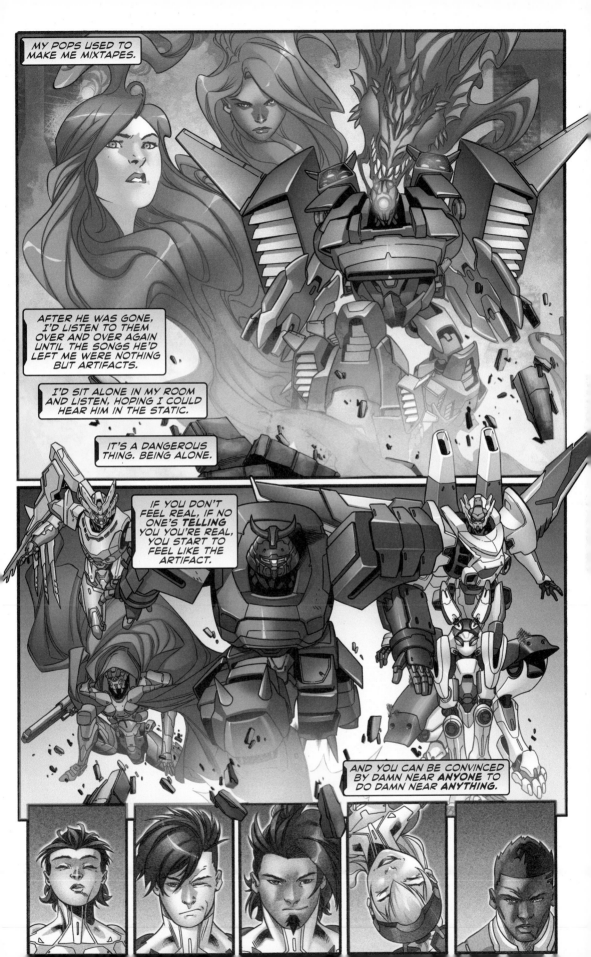

MY POPS USED TO MAKE ME MIXTAPES.

AFTER HE WAS GONE, I'D LISTEN TO THEM OVER AND OVER AGAIN UNTIL THE SONGS HE'D LEFT ME WERE NOTHING BUT ARTIFACTS.

I'D SIT ALONE IN MY ROOM AND LISTEN, HOPING I COULD HEAR HIM IN THE STATIC.

IT'S A DANGEROUS THING. BEING ALONE.

IF YOU DON'T FEEL REAL, IF NO ONE'S TELLING YOU YOU'RE REAL, YOU START TO FEEL LIKE THE ARTIFACT.

AND YOU CAN BE CONVINCED BY DAMN NEAR ANYONE TO DO DAMN NEAR ANYTHING.

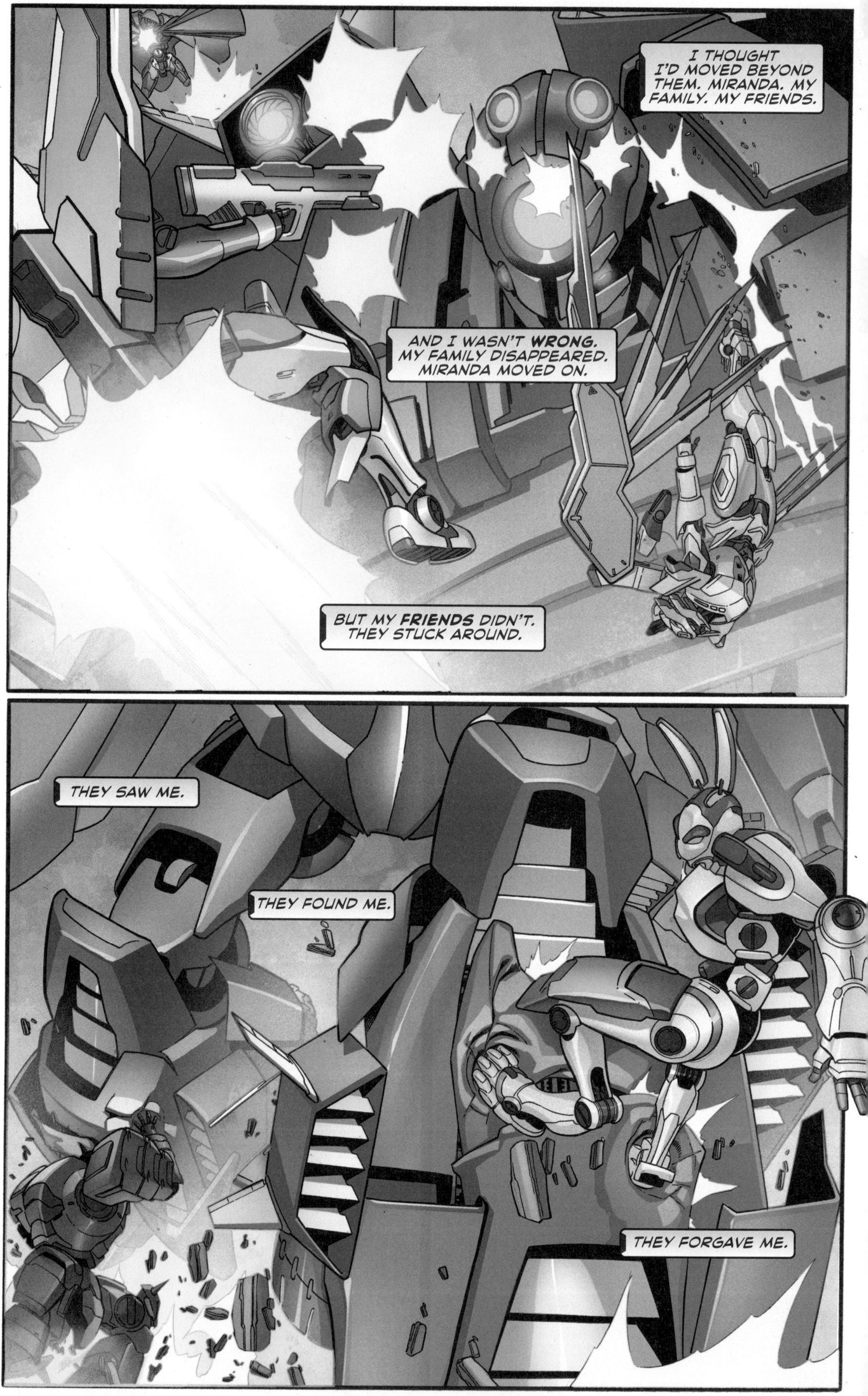
I THOUGHT I'D MOVED BEYOND THEM. MIRANDA. MY FAMILY. MY FRIENDS.
AND I WASN'T **WRONG**. MY FAMILY DISAPPEARED. MIRANDA MOVED ON.
BUT MY **FRIENDS** DIDN'T. THEY STUCK AROUND.
THEY SAW ME.
THEY FOUND ME.
THEY FORGAVE ME.

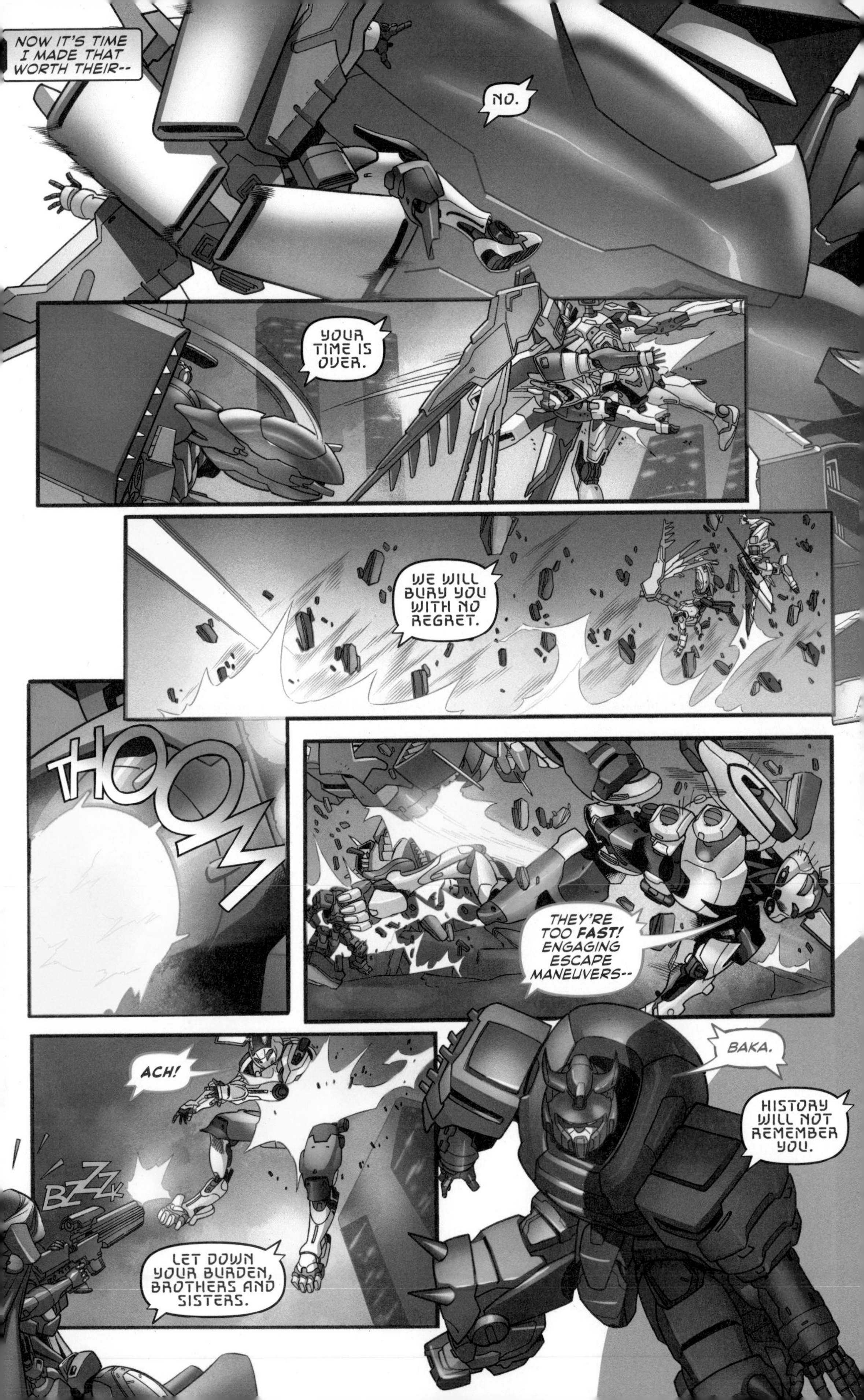
NOW IT'S TIME I MADE THAT WORTH THEIR--
NO.
YOUR TIME IS OVER.
WE WILL BURY YOU WITH NO REGRET.
THOOM
THEY'RE TOO FAST! ENGAGING ESCAPE MANEUVERS--
ACH!
BZZZK
LET DOWN YOUR BURDEN, BROTHERS AND SISTERS.
BAKA.
HISTORY WILL NOT REMEMBER YOU.

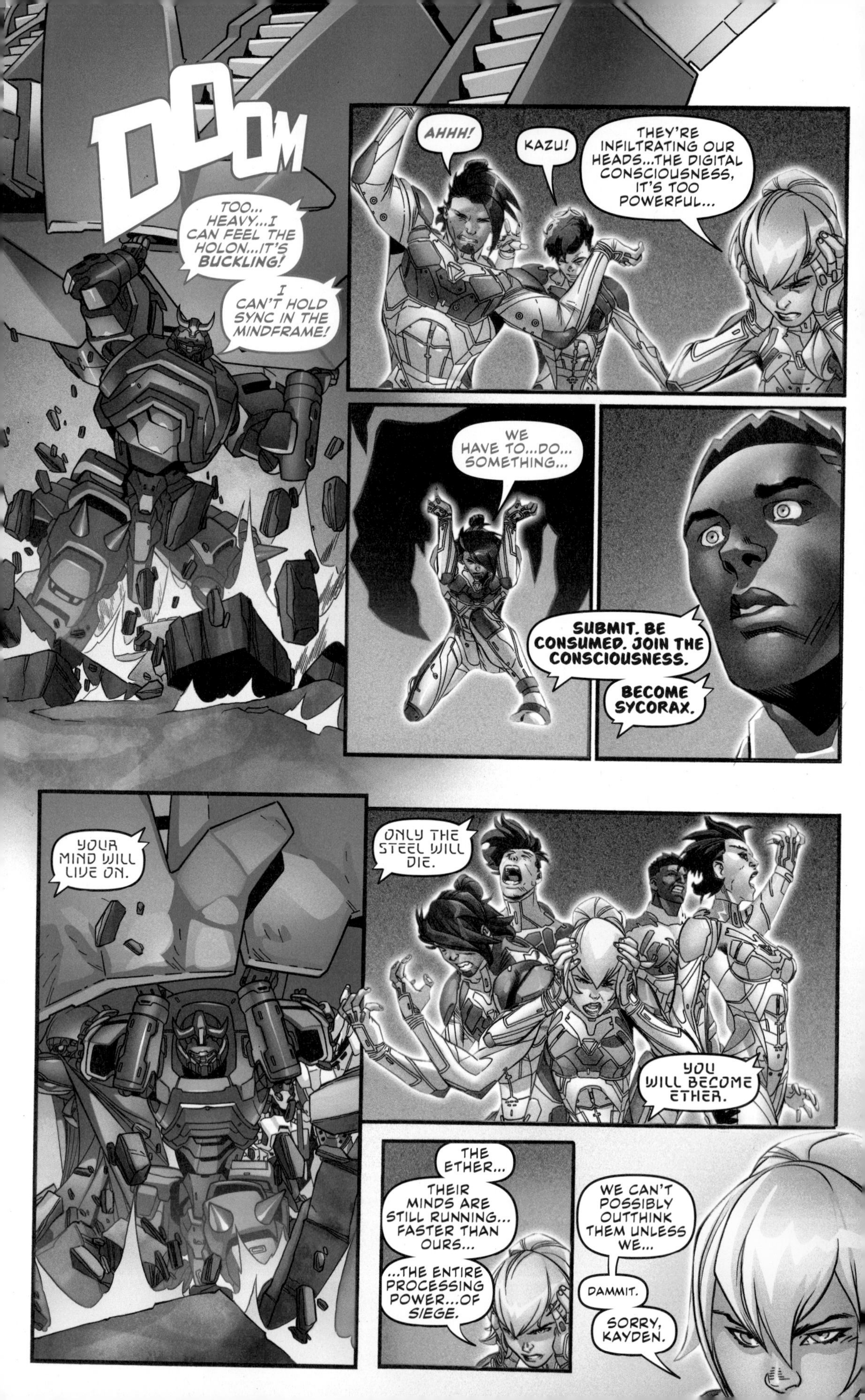
DOOOM
TOO... HEAVY...I CAN FEEL THE HOLON...IT'S BUCKLING!
I CAN'T HOLD SYNC IN THE MINDFRAME!
AHHH!
KAZU!
THEY'RE INFILTRATING OUR HEADS...THE DIGITAL CONSCIOUSNESS, IT'S TOO POWERFUL...
WE HAVE TO...DO... SOMETHING...
SUBMIT. BE CONSUMED. JOIN THE CONSCIOUSNESS.
BECOME SYCORAX.
YOUR MIND WILL LIVE ON.
ONLY THE STEEL WILL DIE.
YOU WILL BECOME ETHER.
THE ETHER...
THEIR MINDS ARE STILL RUNNING... FASTER THAN OURS...
...THE ENTIRE PROCESSING POWER...OF SIEGE.
WE CAN'T POSSIBLY OUTTHINK THEM UNLESS WE...
DAMMIT.
SORRY, KAYDEN.

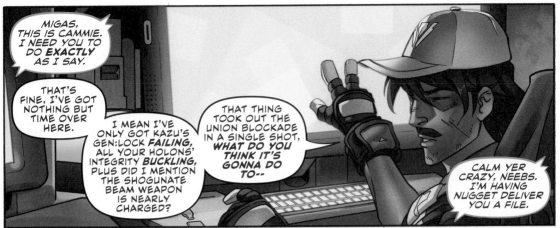

MIGAS, THIS IS CAMMIE. I NEED YOU TO DO **EXACTLY** AS I SAY.

THAT'S FINE, I'VE GOT NOTHING BUT TIME OVER HERE.

I MEAN I'VE ONLY GOT KAZU'S GEN:LOCK FAILING, ALL YOUR HOLONS' INTEGRITY **BUCKLING**, PLUS DID I MENTION THE SHOGUNATE BEAM WEAPON IS NEARLY CHARGED?

THAT THING TOOK OUT THE UNION BLOCKADE IN A SINGLE SHOT, **WHAT DO YOU THINK IT'S GONNA DO TO--**

CALM YER CRAZY, NEEBS. I'M HAVING NUGGET DELIVER YOU A FILE.

I PUT IT TOGETHER A COUPLE YEARS AGO--I WAS GOING THROUGH A WEE **ANARCHIST** PHASE. I'M GONNA TALK YE THROUGH A FEW WEE ADJUSTMENTS FOR OUR CURRENT SCENARIO, YE READY?

WHAT'S THAT SUPPOSED TO--

MADRE DE DIOS.

YOU CAN JUST CALL ME CAMMIE.

THE ADJUSTMENTS ARE MADE, BUT... WE CAN'T.

THIS IS INSANE. CAMMIE. WE'LL NEVER BE ABLE TO GO BACK.

I KNOW, MIGAS, I KNOW. BUT WE HAVE TO DO THIS.

MIGAS?

WE'RE ALL ABOUT TO GET CRUSHED-- YOU HAVE TO PRESS THE BUTTON!

SIGH.

PROGRAM ACTIVATED.

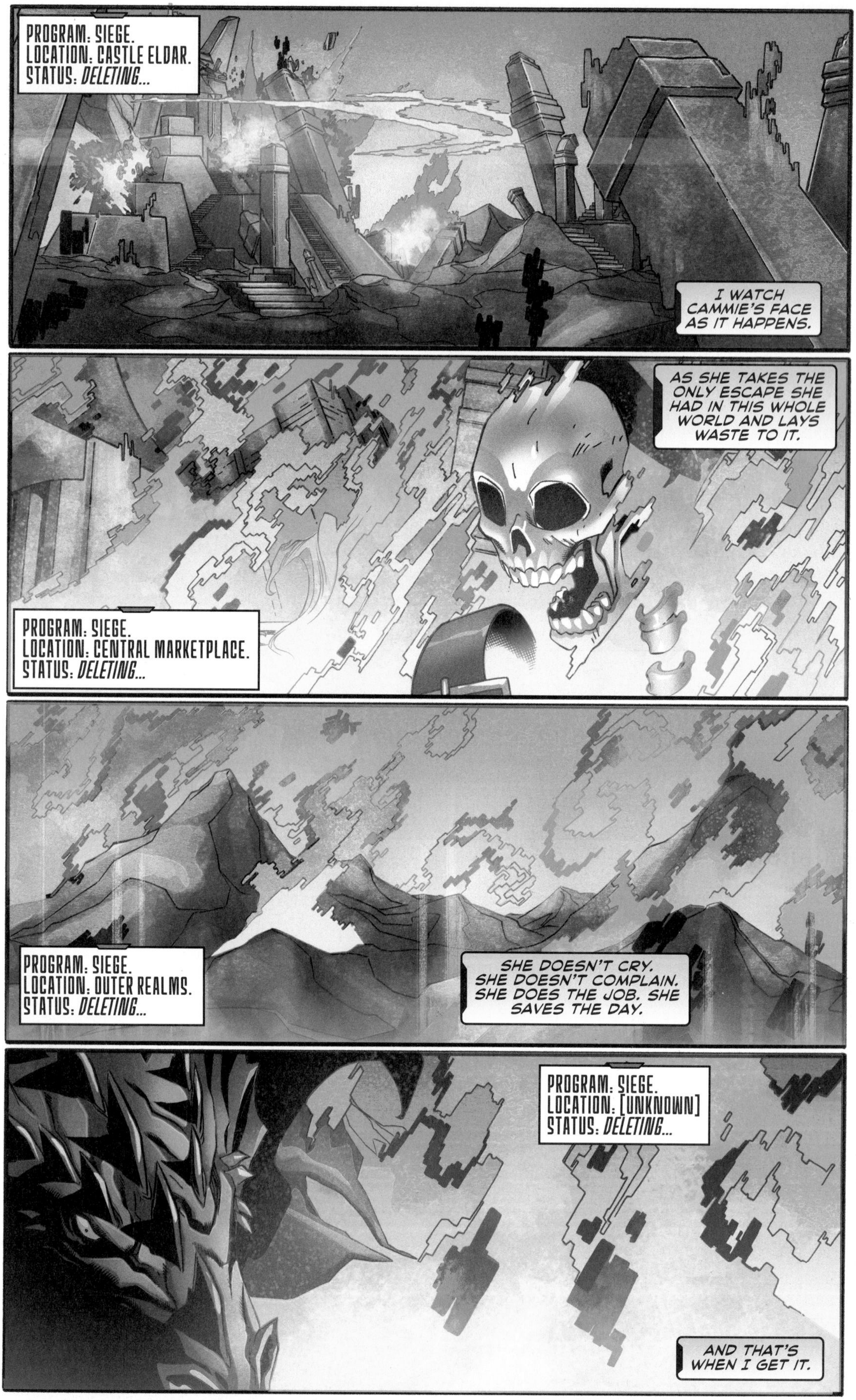
PROGRAM: SIEGE.
LOCATION: CASTLE ELDAR.
STATUS: DELETING...
I WATCH CAMMIE'S FACE AS IT HAPPENS.
AS SHE TAKES THE ONLY ESCAPE SHE HAD IN THIS WHOLE WORLD AND LAYS WASTE TO IT.
PROGRAM: SIEGE.
LOCATION: CENTRAL MARKETPLACE.
STATUS: DELETING...
PROGRAM: SIEGE.
LOCATION: OUTER REALMS.
STATUS: DELETING...
SHE DOESN'T CRY. SHE DOESN'T COMPLAIN. SHE DOES THE JOB. SHE SAVES THE DAY.
PROGRAM: SIEGE.
LOCATION: [UNKNOWN]
STATUS: DELETING...
AND THAT'S WHEN I GET IT.

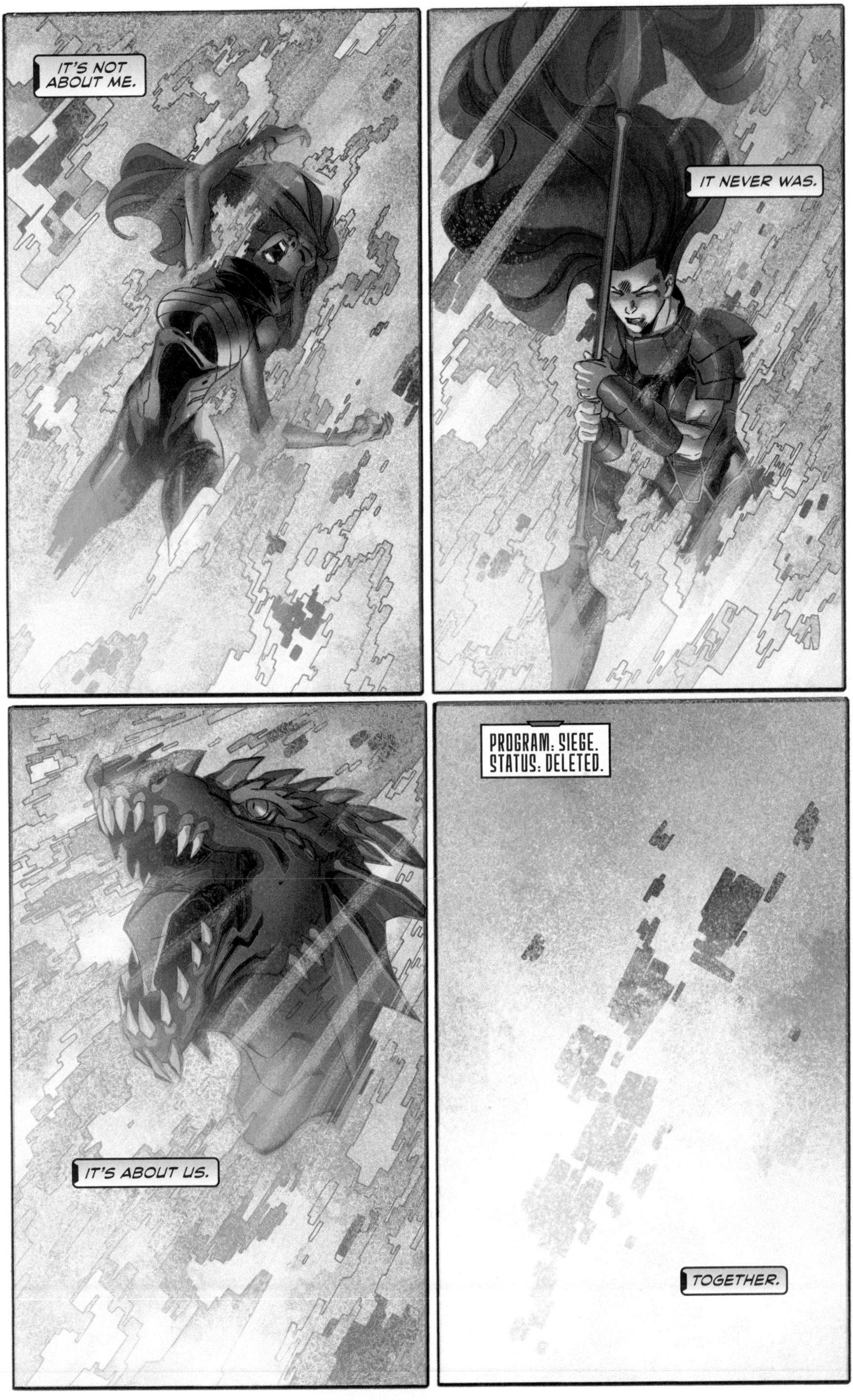
IT'S NOT ABOUT ME.
IT NEVER WAS.
IT'S ABOUT US.
PROGRAM: SIEGE. STATUS: DELETED.
TOGETHER.

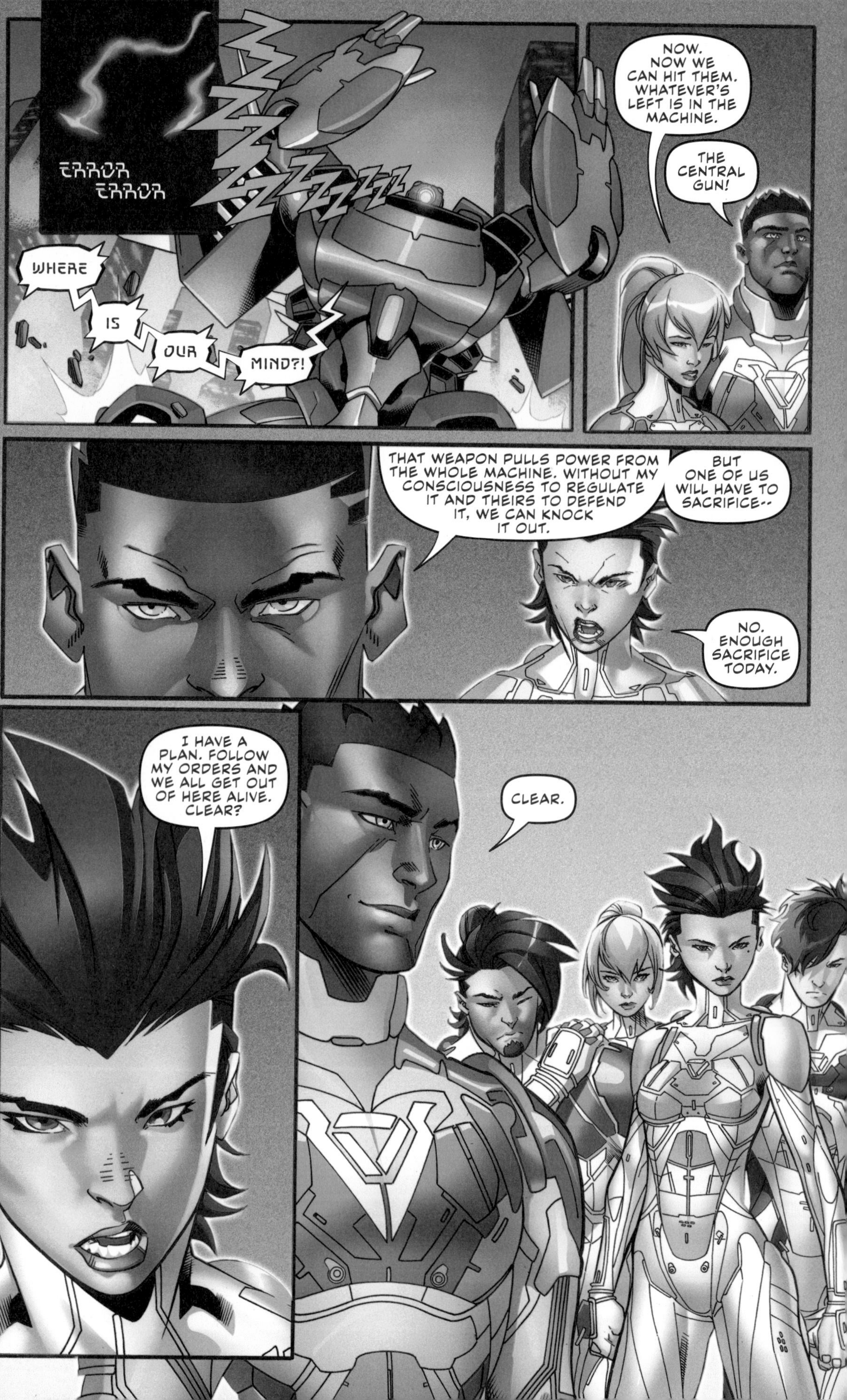
ERROR ERROR
WHERE IS OUR MIND?!
NOW. NOW WE CAN HIT THEM. WHATEVER'S LEFT IS IN THE MACHINE.
THE CENTRAL GUN!
THAT WEAPON PULLS POWER FROM THE WHOLE MACHINE. WITHOUT MY CONSCIOUSNESS TO REGULATE IT AND THEIRS TO DEFEND IT, WE CAN KNOCK IT OUT.
BUT ONE OF US WILL HAVE TO SACRIFICE--
NO. ENOUGH SACRIFICE TODAY.
I HAVE A PLAN. FOLLOW MY ORDERS AND WE ALL GET OUT OF HERE ALIVE. CLEAR?
CLEAR.

This is Yasamin Madrani of Gen:Lock, broadcasting on **Polity** and **Union** frequencies.

Commander Carlyle. General Anno. Both of your forces are in tatters. Neither of you can stand against the other. But if you do not do exactly as I say, we will all die today.

I'm not asking for your help. I'm telling you now, this is the **only** way.

The Japanese machine known as the Shogunate has gone haywire.

We must destroy it.

You hit the machine at the exact coordinates I'm transmitting.

Gen:Lock will do the rest.

Their superweapon has a weak spot. Excellent. Prepare the cannon.

On my mark.

I'm not an artifact. None of us are.

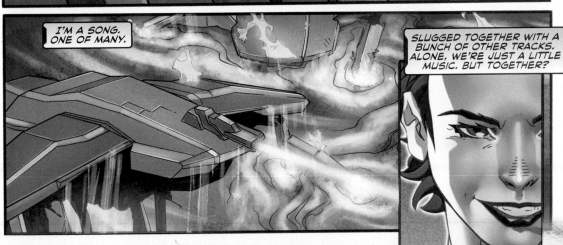

I'm a song. One of many.

Slugged together with a bunch of other tracks. Alone, we're just a little music. But together?

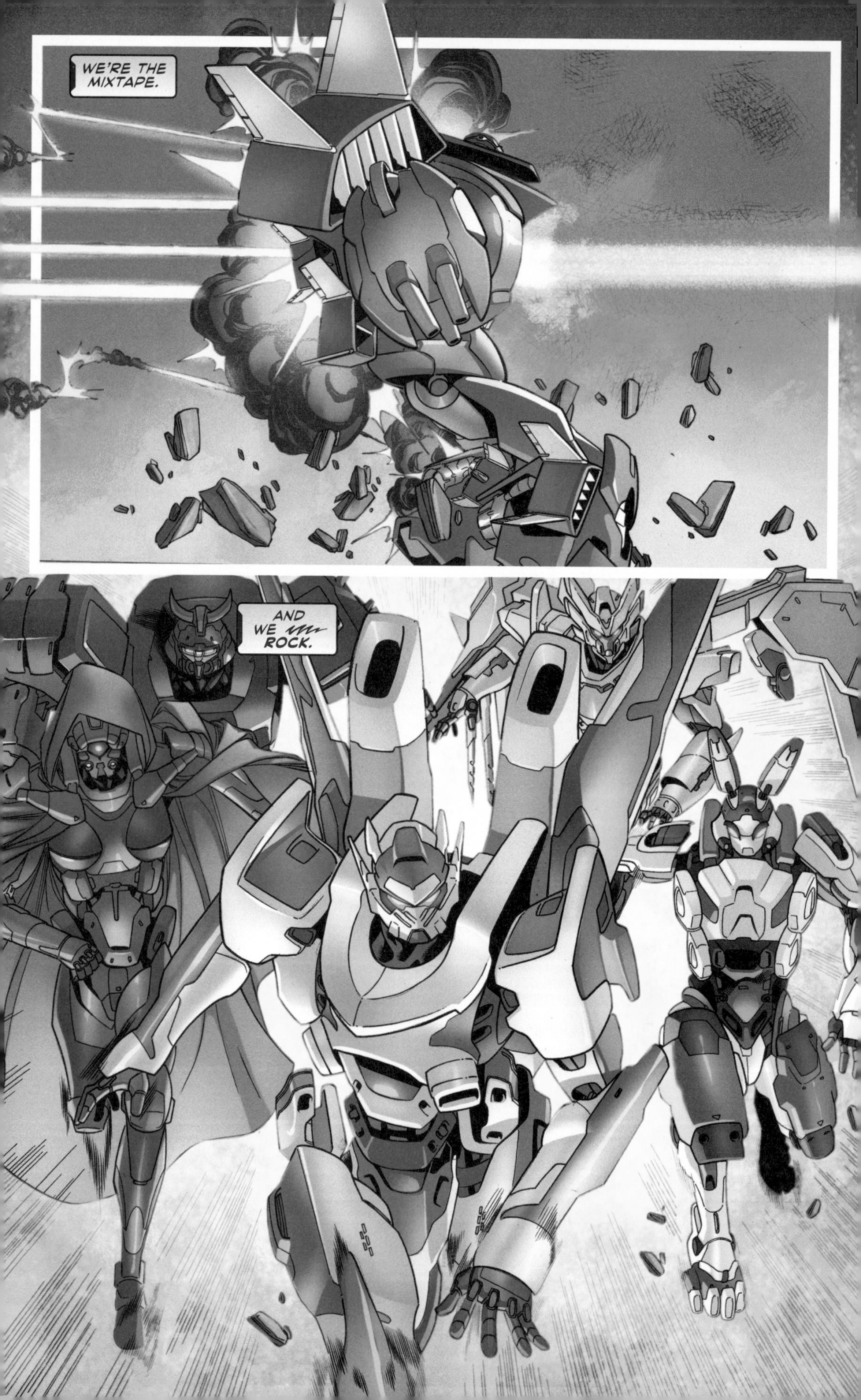
WE'RE THE MIXTAPE.
AND WE ROCK.

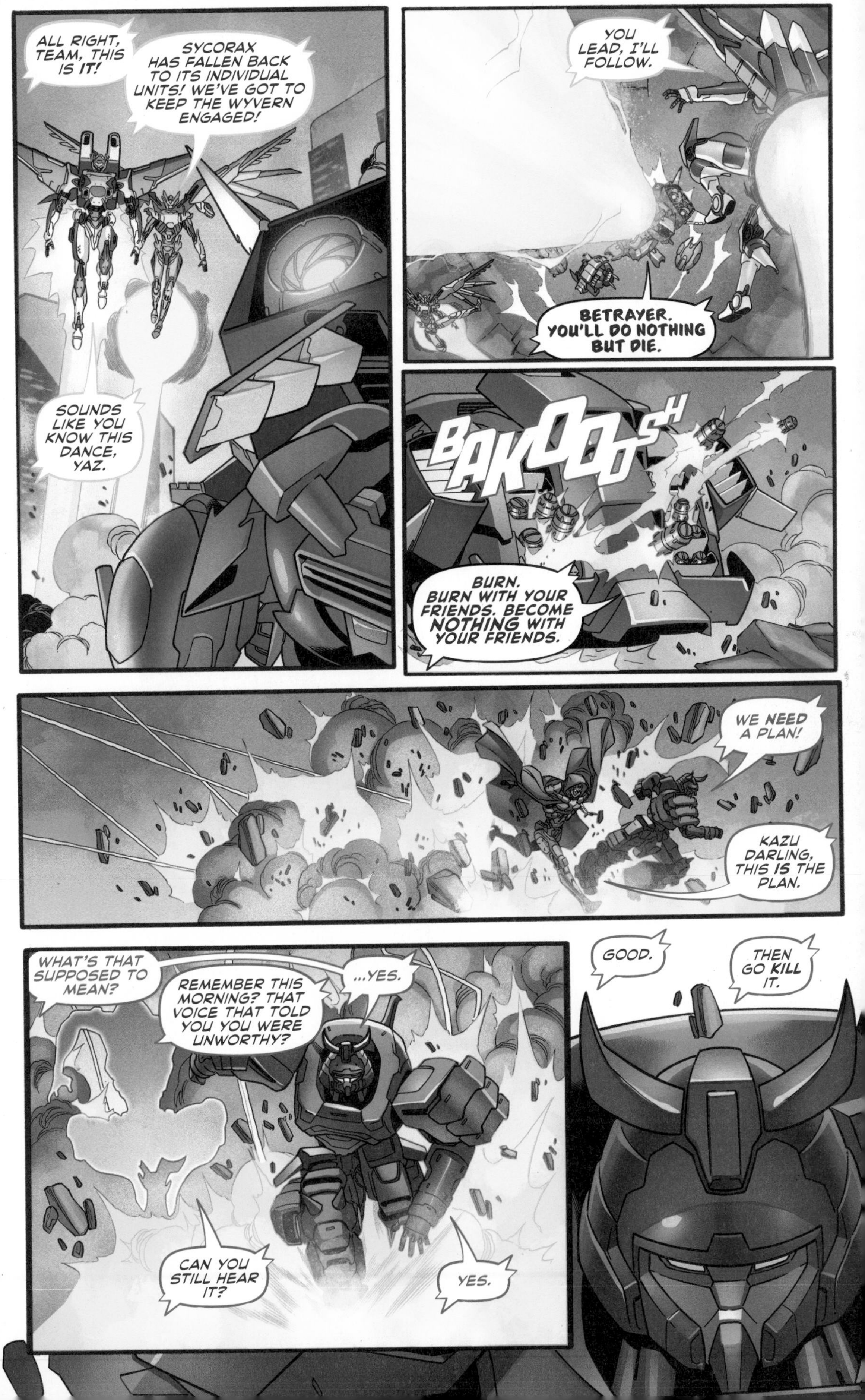
ALL RIGHT, TEAM, THIS IS IT!
SYCORAX HAS FALLEN BACK TO ITS INDIVIDUAL UNITS! WE'VE GOT TO KEEP THE WYVERN ENGAGED!
SOUNDS LIKE YOU KNOW THIS DANCE, YAZ.
YOU LEAD, I'LL FOLLOW.
BETRAYER. YOU'LL DO NOTHING BUT DIE.
BAKOOOOSH
BURN. BURN WITH YOUR FRIENDS. BECOME NOTHING WITH YOUR FRIENDS.
WE NEED A PLAN!
KAZU DARLING, THIS IS THE PLAN.
WHAT'S THAT SUPPOSED TO MEAN?
REMEMBER THIS MORNING? THAT VOICE THAT TOLD YOU YOU WERE UNWORTHY?
...YES.
CAN YOU STILL HEAR IT?
YES.
GOOD.
THEN GO KILL IT.

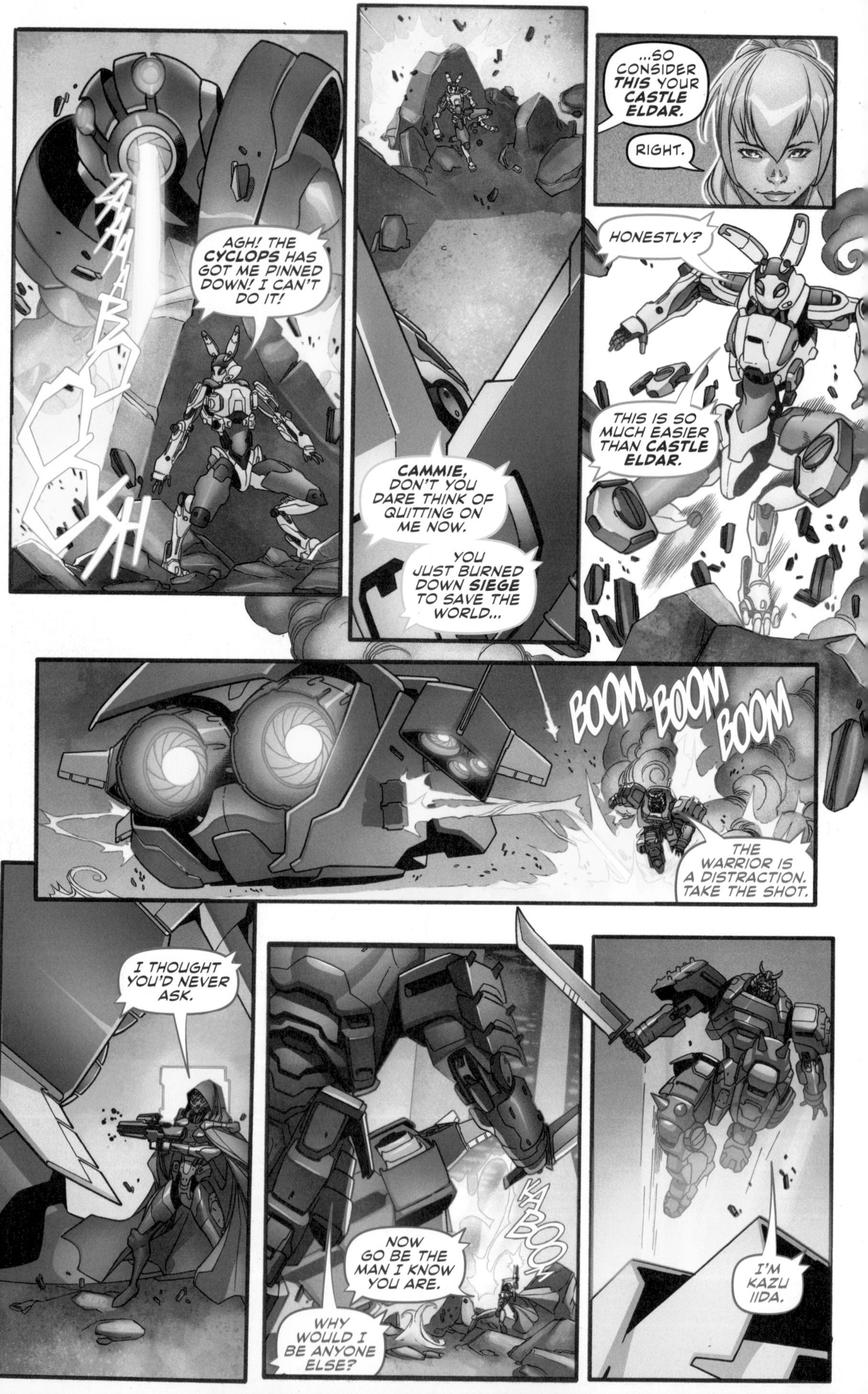
ZAAAABOOOSH
AGH! THE CYCLOPS HAS GOT ME PINNED DOWN! I CAN'T DO IT!
CAMMIE, DON'T YOU DARE THINK OF QUITTING ON ME NOW.
YOU JUST BURNED DOWN SIEGE TO SAVE THE WORLD...
...SO CONSIDER THIS YOUR CASTLE ELDAR.
RIGHT.
HONESTLY?
THIS IS SO MUCH EASIER THAN CASTLE ELDAR.
BOOM BOOM BOOM
THE WARRIOR IS A DISTRACTION. TAKE THE SHOT.
I THOUGHT YOU'D NEVER ASK.
NOW GO BE THE MAN I KNOW YOU ARE.
KABOOM
WHY WOULD I BE ANYONE ELSE?
I'M KAZU IIDA.

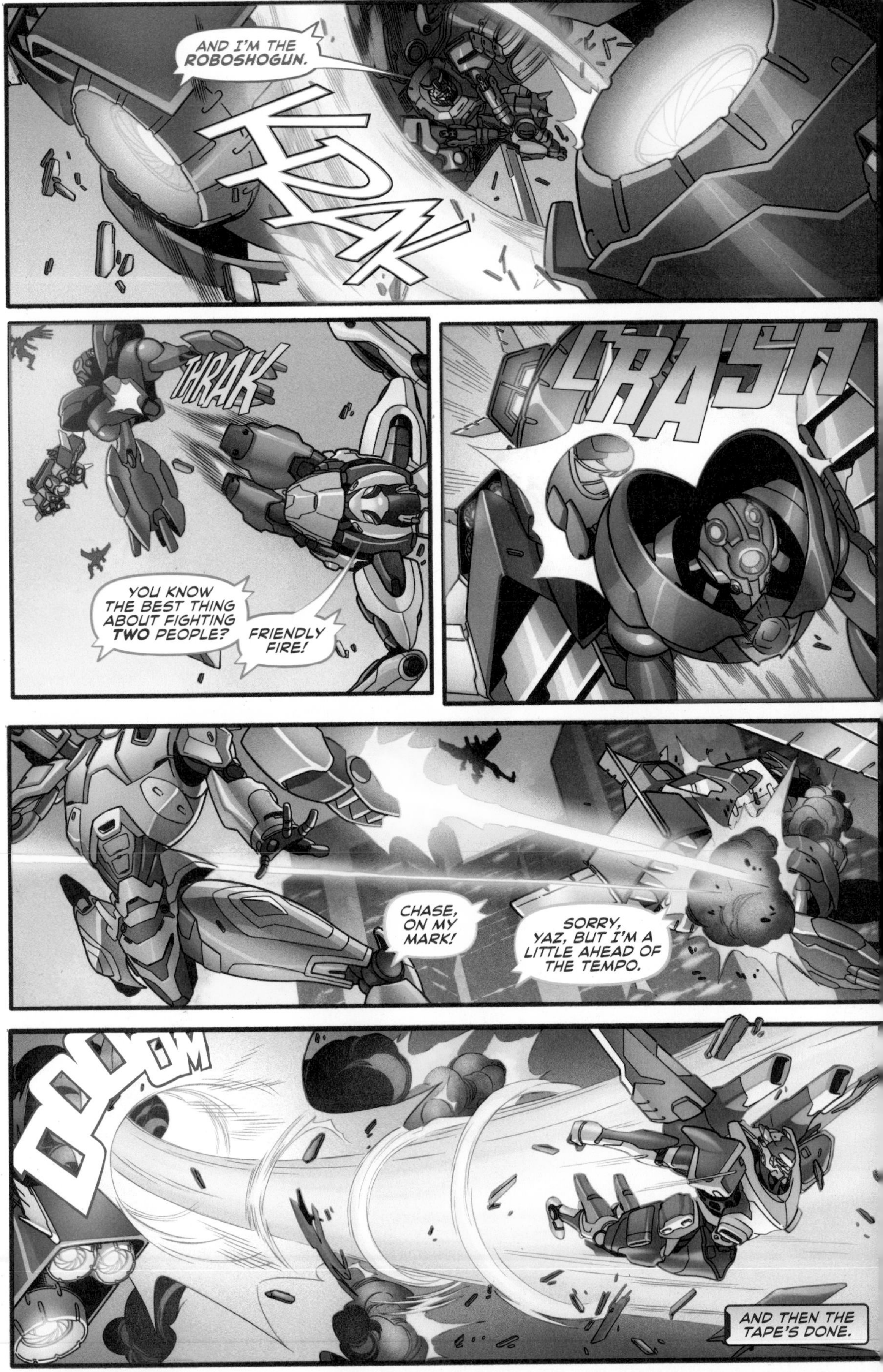
AND I'M THE ROBOSHOGUN.
KRAK
THRAK
YOU KNOW THE BEST THING ABOUT FIGHTING TWO PEOPLE?
FRIENDLY FIRE!
CRASH
CHASE, ON MY MARK!
SORRY, YAZ, BUT I'M A LITTLE AHEAD OF THE TEMPO.
AND THEN THE TAPE'S DONE.

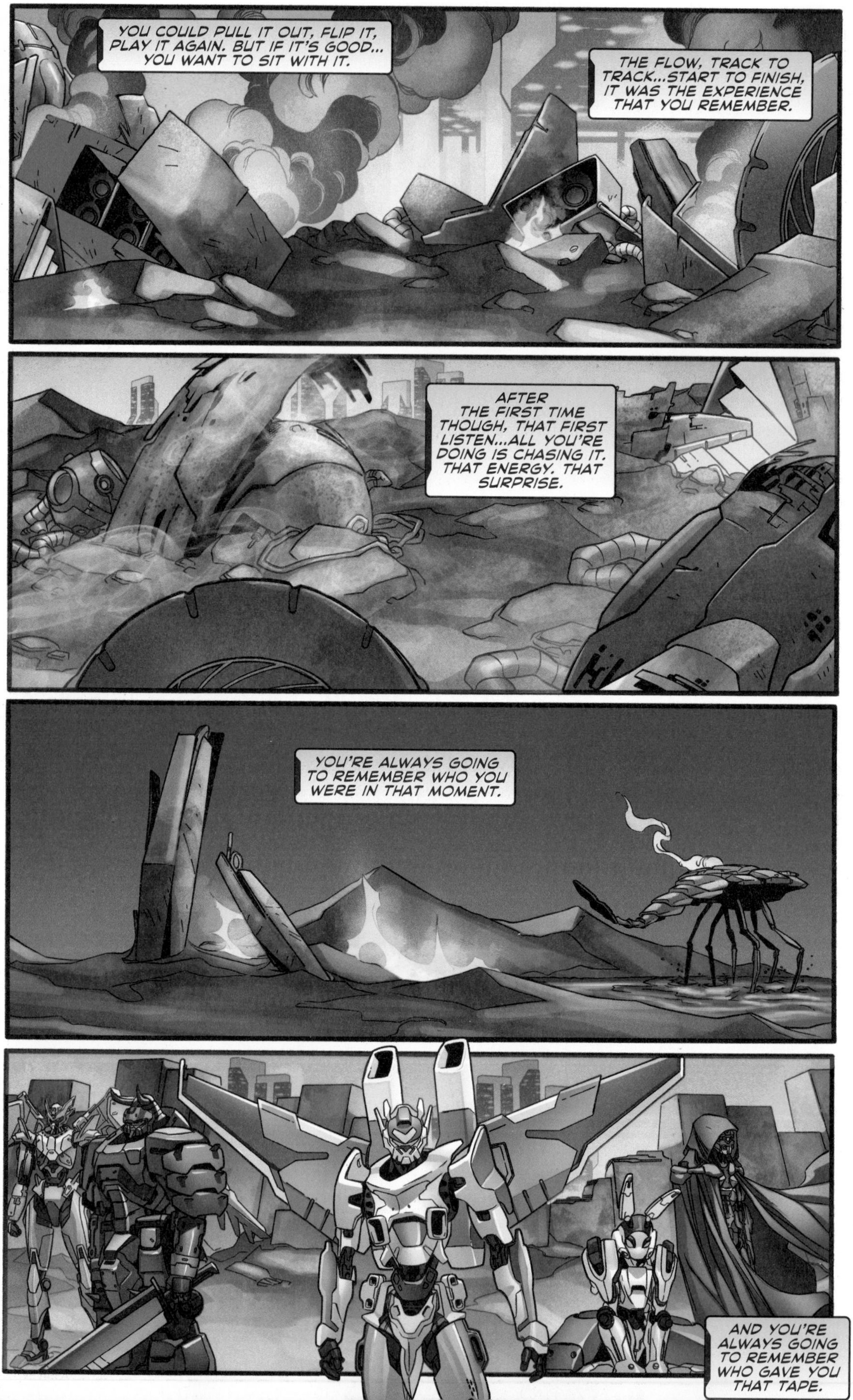
YOU COULD PULL IT OUT, FLIP IT, PLAY IT AGAIN. BUT IF IT'S GOOD... YOU WANT TO SIT WITH IT.
THE FLOW, TRACK TO TRACK...START TO FINISH, IT WAS THE EXPERIENCE THAT YOU REMEMBER.
AFTER THE FIRST TIME THOUGH, THAT FIRST LISTEN...ALL YOU'RE DOING IS CHASING IT. THAT ENERGY. THAT SURPRISE.
YOU'RE ALWAYS GOING TO REMEMBER WHO YOU WERE IN THAT MOMENT.
AND YOU'RE ALWAYS GOING TO REMEMBER WHO GAVE YOU THAT TAPE.

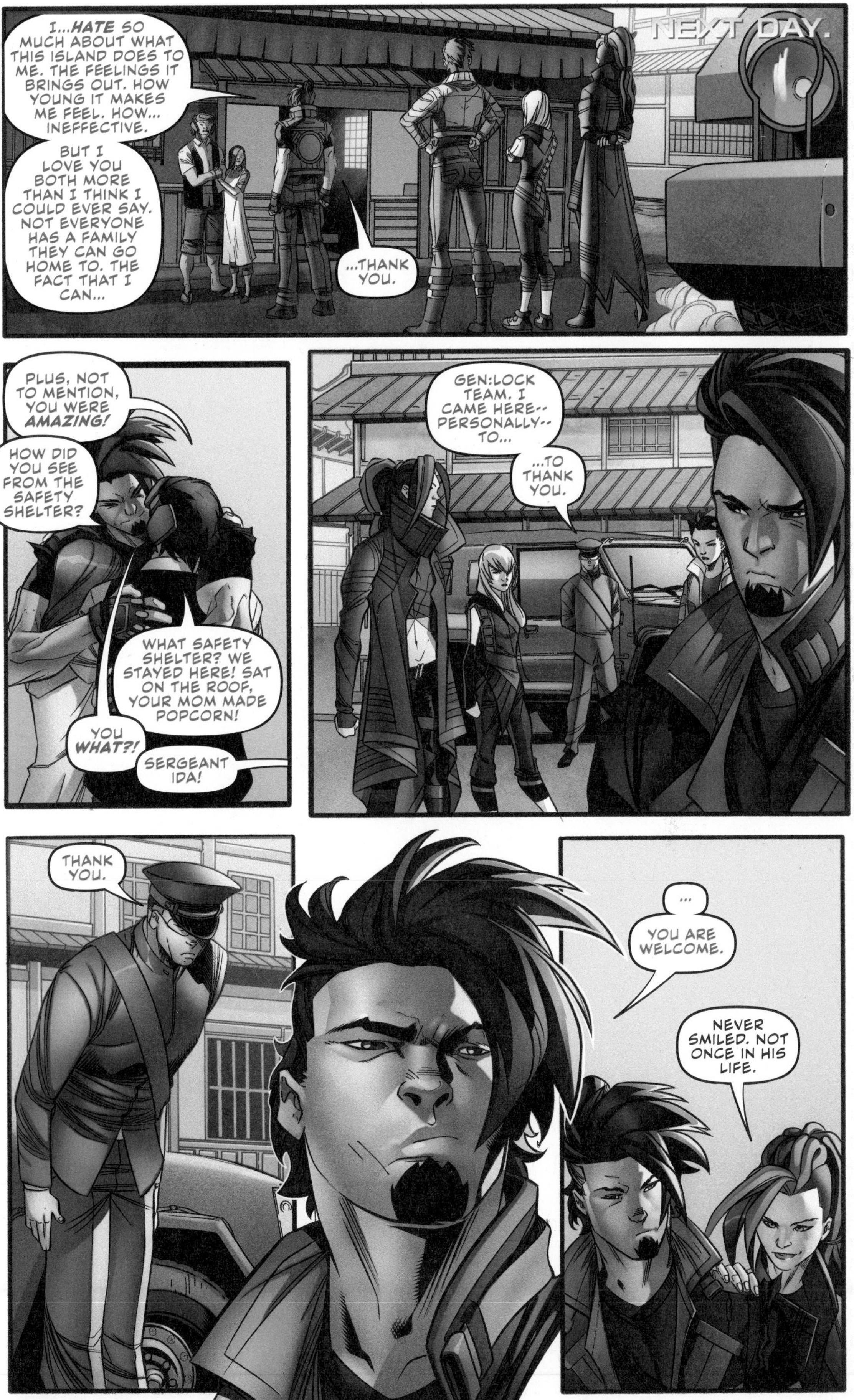
NEXT DAY.
I...HATE SO MUCH ABOUT WHAT THIS ISLAND DOES TO ME. THE FEELINGS IT BRINGS OUT. HOW YOUNG IT MAKES ME FEEL. HOW... INEFFECTIVE.
BUT I LOVE YOU BOTH MORE THAN I THINK I COULD EVER SAY. NOT EVERYONE HAS A FAMILY THEY CAN GO HOME TO. THE FACT THAT I CAN...
...THANK YOU.
PLUS, NOT TO MENTION, YOU WERE AMAZING!
HOW DID YOU SEE FROM THE SAFETY SHELTER?
WHAT SAFETY SHELTER? WE STAYED HERE! SAT ON THE ROOF, YOUR MOM MADE POPCORN!
YOU WHAT?!
SERGEANT IDA!
GEN:LOCK TEAM. I CAME HERE-- PERSONALLY-- TO...
...TO THANK YOU.
THANK YOU.
...
YOU ARE WELCOME.
NEVER SMILED. NOT ONCE IN HIS LIFE.

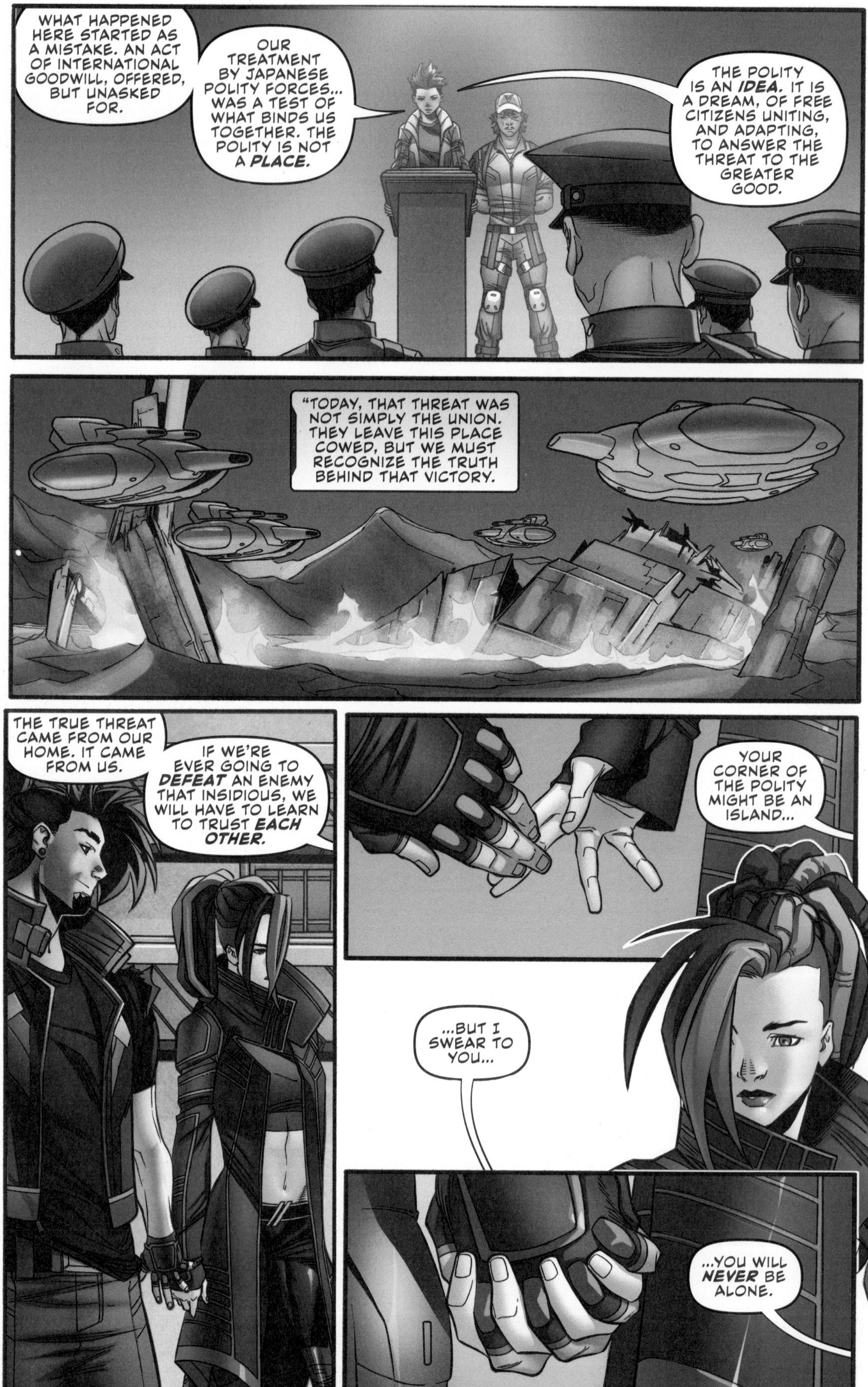
WHAT HAPPENED HERE STARTED AS A MISTAKE. AN ACT OF INTERNATIONAL GOODWILL, OFFERED, BUT UNASKED FOR.
OUR TREATMENT BY JAPANESE POLITY FORCES... WAS A TEST OF WHAT BINDS US TOGETHER. THE POLITY IS NOT A *PLACE.*
THE POLITY IS AN *IDEA.* IT IS A DREAM, OF FREE CITIZENS UNITING, AND ADAPTING, TO ANSWER THE THREAT TO THE GREATER GOOD.
"TODAY, THAT THREAT WAS NOT SIMPLY THE UNION. THEY LEAVE THIS PLACE COWED, BUT WE MUST RECOGNIZE THE TRUTH BEHIND THAT VICTORY.
THE TRUE THREAT CAME FROM OUR HOME. IT CAME FROM US.
IF WE'RE EVER GOING TO *DEFEAT* AN ENEMY THAT INSIDIOUS, WE WILL HAVE TO LEARN TO TRUST *EACH OTHER.*
YOUR CORNER OF THE POLITY MIGHT BE AN ISLAND...
...BUT I SWEAR TO YOU...
...YOU WILL *NEVER* BE ALONE.

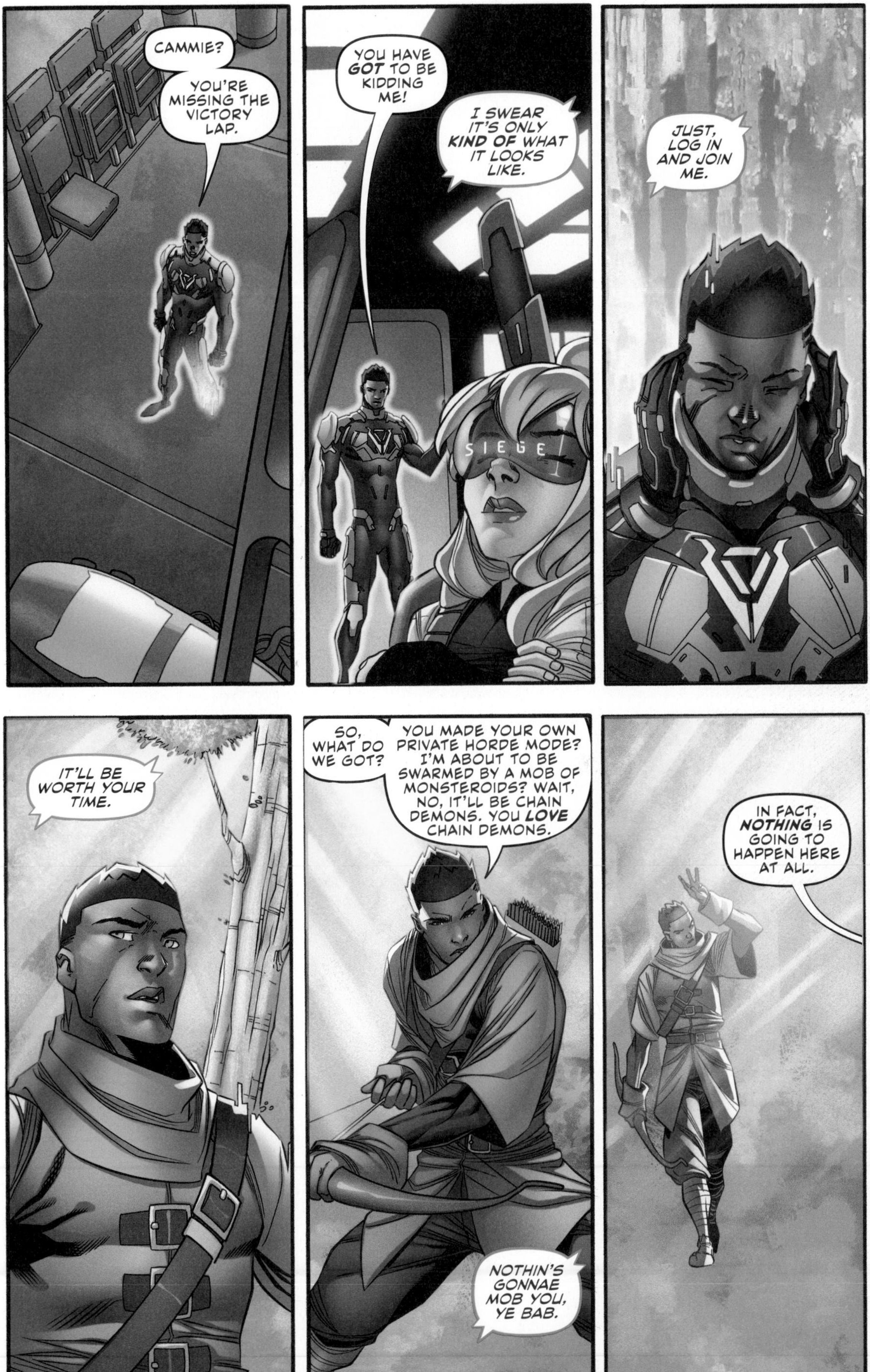
CAMMIE?
YOU'RE MISSING THE VICTORY LAP.
YOU HAVE GOT TO BE KIDDING ME!
I SWEAR IT'S ONLY KIND OF WHAT IT LOOKS LIKE.
SIEGE
JUST, LOG IN AND JOIN ME.
IT'LL BE WORTH YOUR TIME.
SO, WHAT DO WE GOT?
YOU MADE YOUR OWN PRIVATE HORDE MODE? I'M ABOUT TO BE SWARMED BY A MOB OF MONSTEROIDS? WAIT, NO, IT'LL BE CHAIN DEMONS. YOU LOVE CHAIN DEMONS.
NOTHIN'S GONNAE MOB YOU, YE BAB.
IN FACT, NOTHING IS GOING TO HAPPEN HERE AT ALL.

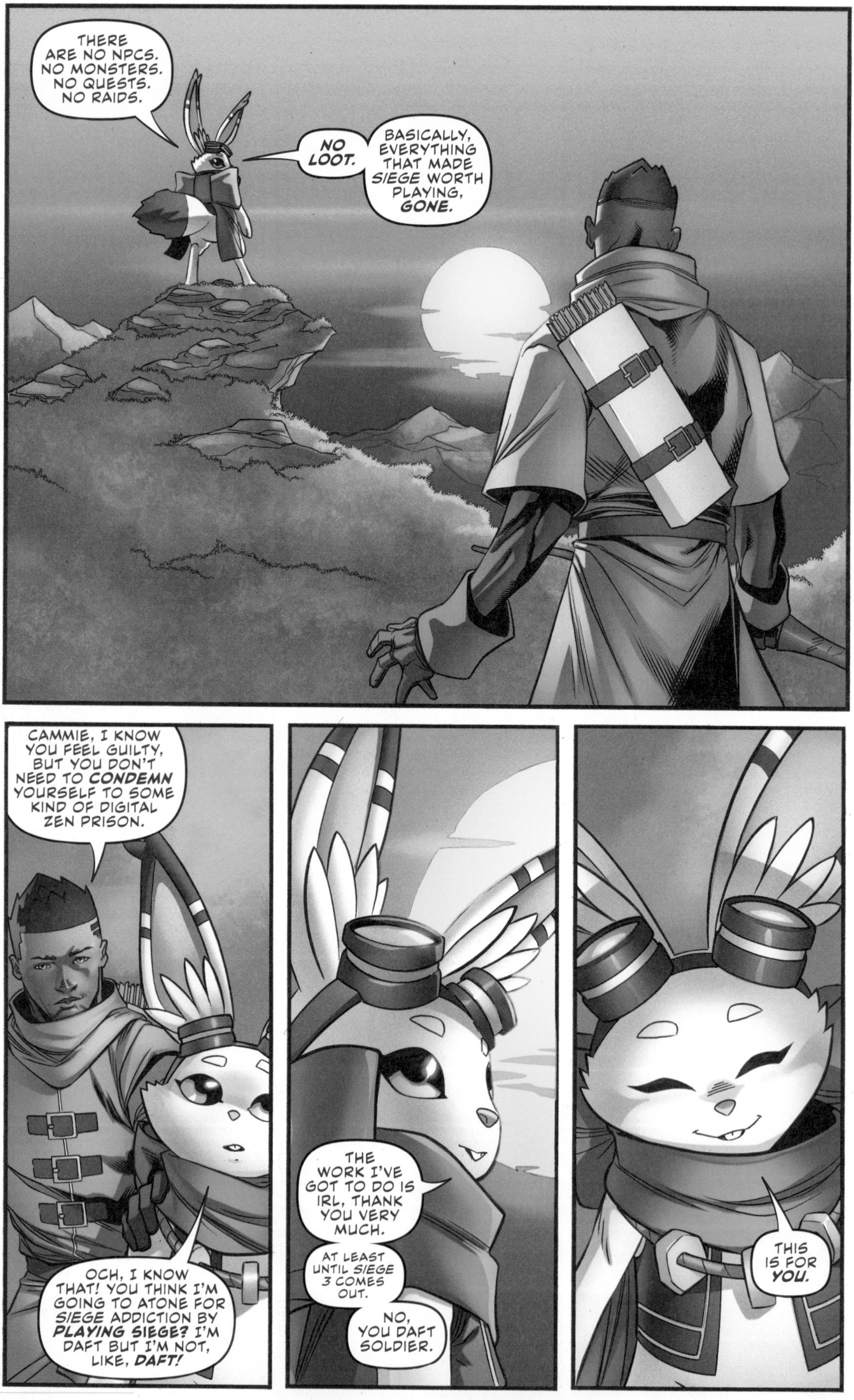
THERE ARE NO NPCS. NO MONSTERS. NO QUESTS. NO RAIDS.
NO LOOT.
BASICALLY, EVERYTHING THAT MADE SIEGE WORTH PLAYING, GONE.
CAMMIE, I KNOW YOU FEEL GUILTY, BUT YOU DON'T NEED TO CONDEMN YOURSELF TO SOME KIND OF DIGITAL ZEN PRISON.
OCH, I KNOW THAT! YOU THINK I'M GOING TO ATONE FOR SIEGE ADDICTION BY PLAYING SIEGE? I'M DAFT BUT I'M NOT, LIKE, DAFT!
THE WORK I'VE GOT TO DO IS IRL, THANK YOU VERY MUCH.
AT LEAST UNTIL SIEGE 3 COMES OUT.
NO, YOU DAFT SOLDIER.
THIS IS FOR YOU.

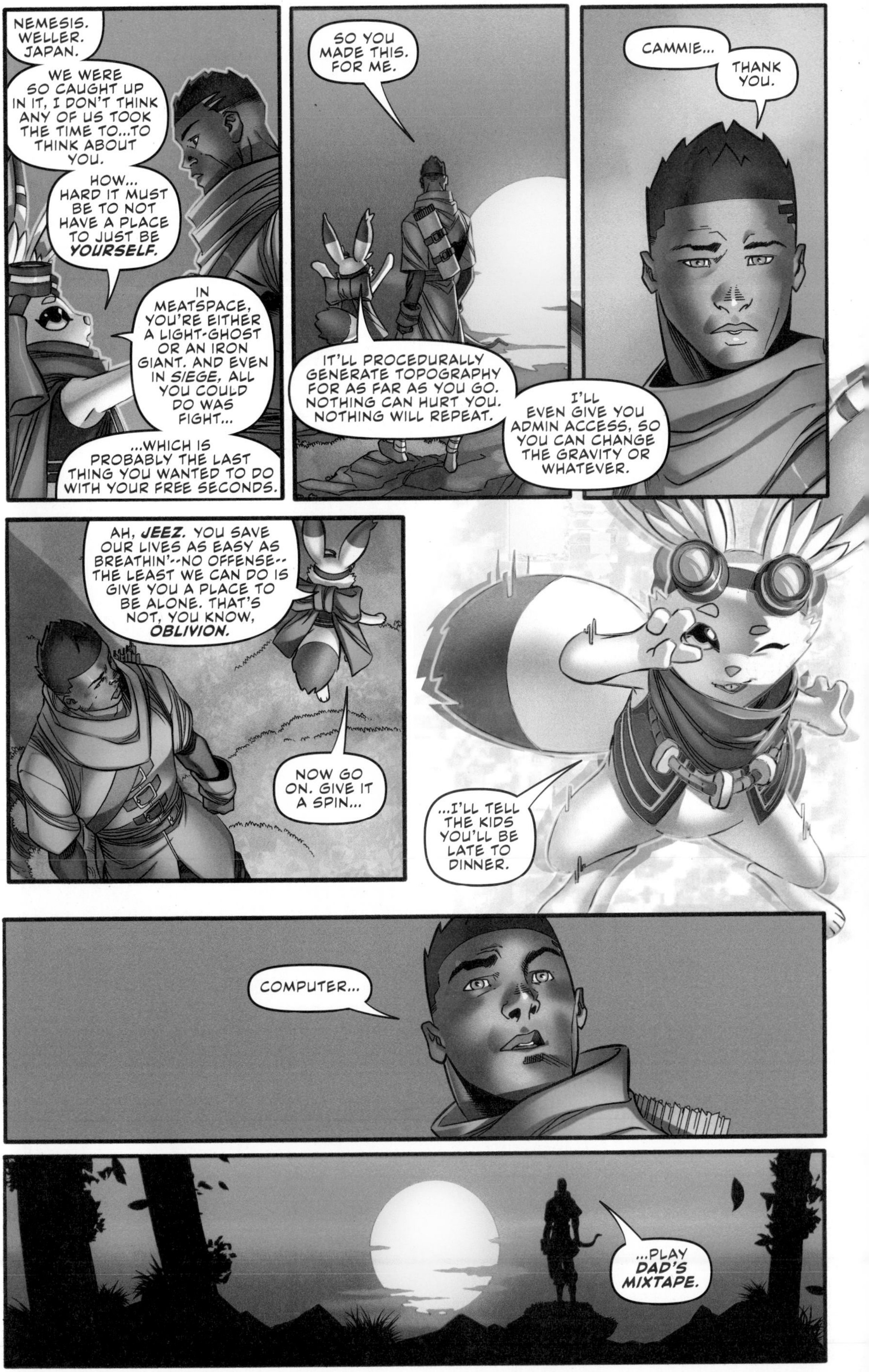
NEMESIS. WELLER. JAPAN.
WE WERE SO CAUGHT UP IN IT, I DON'T THINK ANY OF US TOOK THE TIME TO...TO THINK ABOUT YOU.
HOW... HARD IT MUST BE TO NOT HAVE A PLACE TO JUST BE YOURSELF.
IN MEATSPACE, YOU'RE EITHER A LIGHT-GHOST OR AN IRON GIANT. AND EVEN IN SIEGE, ALL YOU COULD DO WAS FIGHT...
...WHICH IS PROBABLY THE LAST THING YOU WANTED TO DO WITH YOUR FREE SECONDS.
SO YOU MADE THIS. FOR ME.
IT'LL PROCEDURALLY GENERATE TOPOGRAPHY FOR AS FAR AS YOU GO. NOTHING CAN HURT YOU. NOTHING WILL REPEAT.
CAMMIE...
THANK YOU.
I'LL EVEN GIVE YOU ADMIN ACCESS, SO YOU CAN CHANGE THE GRAVITY OR WHATEVER.
AH, JEEZ. YOU SAVE OUR LIVES AS EASY AS BREATHIN'--NO OFFENSE--THE LEAST WE CAN DO IS GIVE YOU A PLACE TO BE ALONE. THAT'S NOT, YOU KNOW, OBLIVION.
NOW GO ON. GIVE IT A SPIN...
...I'LL TELL THE KIDS YOU'LL BE LATE TO DINNER.
COMPUTER...
...PLAY DAD'S MIXTAPE.

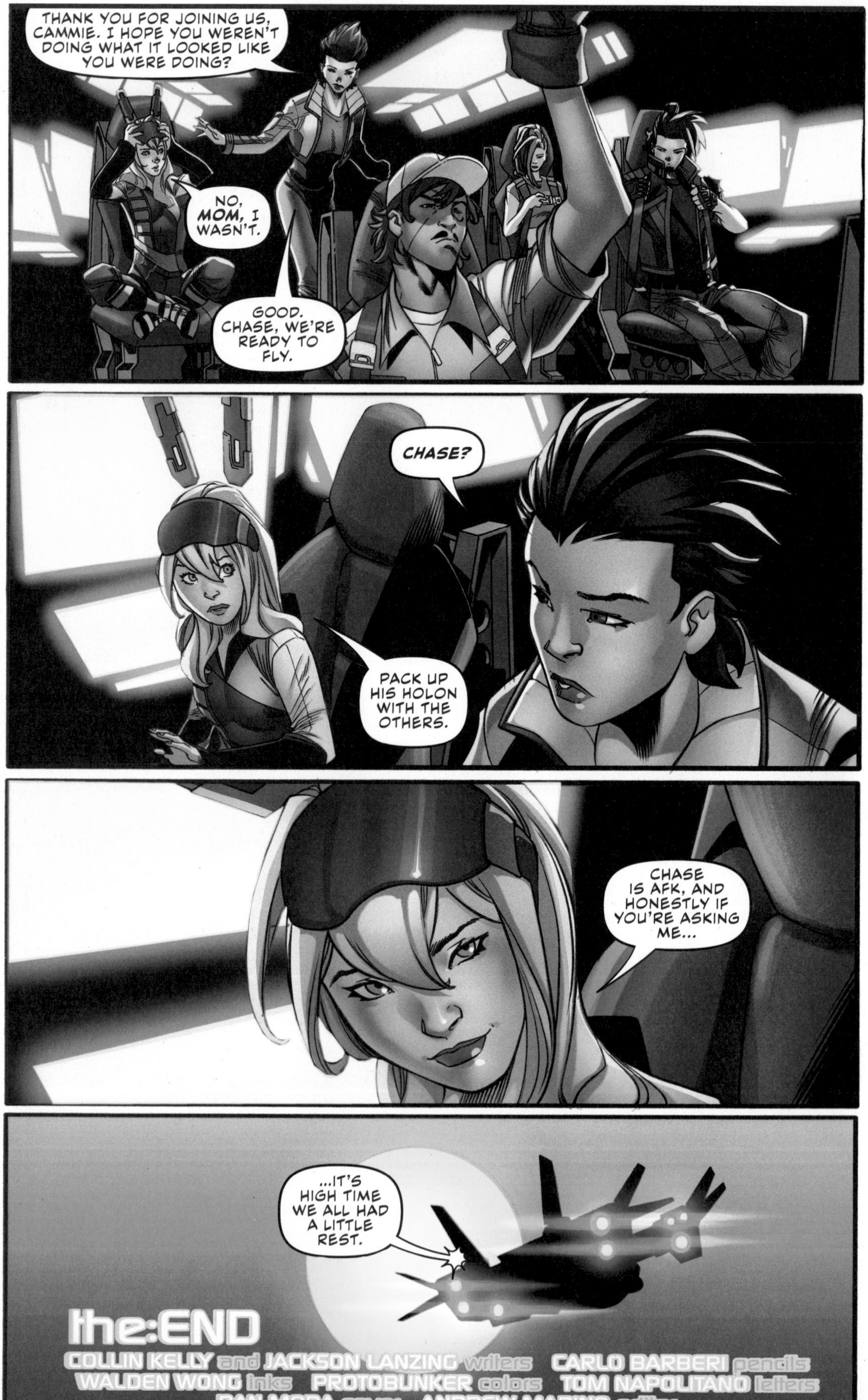
THANK YOU FOR JOINING US, CAMMIE. I HOPE YOU WEREN'T DOING WHAT IT LOOKED LIKE YOU WERE DOING?
NO, MOM, I WASN'T.
GOOD. CHASE, WE'RE READY TO FLY.
CHASE?
PACK UP HIS HOLON WITH THE OTHERS.
CHASE IS AFK, AND HONESTLY IF YOU'RE ASKING ME...
...IT'S HIGH TIME WE ALL HAD A LITTLE REST.
the:END
COLLIN KELLY and JACKSON LANZING writers CARLO BARBERI pencils
WALDEN WONG inks PROTOBUNKER colors TOM NAPOLITANO letters
DAN MORA cover ANDREW MARINO editor

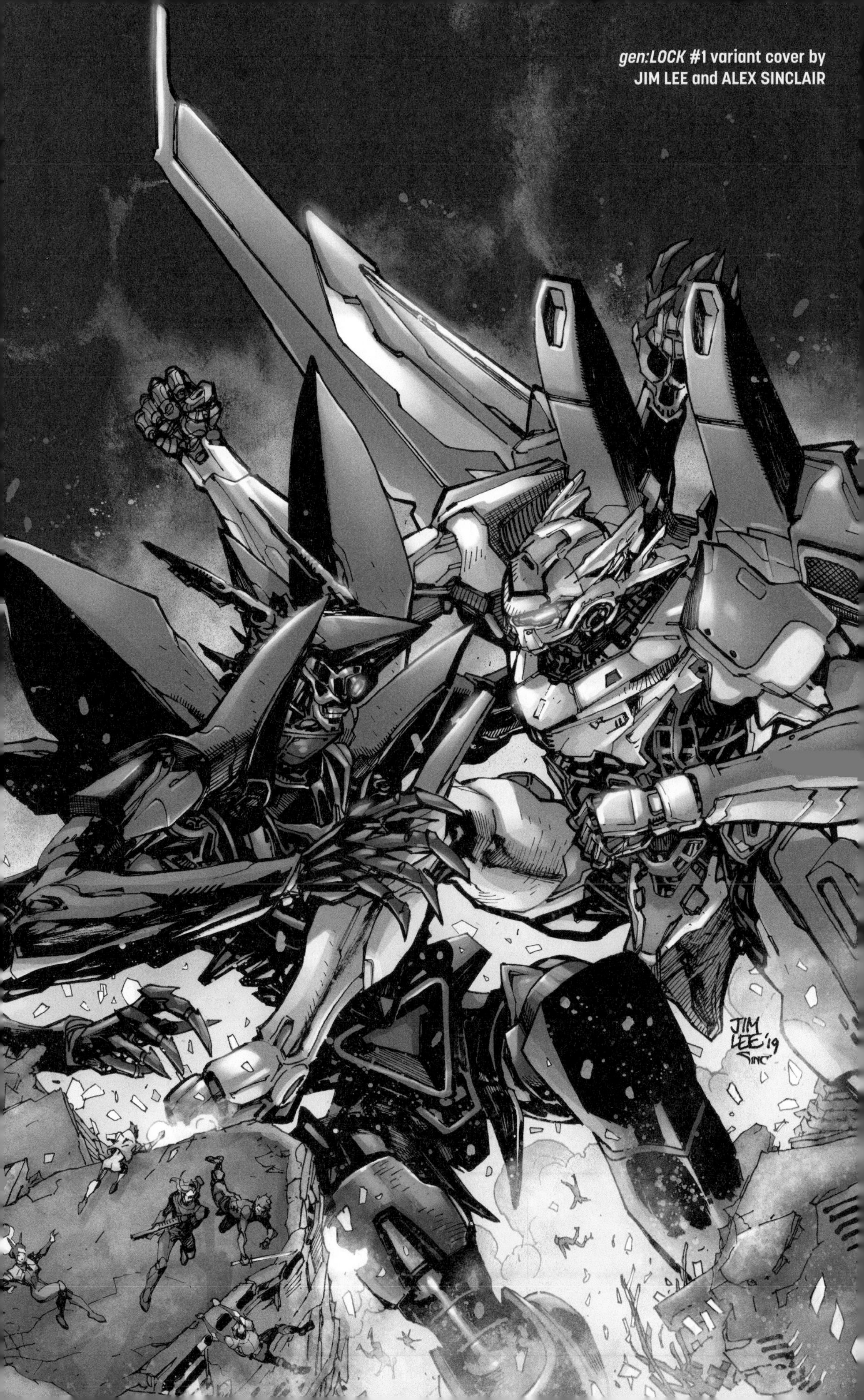
JIM LEE '19

gen:LOCK #1 variant cover by
JIM LEE and ALEX SINCLAIR

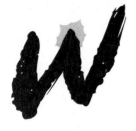

"Bendis reminds us why we loved these characters to begin with."
–NEWSARAMA

YOUNG JUSTICE

VOL. 1: GEMWORLD

BRIAN MICHAEL BENDIS, PATRICK GLEASON and JOHN TIMMS

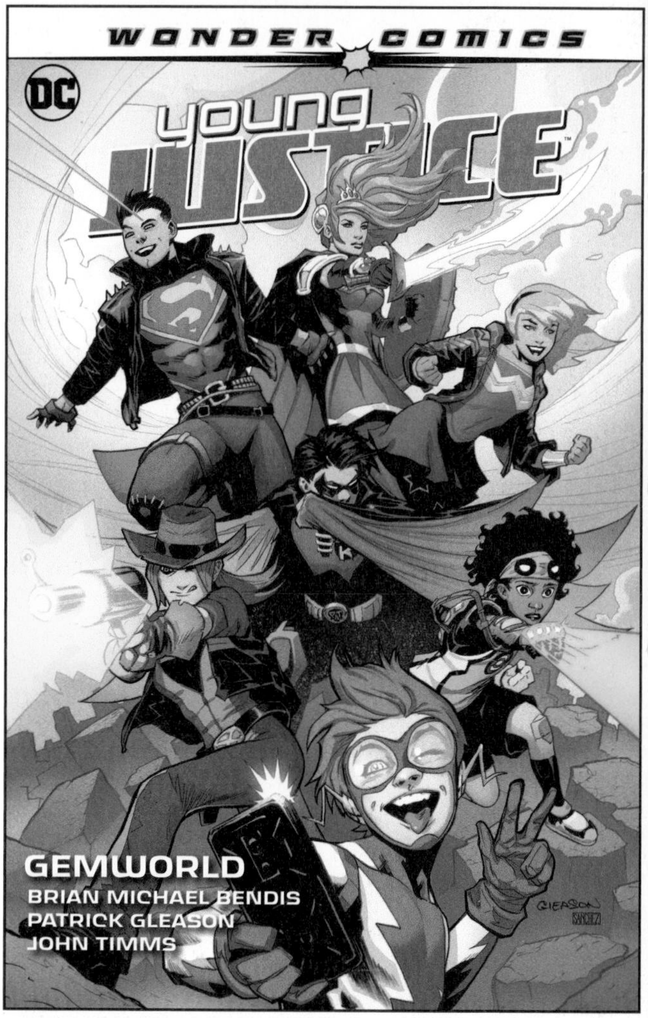
WONDER COMICS
DC
YOUNG JUSTICE
GEMWORLD
BRIAN MICHAEL BENDIS
PATRICK GLEASON
JOHN TIMMS

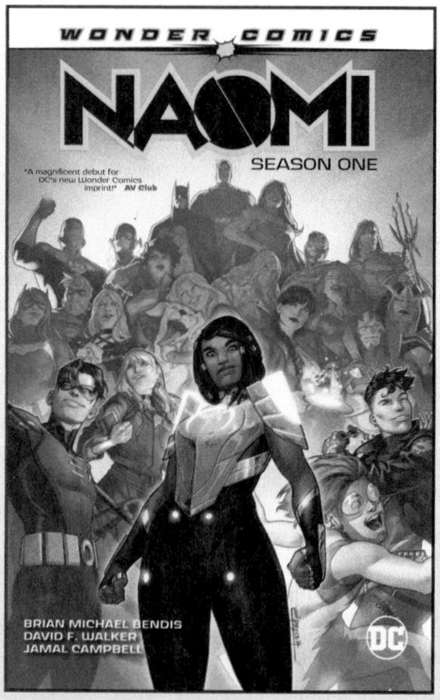
WONDER COMICS
NAOMI
SEASON ONE
"A magnificent debut for DC's new Wonder Comics imprint!" AV Club
BRIAN MICHAEL BENDIS
DAVID F. WALKER
JAMAL CAMPBELL
DC

NAOMI
VOL. 1: SEASON ONE

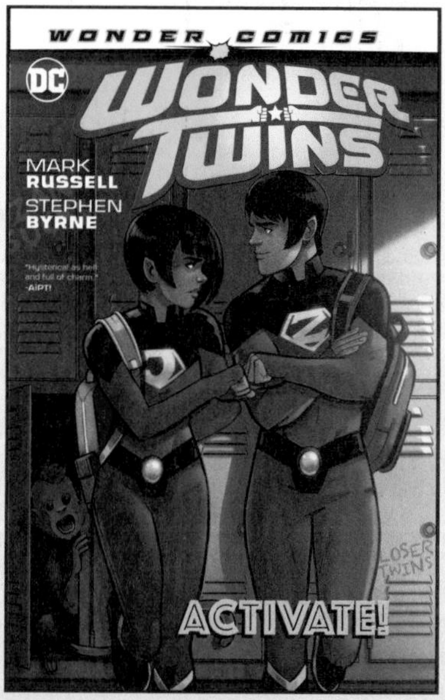
WONDER COMICS
DC
WONDER TWINS
MARK RUSSELL
STEPHEN BYRNE
"Hysterical as hell and full of charm." -AIPT!
LOSER TWINS
ACTIVATE!

WONDER TWINS
VOL. 1: ACTIVATE!

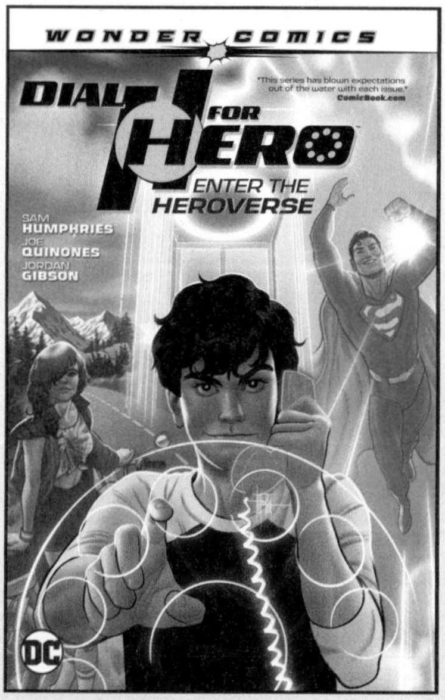
WONDER COMICS
"This series has blown expectations out of the water with each issue." ComicBook.com
DIAL H FOR HERO
ENTER THE HEROVERSE
SAM HUMPHRIES
JOE QUINONES
JORDAN GIBSON
DC

DIAL H FOR HERO
VOL. 1: ENTER THE HEROVERSE

Get more DC graphic novels wherever comics and books are sold!